Continued on next page

Contents at a Glance

Continued from previous page

Windows® XP

Preston Gralla

Teach
Yourself

800 East 96th Street, Indianapolis, Indiana 46240

Windows® XP in a Snap

International Standard Book Number: 0-672-32671-X

Library of Congress Catalog Card Number: 2003099243

Printed in the United States of America

First Printing: August 2004

07   06   05   04   4   3   2   1

Trademarks

All terms mentioned in this book that are known to be trademarks or service marks have been appropriately capitalized. Sams Publishing cannot attest to the accuracy of this information. Use of a term in this book should not be regarded as affecting the validity of any trademark or service mark.

Windows is a registered trademark of Microsoft Corporation.

Warning and Disclaimer

Every effort has been made to make this book as complete and as accurate as possible, but no warranty or fitness is implied. The information provided is on an "as is" basis. The author and the publisher shall have neither liability nor responsibility to any person or entity with respect to any loss or damages arising from the information contained in this book.

Bulk Sales

Sams Publishing offers excellent discounts on this book when ordered in quantity for bulk purchases or special sales. For more information, please contact

U.S. Corporate and Government Sales

1-800-382-3419

corpsales@pearsontechgroup.com

For sales outside of the U.S., please contact

International Sales

international@pearsoned.com

Acquisitions Editor
Betsy Brown

Development Editor
Alice Martina Smith

Managing Editor
Charlotte Clapp

Project Editor
Dan Knott

Production Editor
Seth Kerney

Indexer
Chris Barrick

Proofreader
Wendy Ott

Technical Editor
Dallas Releford

Publishing Coordinator
Vanessa Evans

Designer
Gary Adair

Page Layout
Kelly Maish

About the Author

Preston Gralla is the best-selling author of nearly 30 books that have been translated into 15 languages, including *eBay in a Snap, How the Internet Works, How to Expand and Upgrade PCs, How Wireless Works*, and many others. A well-known technology guru, he has made many television and radio appearances on many shows and networks, including the *CBS Early Show*, CNN, MSNBC, and *ABC World News Now*. He has done occasional commentaries about technology for National Public Radio's *All Things Considered*.

Gralla has also published articles about technology for many national newspapers and magazines, including *USA Today*, the *Los Angeles Times*, the *Dallas Morning News* (where he was a technology columnist), and *PC Magazine*. He was the founding managing editor of *PC Week*, and founding editor and then editor and editorial director of *PC/Computing*, and received the award for the Best Feature in a Computer Publication from the Computer Press Association.

Gralla is also editor-in-chief of the Case Study Forum, which specializes in writing case studies for technology companies. He lives in Cambridge, Massachusetts, with his wife Lydia, son Gabe, and daughter Mia, who occasionally visits from college.

Acknowledgments

Thanks, as always to my wife Lydia, son Gabe, and daughter Mia. And thanks again to Betsy Brown for entrusting me with another project; to Alice Martina Smith for her sharp editing; to Dan Knott for keeping the project on track; and to Seth Kerney for eagle-eyed attention to conventions. Thanks also to Chris Barrick, Wendy Ott, and Kelly Maish.

We Want to Hear from You!

As the reader of this book, *you* are our most important critic and commentator. We value your opinion and want to know what we're doing right, what we could do better, what areas you'd like to see us publish in, and any other words of wisdom you're willing to pass our way.

You can email or write me directly to let me know what you did or didn't like about this book—as well as what we can do to make our books stronger.

Please note that I cannot help you with technical problems related to the topic of this book, and that due to the high volume of mail I receive, I might not be able to reply to every message.

When you write, please be sure to include this book's title and author as well as your name and phone or email address. I will carefully review your comments and share them with the author and editors who worked on the book.

Email: consumer@samspublishing.com

Mail: Mark Taber
           Associate Publisher
           Sams Publishing
           800 East 96th Street
           Indianapolis, IN 46240 USA

Reader Services

For more information about this book or others from Sams Publishing, visit our website at **www.samspublishing.com**. Type the ISBN (excluding hyphens) or the title of the book in the Search box to find the book you're looking for.

PART I

Making Windows XP Work the Way You Want

IN THIS PART:

1

✔ Start Here

Windows XP does more things, more easily, in more different ways than any previous version of Windows—and as part of the bargain, it's easier to use and more fun as well.

It's also the most stable version of Windows to date. You'll rarely, if ever, crash the operating system, and you'll most likely never see the infamous "Blue Screen of Death" (BSOD) screens that used to bedevil earlier versions of Windows. In fact, you'll most likely be able to keep XP running nonstop for as long as you want, without having to restart it frequently, as was often required by earlier versions of Windows.

All that is because XP combines the stability of Windows NT/2000 with the general user-friendliness of a spruced-up interface. XP actually combines two different operating systems—the consumer versions of Windows—such as Windows Me and Windows 98/95—and the business-oriented Windows NT/2000 versions.

XP does more than just offer more stability under the hood. It also features a far more visually appealing interface and sports more features and more customizability than any other version of Windows. Multimedia and graphics have been built directly into the operating system so that it's far easier to do things such as record music, copy CDs, draw pictures, and make videos.

All this is great, but the very strength of XP is sometimes its Achilles' heel as well. It lets you do many different things in many different ways, and because of that, often it's not obvious how to do them. In fact, Windows XP lets you do so much that you often won't even know that there are things the operating system lets you do.

In this book, you'll learn how to get far more out of XP, and you'll be able to do it with ease—as the title says, you'll do it in a snap. But before you embark on the journey, you should know some basics of how XP works. So in this chapter, you'll learn everything you need to know to get started. You'll get a guided tour of XP, as well as a basic grounding on how to use the operating system. That way, it'll be easier to delve into the more advanced topics throughout the rest of the book.

Coming from Earlier Versions of Windows

If you're coming from an earlier version of Windows, XP will seem both familiar and foreign as well. The basic screen layout is the same, with a desktop filled with icons, a **Start** button on the lower right, a **Taskbar** along the bottom, and a **Notification Area**, also called the **System Tray**, on the lower right.

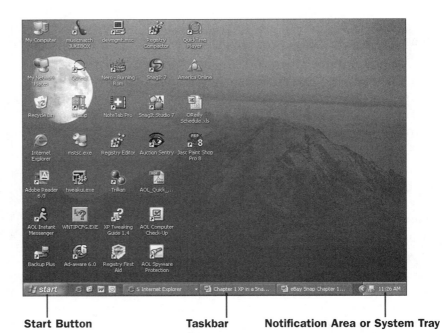

Start Button   **Taskbar**   **Notification Area or System Tray**

The same, but different: The Windows XP desktop is organized in the same basic way as previous Windows versions, but has a more graphical, up-to-date look.

However, there will be a lot that's unfamiliar as well. Window edges are rounded and almost cartoon-like; the **Start** menu (which you can access by clicking the **Start** button in the lower-left corner of the desktop) is far larger and filled with graphics and icons; the **Control Panel** has been completely redesigned; and there are many other changes as well.

What's New in XP

If you're coming from a previous version of Windows, you should take some time to familiarize yourself with what's new in XP. Here are the most important changes:

- **New visual design.** The first difference you'll notice in XP is its new look. It includes brighter colors that take advantage of high-end video hardware, 3D style rounded windows and buttons, and brighter, richer-looking icons. If you prefer the old "classic" style with square buttons and non-3D windows, however, XP will let you revert to it. For details, see **11** **Change Your Desktop's Appearance**.

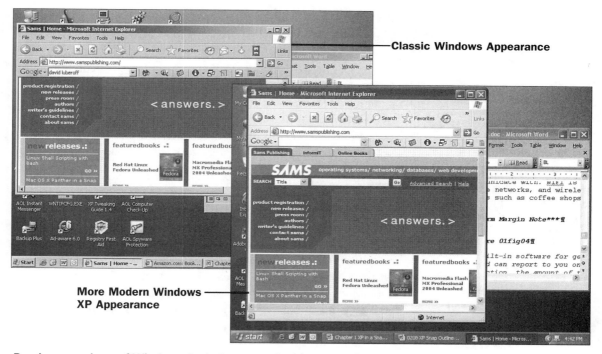

Classic Windows Appearance

More Modern Windows XP Appearance

Previous versions of Windows include square-looking, two-dimensional windows. Windows XP features a much brighter look, richer icons, and three-dimensional, rounded windows.

NOTE

The **Start** menu is one of the most customizable parts of Windows XP. You can change almost everything about the way it looks and works, and even make it look exactly like the old familiar **Start** menu from previous versions of Windows. To learn how to customize it, turn to **18** **Rearrange the Start Menu.**

NOTE

This book covers both Windows XP Home Edition and XP Professional, so almost everything you read applies to both editions. When we tell you about a feature available only in XP Professional, we'll let you know, so that you won't waste your time with the information if you're working with the Home Edition.

NOTE

If you make many changes to your PC, such as upgrading the processor, adding a new hard disk, adding more memory, and so on, you might have to "reactivate" Windows XP. You'll get a warning from XP that you need to reactivate, and you'll then be led through the reactivation process. This happens only when you change a good deal of your hardware, though. If you only add a hard disk and extra memory, and add a scanner and printer, for example, you won't have to reactivate.

- **Two versions of XP.** There are two versions of the operating system, Windows XP Home Edition and Windows XP Professional. The guts of the operating system is the same, and both versions work the same basic way; XP Professional offers everything that the Home Edition does, and offers some extras, as you'll see in **The Difference Between Home Edition and XP Professional** section later in this chapter. The Professional Edition adds some security and networking features; home users, and even many business users, will be perfectly happy without paying the extra $100 or so for XP Professional, compared to the XP Home Edition.

- **System Restore.** This new feature is a godsend for anyone who ever installs software, and that pretty much covers all of us. When this feature is enabled (which it is when you install XP), it takes a snapshot of your system at regular intervals, and if you then run into system problems, you can roll your system back to the state it was in before the problems occurred. For information on how to make the best use of System Restore, turn to **124 Protect Your System with System Restore**.

- **Better reliability and security.** Under the hood, XP adds a whole host of security and reliability features. It includes an entirely new "engine," and gets rid of its DOS-based heritage, instead relying on the more stable Windows 2000. It also includes some very clever system protection tools that won't allow newer system files to be overwritten by older system files, for example. And it lets you roll back to earlier versions of hardware *drivers* (software that makes your hardware, such as a printer, work with Windows) if newer ones cause problems. For more information about drivers, see **117 About Updating Drivers**.

- **Easier sharing of a single computer.** It's now easier than ever for several people to share a single PC. XP includes the capability to set up multiple accounts on a single computer, provides password-protection for each account, and lets people share files and folders with each other—or block each other from using their own files and folders. For more details, see **5 Create a New User Account** and **34 About Sharing Files and Folders with Other Accounts**.

- **Built-in Internet protection.** The Internet exposes you to many dangers, and so XP includes a built-in *firewall* that can stop hackers and other malcontents from invading your PC. For more information, turn to **66** About Firewalls and Routers, **67** Protect Yourself with the Windows Firewall, and **68** Customize the Windows Firewall for Maximum Protection.

- **Easier networking.** Networking used to be only for computer gurus. No longer. XP makes it easy for anyone to set up and use their own network, including wireless networks. For more information, see Chapter 6, "Networking Your PC."

- **Easier Internet access.** XP was built from the ground up with the Internet in mind, so getting online is easier than ever. A "wizard" helps you set up new Internet connections with ease, and you can easily manage multiple connections. In addition, Internet Explorer includes countless improvements. If you have the most recent version of XP, it will even block annoying pop-up ads. For more information, see Chapter 7, "Surfing the Web," and Chapter 9, "Keeping Yourself Safe Online."

- **Built-in wireless access.** The world is going wireless, and XP has helped lead the way. It includes built-in software for getting access to the Internet and networks using the wireless technology known as *Wi-Fi*, or 802.11. It can also report to you on the strength of your wireless connection, the amount of time you've been connected, and similar data. For more information, see **59** About Wireless (Wi-Fi) Computing.

- **Better tools for working with graphics, music, and video.** Using Windows XP, it's easy to play music CDs, copy music from those CDs, and make your own CDs, using Windows Media Player. For more information, see **93** About Windows Media Player. It's a snap to use digital cameras and scanners to import pictures, using the **Scanner and Camera** wizard, as you'll see in **105** Import Photos from a Digital Camera, and **106** Scan In Photos. And Windows Movie Maker lets anyone make their own movies and copy them onto DVDs.

NOTE

Windows XP has been available for several years, and over time, Microsoft has made upgrades and changes to the operating system. It has released two "Service Packs"—called SP-1 (the first one) and SP-2 (the second). Depending on when you bought your version of XP, you might have the original version of Windows XP, XP SP-1, or XP SP-2 (which is the most current version). To make things more confusing, if you have the original version of Windows XP, you can upgrade to SP-1 and SP-2 by downloading and installing an upgrade. The basic functioning and overall look of XP hasn't changed since its release. Instead, smaller, although helpful, changes have been made, such as adding a pop-up blocker to Internet Explorer, and improvements to Windows Internet security.

The Difference Between Home Edition and XP Professional

Microsoft makes the sweeping generalization that business users should use XP Professional, whereas home users should buy the XP Home Edition. In many cases that's true, but not always—for example, small office or home office users might not need the extra features of the Professional Edition, and so won't want to pay the extra $100 or so it costs compared to the Home Edition. And home users who want the extra features, such as security extras, might want to fork over the extra money for the Professional Edition.

The core of both operating systems is the same—they have the same interface, the same software powering them both. However, the Professional Edition comes with a number of extras that make it worthwhile not only for many business users, but for some "power home users" as well. These extras include security, computer administration, networking, remote access, and more.

Here are the primary extras you get when you use Windows XP Professional. This book is primarily concerned with the Home Edition; if you have the Professional Edition, refer to Microsoft's online help if you desire more information about any of the following features of Windows XP Professional:

- **Remote Desktop Connection.** This feature lets you control an XP Professional-equipped PC remotely, from another computer, either across the Internet or across a local area network. When you control a PC in this way, it's as if you are sitting at its keyboard and have full access to its programs, files, printers, and other resources. The figure here shows a PC being controlled remotely. (The remote PC is in the window titled **Remote Desktop**.) Additionally, you can transfer files between the remote and local PC. XP Home Edition includes software that lets you remotely control an XP Professional PC, but an XP Home Edition PC can't be controlled remotely. Software is also available for earlier versions of XP that let you control an XP Professional PC, but such updated PCs can't be controlled remotely, either.

NOTE

If you're not sure which version of XP you currently have, you can find out by clicking the **Start** menu, choosing the **Control Panel**, clicking the **Performance and Maintenance** icon, and then clicking **System**. You will be looking at the **System Properties** dialog box. Look at the **General** tab, which will display your version of XP.

Local PC

Remote PC

A PC with XP Professional can be controlled remotely using the
Remote Desktop Connection feature.

- **Security features.** XP Professional has security features that aren't found in the Home Edition. XP Professional's Encrypting File System lets you encrypt files and folders so that only you can read them—or you can let other specified people use them. To learn how to use the Encrypting File System, turn to **36 Protect a File or Folder with Encryption**.

- **Group Policy Editor.** XP Professional includes the **Group Policy Editor**, which lets you control how different people can use the computer. It also lets you customize the way that XP works and looks in ways that can't be done with the XP Home Edition.

- **Internet Information Services (IIS).** XP Professional includes the capability to host web and FTP sites using Internet Information Services (IIS).

- **Domain membership.** XP Professional PCs can join a *domain* on a corporate network and use all of the domain's resources, as well as take advantage of domain features such as centralized security. XP Home Edition PCs can't join domains, but they can use certain domain resources, such as printers.

- **Offline files.** XP Professional users can copy network files and folders to their local PC, work with them when they're not connected to the network, and then synchronize their work when they reconnect to the network.

- **Better backup.** XP Professional can use the **Automated System Recovery** feature of XP's built-in backup software to automatically recover data and programs from crashed hard disks and other system disasters. Although the Home Edition comes with backup software, it doesn't include **Automated System Recovery**. See **123** **About Backing Up Your Hard Disk** and **124** **Protect Your System with System Restore** for more information.

The Nickel Tour of Windows XP

In this book, you'll learn how to master XP, but before you get around to mastering it, you need to know some basics. At this point, take the quick nickel tour of XP.

Start with the Desktop

Let's start off with the *desktop*, the main screen you'll see when you start XP and log in. The following figure shows a typical desktop, with all the primary areas labeled. Here's more information about each:

- **Start button.** Click the **Start button** to bring up the **Start** menu, which is in essence command central for XP. You'll learn more about the **Start** menu a little later in this section. If you want to change how the **Start** menu looks and works, turn to **18** **Rearrange the Start Menu**.

- **Taskbar.** Across the bottom of the screen is the *Taskbar*, on which the **Start** button is located, as well as a series of icons. Additionally, whenever you run a program or open a file, tiles representing the program or file windows appear on the **Taskbar**. To go to any particular window, click its tile in the **Taskbar**. You'll frequently use the **Taskbar** to switch between files and programs and to launch your favorite programs.

- **Quick Launch toolbar.** Along the **Taskbar**, to the right of the **Start** button, you'll find the *Quick Launch toolbar*, which can be a big time-saver. It contains icons of programs you frequently use. Click any icon to run the associated program.

 KEY TERMS

Desktop—The main screen that appears when you start XP and log in. It includes all the important components of the operating system.

Start button—The button on the lower-left corner of the screen that you click to bring up the **Start** menu.

TIP

A quicker way to launch the **Start** menu is to press the **Windows** key on your keyboard—the key with the Windows symbol on it. On desktop computers, the **Windows** key is often found on the lower-left corner of the keyboard between the **Ctrl** and **Alt** keys.

Desktop Icons

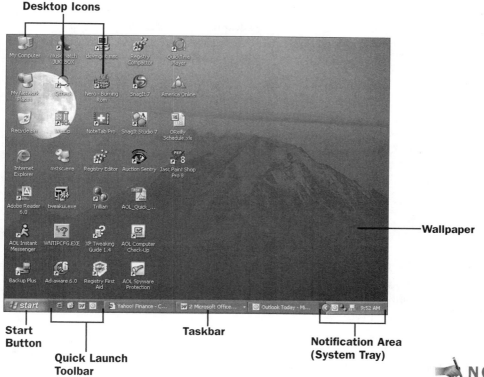

Wallpaper

**Start
Button**

**Quick Launch
Toolbar**

Taskbar

**Notification Area
(System Tray)**

Here's XP's desktop—what you see when you boot up and log into XP.

- **Notification Area (also called the System Tray).** This area of the **Taskbar** handles several different tasks. If Windows sends you alerts for any reason, they'll show up here (for example, when Windows tells you that an update is available, or there's a security patch you should download, the notification appears here). The area also shows you that certain programs are running in the background, doing tasks without you having to know about them. For example, the *Notification Area* shows you that your antivirus software is invisibly working behind the scenes to keep you safe. The area also shows you the Windows clock, which shows the time of day.

  You can build your own toolbars to sit on the **Taskbar**, which can do things such as give you quick access to certain files and folders, among other tasks. To learn how to do it, turn to **20 Build Your Own Toolbar.**

NOTE

To change how the **Taskbar** looks and works, and to add icons to it and take away icons from it, turn to **19 Customize the Taskbar.**

KEY TERM

Notification Area—The right-most portion of the **Taskbar**, which displays alerts (such as when an update for XP is available) and also shows you what programs are running in the background (such as your antivirus software). It also contains the Windows clock, which shows the time of day.

- **Desktop icons.** Icons on the desktop let you quickly launch programs or gain access to certain Windows XP features. To run a program or access the feature, double-click the icon on the desktop. You can add and delete desktop icons, change the way the icons look, and rearrange them as well. For details, see **14** **Clean Up Your Desktop Icons** and **15** **Change Your Desktop Icons**.

- **Background.** The background to your Windows XP desktop is often called the *wallpaper*. XP ships with many different backgrounds from which you can easily choose. You can also download many new background files from the Internet. You can also use any graphic on the web as your wallpaper. For more information, see **11** **Change Your Desktop's Appearance** and **13** **Use a Picture from the Web as Your Background Wallpaper**.

On To the Start Menu

The *Start menu* is command central for Windows XP. Click the **Start** button or press the **Windows** key on your keyboard to bring up the **Start** menu.

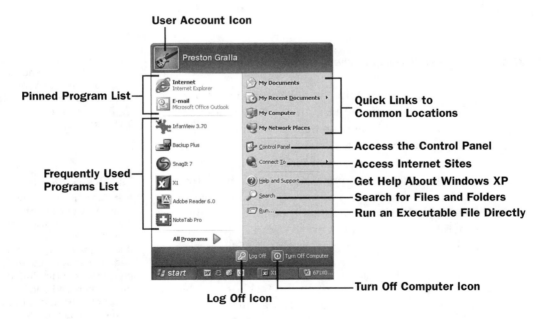

*The **Start** menu is command central for Windows XP.*

KEY TERMS

Wallpaper—The background on your Windows desktop, frequently a picture or photograph.

Start menu—The menu that appears when you click the **Start** button; it gives you access to your programs and files, lets you turn your computer off, and log off of XP, among other functions.

There are many different sections of the **Start** menu, and they contain links to a variety of folders, files, and XP features. Here are the ones on the left side of the two-column menu, and what happens when you click them:

- **Pinned Programs list.** Near the top of the **Start** menu on the left side is a group of icons that are *pinned*—they stay pinned there permanently because they're icons of programs that you use the most often. Click any of these icons to run their associated programs.

- **Frequently Used Programs list.** Just below the pinned programs is a list of frequently used programs. XP calculates which ones you use most often and puts them here in the **Start** menu for you. Unlike the icons on the Pinned Programs list, the icons here change as you use different programs. XP automatically rotates icons in and out of this list as you use programs. Click any of the icons to run the programs associated with them.

The right side of the screen contains a wider variety of links:

- **My Documents** brings you to the **C:\Documents and Settings*Your Name*\My Documents** folder, where ***Your Name*** is your account name in XP. Many people use this folder to organize all their files; XP uses this folder as the default folder for your saved files. You can change the default folder for saving files. For information on this, see **42 Change the Default Folder for Saving Files**.

- **My Recent Documents** brings up a list of the documents you've recently used.

- **My Computer** brings you to a folder that lists all your computer's drives and similar resources.

- **My Network Places** brings you to a folder that lists common places you use on a network, if you're attached to one. (For more information, turn to **48 Browse the Network with My Network Places**.)

- **Control Panel** brings you to the *Control Panel*, which contains a wide variety of utilities that help you control many aspects of how XP works. Later in this chapter, you'll learn more about **Control Panel**.

TIP

You can change just about every aspect of the way the **Start** menu looks and works, including what programs are pinned, among other things. To find out how to do it, turn to **18 Rearrange the Start Menu**.

- **Connect To** brings you to a list of your Internet connections; to connect to any, click on it in the list when it appears. For example, if you have America Online, when you click **Connect To**, you'll see America Online on the list. Click **America Online**, and you'll connect to it.

- **Help and Support** brings you to XP's built-in **Help and Support Center**, which offers comprehensive help when you run into trouble or want to find out more about a particular feature of XP.

- **Search** brings you to XP's built-in search feature. For more information about doing better searching, turn to **39** **About Windows XP Search**, **40** **Kill the Search Dog**, and **41** **Find Files and Folders Faster**.

- **Run** brings up the **Run** dialog box. You can type the name of a file that runs a program, such as **Winword.exe** to run Word, and the program will run. In some instances, you'll have to include the full name of the file and folder, such as **C:\Irfanview\ Irfanview.exe**.

There are also icons at the top and bottom of the **Start** menu:

- **The user account icon**—Located at the top of the **Start** menu next to your user name, clicking this icon lets you manage your user account to do things such as change your icon picture. (For more information about using your own picture for this icon, turn to **6** **Use Your Own Picture for a User Account**.)

- **All Programs**—When clicked, this icon brings up a list of all the programs on your computer. From here, you'll be able to run any piece of software on your system.

- **Log Off**—Clicking this icon logs you out of XP, but won't turn off your computer. You can then log on again later, or someone else who has an account on your computer can log on.

- **Turn Off Computer**—Clicking this icon lets you turn off your PC, restart it, or put it into **Standby Mode**, which is a kind of suspended animation, so that you can quickly restart your computer without having to go through the normally lengthy startup process.

Netscape SmartUpdate	Norton AntiVirus ▸	NewsGator
New Office Document	PhoneTools ▸	PrintMe Internet Printing
Open Office Document	Powertoys for Windows XP ▸	XP-Tweaks
Set Program Access and Defaults	PRO200WL ▸	Adobe Reader 6.0
Windows Catalog	Real ▸	Auction Sentry
Windows Update	Roxio Easy CD Creator 5 ▸	Logitech
WinZip	Startup ▸	NoteTab Pro
AOL for Broadband	SurfSaver ▸	Registry Compactor
America Online 9.0	Trillian ▸	Registry First Aid
Yahoo! Messenger	WinZip ▸	SnagIt 7
Accessories ▸	WS_FTP Pro ▸	StuffIt Standard
Ahead Nero ▸	DellTouch	Microsoft Baseline Security Anal
America Online ▸	Internet Explorer	Yahoo! Messenger
AOL Instant Messenger ▸	Microsoft FrontPage	PerfectDisk 6.0
Backup Plus ▸	Microsoft Money 2002	AnalogX
Dell Accessories ▸	Microsoft Visio	Jasc Software
Games ▸	Outlook Express	Microsoft Office
IrfanView ▸	RealOne Player	NTI Backup NOW!
Java 2 Runtime Environment ▸	Remote Assistance	MSN Messenger 6.1
MailWasher ▸	Solution Center	
Microsoft Interactive ▸	TextPad	
Microsoft Office Tools ▸	Windows Media Player	
Modem Helper ▸	Windows Messenger	
MusicMatch ▸	NetIQ Qcheck ▸	
Netscape 6.2 ▸	Lavasoft Ad-aware 6 ▸	

*Get access to all the programs on your computer by using the **All Programs** icon on the **Start** menu.*

Control XP with the Control Panel

The great thing about XP is how customizable it is—don't like the way something works or looks? No problem. You most likely can change it, and you'll learn how to do all that with this book.

There are many ways to change and control XP, but in many cases, the easiest way is to go through the *Control Panel.*

A set of icons guides you through the **Control Panel**—click one to get to a group of related settings and controls. If you click the **Printers and Other Hardware** icon, let's say, you'll be sent to a page that has another set of icons, each of which represents a particular type of hardware.

Now click the particular piece of hardware that you want to change settings for or customize in some way, such as **Mouse.** You'll come to a *dialog box* of some sort. Select options in the dialog box and then click **OK** to make your changes.

KEY TERMS

Control Panel—The primary place to go when you want to change or customize XP settings.

Dialog box—A screen in XP in which check boxes, buttons, and text boxes are used to control a particular feature or function of XP, such as how your mouse should work.

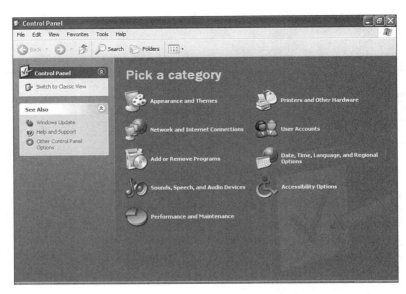

*When you need to customize XP or change settings, the **Control Panel** is often the place to turn.*

TIP

In some instances, you'll see a dialog box with only an **OK** button, but you don't want to have to click it because you don't want XP to do what it's telling you it's going to do. In that case, try clicking the small **X** in the upper-right corner of the dialog box. Sometimes that will close the dialog box. Other times, however, it won't, and your only choice is to click **OK**.

Get used to looking at dialog boxes—it's the main way you communicate with Windows XP. The purpose of a dialog box is simple: To have a "dialog" with you and ask you for information so that you can do something with XP. Most dialog boxes have at least three basic buttons: **OK**, **Cancel**, and **Apply**. When you click the **OK** button, you're telling the dialog box to go ahead and make the selection you've chosen, and then close itself. When you click the **Cancel** button, you're telling the dialog box to *not* make the selection, and then to close itself. When you click **Apply**, you're telling the dialog box to go ahead and make the selection, but not to close itself. Use the **Apply** button when you want to see the results of making a change; that way, the dialog box won't close down, and you can use it to change the option back to the way it used to be or make a new selection.

In some instances, you might get a dialog box that isn't really a dialog at all—you only get a choice to close down the dialog box by clicking **OK**. (For example, you'll get this kind of dialog box when Windows XP is closing down a program that stubbornly tries to remain open.)

The Structure of a Hard Disk

Throughout this book, we'll talk about your hard disk and folders, and so it's a good idea before we begin to get a better sense of how a hard disk is organized.

Each hard disk is identified by a letter, most commonly, **C**. If you have more than one hard disk on your computer, they are identified by letters as well. So, for example, if you have two hard disks, one will be **C** and one will often be **D**. Your CD and/or DVD drives are assigned drive letters as well, and are often labeled **E**. In fact, you can have many drives, all the way up to **Z**.

The same holds true for removable media drives such as CD drives or DVD drives. These storage locations are identified by letters, too. So if you have one hard disk and one CD drive, the hard disk is usually identified as **C** and the CD drive as **D**.

Each hard disk is organized into a series of folders, and each of those folders can have folders inside of them, and so on. The first folder on your computer is called the *root folder*, and it's identified like this: **C:**.

A folder underneath the root folder called **8Wire** would be identified like this: **C:\8Wire**. And a folder underneath **8Wire** called **Latest** would be identified like this: **C:\8Wire\Latest**.

The best way to see the entire structure of your hard disk is to run **Windows Explorer**. (There are a number of ways to run Windows Explorer. The program may be on your **Start** menu or on your **All Programs** menu. You can also launch it by pressing the **Windows+E** key combination.)

You'll notice that Windows Explorer has small + icons next to some folders. These signs mean that the folder has one or more folders inside it. Click the + icon in the left pane, and you'll see the contents of the folder displayed in the right pane, including any folders inside it. When you click a + sign, it turns into a – sign. To close the folder, so that the folders inside it are hidden, click on the – sign. The + sign will then appear.

KEY TERM

Root folder—The first folder on your hard disk, under which all other folders can be found.

Working with Folders

You'll often need to make new folders and move files and folders around on your hard disk. To do all this, you use Windows Explorer. To create a new folder, first highlight the folder underneath which you want to create a new folder. So, for example, if you want to create a folder underneath **C:\Pictures**, you'd first highlight **C:\Pictures** in Windows Explorer.

TIP

Later on, if you want, you can rename the folder by highlighting it and choosing **File, Rename**. Again, the mouse pointer will be in a position so that you can type a new name for the folder. To delete a folder, highlight it and press the **Delete** key.

From the **File** menu, choose **New, Folder**. A new folder will be created called **New Folder**. The insertion point (the mouse pointer) will be in a position so that you can type a new name for the folder.

To *move* a file between folders, highlight the file and while you hold down the left mouse button, drag it to the new folder where you want it. You can move folders in the same way. To *copy* a file or folder, highlight it and choose **Edit, Copy**. Then go to the folder where you want to copy the item, click to position the mouse pointer in the folder, and choose **Edit, Paste**.

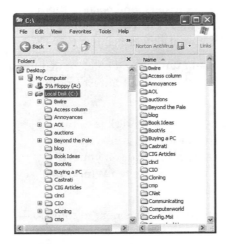

Here's the structure of a typical hard disk, shown in Windows Explorer.

How Windows Is Organized

Windows XP is built so that multiple people can use the same computer. Normally, this would be a problem if every person could see all the files of every other person. It could also mean that when other people use the computer after you, any changes they've made to XP—for example, to the background or the screensaver to use—you will have to live with.

Windows XP, though, solves the problem of multiple users neatly. Every person gets his own account, with his own settings, and even his own special area set aside for files and folders. That way, when you change *your* XP settings, they stay that way until *you* change them. When someone else uses the computer with her account, the changes she makes only affect her.

Each person's private files and folders are found in his own **My Documents** folder. Any file or folder you put there can be seen by you and you alone—no one else can see these items. It's your own private area.

Everyone gets her own **My Documents** folder, and this can lead to some confusion when you're using Windows XP. To clarify it for you, let's take an imaginary example. Say that two people use the computer, one named Gabe and one named Mia. Each has their own logons, and so they have separate accounts, one called **Gabe** and one called **Mia**. Whenever Mia logs on, she will see her own private area as **My Documents**. When Gabe logs on, he will see his own private area as **My Documents**. So how can they each have their own private areas, if both are called **My Documents**?

It's because the **My Documents** folder is in a different location for different users of the computer. Mia's **My Documents** folder is in reality the **C:\Documents and Settings\Mia\My Documents** folder, and Gabe's is the **C:\Documents and Settings\Gabe\My Documents** folder. However, when you save or open files, you don't have to go through that long folder list. In essence, whenever you see **My Documents** in Windows XP, it's a shortcut to your own private folder.

Opening, Saving, and Browsing for Documents

When you use a program such as Word, you often have to open a file. You open it by choosing **Open** from the **File** menu. When you do that, the **Open** dialog box appears. You'll see a list of files that the program commonly uses: in this instance, **.doc**, **.dot**, **.htm**, **.html**, and **.url** files. Even though many other kinds of files might be found in a particular folder, each program filters out files, and only shows those of a certain type. To see more file types, click the **Files of type** arrow and choose other files to show from the drop-down list.

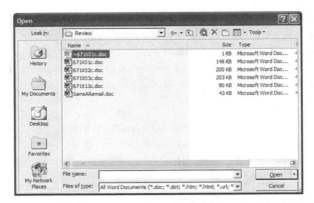

*Whenever you open a file in a program such as Word, the **Open** dialog box appears, letting you browse through your hard disk for the file you want to open.*

The **Open** dialog box lets you navigate through your hard disk to find the file you want. To move to another folder, click the down arrow near the **Look In** box to see a list of folders on your hard disk. From that list, double-click the folder to which you want to browse. When you find the file you want, double-click it to open it.

If you just want to move up to the folder directly above the folder in which you're currently located—say that you want to move from **C:\Pictures\Family** to **C:\Pictures**—click the icon of a folder with an up-arrow on it.

Basic Mouse Operations

The main way you navigate through XP is by using the mouse. Depending on the mouse you have, it may have a variety of different buttons on it. However, you only need two buttons to use XP: the left button and the right button.

Using the Left Mouse Button

You'll mainly use the left button, and you'll use it in several different ways, either by single-clicking or double-clicking with it. Here are the main things to remember about the left mouse button:

- **Double-click** a desktop icon to launch the icon's associated program. If there's an icon for Microsoft Word on your desktop, double-click it to run the program.

- **Single-click** an icon in the **Quick Launch** toolbar to launch the icon's associated program. If there's an icon for Microsoft Word on your **Quick Launch** toolbar, single-click it to launch it.

- **Single-click** check boxes and buttons in dialog boxes to make choices.

- **Single-click** links (blue underlined text) on Internet sites to visit them. If you're on a page and see a link, click that link just once.

Using the Right Mouse Button

The right mouse button isn't used as frequently as the left mouse button, but it serves an important purpose, primarily to access pop-up menus (called *context menus*) from which you can make a choice. For example, if you're in Windows Explorer and right-click a file, you'll get a menu of choices that can be directly applied to the selected file.

TIP

The context menu shows only those choices that can be applied to the selected file—it won't show any options you can't use.

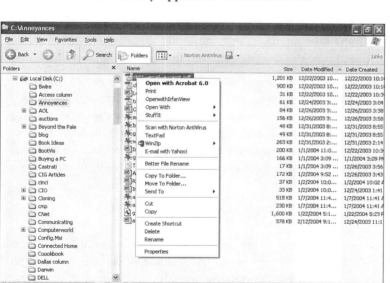

Right-clicking a file or some other object pops up a context menu, from which you can make a choice.

Basic Window Operations

At the heart of XP are individual windows. Whenever you open or create a file, run a program, open a dialog box, run the **Control Panel**—in fact, whenever you do just about anything—you open a window and work inside it.

You typically run many different windows on your computer at the same time, and there are a number of different ways to control those windows and switch between them.

We'll start off with the basics. On the upper-right corner of any window are three small buttons. Here's what each does:

Here are the buttons you'll use for minimizing, maximizing, and closing windows.

 • Click the **Minimize** button to minimize the window—that is, shrink it down so that it is reduced to a tile on the **Taskbar**.

 • When the window is maximized, you'll see icons of two overlapping windows, not just the single **Maximize** button shown here. Click the button of the two overlapping windows to make the window smaller without completely minimizing it. When the window is small, but not completely minimized, you see the icon of just one window, as shown here. Click the **Maximize** button and the window maximizes.

 • Click the **Close** button to close the window.

There are several ways to switch among open windows in XP. Each window you have open shows up as a tile on the **Taskbar**, so you can just click its tile to open that window. You can also cycle through your open windows by pressing **Alt+Tab**. Each time you press that keyboard combination, you'll switch to a new window. Many applications have their own methods of switching between open windows (in Microsoft Word, for example, you can press **Shift+F6** to switch between open windows); refer to the documentation for the application you are using for additional methods.

2

Mastering Startup, Login, and Shutdown

IN THIS CHAPTER:

When you turn on or turn off a light at home, you flip a switch and don't think much more about it. After all, that's the way appliances are supposed to work.

But when it comes to Windows XP, there's a lot more to think about. Because XP allows multiple people to use a computer, and because it offers all kinds of ways to make startup, login, and shutdown easier, there's a whole lot to learn. In fact, taking control of these processes is a great way to get more out of your PC, as you'll see in this chapter.

1 About Windows XP Startup and Login

See Also

→ **7** Log On Automatically

→ **9** About Windows XP Shutdowns

Starting up and using your PC should be as simple as pressing the power button, waiting a moment or two, and then getting to work with your keyboard and mouse. You might think that's the way it should work. But that's not the way it does work—and with good reason, actually.

One of XP's great benefits is that it allows several people to share the same computer, each with his own separate account. That means that each person can change the way the desktop looks, can change the way XP works, and can have his own private files that no one else on the computer can use. So for each person, the operating system and computer seems to be his own.

For all this to work, there must be some way for each person to log in individually. This means that startup in Windows XP is actually a two-step process. In the first part of the process, the operating system starts up and a login screen appears. The second part of the process is when someone logs in by clicking her account icon and typing a password; the familiar XP desktop appears.

When the person is done using XP, she can completely shut down the computer, log out, or switch to another account. For more information, see **8** Turn On Fast User Switching, **9** About Windows XP Shutdowns, and **10** Use Hibernation and Standby.

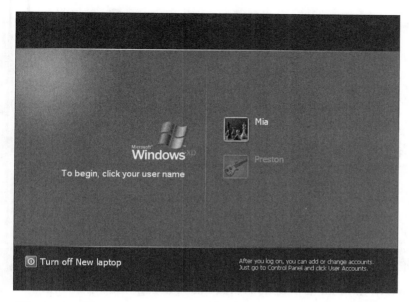

When multiple people share a computer using XP, each has her own separate login, allowing her to customize the operating system exactly the way she wants.

This is actually a greatly simplified version of what really happens when you turn on your PC. In fact, a much more complicated procedure takes place, and it's worthwhile to understand it before you can take full control of how your computer starts. So here's the rundown: Whenever you turn on your PC, it goes through a multiple-step startup process:

1. It starts with the *power-on self test (POST)*, which tests the PC's hardware to make sure that it is working properly.

2. The system *Basic Input Output System (BIOS)* reads the Master Boot Record (MBR), which is the first sector (a special spot) on the hard drive. The BIOS then transfers control of the system to Windows XP, and XP takes control of the startup process.

3. XP looks for a special file named **Boot.ini**. This file contains information that tells the operating system your preferences for startup. If you've created a special boot menu that lets you choose your preferences for startup (see  **Create a Multiboot Menu for Customized Startups**), the boot menu is displayed, and you can make your choice for how to start up XP.

KEY TERMS

Power-on self test (POST)—The process your computer goes through every time you start it, to make sure that all the hardware is working properly.

Basic Input Output System (BIOS)—Built-in software in your computer that handles the hardware's basic functions, such as controlling the keyboard, screen display, and disk drives. The BIOS loads before the operating system.

4. The **Welcome** screen or the login dialog box is displayed, depending on whether you have multiple people using your computer or if you've instead turned on automatic login. For more information, turn to **7** **Log On Automatically**. As a practical matter, you'll be able to create logins for as many people as you need to share the computer.

2 Create a Multiboot Menu for Customized Startups

Before You Begin

✔ **1** About Windows XP Startup and Login

See Also

→ **3** Build Your Own Welcome Screen

→ **6** Use Your Own Picture for a User Account

As you know, XP goes through a fairly complicated startup process before anything actually shows up on your computer screen. Hidden away in that startup process are many options you can set to determine how Windows XP will start; for example, whether to start in "Safe Mode" (if you're troubleshooting problems), whether to use a special fast XP startup option, and so on.

Normally, these kinds of options are hidden, or can be accessed only with difficulty. However, you can build a multiboot text menu that will pop up when you start XP. The menu lets you choose exactly how you want the operating system to start. Each menu entry has a number next to it; to choose the option you want, either scroll down to the entry with your keyboard and press **Enter** or type the number of the entry on your keyboard and then press **Enter**. XP then starts up with the options associated with that menu choice. Here's how to create and use a multiboot menu.

1 Decide on Your Startup Options

KEY TERM

Safe Mode—When XP starts up in this mode, it uses only the minimum amount of software and special services required to run the operating system. If you run into problems with XP, or have hardware issues, using Safe Mode is a good idea because it can help you track down the source of your troubles. For information, see **115** **Troubleshoot Hardware Problems**.

There are many different ways you can customize how XP starts up, so before building your multiboot startup menu, decide which options you want to use.

Many of the choices are rather esoteric and are for programmers or computer professionals, so you don't need to know all of your choices. However, here are the most important options:

- **Boot into Safe Mode.** Sometimes XP will run into very serious problems, and every time you run it, it might crash or exhibit other problems. In those cases, you should boot into *Safe Mode*. If you create a special menu entry for Safe Mode, it's very easy to boot into it whenever you restart your computer.

- **Bypass the splash screen.** When XP starts up, you see Microsoft's familiar "splash screen" that greets you before you see the login screen or before you automatically log into XP, depending on how you've set up your system. You can bypass this screen, however.

- **Change the amount of time the multiboot menu appears.** After a certain amount of time after the multiboot menu appears on your screen, XP boots using the first entry on the menu. You can change the length of this pause and arrange the options on your multiboot menu so that the most common boot option is the first item in the menu.

② Open Notepad

You'll create the multiboot menu by editing the **Boot.ini** file. This file tells your computer how to start up XP. It's a normal text file, and you can edit it using a text editing program such as Notepad.

To open Notepad, click the **Start** button and then choose **All Programs** to display the **All Programs** menu. From the **Accessories** listing, choose **Notepad**.

③ Display Hidden System Files

After you've opened Notepad, you must find and open the **Boot.ini** file. **Boot.ini** is a hidden file—that is, Windows doesn't normally display it in file listings such as Windows Explorer. To tell Windows to display hidden files, open Windows Explorer and choose **Folder Options** from that program's **View** menu. Click the **View** tab and enable the **Show hidden files and folders** option underneath the **Hidden files and folders** section.

NOTE

Windows hides **Boot.ini** and other system files so that you can't damage them. But if you're careful, you can view and edit these files.

④ Open Boot.ini in Notepad

Now that you'll be able to see **Boot.ini**, it's time to open it. Typically, you'll find the file in the **C:** folder, so look for it there. To open it in Notepad, switch to the Notepad window and choose **Open** from the **File** menu. In the **Open** dialog box that appears, choose **Local Disk (C:)** from the **Look in** drop-down list at the top of the dialog box.

Notepad normally shows only those files that end in a **.txt** extension, so at first it won't show the **Boot.ini** file. From the **Files of**

TIP

Before editing the **Boot.ini** file, make a backup copy of it, so that if you make an error when editing it, you'll still have the original that you can revert to. Copy it and give it a different name that you'll remember, such as **Boot.bak**. To make a copy of the file, open it in Notepad, select **File, Save As**, and then save the file as **Boot.bak**. To edit **Boot.ini**, open it again in Notepad.

Type drop-down list at the bottom of the **Open** dialog box, choose **All Files**, and you'll be shown all the files in the directory. When you find **Boot.ini**, double-click to open it (alternatively, click once to select the file and then click **Open**).

5 Edit the File to Change Pause Time

When you open the **Boot.ini** file in Notepad, you'll see a listing that looks something like this:

[boot loader]

timeout=30

default=multi(0)disk(0)rdisk(0)partition(2)\WINDOWS

[operating systems]

multi(0)disk(0)rdisk(0)partition(2)\WINDOWS="Microsoft Windows XP Home Edition" /fastdetect

The listing you'll see won't be for a multiboot menu—the original version of **Boot.ini** just boots you straight into the operating system. You're going to add items that will create a menu.

The first entry you might want to edit is the **timeout** entry. It tells XP how many seconds to display the multiboot menu before booting using the first menu item. In the example shown here, the system will wait 30 seconds (**timeout=30**). If you want to increase the time, use a larger number; if you want to decrease the time, choose a smaller number. In this example, let's use the larger number of 45 seconds: Edit the second line of the **Boot.ini** file in Notepad so that it reads **timeout=45**.

6 Copy and Paste Original Code

Next it's time to create the menu itself. To do it, you'll add new entries underneath the **[operating systems]** section. In the example shown here, there is only one entry, and so no menu appears. We're going to add two new entries, one of which will boot you into Safe Mode, and the other of which will start up XP without displaying the splash screen.

To create a new entry for the multiboot menu, copy the original entry and then edit it. In Notepad, select the following line of code (the first line following the **[operating systems]** section break):

multi(0)disk(0)rdisk(0)partition(2)\WINDOWS="Microsoft Windows XP Home Edition" /fastdetect

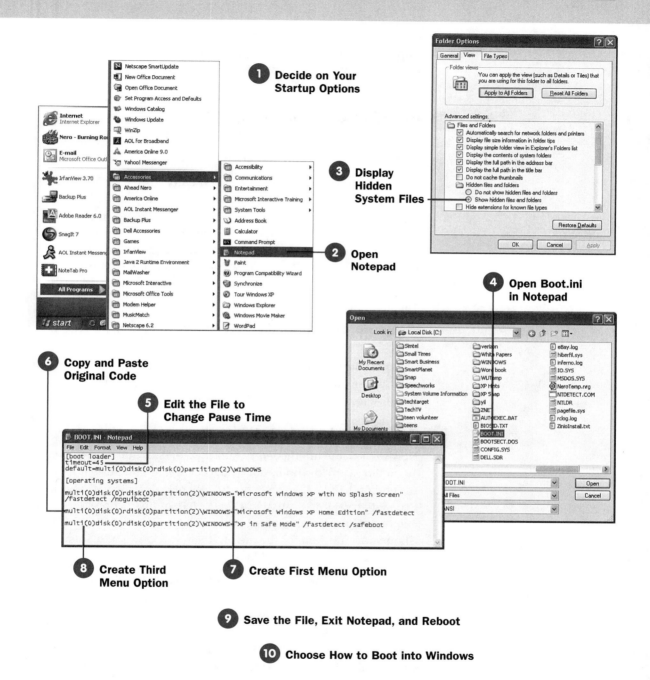

Press **Ctrl+C** (or choose **Edit, Copy**) to copy this block of text to the Clipboard. Then press **Ctrl+V** (or choose **Edit, Paste**) to insert a copy of the line of code immediately after the original block of code.

7   Create First Menu Option

You edit only the last part of the entry—the part after the first quotation mark. Leave the entire front part of the entry as is.

In this example, we're going to add an entry that starts XP without a splash screen. To do that, you add the **/noguiboot** instruction (which in English translates to "don't show the splash screen") to the end of the line, leaving a space between it and **/fast detect**. Inside the quotation marks, put the words you want to appear on the menu for that entry—for example, **"XP with No Splash Screen"**/.

The new entry looks like this:

multi(0)disk(0)rdisk(0)partition(2)\WINDOWS="XP with No Splash Screen" /fastdetect /noguiboot

The first entry is the default, the one that XP will use unless you tell it to use another. In this example, we'll have this new, no-splash-screen menu entry as the first choice.

8   Create Third Menu Option

Now we'll create another entry, this time to boot into Safe Mode. To do that, copy the original line of code again and paste it in at the end of the file, after the original line of code. (Use **Ctrl+C** and **Ctrl+V** to copy and paste.) Add the **/safeboot** instruction to the end of the line, leaving a space between it and **/fast detect**. Change the label on for the menu option to read **"XP in Safe Mode"**. The third entry will look like this:

multi(0)disk(0)rdisk(0)partition(2)\WINDOWS="XP in Safe Mode" /fastdetect /safeboot

Here is what the entire **Boot.ini** file will look like after you've edited it to include two new startup options. This code will create a menu with three items, and will take 45 seconds before automatically booting into the first menu choice (Windows XP without a splash screen):

```
[boot loader]
timeout=45
default=multi(0)disk(0)rdisk(0)partition(2)\WINDOWS
[operating systems]
multi(0)disk(0)rdisk(0)partition(2)\WINDOWS="Microsoft Windows
XP with No Splash Screen" /fastdetect /noguiboot
multi(0)disk(0)rdisk(0)partition(2)\WINDOWS="Microsoft Windows
XP Home Edition" /fastdetect
multi(0)disk(0)rdisk(0)partition(2)\WINDOWS="XP in Safe Mode"
/fastdetect /safeboot
```

9 Save the File, Exit Notepad, and Reboot

After you've made your changes to **Boot.ini** in Notepad, save them (choose **File, Save**). If you forget to save the file, none of your changes will go into effect. Now exit Notepad (choose **File, Exit**), close down any other open programs, and reboot by clicking the **Start** button, choosing **Turn Off Computer**, and then choosing **Restart**.

10 Choose How to Boot into Windows

When you reboot, a menu will appear, based on the **Boot.ini** file you just edited. To choose which way XP should boot, scroll down to the entry you want using the keyboard arrow keys and press **Enter**; alternatively, type the number of the entry on your keyboard and then press **Enter**. XP will now boot the way you told it to.

3 Build Your Own Welcome Screen

The XP **Welcome** screen (also called the logon screen) is the screen you see whenever you turn on your computer, restart it, log off, and switch users. It's a pretty boring screen, and if you're tired of looking at it constantly, join the club—you're not alone.

But you don't have to settle for the same old **Welcome** screen whenever you start up, restart, log off, or switch users. You can build one of your own, using a different picture, different text—pretty much different everything.

Before You Begin

✔ **1** About Windows XP Startup and Login

See Also

→ **6** Use Your Own Picture for a User Account

→ **7** Log On Automatically

To do it, you'll use a free program called **Stardock LogonStudio** that lets you edit, change, and apply new screens. It even includes a graphics tool for building your own screens. Here's how to use it to build your own Welcome screen.

❶ Download, Install, and Run LogonStudio

LogonStudio is free, so you won't have to pay for it. Go to **www.stardock.com/products/logonstudio** and download the software by clicking the **Download** button and following the instructions. When you save it on your hard disk, remember where you put the file. Then double-click the filename and follow the installation instructions.

After you've installed the program, run it by clicking the **Start** button and choosing **All Programs**, **WinCustomize**, and then clicking **LogonStudio**. You'll be asked whether you want LogonStudio to be registered as your screen editor. Click the **Yes** button.

❷ Fill In Basic Information About the Screen

To create a new **Welcome** screen, click the **New** button on the left side of the LogonStudio screen. The **Create New Logon** dialog box appears. It asks for information about you and the screen itself. In the **Name** box, type the name you want to give the screen. This name won't appear on the screen itself. Instead, you'll use it to identify the screen inside LogonStudio. The program lets you create multiple screens and choose among them; the name you type here should be descriptive so that you can easily identify it when choosing it from your list.

In the rest of the boxes, fill in the required information, including your name, email address, web page URL if you have one, and so on. If you plan to create multiple versions of the screen you're about to create, give the screen a version number and a revision number or letter. Type any extra information about the screen in the **Notes** field.

When you're done filling in the form, click the **Create** button.

NOTE

The information such as your email address and author name isn't strictly required to create a logon screen. You can trade logon screens with others, howeverer, and this information is a way to identify yourself and the screens you create when you trade them with others. You can trade with others by uploading the screens to a site that allows people to share screens, such as **http://www. wincustomize.com/skins. asp?library=26&u=0**, and downloading the screens that others have created.

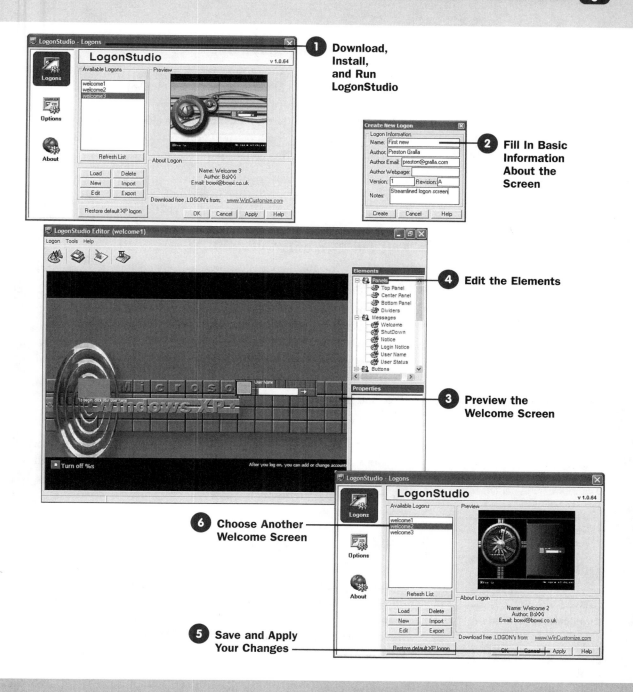

1 Download,
Install,
and Run
LogonStudio

2 Fill In Basic
Information
About the
Screen

4 Edit the Elements

3 Preview the
Welcome Screen

6 Choose Another
Welcome Screen

5 Save and Apply
Your Changes

③ Preview the Welcome Screen

After you click the **Create** button, you'll see a preview of your screen on the left side of the program window. This is the screen you'll see when you turn on Windows. On the right side of the program window is the **Elements** list of all the elements that you can change on the screen, such as the **Login Notice**, the **Shutdown Notice**, the **Buttons**, the **Welcome** message, and so on.

This preview of the **Welcome** screen opens up in a new window. While that preview screen opens in a new window, the current LogonStudio window remains running.

④ Edit the Elements

Change any of the elements of the screen by clicking the option in the **Elements** list and then filling out the form that appears.

For example, to change the login notice, click **Login Notice** under **Messages** in the **Elements** list and type the text that you want to appear when you log in. Press the **Enter** key when you want to start a new paragraph. So, for example, you might want to enter a login notice like this one:

Welcome to XP again, Preston. Glad that you decided to visit again.

This text will appear on the left side of the **Welcome** screen.

Continue to make as many changes to the various screen elements as you want. If you want a message to appear at the bottom of the **Welcome** screen, for example, click the **Notice** option under **Messages** in the **Elements** list and type the message where you want it to appear.

⑤ Save and Apply Your Changes

LogonStudio does not automatically save your changes for you, so if you exit the program now, nothing will happen and you'll lose all the work you've done. Choose **Save and Apply** from the **Logon** menu to save your changes, log off Windows, and go straight to the new **Welcome** screen. You don't have to do anything to use your new **Welcome** screen—it shows up automatically when you start Windows.

NOTE

If you choose **Save** from the **Logon** menu, the Welcome screen you've been working on is saved, but XP won't yet use it.

To create another **Welcome** screen, restart LogonStudio, and follow steps 2 through 5 to create another new **Welcome** screen. Make sure that you give this screen a descriptive title, different from the first screen you named and created.

6 Choose Another Welcome Screen

To choose a different **Welcome** screen, restart LogonStudio, and from the **Available Logons** list, select the screen you want to use and click **Apply**. Windows logs you off, and then logs back on, displaying the **Welcome** screen you just selected.

4 Use Passwords for Better Security

How easy is it for someone to get unauthorized access to your computer when you use XP? As Windows is set up to work as soon as you install it, all anyone has to do is sit down at the keyboard to access your files.

From the **Welcome** screen, all someone has to do is to click your account name to immediately log in, with full access to everything on your computer.

However, for more security, you can create a password, so that the only way to access your computer through your account is to type your password. Here's how to protect yourself by creating and using a password.

1 Choose a Secure Password

Most people imagine that nefarious hackers must spend untold hours of top-secret programming to break into networks and computers. The truth is much more mundane. Hackers frequently break in by simply guessing people's passwords or by using a piece of software that automatically tries many passwords until it finds the right one.

The most important part of choosing a password is choosing one that's not easy to guess. That means you shouldn't choose the following:

- **The word *password*.** Yes, believe it or not, quite a few people use the word *password* as their password. Maybe you've even done it. If you do, stop. It's very easy to guess.

Before You Begin

✔ **1** About Windows XP Startup and Login

See Also

→ **5** Create a New User Account

- **Any combination of your first and last name.** If someone can see or guess your username or knows your real name, it'll be easy for him to guess your password.

- **Any common words or names.** They're simply too easy to guess, so avoid them.

WEB RESOURCE

This site can create a hard-to-crack random password for you. Type characters at random, and it creates the password.

www.world.std.com/~reinhold/passgen.html

So how do you create a password that's hard to guess? Follow this advice:

- **Never use the name of your spouse, children, pets, or anything else associated with you.** If someone knows anything about your life, these names will be the first passwords they'll try. Also, do not use your address, Social Security number, license plate, initials, or similar information. Remember the principle of "security through obscurity."

- **Use at least eight characters in your password.** The longer the password, the harder it is to guess.

- **Mix letters and numbers.** When you mix alphabetic and numeric characters, it's that much harder to guess a password than if you use only letters or only numbers.

TIP

For safety's sake, never use letters or numbers in sequence such as DAL-REL1234. A better one would be ALDELR3224.

- **If you can use uppercase and lowercase characters, use both.** Sometimes passwords are case sensitive, which means that the only way to type them correctly is if the proper case is used. If you can create a case-sensitive password, make sure to mix uppercase and lowercase letters.

② Go to the User Account You Want to Change

Get to the **User Accounts** screen (which lets you manage all aspects of your user accounts, including setting passwords for them) by clicking the **Start** button and choosing **Control Panel**. From the **Control Panel**, click **User Accounts**.

You'll see a list of all the accounts on your system. Click the account to which you want to add a password.

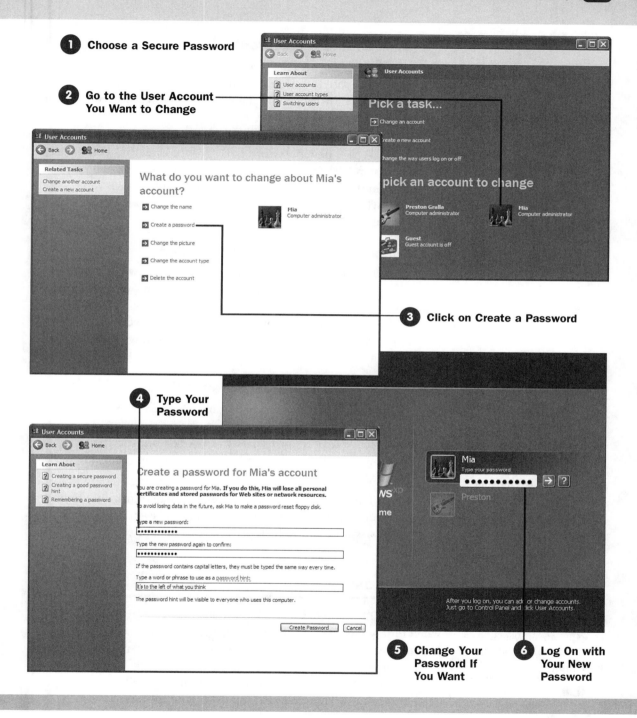

1 Choose a Secure Password

2 Go to the User Account You Want to Change

3 Click on Create a Password

4 Type Your Password

5 Change Your Password If You Want

6 Log On with Your New Password

3 **Click Create a Password**

Windows displays a **User Accounts** screen with a list of options you can choose to perform on the selected account. Click the **Create a password** option; the **Create a password** screen appears.

TIP

If you want to use a password hint for Windows to show you if you forget your password, type the hint into the box at the bottom of the screen.

4 **Type Your Password**

In the **Type a new password** box, type the password you decided on in step 1. In the second text box, type the password again to confirm it. When you're done, click **Create Password**. Your password will be created, and you'll be sent back to your **User Accounts** screen.

5 **Change Your Password If You Want**

If after you create the password, you decide you want a different one, start by opening the **User Accounts** screen (see step 2 for instructions). Click the account you want to work with, and then click **Change the password**. The **Create a password** screen appears. Create your new password the same way you created your first password.

NOTE

If after you create a password you decide you don't want one for the account any longer, from the **User Accounts** screen for your account, click **Remove the password**. From the screen that appears, click **Remove Password**.

6 **Log On with Your New Password**

To make sure that the password took effect, log off XP or restart the computer. When the **Welcome** screen appears, click the account for which you've created a password. A box appears beneath the account name and icon. Type your password and press **Enter** to log into XP.

If you forget your password, click the question mark next to the box that appears for you to type in your password. XP will display your password hint to help prompt your memory.

---

5 **Create a New User Account**

Before You Begin

✔ **1** About Windows XP Startup and Login

See Also

→ **6** Use Your Own Picture for a User Account

Often, you'll have to create more than one user account—for example, when family members suddenly decide they'd like to use your computer. Having two or more people share a single account often leads to problems. One person might like a particular desktop background and icons, whereas another likes different background images and icons. And you might not want to share all your files with other people.

The best answer is to create separate accounts, one for each person who uses the computer. It's easy to set up a new user account—here's how to do it.

1 Go to the User Accounts Screen

The **User Accounts** screen lets you manage all aspects of accounts on your system, including setting up and deleting user accounts. To get to it, click the **Start** button and then choose **Control Panel**. From the **Control Panel**, click the **User Accounts** icon. The **User Accounts** screen opens.

2 Name the New Account

From the **Pick a task** list at the top of the **User Accounts** screen, click **Create a new account**. The **Name the new account** screen appears. Type a name for the new account. This name will appear on the **Welcome** screen as well as at the top of the **Start** menu when the person who uses the account is logged on. When you're done, click **Next**.

3 Choose the Account Type

The **Pick an account type** screen appears. You can choose to make the account one of two different types:

- **Limited.** This account doesn't give full privileges to the person. He'll be able to customize his own account, but he won't be able to make systemwide changes. He'll be able to change or delete his password, change his account picture, customize his XP desktop, view and use files he creates, and also use files in the *Shared Documents folder*. He can also install software, although some programs require users to have administrator privileges before they can be installed.

- **Computer administrator.** This account gets full access and control of the PC. It can do everything that a **Limited** account can do, plus create, change, and delete any account; make any systemwide changes; install any software; and get access to any file.

Think carefully before choosing to make the account a **Computer administrator** account, because it means that the person has full access to the computer and everything on it, including the capability to delete your account.

KEY TERM

Shared Documents folder—A folder that contains files that can be shared by any account on the computer, even if those accounts are **Limited** accounts.

1 Go to the User Accounts Screen

2 Name the New Account

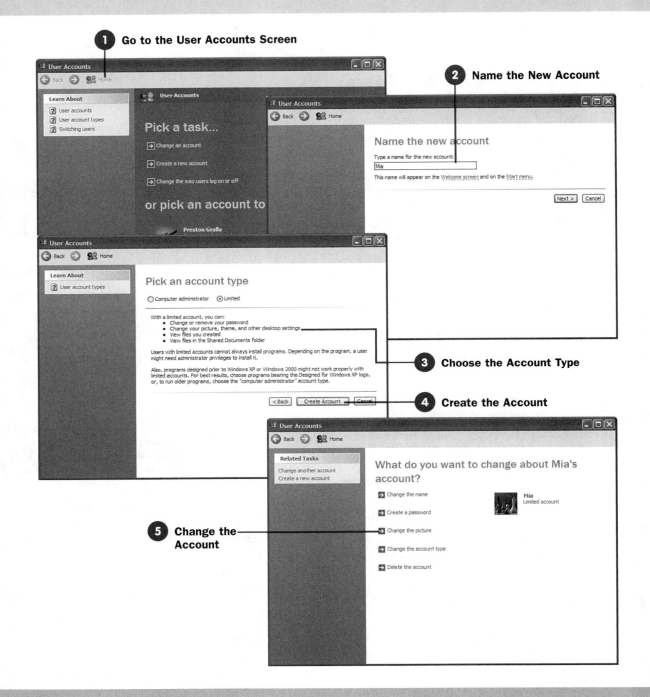

3 Choose the Account Type

4 Create the Account

5 Change the Account

④ Create the Account

When you've chosen the account type, click the **Create Account** button. You'll be sent back to the **User Accounts** screen, and the new account will now be listed there.

⑤ Change the Account

If you want to change anything about the account, click the account icon to come to a screen that will let you change the name of the account, create a password for the account, choose a picture for the account, change the account type, and delete the account. Click the appropriate option and follow the instructions for changing the account.

⑥ Use Your Own Picture for a User Account

Each user account has a picture associated with it that appears on the **Start** menu and on the **User Accounts** screen. But you're not stuck with that picture—XP lets you choose from quite a few different images from its collection. However, you're not limited to the pictures that ship with XP—you can use any picture you want. Here's how to do both.

① Create or Take a Picture

If you want to use your own picture for your user account, you'll first have to create it or find one online. Take the photograph with a digital camera or scan it in with a scanner. You can also create a picture from scratch using a graphics program. Keep in mind that the picture will be displayed as a small square, so size it accordingly.

After you have the picture, put it on your computer's hard disk; remember its filename and where you stored it.

② Choose the Account to Change

Now choose the account whose picture you want to change. Click the **Start** button, choose **Control Panel** from the **Start** menu, and click **User Accounts**. If you want to change the picture on your own account, the one under which you're currently logged on, click the **Change my picture** option from the **Pick a task** list on the **User Accounts** screen.

Before You Begin

✔ ⑤ Create a New User Account

See Also

→ ① About Windows XP Startup and Login

TIP

When you import photos from a digital camera or scan them in with a scanner, Windows XP frequently defaults to putting the files in your **My Pictures** folder. If you want, you can put them in any folder of your choice. You might, however, want to create separate folders for different types of pictures (for example, a **User Accounts** folder for pictures you might want to use on a user account).

1 Create or Take a Picture

2 Choose the Account to Change

3 Choose a Picture from Those That Appear

4 Browse for a Different Picture

6 See How the New Picture Looks

5 Choose the New Picture

If you instead want to change the picture on another account, click the **Change an account** option and, from the screen that appears, choose the account you want to give a new picture. On the **What do you want to change about your account?** screen for the account you've selected, click **Change the picture**.

③ Choose a Picture from Those That Appear

Windows displays the **Pick a new picture for your account** screen. You'll see thumbnail pictures that you can use for your account. To choose any of the Windows-supplied images, click the picture and then click **Change Picture**.

④ Browse for a Different Picture

If you instead want to use a different picture (such as the one you prepared in step 1 of this task), click **Browse for more pictures**. The **Open** dialog box appears. Browse through your hard disk for a picture you want to use. If you've already created a picture you want to use, browse to that folder.

⑤ Choose the New Picture

When you find the picture you want to use, click to select it and then click **Open**. When you do that, you'll be sent back to the **What do you want to change about your account?** screen, and your new picture will show up next to your name.

⑥ See How the New Picture Looks

Click the **Start** button and look at the top of the screen. Your new picture will be displayed at the top of the **Start** menu. If you're satisfied with it, leave it as is. If you're not, go back to the **What do you want to change about your account?** screen (as described in step 2) and follow the directions for choosing a new picture.

TIP

The **Open** dialog box that appears from the **User Accounts** screen displays pictures with only certain file formats: **.gif**, **.jpg**, **.png**, and **.bmp**. You can use pictures in other graphics formats as well, such as **.tif** and **.pcx**. To do so, in the **Open** dialog box, choose **All Files (*.*)** from the **Files of type** drop-down list and you'll see *all* picture files. Also, if you have a picture in another format, you can convert it to one that you can use for a user account. To learn how, see **107 Convert Between Image Formats**.

NOTE

If you're changing the picture of an account that you're not currently using, you'll have to log off XP and log into that account to see what the picture looks like in its place.

Log On Automatically

Before You Begin

✔ **①** About Windows XP Startup and Login

<hr>

KEY TERM

Run box—A dialog box that lets you issue commands to run programs without having to click or double-click icons or files. Some programs and utilities can't be started any other way except from the **Run** box.

<hr>

NOTE

If you're worried about computer security, don't allow automatic logons. With automatic logons, anyone who wants to can log on to your PC just by turning on the computer. If you have a computer in a secure place that only you can access, there's no problem with enabling automatic logon.

If you're the only person who uses your computer, or if you're the main user of your computer and others don't use it that frequently, you might find having to log on every time you restart to be a bit annoying. Perhaps you'd prefer that whenever you start your computer, you're automatically logged in, so that you go straight to your XP desktop—a process called *automatic logon*. Windows can be configured so that only one user is automatically logged on.

If multiple people use your computer, you can enable automatic logon so that you're logged on whenever the computer starts. If others want to use the machine, you can log off, which brings you to the **Welcome** screen, from which other users can then log on.

① Start the Run Box

You're going to use the *Run box* to get to a dialog box that will allow you to control logons. To get to the **Run** box, click the **Start** button and choose **Run** from the **Start** menu.

② Type Command

Type the command **control userpasswords2** and press **Enter** or click the **OK** button. This command brings up the **User Accounts** dialog box, which lets you customize user account functionality in ways not possible when using the normal **User Accounts** screen that you've used in **④ Use Passwords for Better Security**, **⑤ Create a New User Account**, and **⑥ Use Your Own Picture for a User Account**.

③ Turn On Automatic Logon and Click OK

To enable automatic logon, disable (remove the check mark from) the **Users must enter a user name and a password to use this computer** check box. When you do that, you'll notice that the background behind the user accounts in the **Users for this computer** list goes from white to gray. You also won't be able to highlight any of the user accounts in this list.

When you click **OK**, you'll turn on automatic logon. If you're the only account on your PC, you won't have to do anything else—from now on, when you turn on your computer, you'll be automatically logged on.

<hr>

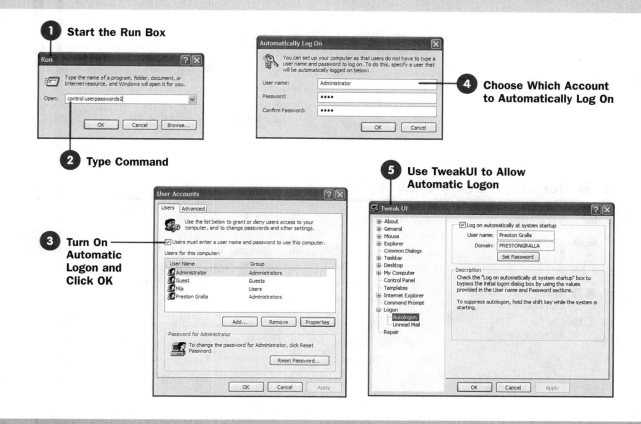

1 Start the Run Box

2 Type Command

3 Turn On Automatic Logon and Click OK

4 Choose Which Account to Automatically Log On

5 Use TweakUI to Allow Automatic Logon

4 ## Choose Which Account to Automatically Log On

If you have more than one account on your PC, after you click **OK**, the **Automatically Log On** dialog box appears, asking which account should automatically log on when your PC starts or restarts. Type the account's username and password, and then confirm the password; then click **OK**. From now on, that account will be automatically logged in when you start your PC. If you don't want the account to have a password, simply type the account's username without filling in the passwords and click **OK**.

If there are several accounts on your system, whenever another person wants to use her account, you can log off, and the **Welcome** screen appears, listing all user accounts. The person can then click her user account to log on. For an even quicker method of switching from one account to another, see **8** **Turn On Fast User Switching**.

5 **Use TweakUI to Allow Automatic Logon**

If you're willing to download a free utility, there's an even quicker way to allow automatic logon. The free Microsoft utility **TweakUI** lets you easily turn on automatic logons, as well as customize many other aspects of XP. For information about how to download and use TweakUI, turn to **24** **About Customizing Your Desktop with TweakUI**.

8 Turn On Fast User Switching

Before You Begin

✔ **5** Create a New User Account

See Also

→ **1** About Windows XP Startup and Login

→ **7** Log On Automatically

One of XP's great features is that it lets several people share a computer—and better yet, it lets them be logged on at the same time, using the **Fast User Switching** feature. With **Fast User Switching** turned on, each person can have her account alive and running programs with files open. So even when one person is using the computer, the other accounts remain open in the background.

Why is this important? Let's say one person wants to download a large file from the Internet, which will take 30 minutes, but otherwise doesn't want to use the computer. That person can log on and start downloading the file, and then you can use Fast User Switching to switch to your account. While the file continues to download in the other person's account, you can still use the computer—and all the files accessible from your account.

Also, if you're using the computer and someone needs to use it for only a few minutes, with **Fast User Switching**, you don't have to shut down all your programs and close all your files. Just switch to the other account, leaving all your programs and files open. When it's your turn to use the computer, all your files and programs are ready for you, just the way you left them.

If **Fast User Switching** isn't turned on, you can still have multiple accounts on your computer, but only one account can be in use at a time. When you log off, all your programs and files are closed. So if you're downloading a file, for example, that file will stop downloading.

For all these reasons, if multiple people use your computer, it's a good idea to turn on **Fast User Switching**. Here's how to do it.

① Check Your PC's Memory

Fast User Switching can use up a lot of memory, because several people can be logged on at the same time, and each of them can be using several programs. If you don't have enough memory, your system will slow to a crawl. If you have less than 128MB of memory (256MB is a more realistic minimum), you shouldn't use **Fast User Switching**. If you have only 128MB, try **Fast User Switching**; you can always turn it off if it slows down your system.

To find out how much *RAM (Random Access Memory)* your computer has, right-click the **My Computer** icon on your desktop, choose **Properties** from the context menu, and click the **General** tab of the **System Properties** dialog box. At the bottom of the box, you'll see how much RAM you have. If you see that you have at least 128MB of memory, you can use **Fast User Switching**. If not, consider installing more memory in your PC.

KEY TERM

RAM (Random Access Memory)—The memory in your PC used when you run XP and programs and open files. Unlike the storage space on a hard disk, when you turn off your computer, all the information in RAM is lost.

② Go to the User Accounts Screen

You turn on **Fast User Switching** from the main **User Accounts** screen. Get there by clicking the **Start** button, choosing **Control Panel** from the **Start** menu, and clicking the **User Accounts** icon.

When the **User Accounts** screen is shown, click **Change the way users log on or off**. You'll come to the **Select logon and logoff options** screen.

③ Turn On the Welcome Screen

To turn on Fast User Switching, XP must be set to use the **Welcome** screen. Unless you've changed the Windows XP options, it already uses the **Welcome** screen. On the **Select logon and logoff options** screen, make sure that the **Use the Welcome screen** check box is enabled.

NOTE

If the **Welcome** screen option is not selected, when you turn on your computer, you'll see a logon prompt instead of the **Welcome** screen. You can't take advantage of the **Fast User Switching** feature unless you use the **Welcome** screen.

④ Turn On Fast User Switching

To turn on the Fast User Switching feature, enable the **Use Fast User Switching** check box and then click **Apply Options**.

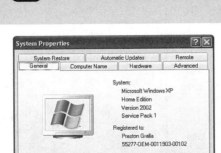

① **Check Your PC's Memory**

② **Go to the User Accounts Screen**

③ **Turn On the Welcome Screen**

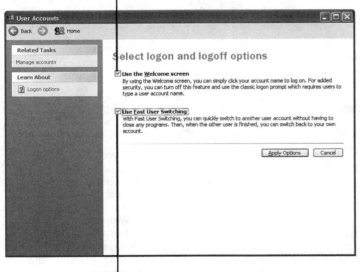

④ **Turn On Fast User Switching**

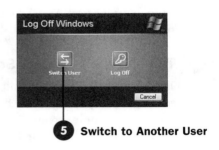

⑤ **Switch to Another User**

5 Switch to Another User

After you're turned on Fast User Switching, it's easy to switch to another user account. Click the **Start** button and choose **Log Off** from the **Start** menu. In the **Log Off Windows** dialog box that appears, click the **Switch User** button. You'll immediately be sent to the **Welcome** screen, which lists all user accounts. Click any account icon to switch to that account, in the same way that you normally use the **Welcome** screen.

9 About Windows XP Shutdowns

Shutting down Windows XP is a simple process. Before shutting down your PC, you should first save and close any files you have open and then close down any programs.

After you do that, you can shut down XP in two different ways:

- Click the **Start** button, choose **Turn Off Computer** from the **Start** menu, and then click the **Turn Off** button. If you want to restart your computer instead of shutting it off, click the **Restart** button instead of the **Turn Off** button, and your computer will shut down and immediately restart. You can also put your computer into Standby or Hibernate mode, each of which in essence puts your computer into a kind of suspended animation that uses very little power; you can restart the computer quickly from these modes. For more information about these modes and how to use them, turn to **10** Use Hibernation and Standby.

Before You Begin

✔ **1** About Windows XP Startup and Login

See Also

→ **10** Use Hibernation and Standby

When you shut down XP, you have a choice of turning it off, restarting it, or putting it into Standby or Hibernation mode.

- Press your PC's power button until your computer turns off.

When you shut down your PC, it alerts any open programs or services that it's shutting down and gives them time to close. Even if you've shut down all the programs you opened (such as word processors or Internet browsers), other programs and services continue to run in the background and must close before Windows XP can shut down. For example, antivirus software runs in the background, as do a variety of services such as one that makes it easy for your PC to be configured to connect to wireless networks.

After XP alerts any running programs and services to shut down, it then starts its shutdown process. If any programs or services are still running, Windows shuts them down itself.

Shutting Down XP If Programs Hang

Sometimes programs or services refuse to close, even after XP tries to force them to do so. If that happens, XP itself may refuse to shut down. Sometimes faulty hardware can be the cause of the problem, as well.

However, there's a way to shut down XP even if it freezes. Press **Ctrl+Alt+Del**, and you'll display the **Task Manager**. From the **Shut Down** menu, hold down the **Ctrl** key and click **Turn Off**. XP will now shut down.

The **Task Manager** also has a way for you to shut down any programs that refuse to close: Click the **Applications** tab, highlight the program you want to close, and click **End Task**.

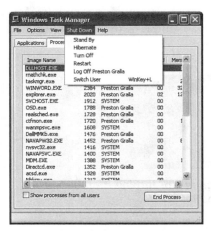

As a last resort, you can use the Task Manager to shut down Windows XP if it refuses to turn off.

10 Use Hibernation and Standby

Desktop computers can suck up a lot of electricity; if you leave your PC on all day and use it for only a few hours, you're paying the electric company a whole lot more than you should. Wouldn't it be nice to save some of that money?

For laptops, conserving power is even more vital. Even the best of laptops has only a limited amount of power in its battery, and you want each battery charge to last as long as possible. You especially want laptops to conserve power when they're not in use.

Windows XP offers two similar ways to save electricity when you're not using your PC, but don't want to turn it off—Hibernation and Standby modes. These special states use little or no electricity and have the added benefit of bringing your PC back to life very quickly. Put your PC into one of these states, and when it comes back to life, it won't have to go through its normal, lengthy startup routine. Instead, it comes on very quickly in the state you left it in. In other words, you won't have to close files and programs before you put your computer into Standby or Hibernation mode, and you won't have to start the programs after the computer comes back to life. Instead, your computer remembers what was opened and what was closed, and starts up in the exact state you left it in.

Here's how to use Hibernation and Standby modes—and how to decide when to use which.

Before You Begin

✔ **9** About Windows XP Shutdowns

See Also

→ **1** About Windows XP Startup and Login

1 Decide Whether to Use Standby or Hibernation

Standby and Hibernation modes are similar to one another, but not quite identical. When you use Standby mode, your PC consumes a very small amount of power. It turns off your hard drives, the *Central Processing Unit (CPU)*, the fans, and any other components that use a lot of power, including the monitor on a laptop.

Standby mode still uses enough power to keep your RAM alive. It saves your files, programs, and other information in RAM, so that when you come out of Standby, your PC almost instantaneously springs back to life. If, however, your PC is turned off for some reason when it's in Standby—for example, if your home or office's electricity goes out—you'll lose all the information in RAM.

KEY TERM

Central Processing Unit (CPU)—The main brains of your PC, this chip does all the computing and processing. A Pentium chip is a CPU.

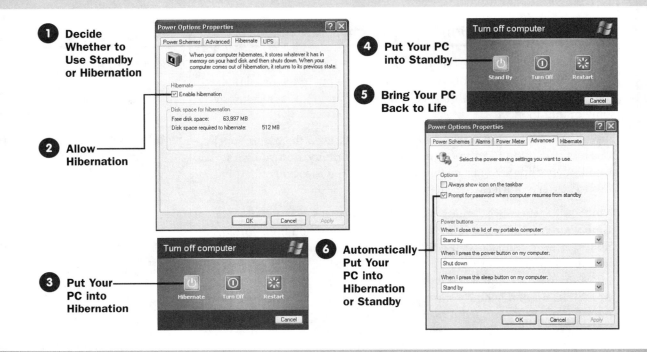

1 Decide Whether to Use Standby or Hibernation

2 Allow Hibernation

3 Put Your PC into Hibernation

4 Put Your PC into Standby

5 Bring Your PC Back to Life

6 Automatically Put Your PC into Hibernation or Standby

Hibernation mode, on the other hand, uses absolutely no power. It saves all the information in RAM to your hard disk and then shuts off your PC. That means absolutely no power is being used. But because your PC is using no power and has to retrieve information from your hard disk when you turn the PC back on, your PC doesn't come back to life as quickly as it does when you use Standby mode. However, because all the information is stored on your hard disk rather than in RAM, if your PC is turned off, you won't lose any of the information.

The following chart details the differences between the two states:

Differences Between Standby and Hibernation Modes

Standby Mode	Hibernation Mode
Uses a small amount of power	Uses absolutely no power
Comes back to life quickly	Comes back to life more slowly
Requires no hard disk space	Requires hard disk space
Powers down quickly	Powers down more slowly
Doesn't save data in RAM if the power goes out	Saves data in RAM even if the power goes out

So which mode should you use, and when? If you'll be leaving your PC off for a relatively short time, such as under an hour, consider Standby mode because it powers down quickly and starts up quickly. The small amount of power you'd save by going into Hibernation mode won't make much of a difference, and your electricity isn't likely to go out within the next hour.

If you're leaving your PC off for longer periods of time, and especially overnight, consider using Hibernation mode. You'll save more electricity and know that you won't lose data if the power goes out. The little extra power down and startup time will be worth the additional security and power savings. As a general rule, Hibernation mode is better for laptops because it uses less power, and you'll use less of your battery life.

2 Allow Hibernation

Your computer might not be set up to allow it to hibernate, and you might have to change a setting to allow for hibernation. To check this setting, click the **Start** button, choose **Control Panel** from the **Start** menu and then click the **Performance and Maintenance** icon. From the screen that appears, click **Power Options**.

The **Power Options Properties** dialog box appears. Click the **Hibernate** tab, enable the **Enable hibernation** check box, and click **OK**. The tab shows you how much free hard disk space you have, and how much hard disk space you'll require for hibernation.

3 Put Your PC into Hibernation

To put your PC into hibernation, click the **Start** button and choose **Turn Off Computer** from the **Start** menu. A screen appears with several options: **Standby**, **Turn Off**, and **Restart**. The **Hibernation** option does not appear. Press the **Shift** key, and **Hibernation** appears where **Standby** used to be. Click the **Hibernation** button to put your PC into Hibernation mode. After several moments during which your PC saves the contents of your RAM to your hard disk, your PC will go into Hibernation mode.

NOTE

You might be unclear about what the terms *cold boot* and *warm boot* mean. To "boot your PC" means to start it. In a warm boot, your computer is already on, and you turn off Windows XP and turn it back on without actually turning off the power to your PC. You do it by clicking the **Start** menu, choosing **Shut Off Computer**, and then choosing **Restart**. In a cold boot, you turn off your computer and its power source. To do this, click the **Start** menu, choose **Shut Off Computer**, and then choose **Turn Off**. When you restart your computer by pressing the power button, you're performing a cold boot—cold, because you're starting it at a point when it isn't using power.

 TIP

If there is not a large difference between the **Free disk space** and the **Disk space required to hibernate** numbers, don't use Hibernation mode. If you do, you'll use up too much disk space.

4 Put Your PC into Standby

You don't have to change any settings if you want to allow your PC to go into Standby mode; it's already capable of doing that. Just click the **Start** button and choose **Turn Off Computer** from the **Start** menu. A screen appears with the three options **Standby**, **Turn Off**, and **Restart**. Click **Standby** to put your PC into Standby mode. Relatively quickly, it will go into Standby mode.

5 Bring Your PC Back to Life

When your PC is in Standby or Hibernation mode, it appears as if no power is coming to it (in fact, in Hibernation mode, no power *is* coming to it). To bring your PC out of Standby or Hibernation mode, press the power button as if you were starting up your PC. If the PC has been in Standby mode, it comes back to life very quickly, and in the state in which you left it when you put it into Standby. If the PC has been in Hibernation mode, it will take a few seconds to come back to life, and in the state in which you left it when you put it into Hibernation mode.

6 Automatically Put Your PC into Hibernation or Standby

If you want, you can tell your PC to go into Hibernation or Standby mode if you haven't used it for a certain amount of time. Start by opening the **Power Options Properties** dialog box as described in step 2. Then click the **Power Schemes** tab. The bottom two drop-down lists let you configure how long your computer should be idle before it enters Standby or Hibernation mode. Choose the amount of time for each mode and click **OK**.

When your system is in Hibernation or Standby mode, anyone can press the power button and bring it back to life—*without knowing your password*. Your PC will start right up in the state it was in when you put it into Standby or Hibernation mode. You can, however, require that someone type the password associated with your user account if they want to bring your PC out of each state. To do that, click the **Advanced** tab and enable the **Prompt for password when computer resumes from standby** check box. Note that this check box may not appear on the **Power Schemes** tab in the **Power Options Properties** dialog box unless you require that a password be used to log into your user account.

3

Customizing Your Desktop

IN THIS CHAPTER:

Don't like the way your *desktop* looks and works? No problem—you can change it easily. XP makes it incredibly easy to change the desktop in many different ways.

In this chapter, you'll delve deep into the desktop, changing just about every aspect of it, from its background, to the appearance of its icons, to how the **Start** menu and **Taskbar** look and function. You use your desktop more than just about any other part of Windows XP, and it's the main way you interact with the operating system. When you change the desktop, to a great extent you change all of XP.

11 Change Your Desktop's Appearance

If you want to change the *desktop*, start with the absolute basics— change its basic appearance, including its background, menu and button style, screen resolution, and more. Here's how to do it.

1 Go to the Display Properties Dialog Box

The **Display Properties** dialog box is the primary place where you'll be able to customize how your desktop looks. Get there by right-clicking a blank space on the desktop, and from the context menu that pops up, choosing **Properties**.

2 Change the Desktop Background

The desktop background, often called *wallpaper*, is the picture or solid color that forms the background to the desktop. It's easy to change to a different color or picture.

Click the **Desktop** tab in the **Display Properties** dialog box. The **Background** list has many different pictures you can use as your background. Scroll through the list to see what's available. As you highlight a picture, you'll see a preview of it on the picture of the monitor at the top of the dialog box. When you find an image you want to use, click **Apply**, and it will be applied to the desktop.

You're not limited to the pictures in the **Background** list, however. You can use any graphics file in the following formats: **.bmp**, **.gif**, **.jpg**, **.jpeg**, **.dib**, **.png**, **.htm**, and **.html**.

To use any other image, click the **Browse** button on the **Desktop** tab of the **Display Properties** dialog box and browse to the directory that holds the graphic you want to use. Choose the graphic file and click **Open**. You'll return to the **Desktop** tab and see a preview of the image you selected in the monitor at the top of the dialog box.

Most pictures you choose are not the same dimensions as your screen and so must be scaled in some way. Most often, the picture is smaller than your screen. You use the **Position** drop-down box on the **Desktop** tab to choose how to scale the picture:

- **Center.** When you choose this option, the picture stays at its original size. If it is smaller than the screen, a background color surrounds it. If it is larger than the screen, only a portion of the picture is displayed.

- **Tile.** When you choose this option, the picture is displayed in *tiles*—multiple copies of the picture displayed like bathroom tiles around a bathtub.

- **Stretch.** When you choose this option, the picture is stretched in both dimensions to fit the screen size.

If you've chosen to center the picture, you can choose the color that surrounds it. Choose the color you want from the **Color** drop-down list box.

When you're done choosing your picture and its display options, click **Apply** to apply your choice to the desktop.

③ Choose Button Style and Color Scheme

XP gives you control over how individual windows will appear, your overall color scheme, and the font size on all your windows. To change all this, click the **Appearance** tab on the **Display Properties** dialog box.

To choose the window and button style, choose one of the two options in the **Windows and buttons** drop-down list:

- **Windows XP Style.** This option uses the familiar XP rounded edges for windows and buttons.

- **Windows Classic Style.** This option uses the old, pre-Windows XP style with squared-off windows and buttons.

TIP
You can also use any picture you find on the Web as your background (see **13** Use a Picture from the Web as Your Background Wallpaper).

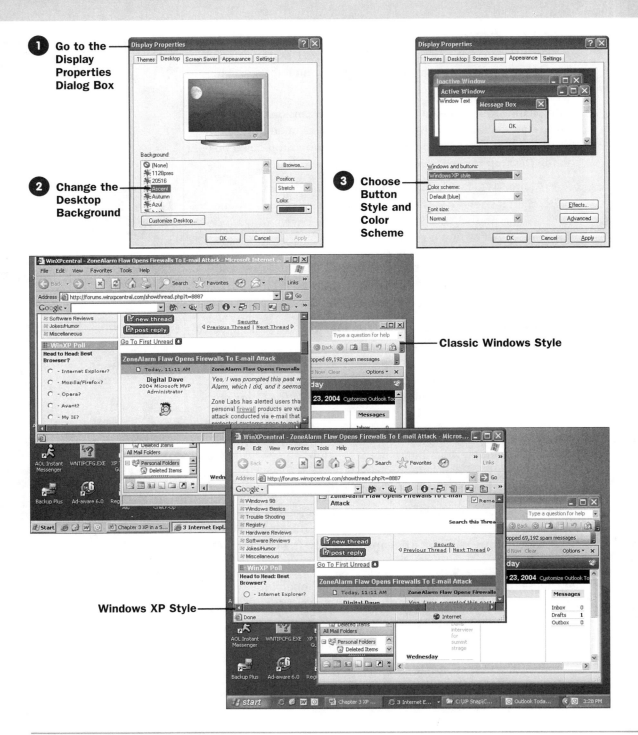

1 Go to the Display Properties Dialog Box

2 Change the Desktop Background

3 Choose Button Style and Color Scheme

Classic Windows Style

Windows XP Style

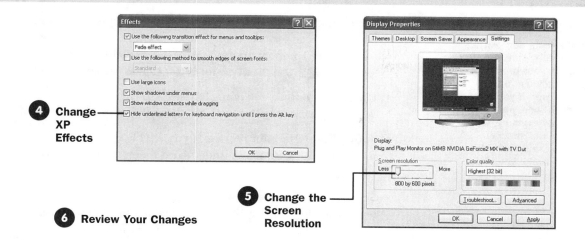

④ Change XP Effects

⑤ Change the Screen Resolution

⑥ Review Your Changes

To choose the colors for dialog boxes and windows, choose from the **Color scheme** drop-down list. Choose a font size for the text displayed in dialog boxes and windows from the **Font size** drop-down box. As you choose colors and font sizes, you'll see the changes in the picture of XP windows and boxes at the top of the dialog box. When you're done, click **OK** to close the dialog box and apply the changes.

④ **Change XP Effects**

Windows XP has a great many options that affect the appearance of the desktop as well as how XP works overall. To get to them, go back to the **Appearance** tab of the **Display Properties** dialog box and click the **Effects** button to display the **Effects** dialog box. Here's what you can change:

- **Transition effects.** From the **Use the following transition effects for menus and tooltips** drop-down list, you can choose either **Fade effect** or **Scroll effect**. With the fade effect, menus appear to slowly fade in and out when you choose them; with the scroll effect, the menus scroll up and down. If you don't want to use any effects, don't enable the box.

- **Screen fonts.** Enable the **Use the following method to smooth edges of screen fonts** check box to choose a method to smooth screen fonts. For more information about smoothing screen fonts, see **121 Use ClearType for Better Laptop Resolution**.

- **Use large icons.** As the name implies, this choice forces Windows to use large icons on the desktop and throughout XP.

- **Show shadows under menus.** If you enable this check box, menus will have shadows underneath them, giving them a richer 3D effect.

- **Show window contents while dragging.** Enable this check box to see the contents of any window as you drag it. If this option is not enabled, you won't see the contents of screens as you drag them.

- **Hide underlined letters for keyboard navigation until I press the Alt key.** Windows XP lets you make menu choices by pressing key combinations. For example, to bring up the File menu, you can press **Alt+F**. The menu normally shows which underlined letter you need to press along with the **Alt** key to bring up the menu. So, for example, the word **File** in most menu bars has the letter **F** underlined. If you enable this option, that underline appears only when you press the **Alt** key. However, just to make things more confusing, this setting doesn't work with every program. For example, it won't work with Microsoft Word, but it does work with Internet Explorer.

When you're done making your choices, click **OK** to close the **Effects** dialog box and click **OK** again when you get to the **Appearances** tab of the **Display Properties** dialog box.

⑤ Change the Screen Resolution

You can also change the resolution of your screen—in other words, how much your screen should display. The resolution is measured in *pixels*. Each pixel represents a single dot on your screen. You can set things up so that your screen displays more pixels or fewer pixels: for example, 800 pixels wide by 600 pixels deep (commonly referred to as 800 × 600), 1024 × 768, or a number of other resolutions. The choices you have are determined by the kind of graphics card and monitor you have.

The higher the resolution, the more you can show on your screen, but the smaller each item will be. At a higher resolution, you'll show more of a Word document, for example, but the words will appear smaller. You can also show more icons on your screen, but each icon will be smaller.

On the **Settings** tab of the **Display Properties** dialog box, drag the **Screen Resolution** slider to choose a resolution. As you move it, you'll see the effect reflected in the monitor at the top of the dialog box.

You can also choose the color quality, from the **Color quality** drop-down box. Choose the highest quality, unless it slows down your computer. High-quality color is not only more appealing, it's also easier on your eyes.

When you're done, click **OK** to apply your changes.

6 Review Your Changes

When you're done, see what your desktop looks like. If you're pleased with it, continue to use your computer. If not, go through the preceding steps again to make changes until you find settings with which you're satisfied.

12 Create Your Own Screensaver

Windows *screensavers* have a long history. A screensaver is a series of pictures or animations that play on a computer screen against a background when the computer is idle for a certain amount of time.

Screensavers were first built because in the earlier days of computing, if the same image stayed on the screen for too long, that image would actually burn itself onto the monitor, and a ghost of the image would always be present.

Monitors haven't had burn-in problems for years, but that hasn't slowed down the popularity of screensavers. You can find screensavers of all kinds, and even Hollywood has gotten into the act, often creating screensavers as a way to promote movies.

NOTE

The actual settings you'll see in the **Color quality** list might say something such as **Highest (32-bit)** and **Medium (16-bit)**. The larger the number of bits, the more colors your computer can use, which means richer, more realistic pictures.

Before You Begin

✔ 11 Change Your Desktop's Appearance

See Also

→ 16 Build Your Own Themes

KEY TERM

Screensaver—A series of pictures or animations that play on a computer screen against a background when the computer is idle for a certain amount of time.

You're not limited to using only the screensavers built into XP or those built by someone else. You can easily create screensavers of your own, using XP's built-in capabilities. To do it, you first must have pictures you want to use for your screensaver. You can take them with a digital camera, scan them in with a scanner, or find them on the Internet. Before creating your screensaver, collect all the pictures you want to use. After you do that, here's how to create a screensaver from them. Keep in mind that the screensaver you create will be a slideshow rather than the animations such as dancing ribbons and fireworks you sometimes see in screensavers.

❶ Put the Pictures in Their Own Folder

Your screensaver will work by using all the image files in a folder. Collect all your picture files and place them in the same folder.

The folder Windows XP normally uses for your screensaver is **C:\Documents and Settings*Your Name*\\My Documents\\My Pictures**, where ***Your Name*** is your XP account name. If you want to go with the system default, put your pictures in the **My Pictures** folder.

However, you can use any folder you want. In fact, you might want to use a different folder, because that way you can set up different folders for different screensavers.

TIP

You're not limited to the screensavers that ship with XP, or one you build yourself. The Internet offers thousands of other screensavers. Find them at popular download sites such as **www.download.com**, **www.tucows.com**, and **www.screensaver.com**. Installation instructions might differ from screensaver to screensaver, so read the directions.

❷ Go to the Screen Saver Tab of the Display Properties

Right-click a blank spot on the desktop and choose **Properties** from the context menu that appears. When the **Display Properties** dialog box opens, click the **Screen Saver** tab.

If you want to use an existing screensaver, choose it from the **Screen saver** drop-down list. You'll see a preview of the selected screensaver on the monitor at the top of the dialog box. If you find one that you want to use and don't want to use your own screensaver, click **OK**.

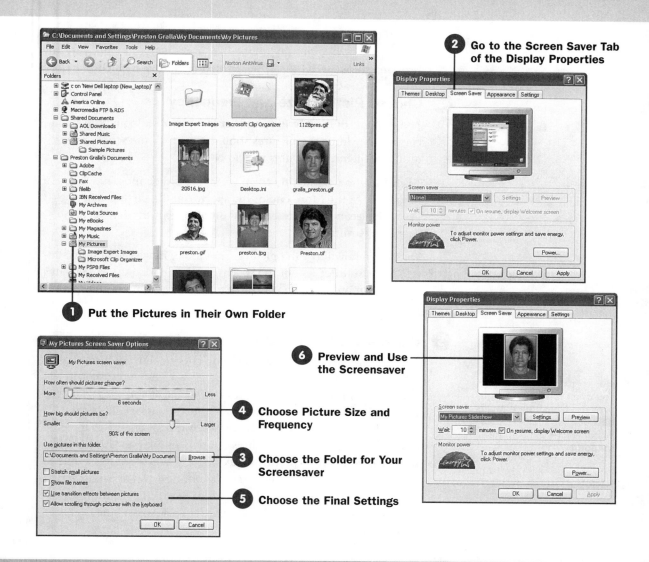

1 Put the Pictures in Their Own Folder

2 Go to the Screen Saver Tab of the Display Properties

6 Preview and Use the Screensaver

4 Choose Picture Size and Frequency

3 Choose the Folder for Your Screensaver

5 Choose the Final Settings

3 ## Choose the Folder for Your Screensaver

If you want to create your own screensaver, choose **My Pictures Slideshow** from the **Screen saver** drop-down list and then click **Settings**. You'll come to the **My Pictures Screen Saver** dialog box. If you've put your pictures into C:**Documents and Settings***Your Name***My Documents****My Pictures**, where *Your Name* is your XP account name, you don't have to choose a different folder. However, if you've put the image files in a different folder, click the **Browse** button, select the appropriate folder, and click **OK**.

4 Choose Picture Size and Frequency

The top part of the **My Pictures Screen Saver** dialog box lets you control how large the pictures should appear in the screensaver and how often the pictures should change.

To change how frequently the pictures should change, move the top slider. At the **More** end of the spectrum, the pictures change every six seconds. At the **Less** end of the spectrum, they'll change every three minutes.

To change how large the pictures should be, move the bottom slider. At the **Smaller** end of the spectrum, they'll take up 25 percent of your computer screen. At the extreme **Larger** end of the spectrum, they'll take up your entire screen.

5 Choose the Final Settings

TIP

You don't have any control over the transition effects between pictures—Windows XP applies them randomly.

The bottom part of the screen lets you choose your final settings. If you have small pictures and want them resized to your screen, enable the **Stretch small pictures** check box. If you want file-names to appear onscreen along with the pictures, enable the **Show file names** check box. If you want transition effects to appear between pictures (such as a fade), enable the **Use transition effects between pictures** check box. If you want to be able to scroll through your pictures using the right arrow key while your screensaver is playing, enable the **Allow scrolling through pictures with the keyboard** check box. Click **OK** when you've chosen all your screensaver options.

6 Preview and Use the Screensaver

Back on the **Screen Saver** tab of the **Display Properties** dialog box, you'll see your screensaver images previewed in the monitor at the top of the dialog box. In the **Wait** box, choose how long you want your computer to be idle before the screensaver kicks in.

If you're satisfied with the preview, click **OK**. Your screensaver will start up after you don't use your computer for the amount of time you specified.

13 Use a Picture from the Web as Your Background/Wallpaper

Windows ships with a good selection of backgrounds (also called *wallpaper*), but you're not limited to what you find there. In fact, the number of pictures you can use as your background is practically unlimited. That's because you can easily use any picture you find on the web as your background. And as you'll see in these steps, using a picture as your background is quite easy to do.

1 Find a Picture on Google

Whenever you're browsing the Web and come across a picture you want to use as your background, you can save it to use (as outlined in the following steps). If you're actively looking for a picture, the best place to find it is on the Google search site, which has a special search area devoted to finding pictures.

Go to **www.google.com** and click the **Images** tab. You'll be brought to the **Image Search** page. Type a word or words that describe the picture you're looking for and press **Enter** or click **Google Search**. You'll be sent to a page with many different pictures. Scroll through until you find an image you might want to use as your background.

2 View the Picture

Click the picture you're interested in using as your background. You'll be sent to a page that shows a thumbnail of the picture at the top and the page on which the picture was found at the bottom.

Just to the right of the thumbnail is the URL of the picture, as well as the size of the picture in pixels. Use the size in pixels to gauge how well the picture will fit as your background. See **11** **Change Your Desktop's Appearance** to determine your screen resolution in pixels so that you have a sense of whether the picture you're currently looking at will fit your screen. It doesn't have to be the same size because you can stretch or tile the picture (as described in **11** **Change Your Desktop's Appearance**), but it's a good idea to know the size of the picture relative to your screen resolution.

Before You Begin

✔ **11** Change Your Desktop's Appearance

See Also

→ **16** Build Your Own Themes

TIP

To fine-tune your Google image search, click the **Advanced Image Search** link above the search text box. You can use the options there to search based on criteria such as image size and file format.

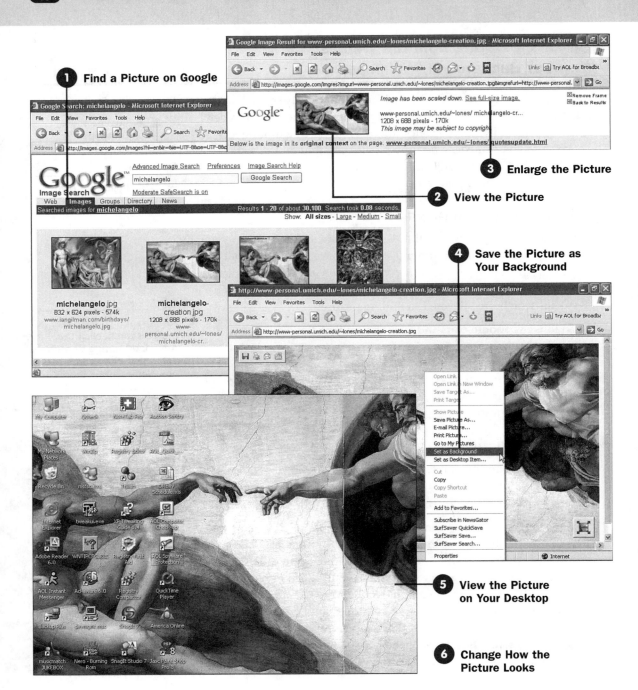

1 Find a Picture on Google

2 View the Picture

3 Enlarge the Picture

4 Save the Picture as Your Background

5 View the Picture on Your Desktop

6 Change How the Picture Looks

❸ Enlarge the Picture

To see the picture full-size instead of as a thumbnail, click the thumbnail of the picture. Alternatively, click the **See full-size image** link. The picture now appears in your browser full size.

❹ Save the Picture as Your Background

Right-click the enlarged picture and choose **Set as Background** from the context menu. The picture will now be set as your background. In fact, as you're browsing the Web, you can save any picture as your background in this way—no need to use Google. When you come across a picture you want to use as your background, right-click it and choose **Set as Background** from the context menu.

✎ NOTE

These instructions for saving a picture from the Web as your background are for Internet Explorer. If you use another browser, the instructions might vary slightly.

❺ View the Picture on Your Desktop

Go to the desktop and see how it is displayed. Because it may not be the exact resolution of your screen, the image might be cut off, stretched, or tiled. If you're pleased with the way it looks, however, leave it as is.

❻ Change How the Picture Looks

If you're not satisfied with how the picture looks, you can change it by tiling it, stretching it, or centering it. Right-click a blank spot on the desktop, choose **Properties** from the context menu, and click the **Desktop** tab of the **Display Properties** dialog box. Refer to **⓫ Change Your Desktop's Appearance** for information on tiling, stretching, or centering the image.

Go back to your desktop and view the picture again. If you're satisfied, leave it as is. If not, repeat this step to change how the picture looks until you are satisfied.

🌐 WEB RESOURCE

www.lycos.com

This search site also has a feature that lets you search for pictures. When you go there and do a search, click the button next to **Pictures** to search for images on the Web.

14 Clean Up Your Desktop Icons

Before You Begin

✔ **11** Change Your
        Desktop's
        Appearance

See Also

→ **15** Change Your
        Desktop Icons

→ **16** Build Your Own
        Themes

Use Windows XP for long enough, and it becomes littered with a variety of desktop icons—icons for programs you've installed, icons for folders, and icons for files you or installation programs have put there for quick reference. Additionally, XP itself puts a fair number of icons on your desktop right from the start.

This means that your desktop can become cluttered with icons that you rarely, if ever, use. Not only does this make for a messy desktop, it also makes it much more difficult to find the icons to programs, files, and folders you *do* want to use.

The solution? Clean up your desktop icons. Delete those that you don't need anymore. Although it's possible to do this manually, there's a simpler way—use XP's built-in feature for cleaning up your desktop.

1 Open the Desktop Items Dialog Box

Right-click a blank spot on the desktop and choose **Properties** from the context menu. Click the **Desktop** tab and then click the **Customize Desktop** button to open the **Desktop Items** dialog box.

2 Run the Desktop Cleanup Wizard

You'll use the **Desktop Cleanup** wizard to clean up desktop icons you rarely use. From the **Desktop Items** dialog box, click **Clean Desktop Now** to launch the **Desktop Cleanup Wizard**.

A **Welcome to the Wizard** screen appears. Click **Next** to continue with the wizard.

3 Delete Desktop Icons

The next page of the wizard lists most of the icons on your desktop. (The wizard calls the icons *shortcuts*.) In the **Date Last Used** column, you'll see the last date and time you clicked the icon. If you've never clicked the icon, the list reads **Never**.

Enable the check boxes next to those icons you want to delete. For icons you want to keep, make sure that there is no check in the box next to them.

> **NOTE**
>
> The **Desktop Cleanup Wizard** does not display or let you delete system icons, such as those for the **Recycle Bin**, **My Network Places**, or **My Computer**. In step 4 in this task, you'll learn how to delete those icons from the desktop or include those icons on your desktop.

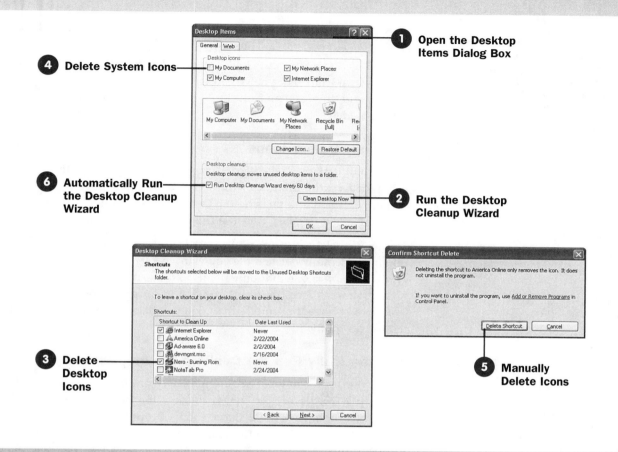

4 Delete System Icons

1 Open the Desktop Items Dialog Box

6 Automatically Run the Desktop Cleanup Wizard

2 Run the Desktop Cleanup Wizard

3 Delete Desktop Icons

5 Manually Delete Icons

After you choose the icons you want deleted, click **Next**. A screen appears, telling you which icons will be deleted. If you want to delete those icons, click **Finish**. The icons will be deleted to a new folder on your desktop called **Unused Desktop Shortcuts**.

4 **Delete System Icons**

After you finish running the **Desktop Cleanup Wizard**, you'll return to the **Desktop Items** dialog box. At the top of the tab, you'll find a list of system icons, including **My Documents**, **My Computer**, **My Network Places**, and **Internet Explorer**. Disable the check boxes next to those icons you don't want to appear on your desktop. Enable the boxes next to those that you want to appear on the desktop.

TIP

If you deleted icons with the **Desktop Cleanup Wizard** that you later decide you want back on the desktop, open the **Unused Desktop Shortcuts** folder on your desktop and drag the icons back onto the desktop.

Click **OK** and then click **OK** again. The icons you chose to be deleted by the **Desktop Cleanup Wizard** are deleted and placed in the **Unused Desktop Shortcuts** folder on your desktop. Additionally, those system icons that you've chosen to be displayed will be displayed, and those system icons that you don't want to be displayed will be hidden.

⑤ Manually Delete Icons

Check your desktop. If there are icons that you didn't clean up using the **Desktop Cleanup** wizard, manually delete them by clicking on them and pressing the **Delete** key. When the confirmation dialog box appears, click the **Delete Shortcut** button.

Be careful to delete only those icons that are shortcuts, or you might accidentally delete a file you want to keep. A shortcut icon on the desktop is one that only points to a file, and is not the file itself. A shortcut icon has small arrow in its lower-left corner. If an icon doesn't have that small arrow and you delete it, you're deleting the actual file itself.

⑥ Automatically Run the Desktop Cleanup Wizard

If you want, you can have XP automatically run the **Desktop Cleanup Wizard** every 60 days. Go back to the **Desktop Items** dialog box (right-click the desktop, choose **Properties**, click the **Desktop** tab, and click the **Customize Desktop** button). Enable the **Run Desktop Cleanup Wizard every 60 days** check box, and the wizard will run every 60 days. Disable the check box, and the wizard won't run automatically. Click **OK** twice to close the dialog boxes.

---

⑮ Change Your Desktop Icons

Before You Begin

✔ ⑪ Change Your Desktop's Appearance

See Also

→ ⑭ Clean Up Your Desktop Icons

Not happy with the desktop icons on your desktop? No problem—you can change them. You can change icons for programs to any other icon on your system, and as you'll see in this task, Windows offers you a lot more icons than you realize.

Before you change your icons, you should understand a little bit about how icons work. Icons can be found in one of three types of files:

- **.ico files.** This special kind of graphics file ends in an **.ico** extension, like this: **Coolpicture.ico**.

- **.exe files.** Some, but not all, of these program files also contain icons.

- **.dll files.** *dll* is short for dynamic link library, and **.dll** files provide functions that programs can use. Some **.dll** files contain icons, and in fact contain entire icon libraries. Most **.dll** files, however, do not contain icons.

With that as a background, here's how to change desktop icons.

1 Right-click the Icon to Change

Right-click the icon you want to change and choose **Properties** from the context menu. The **Properties** dialog box for that icon appears. Click the **Shortcut** tab—it's from this tab that you'll change your icon. Recall that Windows also refers to desktop icons as "shortcuts."

2 Open Change Icon Dialog Box

In the **Properties** dialog box, click the **Change Icon** button to display the **Change Icon** dialog box. At the top of the dialog box, in the **Look for icons in this file** box, you'll see the filename and location of the file in which the current icon can be found.

In the **Select an icon from the list below** box are thumbnails of all the icons in the current file. There may only be one icon shown here or there may be many icons. If there is more than one icon shown, click the icon you want to use and then click **OK**.

NOTE
You won't be able to change system icons, such as for **My Computer** or **Network Places**, using this method. To find out how to change those icons, see step 5 in this task.

3 Browse for a Different Icon

If there's only one icon in the list for the current file, or if you don't see an icon you want to use, click the **Browse** button to browse for more icons. Look for files in the **.ico** format (that is, files that end with the **.ico** extension). Some **.exe** files and some **.dll** files also have icons, although many do not.

If you're looking for a sizable collection of icons from which to choose, browse to the **CL\Windows\System32** folder and open the file **shell32.dll**. Open the file, and a list of icons will appear.

NOTE
There's no way to know ahead of time whether the **.exe** and **.dll** files contain icons, so when you click one of these files, you might not find any icons inside.

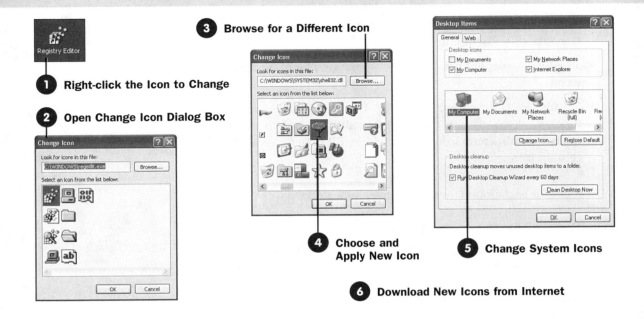

Registry Editor

1 Right-click the Icon to Change

2 Open Change Icon Dialog Box

3 Browse for a Different Icon

4 Choose and Apply New Icon

5 Change System Icons

6 Download New Icons from Internet

4 Choose and Apply New Icon

Choose your icon from the list and then click **OK** twice. On your desktop, the new icon will be applied.

5 Change System Icons

The icons for **My Documents**, **My Computer**, **Network Places**, and the **Recycle Bin** (separate icons for the full bin and the empty bin) cannot be changed using the **Change Icons** dialog box. Instead, right-click a blank space on the desktop and choose **Properties** from the context menu. When the **Display Properties** dialog box opens, click the **Desktop** tab and then click the **Customize Desktop** button. In the middle of the **General** tab of the **Desktop Items** dialog box, you'll see icons for **My Documents**, **My Computer**, **Network Places**, and the **Recycle Bin** (separate icons for the full bin and the empty bin). Click the icon you want to change, click the **Change Icon** button, choose an icon you want to use, and click **OK** twice to close the dialog boxes. The new icon will be applied.

6 **Download New Icons from Internet**

You're not limited to icons included in Windows XP. You can find thousands of icons and icon collections on the Internet. Sites such as **www.iconbazaar.com** and the popular download sites **www.tucows.com** and **www.download.com** have icon files, and many are free. Download them and follow the instructions for installing them. Remember the folder where you put them, and then when you want to use the icons, browse to that folder, following the steps outlined in this task.

16 **Build Your Own Themes**

As you've already seen in this chapter, and you'll see throughout the rest of this book, XP is almost infinitely customizable, especially the way it looks and sounds. It's easy to change the desktop background (wallpaper), the screensaver, system sounds, icons, and much more.

Even after you get XP looking the way you want, though, you might get tired of it. Perhaps you want a completely different look and feel—but then again, maybe you'll want to revert to the way it currently looks on occasion.

There's an answer to your problem—use *themes*. Themes package together XP's entire look and feel, so that with a few clicks you can choose a new theme and entirely change the way XP looks. There are many themes you can find and buy; for example, themes related to movies can include backgrounds and screensavers from the movie, sounds from the movie, and so on. (For information on how to find and download themes from the Internet, see **17** **About Getting More Themes Online**.)

Although most people are familiar with themes, many don't realize that it's easy to create your own. Follow these steps to do it.

1 **Customize Your Desktop**

First, customize your desktop, including the button style and color, screen resolution, and XP special effects. You change all this from the **Display Properties** dialog box (right-click a blank spot on your desktop and choose **Properties** from the context menu). For details on how to use the dialog box to make changes, see **11** **Change Your Desktop's Appearance**.

Before You Begin

✔ **11** Change Your Desktop's Appearance

✔ **12** Create Your Own Screensaver

✔ **13** Use a Picture from the Web as Your Background/Wallpaper

✔ **25** Change Your System Sounds

✔ **27** Change Your Mouse Settings

See Also

→ **15** Change Your Desktop Icons

→ **17** About Getting More Themes Online

KEY TERM

Theme—A collection of pictures, sounds, background, and cursors that give XP a particular look and feel. You can easily switch from theme to theme with a few clicks.

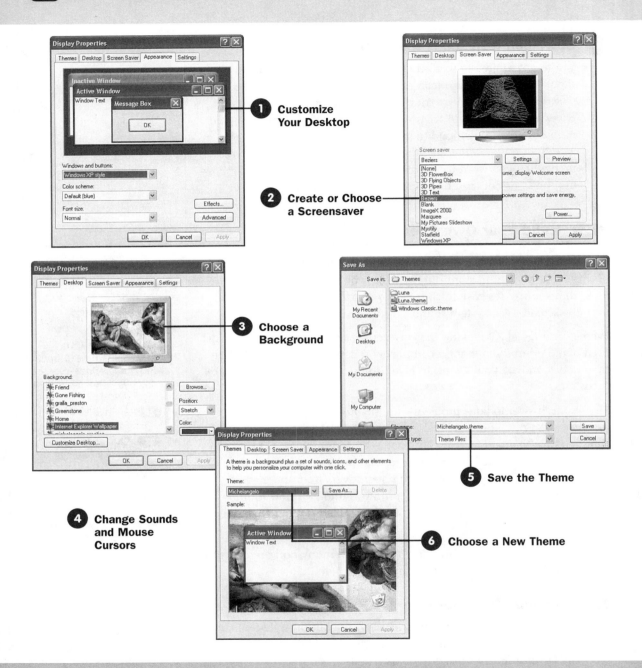

1 Customize Your Desktop

2 Create or Choose a Screensaver

3 Choose a Background

4 Change Sounds and Mouse Cursors

5 Save the Theme

6 Choose a New Theme

2 Create or Choose a Screensaver

Choose or create a screensaver that you want to use for your theme. In the **Display Properties** dialog box, click the **Screen Saver** tab, and choose a screensaver from the **Screen saver** drop-down list. To create your own screensaver, see 12 **Create Your Own Screensaver**.

3 Choose a Background

You spend a lot of your computing time looking at your desktop background, and so choosing a background for your theme is important. To choose a background (also called the *wallpaper*), from the **Display Properties** dialog box, click the **Desktop** tab and choose a background from the **Background** box.

You can also use a picture from the Web as your background. For information, turn to 13 **Use a Picture from the Web as Your Background/Wallpaper**.

4 Change Sounds and Mouse Cursors

Themes can have sounds and mouse cursors associated with them. To change your system sounds, see 25 **Change Your System Sounds** and 26 **Record and Use Your Own System Sounds**. To change your mouse cursors, see 27 **Change Your Mouse Settings**.

5 Save the Theme

You've now created an entire theme. To save it so that you can call it up for later use if you change to another theme or customize XP, click the **Themes** tab in the **Display Properties** dialog box. Click the **Save As** button; in the **File name** box in the **Save As** dialog box, give the theme a descriptive name and end it with the **.theme** extension. When you click the **Save** button, a dialog box opens into the **My Documents** folder. You can save the theme there, in the **C:\Windows\Resources\Themes** folder, where the rest of XP's themes are stored, or in any other folder. Many people prefer to store their themes in the **C:\Windows\Resources\Themes** folder so that all themes are in one place.

💡 TIP

If you use pictures from the Web as backgrounds for different themes, XP uses only the most recent background you've chosen for all themes. To use different pictures from the Web for different themes, you need a workaround. Follow the instructions for finding a picture on the Web in the first part of 13 **Use a Picture from the Web as Your Background/Wallpaper**. When you find a picture, right-click it and choose **Save Picture As** from the context menu. Save the picture file to a folder and remember where you saved it. When you want to use it as a background, go to the **Desktop** tab of the **Display Properties** dialog box, click the **Browse** button, and then go to the folder where you saved the picture. Open the picture and click **OK** to make it a background that can be saved as part of a theme.

6 Choose a New Theme

To choose a different theme than the current one you're using, go to the **Themes** tab of the **Display Properties** dialog box. From the **Themes** drop-down list, choose a theme and click **OK**.

17 About Getting More Themes Online

Before You Begin

✔ 16 Build Your Own Themes

See Also

→ 11 Change Your Desktop's Appearance

→ 12 Create Your Own Screensaver

→ 13 Use a Picture from the Web as Your Background/Wallpaper

→ 25 Change Your System Sounds

→ 27 Change Your Mouse Settings

Although it's easy to build your own themes, as you've seen in 16 **Build Your Own Themes**, the best way to get new themes is to find them online. There are literally thousands of prebuilt themes out there, waiting for you to download them. Most are free, so you shouldn't have to pay for them. Some, however, ask for payment.

There's no single way to install the themes you'll find online; different ones require different installations. Some come as files that end in **.exe**; to install those after you download them, double-click them, and an installation process launches. Check the Help area of the download site for information.

If you download a theme file that ends in a **.theme** extension, you should save it to your **C:\Windows\Resources\Themes** folder. Usually, the related art, sound, icon, wallpaper, and cursor files will be installed into a subfolder. After you've installed the theme, choose it like you do any other theme, as outlined in 16 **Build Your Own Themes**.

Not infrequently, commercial movies create themes as a way to publicize the movie. These days, just about every movie released has an associated website. You can usually find the site locations by looking in newspaper ads or by going to the website of the studio that produced the movie. The themes may be located in different areas of the movie website. If there's a **Downloads** area, check there.

 WEB RESOURCE

Visit any of these sites for selections of themes you can download. Also visit general download sites, such as www.download.com.

www.themeworld.com

www.topthemes.com

www.theme.org

www.tucows.com

Sometimes, movies don't make available entire themes, but they do offer desktop backgrounds, screensavers, and sometimes sounds. If that's the case, download and use those elements to build your own theme as described in **16** **Build Your Own Themes**.

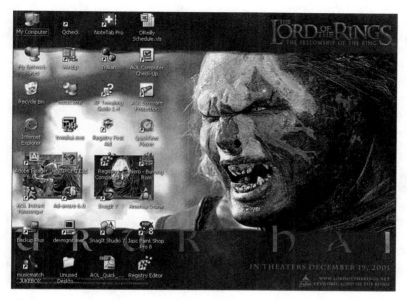

Movies such as **Lord of the Rings** *often make screensavers and background available—using these elements, you can build your own themes. This background was downloaded from* **www.lordoftherings.net***.*

By the way, you should realize that a significant number of the movie- and entertainment-related backgrounds, themes, and screensavers that you find online probably violate copyright laws. Frequently, fans create the themes or elements without asking permission from the movie studios and then upload them. You won't be prosecuted for using them, but you should realize that they are frequently in violation of copyright. If you download themes or elements from the official movie sites, however, you won't violate copyright laws.

NOTE

When you change a theme, as outlined in **16** **Build Your Own Themes**, you'll see an entry in the drop-down **Themes** menu titled **More themes online...** The wording of that item implies that if you choose it, you'll be sent online to a site with themes you can download. However, that's not the case. In fact, when you choose it, you're sent to a site advertising Microsoft's Plus for Windows XP. Plus is a series of software that has a collection of screen-savers, themes, games, and similar content, but you'll have to pay $29.95 for it. Although the content is good, first consider trying to find themes for free, as outlined in this task.

18 Rearrange the Start Menu

See Also

→ **6** Use Your Own Picture for a User Account

→ **19** Customize the Taskbar

→ **22** Use the Quick Launch Toolbar

![KEY TERMS]

Pinned Programs list—A list of programs, at the top-left side of the **Start** menu, that stay there permanently until you remove them or put new ones there.

Frequently Used Programs list—A list of programs you use frequently, located just below the Pinned Programs List. The programs are moved in and out by XP automatically.

The **Start** menu packs an astonishing number of features into a small amount of screen real estate. Using it, you can log on and log off Windows XP, start your favorite programs quickly, find any program on your computer, open your favorite documents, get to the **Control Panel**, and more.

But many people overlook the **Start** menu except when they want to log off or run a program they rarely use. There seems no way to customize it, to make it work the way you want, and so people very quickly find other ways of using XP, even though those other ways may be less effective and more time-consuming than using the **Start** menu.

Most people don't realize that the **Start** menu is extremely customizable—as you'll see in this task, you can change it in many different ways. Before learning how to customize it, though, take a moment to learn about some confusing terminology. On the left side of the menu are two groups of programs, separated by a faint horizontal line. The programs above the line are called *Pinned Programs*, and those at the bottom are called *Frequently Used Programs*. When you put a program in the **Pinned Programs** list, it stays there permanently until you decide you want to move it out or put different programs there. **Frequently Used Programs**, on the other hand, move in and out automatically, depending on how often you use them.

As you'll see in this task, you can customize both those sections, as well as most other parts of the XP **Start** menu.

1 Unpin Programs from the Pinned Programs List

The **Pinned Programs** list should contain programs you use frequently and to which you want quick access. When you install XP, Internet Explorer and Outlook Express are put there automatically because Microsoft assumes that you'll want to use your browser and email program frequently—and that you'll want to use Internet Explorer as your browser and Outlook Express as your email program.

However, you can instead display icons for a different browser and email program, or you can get rid of those icons entirely. You can add different programs to the list, as well.

To change which browser and email program show up on the list, or to delete them entirely, first right-click the **Start** button and choose **Properties** from the context menu. Click the **Start Menu** tab, make sure that the **Start menu** option is selected (not the **Classic Start menu** option), and then click the **Customize** button to display the **Customize Start Menu** dialog box. In the **Show on Start menu** section of the dialog box are two entries, one for **Internet,** and one for **E-mail.** To change the browser or email program that appears on your **Pinned Programs** list, choose the appropriate program from the drop-down menu to the right of the **Internet** or **E-mail** label.

To keep any browser or email program from appearing in the **Pinned Program** list, disable the check box to the left of **Internet** or **E-mail** label, click **OK,** and then click **OK** again.

You can also unpin any icon from the **Pinned Programs** list, not just your browser and email program. Right-click the icon in the **Start** menu you want to unpin and choose **Remove from This List** from the context menu. The icon is removed from the list, but the program itself isn't deleted; you'll only remove the icon shortcut to the program.

❷ Add Items to the Pinned Programs List

You can also easily add items to the **Pinned Programs** list, and those items don't have to be programs. They can be programs, folders, or files.

To add an item to the list, open Windows Explorer and locate the item you want to move to the list. Right-click the item and drag it to the **Start** button. The **Start** menu opens. Drag the item to the location on the **Pinned Programs** list where you want it displayed. As you drag the item, it appears semitransparent and has the small jagged arrow on the icon, indicating that it's a shortcut.

Make sure that you *right-click and drag* the icon from Windows Explorer to the **Start** menu. If you drag the icon without right-clicking it, you actually *move* the item to the **Pinned Programs** list instead of creating a shortcut there. Then, if you end up removing the item, you'll actually delete it, rather than deleting a shortcut to it.

💡 TIP

Keep in mind when deciding which programs to put on the **Pinned Programs** list, that you don't want duplicate programs on that list and on the **Quick Launch** toolbar, a section of the **Taskbar** that has shortcuts to programs. If you're going to put a program on the **Quick Launch** toolbar, put different programs on the **Pinned Programs** list. To learn how to add programs to the **Quick Launch** toolbar, see **22** Use the **Quick Launch Toolbar.**

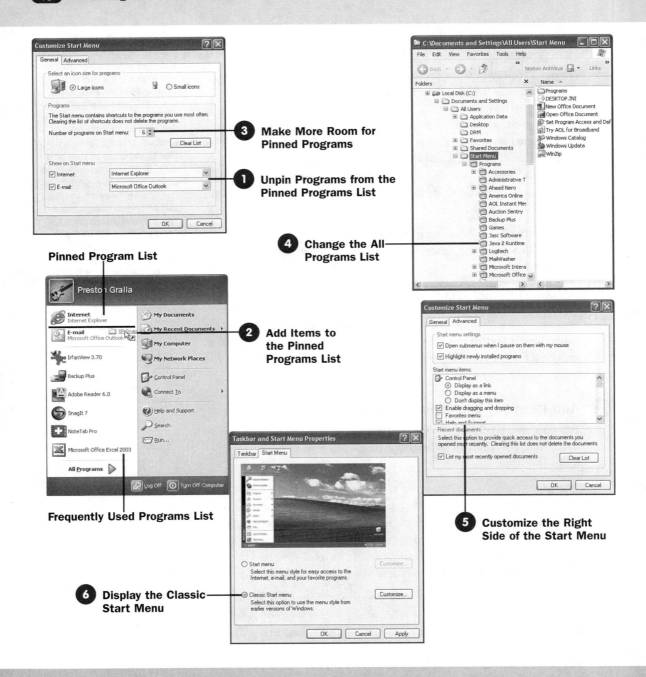

3 Make More Room for Pinned Programs

1 Unpin Programs from the Pinned Programs List

4 Change the All Programs List

Pinned Program List

2 Add Items to the Pinned Programs List

Frequently Used Programs List

5 Customize the Right Side of the Start Menu

6 Display the Classic Start Menu

3 Make More Room for Pinned Programs

The left side of the **Start** menu is divided between the **Pinned Programs** list and the **Frequently Used Programs** list. There is room for six programs on the **Frequently Used Programs** list and for two items on the **Pinned Programs** list. You can, however, give more space to the **Pinned Programs** list and less space to the **Frequently Used Programs** list.

Right-click the **Start** button and choose **Properties** from the context menu. Click the **Start Menu** tab and click the **Customize** button. The **Customize Start Menu** dialog box appears. Click the **General** tab. In the **Number of programs on the Start menu** list box, decrease the number of programs on the **Frequently Used Programs** list and increase the space for programs in the **Pinned Programs** list; choose a number less than **6**. To increase the number of programs on the **Frequently Used Programs** list and decrease the number of programs available for the **Pinned Programs** list, choose a number up to **6**. Click **OK** twice to close the dialog boxes.

4 Change the All Programs List

When you click **All Programs** on the **Start** menu, a list of folders and programs appears, letting you run any program on your computer. As you install and uninstall programs, the list and order of programs in the **All Programs** list changes. You can organize the programs however you want, and you can add and remove items to and from the list, including folders and programs.

Right-click the **Start** button and choose **Explore All Users**. Windows Explorer opens to the **C:\Documents and Settings\Start Menu** folder. Open the **Programs** folder located under this folder. The **Programs** folder lists all the programs and items on the **All Programs** menu that are displayed for all users of the computer. (You'll also be able to change which programs and items specifically appear on *your* account, and not for all users, as you'll see later in this step.) Rearrange items on the menu, delete them, and add to the folder, the way you would any other files in Windows Explorer. When you're done, close Windows Explorer to put your changes into effect.

TIP

To clear all entries from the **Frequently Used Programs** list, click the **Clear List** button. You've not deleted any of the programs, just the shortcut icons that appear on the **Start** menu.

To change items specific to *your* XP account, right-click the **Start** button and choose **Explore** from the context menu. Windows Explorer opens to the **C:\Documents and Settings*Your Name*\Start Menu** folder, where ***Your Name*** is your user account name. Open the **Programs** folder underneath this folder. Rearrange items on the menu, delete them, and add to the folder, the way you would any other files in Windows Explorer. When you're done, close Windows Explorer to put your changes into effect.

⑤ Customize the Right Side of the Start Menu

The right side of the **Start** menu has a variety of entries on it, including links to **My Documents**, **My Computer**, **My Network Places**, **Control Panel**, and many others. You can customize what items show up on the right side of the menu.

Right-click the **Start** button and choose **Properties** from the context menu to display the **Taskbar and Start Menu Properties** dialog box. Click the **Start Menu** tab and then click the **Customize** button. In the **Customize Start Menu** dialog box, click the **Advanced** tab. In the **Start menu items** section, look for the entries for **My Computer**, **My Documents**, **My Music**, **My Network Places**, **My Pictures**, **Network Connections**, and other items. Some of these items, such as **Control Panel**, let you choose whether to display them as a link, as a menu, or not display them at all. If you don't want one of these items displayed, choose **Don't display this item**. If you want it displayed only as a link—in other words, when you click on it, you'll open it—choose **Display as a link**. If you want the item displayed as a menu—in other words, so that an arrow appears next to it, and when you click the arrow, you see all the items contained within it so that you can choose from those elements—click **Display as a menu**.

Some items, such as **My Network Places**, only let you either display them or not. To display an item, enable the check box next to the item. To "hide" an item from the **Start** menu, disable the check box next to the item.

When you're done, click **OK** and then click **OK** again to close the dialog boxes and apply your selections.

6 **Display the "Classic" Start Menu**

If you don't like the new look of the **Start** menu in Windows XP and prefer the old-style "classic" Windows look (in which items are displayed in a single column), right-click the **Start** button and choose **Properties** from the context menu. In the **Taskbar and Start Menu Properties** dialog box, click the **Start Menu** tab and select the **Classic Start menu** option. Then click **OK**. Your **Start** menu will now look like the **Start** menu used in previous versions of Windows.

19 Customize the Taskbar

The *Taskbar*, the bar that runs across the bottom of the XP screen, is one of XP's niftiest features. When you run multiple programs and open multiple files in those programs, the **Taskbar** displays little "tiles" of each program and file so you can easily switch among them simply by clicking the tiles.

The **Taskbar** helps in other ways as well, such as letting you launch programs quickly from the **Quick Launch** toolbar area, just to the right of the **Start** button where a series of icons is located. (To learn more about using these icons, see **22** **Use the Quick Launch Toolbar**.) Not surprisingly, the **Taskbar** can be customized.

1 **Unlock the Taskbar**

You can't make some basic changes to the **Taskbar**—such as moving or resizing it—unless you unlock it. To unlock the **Taskbar**, right-click an empty portion of the bar, and choose **Lock the Taskbar** from the context menu to remove the check mark from that menu item. You'll notice that a small dotted area appears between sections of the **Taskbar** (for example, between the **Start** button and the **Quick Launch** toolbar). This dotted area indicates that the **Taskbar** has been unlocked.

2 **Reposition the Taskbar**

You can now change the height of the **Taskbar** and even reposition it so that it appears along the right side of the desktop, the left side of the desktop, or at the top of the desktop.

See Also

→ **20** Build Your Own Toolbar

→ **21** Turn On the Address Bar

→ **22** Use the Quick Launch Toolbar

KEY TERM

Taskbar—The bottom portion of the XP desktop on which the **Start** button is located, as well as a series of icons and tiles representing open windows. It's used to make it easy to run programs, to get access to files you currently have open, and to receive notifications from XP about things such as updates to the operating system.

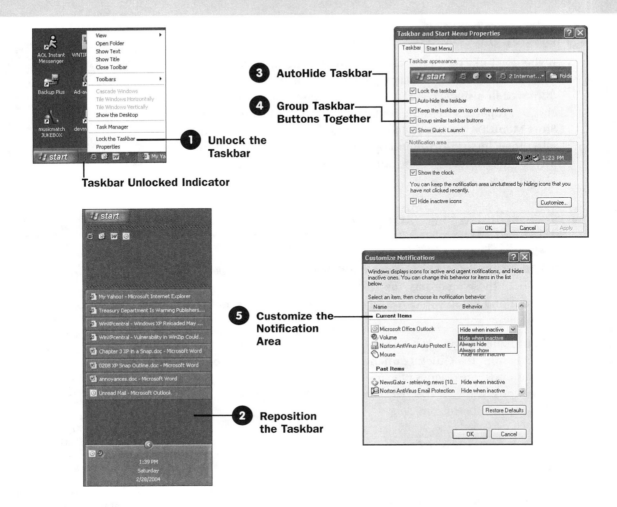

AutoHide Taskbar

Group Taskbar Buttons Together

Unlock the Taskbar

Taskbar Unlocked Indicator

Customize the Notification Area

Reposition the Taskbar

To change the height of the **Taskbar**, hover your mouse pointer over the top of the **Taskbar** until a double-headed arrow appears, and then drag the top of the **Taskbar** up. It will grow to whatever size you want.

To reposition the **Taskbar** to the right, left, or top of the screen, click an empty portion of the **Taskbar** and drag it to the location where you want it to be.

3 Auto-Hide the Taskbar

The **Taskbar** normally appears at the bottom of your screen, no matter what you're doing in XP. That way, it's easy to switch between what you're doing and any other running program or window, by clicking the appropriate tile.

Perhaps you don't want the **Taskbar** to take up part of your screen when you're working in documents because it takes away precious screen real estate. You can hide the **Taskbar** so that it appears only when you want it to. When you hide the **Taskbar** this way, it appears when you hover your mouse over the part of the screen where the **Taskbar** normally appears. Move the mouse away, and the **Taskbar** disappears.

Right-click the **Start** button, choose **Properties** from the context menu, and click the **Taskbar** tab of the **Taskbar and Start Menu Properties** dialog box. Enable the **Auto-hide the taskbar** check box.

4 Group Taskbar Buttons Together

You also have control over how individual windows appear on the **Taskbar**. You can have each window appear individually, or you can have windows appear in related groups. For example, if you have three browser windows open, you can have each window appear by itself as a button on the **Taskbar**, or you can have them all appear grouped together in a single button on the taskbar, with a number on it indicating the number of windows that program has open. When you click the program's button on the **Taskbar**, a menu of all the windows open in that program appears. To go to any window, click its title.

If you frequently keep many windows open, it's a good idea to group **Taskbar** buttons together. On the **Taskbar** tab of the **Taskbar and Start Menu Properties** dialog box, enable the **Group similar taskbar buttons** check box.

5 Customize the Notification Area

The **Notification Area** is the far-right portion of the **Taskbar**. It shows icons for programs that are running in the background, such as your antivirus program, as well as the time. Double-click any icon in the **Notification Area** to run that program.

NOTE

When you're done resizing and repositioning the **Taskbar**, lock it again: Right-click an empty portion of the bar and choose **Lock the Taskbar** from the context menu to place a check mark next to the menu item. If you don't lock it, you might accidentally resize it and reposition it when you don't want to do so.

You can customize how the **Notification Area** works by showing the icons of only some programs running in the background and not others. And you can hide "inactive icons"; that is, icons of programs running in the background that are not currently active and performing a task.

On the **Taskbar** tab of the **Taskbar and Start Menu Properties** dialog box, enable the **Show the clock** check box if you want the clock to appear; disable the check box if you don't want the clock to appear. If you don't want inactive icons to appear, enable the **Hide inactive icons** check box.

You can further customize whether inactive icons are displayed by choosing to display some and not others. Click the **Customize** button at the bottom of the dialog box. In the **Customize Notifications** dialog box that opens, click any icon in the **Current Items** area; from the drop-down menu that appears, choose whether to hide it when inactive, to always hide it, or to always show it. Repeat this action for all the current items in the **Notification Area**. You can also customize icons that have appeared in the **Notification Area** in the past by doing this to items in the **Past Items** area. When you're done, click **OK** and then click **OK** again to close the dialog boxes and reset the **Start** menu and **Taskbar**.

20 Build Your Own Toolbar

Before You Begin

✔ **19** Customize the Taskbar

See Also

→ **21** Turn On the Address Bar

→ **22** Use the Quick Launch Toolbar

KEY TERM

Toolbar—A link to a folder, file, or URL placed directly on the **Taskbar**.

One of the **Taskbar**'s more useful features is its capability to use *toolbars*, which give you immediate access to a folder, file, or Windows XP feature directly from the **Taskbar**.

The **Taskbar** has a number of toolbars built into it, such as the Address bar (for more details, see **21** **Turn On the Address Bar**). However, you can easily build one of your own.

1 Right-click an Unused Portion of the Taskbar

Right-click an empty area on the **Taskbar** and choose **Toolbars** from the context menu. Then choose **New Toolbar** from the context submenu. The **New Toolbar** dialog box appears.

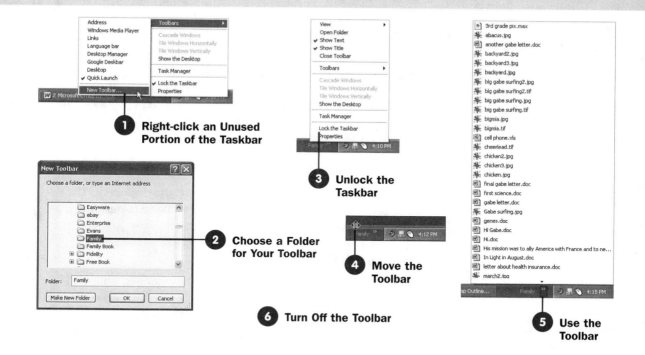

1 Right-click an Unused Portion of the Taskbar

2 Choose a Folder for Your Toolbar

3 Unlock the Taskbar

4 Move the Toolbar

6 Turn Off the Toolbar

5 Use the Toolbar

2 Choose a Folder for Your Toolbar

Navigate to the folder that you want for your new toolbar and click **OK**. Your new (empty) toolbar appears on the **Taskbar**. The name of the new toolbar is the same as the folder you selected, and next to it is a double arrow.

3 Unlock the Taskbar

You might not want your new toolbar to stay where XP put it on the **Taskbar**, so you can move it. Before you can move the toolbar, however, you must unlock the **Taskbar**. Right-click an unused portion of the **Taskbar** and choose **Lock the Taskbar** from the context menu to remove the check mark from that option. Look for the dotted area next to the **Start** menu, which indicates that the **Taskbar** is unlocked.

4 Move the Toolbar

Click the new toolbar you've just created. A four-headed arrow appears. Drag the toolbar to the position in the **Taskbar** where you want it to be. After you've moved the toolbar to its new location, lock the **Taskbar** by right-clicking an unused portion of the bar and choosing **Lock the Taskbar** from the context menu to place a check mark next to that option.

5 Use the Toolbar

Click the double arrow next to the toolbar; the contents of the folder appear as a pop-up menu. To open any file or folder that appears in the toolbar's list, click the option.

6 Turn Off the Toolbar

When you don't want to use the toolbar any longer, right-click an unused portion of the **Taskbar** and choose **Toolbars** from the context menu. From the submenu of named toolbars that opens, select the toolbar you want to remove from the Taskbar so that you take away the check mark next to the toolbar you just created. The toolbar vanishes from the **Taskbar**. It will, unfortunately, vanish permanently, so if you want to use that toolbar again, you'll have to re-create it from scratch.

21 Turn On the Address Bar

Before You Begin

✔ **19** Customize the Taskbar

✔ **20** Build Your Own Toolbar

See Also

→ **22** Use the Quick Launch Toolbar

One of Windows XP's most convenient toolbars is the *Address bar*, a toolbar on the **Taskbar** that lets you type a web address, a command, or the name of a file or folder, and then sends you to the address, runs the command, or opens the file or folder. The **Address bar** looks like a blank input box into which you type your address, command, filename, or folder name.

For example, to visit a website, you could type **www.cnn.com** and press **Enter**. To open a folder, you could type **C:\Family** and press **Enter**, and the folder opens in Windows Explorer. To open a file, you could type the filename and path (in other words, include the folder name) **C:\Family\Vacation.doc** and press **Enter**. The application that created the file launches and opens the file.

1 **Put the Address Bar on the Taskbar**

Right-click a blank area on the **Taskbar** and choose **Toolbars** from the context menu. From the submenu that opens, choose **Address**.

The word **Address** appears to the left of the **Notification Area**. However, you won't see an input box, and you can't use the **Address bar** at this point. You have to reposition it before you can use it.

2 **Unlock the Taskbar**

Before you can move the **Address bar**, you must first unlock the **Taskbar**. Right-click an unused portion of the bar and choose **Lock the Taskbar** from the context bar to remove the check mark next to the option. Look for the dotted area next to the word **Address**, which indicates that the **Taskbar** is unlocked.

3 **Move the Address Bar**

Drag the dotted area next to the word **Address** to the left until the input box appears. The more you drag, the larger the input box will be.

4 **Eliminate the Go Button**

One problem with the **Address bar** is that it takes up so much space on the **Taskbar**. As you open more windows and programs, the space devoted to the **Address bar** becomes smaller and smaller, until it can become unusable. To give it more room, you can eliminate the **Go** button next to it. The button serves no purpose—after you type a URL, command, folder name, or filename into the box, you can press **Enter** instead of clicking **Go**.

To eliminate the **Go** button, click the **Start** button and choose **Control Panel**. From the **Control Panel**, click the **Network and Internet Connections** icon and then click **Internet Options** to open the **Internet Properties** dialog box. Click the **Advanced** tab. Scroll through the **Settings** list toward the end of the **Browsing** section and disable the **Show Go button in Address bar** check box. Then click **OK**.

KEY TERM

Address bar—A toolbar on the **Taskbar** that lets you type in a web address, a command, or the name of a file or folder, and then sends you to the address, runs the command, or opens the file or folder.

TIP

Don't lock the **Taskbar** yet. The bar must be unlocked so that you can finish customizing how the **Address bar** will look.

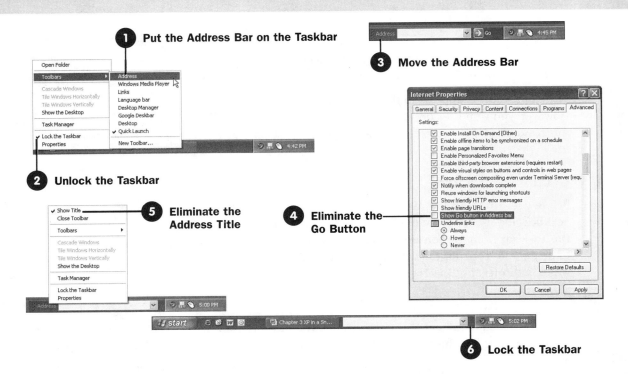

1 Put the Address Bar on the Taskbar

3 Move the Address Bar

2 Unlock the Taskbar

5 Eliminate the Address Title

4 Eliminate the Go Button

6 Lock the Taskbar

TIP

If you right-click the word **Address** and don't see an entry for **Show Title** in the context menu that appears, it means that you've locked the **Taskbar**. Unlock it and then right-click the word **Address**.

5 **Eliminate the Address Title**

Eliminating the **Go** button gives you more space for the **Address bar** but the Taskbar can still be somewhat cramped. To give it even more space, get rid of the word **Address** to its left. Right-click the word **Address** and choose **Show Title** from the context menu to remove the check mark from that option.

6 **Lock the Taskbar**

When you're satisfied with the size and location of the **Address bar** in the **Taskbar**, lock the **Taskbar** by right-clicking an unused portion of the bar and choosing **Lock the Taskbar** from the context menu so that a check mark appears next to that option.

---

22 Use the Quick Launch Toolbar

Running your favorite programs can sometimes be a chore. Going the way of the **All Programs** menu is annoying and time-consuming, and even using the **Pinned Programs** list or **Frequently Used Programs** list isn't that convenient for programs you run almost constantly.

There's a better way—use the *Quick Launch* toolbar. This toolbar contains a series of icons just to the right of the **Start** menu. Click any icon to immediately launch its associated program. You can turn the toolbar on and off, and you can add and delete programs to it.

1 Turn On the Quick Launch Toolbar

The **Quick Launch** toolbar might not be turned on. To turn it on, right-click an empty portion of the **Taskbar**, choose **Toolbars** from the context menu, and choose **Quick Launch** from the submenu so that a check mark applies next to the option. The **Quick Launch** toolbar now appears to the right of the **Start** menu.

2 Find a Program You Want to Add

When you turn on the **Quick Launch** toolbar, it will have several icons on it, most likely Internet Explorer, an icon that brings you to your desktop, and possibly Windows Media Player. If you've installed Outlook, an icon for that program might appear on the toolbar as well. Other programs may or may not appear there.

If you're not happy with the collection of icons in the toolbar and want to add one or more of your own, start by finding the program on the **All Programs** menu, accessed from the **Start** menu.

3 Add the Icon to the Quick Launch Toolbar

Right-click the program in the **All Programs** menu and drag it to the **Quick Launch** toolbar. An I-beam appears on the toolbar where the icon will be placed. Release the icon and choose **Copy Here** from the context menu that pops up.

Before You Begin

✔ **19** Customize the Taskbar

See Also

→ **18** Rearrange the Start Menu

→ **21** Build Your Own Toolbar

→ **22** Turn On the Address Bar

ꓘEY TERM

Quick Launch toolbar—A toolbar on the **Taskbar**, just to the right of the **Start** menu, that has icons of programs you want to quickly launch. Click any icon to run the associated program.

TIP

When you release the icon, make sure to choose **Copy Here** rather than **Move Here**. If you choose **Move Here**, the icon on the **All Programs** menu will disappear, because you've *moved* it to the **Quick Launch** toolbar rather than copied it. If you do that accidentally, drag the icon back to the **All Programs** menu.

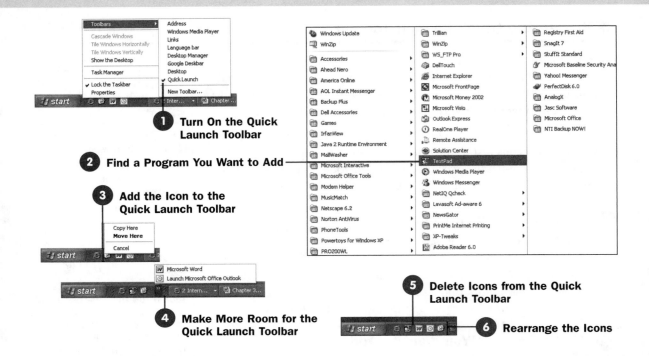

1 Turn On the Quick Launch Toolbar

2 Find a Program You Want to Add

3 Add the Icon to the Quick Launch Toolbar

4 Make More Room for the Quick Launch Toolbar

5 Delete Icons from the Quick Launch Toolbar

6 Rearrange the Icons

4 **Make More Room for the Quick Launch Toolbar**

There might not be enough room on the **Quick Launch** toolbar to accommodate your new icon or icons. If that's the case, not all the icons will appear. A double-headed arrow shows up at the far right of the **Quick Launch** toolbar to indicate that other icons are hiding. To see the other icons, click the double arrow. The icons (and their labels) appear above the double arrow. To launch any of the programs associated with the icons, launch them as you would any other icon on the **Quick Launch** toolbar by clicking them.

If you want to make more room for the **Quick Launch** toolbar so that all your icons show up, unlock the **Taskbar** by right-clicking it and choosing **Lock the Taskbar** from the context menu so that the check mark is removed from the option. A dotted area appears on the right edge of the **Quick Launch** toolbar. Drag this dotted area to the right until there's enough room for all the icons. When the toolbar is the right size, lock the **Taskbar** by right-clicking it and choosing **Lock the Taskbar** from the context menu again.

5 Delete Icons from the Quick Launch Toolbar

If there is an icon you don't want to appear on the **Quick Launch** toolbar, right-click it and choose **Delete** from the context menu. Although the icon is deleted from the **Quick Launch** toolbar, the program itself isn't deleted.

6 Rearrange the Icons

You can rearrange the order of the icons in the **Quick Launch** toolbar by dragging any icon to a new spot on the toolbar. As you drag the icon, a semitransparent copy appears, and an I-beam appears on the toolbar. When you find the location where you want it to appear on the toolbar (when the I-beam is positioned where you want to drop the icon), release the mouse.

Launch programs by clicking their icons on the toolbar. Hover the mouse pointer over any icon in the **Quick Launch** toolbar, and the name of the program appears above its icon so that you know the name of the program.

23 Customize the Date and Time

One of Windows XP's nicer small conveniences is the small time indicator that appears at the far right of the **Notification Area**. It's a humble little piece of real estate, but surprisingly useful. Here's how to customize how the clock looks and behaves.

Before You Begin

✔ **19** Customize the Taskbar

1 Turn the Clock On and Off

There are times when you might not want the clock to appear at all. For some people, a clock can be a distraction, especially when you're working, because you're so conscious of time you have a difficult time concentrating on the work to be done.

To make the clock disappear, right-click the **Start** button and choose **Properties**. In the **Taskbar and Start Menu Properties** dialog box, click the **Taskbar** tab. Disable the **Show the clock** check box. In the picture of the **Notification Area** in the center of the dialog box, the clock disappears. Click **OK**. The clock is no longer visible in the **Notification Area** of the **Taskbar**. To make the clock reappear, repeat this step and enable the **Show the clock** check box.

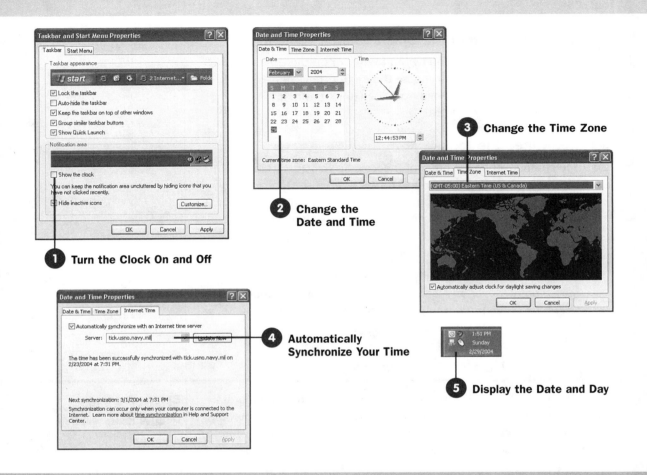

3 Change the Time Zone

2 Change the Date and Time

1 Turn the Clock On and Off

4 Automatically Synchronize Your Time

5 Display the Date and Day

2 Change the Date and Time

If the time displayed is wrong, you can change it—and the date as well. Double-click the clock in the **Notification Area** of the **Taskbar**. The **Date and Time Properties** dialog box appears. Click the **Date & Time** tab. Change the date by choosing a new date from the drop-down boxes or by clicking a date on the calendar. Choose a new time by clicking the spin arrows under the clock or by dragging the hands of the clock. When you're done, click **OK**.

③ Change the Time Zone

If you're using a laptop and traveling to a different time zone or want to display the time in a different time zone, click the **Time Zone** tab of the **Date and Time Properties** dialog box and choose a new time zone from the drop-down box at the top. Then click **OK**.

④ Automatically Synchronize Your Time

Computers use a built-in clock to keep the date and time. These clocks are not always perfect timekeepers and might be slightly slow or slightly fast. You might want your clock to keep as close to perfect time as possible—for example, if you're bidding at auction sites like eBay, because it's important that you can bid in the moments before the auction closes.

You can have XP automatically synchronize its clock with an Internet time server (a computer that keeps the precise time). Click the **Internet Time** tab of the **Date and Time Properties** dialog box and enable the **Automatically synchronize with an Internet time server** check box and click **OK**. XP will automatically synchronize its time with the time server listed in the dialog box once a week.

You can also have XP synchronize the time manually, at any point. To do it, on the **Internet Time** tab of the **Date and Time Properties** dialog box, click **Update Now**. If for some reason, Windows will not synchronize, choose a different time server from the drop-down list and click **Update Now** again.

⑤ Display the Date and Day

XP only shows the time, not the date and day of the week in the **Notification Area**. However, you can make it display both of those bits of information as well. To do it, you'll have to make the **Taskbar** larger. When you make it larger, the date and day of the week automatically appear.

Unlock the **Taskbar** by right-clicking an empty section of the bar and choosing **Lock the Taskbar** from the context menu to remove the check mark from that option. Then hover your mouse over the top portion of the **Taskbar** until a double-headed arrow appears. Drag the top of the **Taskbar** upward until it is twice the height it was previously. The time, date, and day of the week are now displayed. Then lock the **Taskbar**.

 NOTE

When you do change the clock, you're not only changing the display of the date and time, you're actually changing your system clock. The system clock is used by Windows XP to add time and date stamps to files and folders when you create and save them, as well as for other tasks, such as automatically inserting times and dates in documents.

 TIP

You can also choose whether to have XP automatically adjust your clock for Daylight Savings Time when the clock is moved forward or back in the spring and fall. Enable the **Automatically adjust clock for daylight savings changes** check box on the **Time Zone** tab of the **Date and Time Properties** dialog box and click **OK**. If you live in an area that does not follow Daylight Savings Time, disable this check box.

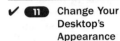

24 **About Customizing Your Desktop with TweakUI**

Before You Begin

✔ **11** Change Your Desktop's Appearance

See Also

→ **43** Customize Windows Explorer with TweakUI

NOTE

TweakUI is one of a set of free Microsoft downloads to help you customize or get more out of Windows XP. The entire set is called **PowerToys,** and you can download the utilities individually. Read the descriptions of each on the **www.microsoft.com/ windowsxp/pro/ downloads/powertoys.asp** page and download others you want to try out.

As you've seen throughout this chapter, there's a lot you can do to customize your desktop using Windows XP's built-in tools. But there's an even more powerful way to customize your desktop—use the free utility TweakUI from Microsoft. Not only does this utility let you customize your desktop, you can use it to customize how XP works in many other ways, such as controlling mouse behavior, how Internet Explorer and Windows Explorer work, how you log on and log off XP, and many other aspects of the operating system.

To use it, you must first download it. Go to **www.microsoft.com/ windowsxp/pro/downloads/powertoys.asp** and look for the link for downloading TweakUI. It's on the right side of the screen. Click the **TweakUI.exe** link and save the file to a folder on your computer. The file you save will be called **TweakUiPowertoySetup.exe** or something similar. After it downloads, go to the folder where you downloaded it, double-click the file, and follow the installation instructions.

After you download TweakUI, find the file or icon for the file (the file is named **tweakui.exe**) and either double-click the file or single-click the icon to launch the TweakUI utility.

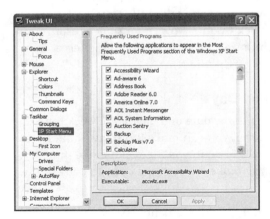

*TweakUI lets you change many aspects of how the desktop and other parts of XP work. Pictured here is a feature that lets you determine which programs can appear on the **Frequently Used Programs** list.*

In the left pane of the TweakUI program window, click the area of Windows XP or the desktop you want to customize: for example, **Taskbar**. There will be a variety of options you can change, and there may also be subchoices beneath the choice. For example, under the **Taskbar** option are choices for ways to customize the **XP Start Menu** as well as **Grouping** (which controls how open windows are grouped on the **Taskbar**). Make your changes by making selections as you do with the rest of Windows XP. For example, in the **XP Start Menu** section, you can determine which programs will be allowed to show up on the **Frequently Used Programs** list. Enable the check boxes next to those programs you want to allow to show up on the list and disable those that you don't want to allow on the list. XP will ignore programs with no checks next to them. Programs you've selected are allowed to show up on the list when they are used frequently enough. For more information about the **Frequently Used Programs** list, see **18 Rearrange the Start Menu**.

You can customize other aspects of the desktop and XP in this manner as well; for example, in the **Desktop** section by determining which system icons should appear on the desktop, and in the **General** section by configuring the behavior of menus (for example, using fades or not) and other XP features.

4

Customizing the Rest of Windows XP

IN THIS CHAPTER:

Your desktop isn't the only thing about Windows XP that's customizable. There's a lot more you can control as well. Want to change the sound your PC makes when you start it up, shut it down, or get mail? No problem—it's easy to do. In fact, you can even record your own sounds and use those for any XP event you want.

You can also change how your mouse works, create shortcuts to launch programs, and start and stop programs from running automatically on startup. You'll learn how to do all that in this chapter.

25 Change Your System Sounds

See Also

→ **16** Build Your Own Themes

→ **26** Record and Use Your Own System Sounds

NOTE

System sounds are in the **.wav** sound file format; you cannot use other sound file formats, such as **.MP3** for your system sounds.

All day as you use your computer, Windows XP makes all kinds of sounds: Turn off XP, and it chimes at you; get new email, and it tinkles at you; for all kinds of different reasons, it beeps at you.

Don't like the system sounds? No problem. You can change any of them. If you don't want to hear sounds for certain events, such as getting email, you can turn the sound off. And you can assign certain events to sounds as well, such as whenever you close a program.

1 Open the Sounds and Audio Devices Properties Dialog Box

Click the **Start** button and choose **Control Panel** from the **Start** menu. Click the **Sounds, Speech, and Audio Devices** icon to open the **Sounds, Speech, and Audio Devices** page. Click the **Sounds and Audio Devices** icon to open the **Sounds and Audio Devices Properties** dialog box.

2 Review Your System Sounds

Click the **Sounds** tab. The **Program events** box lists all system events to which sounds can be associated. Any events that already have sounds associated with them have a small speaker icon next to them. Events that don't play sounds have no icon.

Click any event. The **Sounds** drop-down list at the bottom of the dialog box shows the name of the sound file associated with that event. To hear the system sound, click the small arrow to the right of the filename.

Review your system sounds until you come across one or more that you want to change.

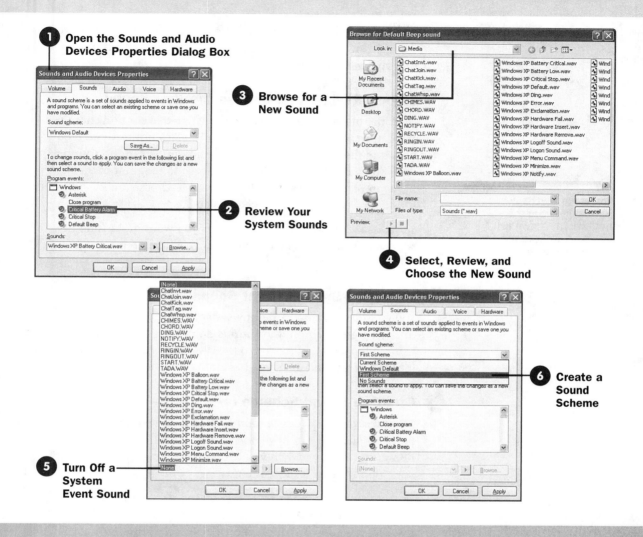

1 Open the Sounds and Audio
Devices Properties Dialog Box

3 Browse for a
New Sound

2 Review Your
System Sounds

4 Select, Review, and
Choose the New Sound

5 Turn Off a
System
Event Sound

6 Create a
Sound
Scheme

---

3 Browse for a New Sound

To choose a new sound for the currently selected event, click the
Browse button. The **Browse** dialog box opens into the
C:\Windows\Media folder, which contains all your system
sounds. Browse through that folder for a sound you want to use in
place of the original sound. Note that you can assign a sound to a
system event that currently doesn't have a sound by selecting the
event and browsing for sound files in this way.

Your system may also have other sound files in **.wav** format. You can use any of those sound files for your system sounds. Browse to any you want to use.

4 **Select, Review, and Choose the New Sound**

Click the file you want to use for the selected event and click **OK**. You return to the **Sounds and Audio Devices Properties** dialog box, and the filename of the new sound appears in the **Sounds** drop-down list box. Click the small arrow to the right of the filename to preview the sound. If you want to choose a different sound, browse to it as described in step 3.

Select as many other system events as you want and assign new sounds in this way. When you're done, click **OK** to put the new sounds into effect.

5 **Turn Off a System Event Sound**

You can turn off sounds for any system event. Choose the event and choose **None** from the **Sounds** drop-down list. The speaker icon no longer appears next to the system event, and that event no longer has a sound associated with it.

6 **Create a Sound Scheme**

XP makes it easy to create *sound schemes*. If you have a laptop, for example, you can have one sound scheme when you're at home, and another when you're on an airplane, when perhaps you don't want to disturb others.

To create a sound scheme, change all the system sounds that you want for your new scheme (as outlined in steps 1 through 5 of this task). In the **Sounds and Audio Devices Properties** dialog box, choose **Save As** from the drop-down box, type a name for your scheme, and click **OK** twice.

TIP

You can quickly select a new sound from the **Sounds** drop-down list if you don't want to use the **Browse** dialog box described in step 3.

KEY TERM

Sound scheme—A collection of system sounds that you group together. You can create many different sound schemes for Windows XP.

26 Record and Use Your Own System Sounds

Windows XP comes with quite a few system sounds, but you're not limited to them. You can use any file in **.wav** format you want for your system sounds.

In fact, for the ultimate in customization, you can easily record your own sounds and use them for your system events. So you could, for example, have your own voice saying, "Welcome to my world," when you start up XP. Here's how to record your own system sounds.

❶ Get a Microphone for Your PC

Some PCs, such as laptops, have microphones built into them, but built-in microphones often aren't of a very high quality—you might have to buy a microphone. Any computer store or website specializing in computer equipment will sell them.

❷ Connect the Microphone to Your PC

Plug the microphone into the microphone jack on your computer. Depending on your computer, you may find the mic jack in different locations. On a desktop model, you'll typically find it on the sound card, which also has a jack for your speakers. Very often, these jacks are located on the back of your PC.

❸ Open the Sound Recorder

You'll use the **Sound Recorder** to record your sound. Click the **Start** button and choose **All Programs**. Then choose **Accessories**, and from the **Accessories** menu, choose **Sound Recorder**.

❹ Start Recording

The **Record** button is the red, round button at the bottom right of the **Sound Recorder** screen. As soon as you click it, you'll start recording your sound.

Speak about six inches away from the microphone. Don't shout or whisper—speak in your normal voice. Keep your clip short, a few seconds at most, because you're going to use it for XP events, and you don't want to have to listen to yourself ramble on for 10 seconds, when all you want is a sound telling you that you've gotten an email.

Before You Begin

✔ **25** Change Your System Sounds

See Also

→ **16** Build Your Own Themes

NOTE

You don't have to spend much money on a microphone—if you're only recording your voice, $10 to $20 will buy a perfectly fine microphone. In fact, if you shop around, you can even find one for less.

TIP

The microphone jack frequently has a small picture of a microphone next to it. Don't confuse it with the headphone jack, which has the exact same kind of connector as the microphone jack. The headphone jack has a small picture of a headphone next to it.

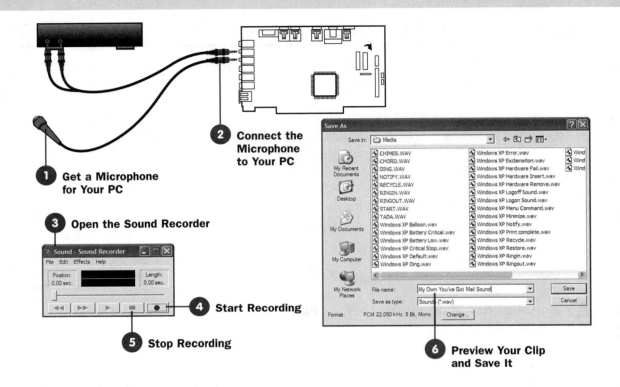

① **Get a Microphone for Your PC**

② **Connect the Microphone to Your PC**

③ **Open the Sound Recorder**

④ **Start Recording**

⑤ **Stop Recording**

⑥ **Preview Your Clip and Save It**

 NOTE

You're not limited to your own voice for system sounds. You can record literally any sound you want, including car sounds, alarms, or anything else that strikes your fancy. The key is getting the sound close enough to the microphone, which is not always possible.

As you record, you'll see the thin green line in the middle of the screen move and change as the volume and intensity of your voice changes. The **Length** section of the screen, to the right of the thin green line, tells you how long, in seconds, your clip is; use that as a guide for knowing how long you've been recording.

⑤ **Stop Recording**

The **Stop** button is the rectangular button to the left of the **Record** button. Click it when you want to stop recording. When you're done recording, the **Length** section tells you the length of the clip.

⑥ **Preview Your Clip and Save It**

Before you save your clip, listen to it to make sure that it's what you want. Click the **Play** button (the single right arrow to the left of the **Stop** button) and listen to the sound you recorded.

If you're not satisfied, re-record it. When you've decided it's what you want, choose **Save** from the **File** menu to save the file. Give the file a descriptive name, one that mentions the system event to which you want to link it. When you save it, it's a good idea to save it in the same **C:\Windows\Media** folder that holds your other system sounds so it'll be easy to find. However, if you want, you can save the file in any other folder; if you do, remember where you put it.

After the sound has been recorded, you can use it as a sound for any system event, as outlined in **25** **Change Your System Sounds**.

27 Change Your Mouse Settings

You most likely don't give much thought to your mouse, but changing the way it works to suit the way *you* work is one of the simplest and most effective ways to get more out of Windows XP.

You can change just about everything about the way your mouse works—its sensitivity to double-clicking, the speed with which it travels across the screen, the size and shape of the pointer, and much more. You can even customize the way your mouse buttons work.

① Install Any Special Software

If you're using the mouse that came with your computer, you won't have to install any special software. However, if you've added a mouse to your system, such as a wireless mouse, a mouse with extra buttons, and so on, you should install the software that came with it. This software will give your computer access to the special features of the mouse.

To install the software, insert the CD disc in your CD or DVD drive and follow installation instructions.

② Go to the Mouse Properties Dialog Box

Click the **Start** button and choose **Control Panel**. Then choose **Printers and Other Hardware**, and from the page that appears, click the **Mouse** icon to open the **Mouse Properties** dialog box.

Depending on your mouse, the dialog box may have a different number of tabs, and what's on each tab may vary. For example, if

See Also

→ **24** About Customizing Your Desktop with TweakUI

NOTE

The mouse pointer is also frequently called a *cursor*.

NOTE

Mice can connect in a variety of ways to your computer. Most often, they'll connect to the mouse port or the USB port on your PC, although some can also connect to the serial port. If you have an option, connect the mouse to your USB or mouse port to avoid hardware conflicts.

you've installed a cordless mouse, you might have a tab labeled **Cordless** that lets you monitor the battery level of the mouse. And if you've installed a mouse with extra buttons, the **Buttons** tab has different options than the **Buttons** tab shown here.

③ Change Your Mouse Pointer

You can easily change the shape and size of your mouse pointer. Click the **Pointers** tab in the **Mouse Properties** dialog box and choose a pointer scheme from the **Scheme** drop-down list. A *scheme* is the complete collection of pointers that XP uses—the normal pointer, the pointer that appears when XP is busy or doing work (normally an hourglass), the pointer that appears when it is working in the background, and so on.

When you choose a pointer scheme, all the pointers associated with that scheme appear in the **Customize** list. When you select a pointer in that list, a close-up of that pointer appears in the square to the right of the **Scheme** area.

If you like a shadow to appear around your pointer, click the **Enable pointer shadow** check box at the bottom of the dialog box.

When you've finished choosing your pointers, click **OK**. If, however, you want to customize your mouse in other ways, click another tab, as outlined in the following steps.

④ Change Your Mouse Speed and Motion

The way you change the speed and motion of your mouse varies according to the mouse you have installed on your system. It may be on a **Pointer Options** tab or a **Motions** tab in the **Mouse Properties** dialog box. Whichever tab your system has, click it.

Depending on your model of mouse, and whether you have a laptop or desktop PC, the options vary on this screen, so what you see may differ from what we describe here. The options shown here are for a laptop.

TIP

If you want to choose an individual pointer rather than an entire scheme, you can do that using the **Browse** button. First highlight the pointer you want to change and then click the **Browse** button. You'll come to a list of pointers. Click the one you want to use, click **Open**, and then click **OK**.

TIP

Because pointers can be difficult to find on laptops, some laptops offer the **Show location of pointer when I press the CTRL key** option. If you enable this option, whenever you press the **Ctrl** key, a bulls-eye appears around your pointer so that you can easily locate it.

In the **Motion** section of the **Mouse Properties** dialog box, drag the slider to a spot on the continuum between **Slow** and **Fast** to control the speed of the pointer. This controls how much the pointer moves in response to how you drag the mouse. At the slowest speed, the pointer moves very little, even when you move your mouse quickly and a great deal. At the fastest speed, the pointer moves very quickly in response to minimal mouse movements. As you drag the slider, move the mouse to test the different speeds to see which one suits you best.

You might see an **Enhance pointer precision** check box. If you enable this option, the pointer more accurately tracks your mouse motions, but it also slows down the pointer slightly.

In the **Snap To** section, you can have the pointer automatically point to the default button whenever you open a dialog box. If you choose this option, whenever you open a dialog box, the mouse pointer immediately jumps to the button that XP defaults to in that box. Some people find this motion disconcerting, especially if they don't always use the default button option. However, others find it a time-saver. Try it out to see whether it's something you want to use.

If you have a laptop, other sections might appear on this tab. You might see a **Visibility** section that lets you choose options of special note to laptop owners. Because laptop screens can be more difficult to read than desktop monitors, the mouse pointer can sometimes be difficult to locate on the screen. This section lets you increase the pointer's visibility. If you enable the **Display pointer trails** check box, as the pointer moves, it leaves behind fading images of itself, in a trail. This makes it easier to see the pointer, although it is a distracting option for some people. If you enable the **Hide pointer while typing** check box, the pointer does not appear when you type. Unless you choose this option, the pointer will look like a thin, capital letter *I* when you type.

When you've finished setting mouse motion options, click **OK** or choose another tab to further customize your mouse.

 **NOTES**

Laptops typically have one or two types of pointing devices on them. The touchpad has become the most common, a rectangular, smooth area over which you move your finger to control the pointer. Underneath the touchpad are two buttons, which correspond to the two buttons of a mouse. Unless you're used to a touchpad, you might move your finger along the touchpad without realizing that part of your thumb has accidentally brushed a touchpad button and clicked it. So you might find items being clicked that you didn't mean to click. To solve the problem, make sure that you raise your thumb enough so that no part of your hand touches a button.

Some laptops have a pointing stick instead of or in addition to a touchpad to control the pointer. The pointing stick is a small red stick or knob in the center of the keyboard. You move your finger over the knob to control the pointer.

Some people don't like using touchpads or pointing sticks. If you're one of them, you can just plug your mouse into your laptop and use that instead. You can even buy a special "travel" mouse that is just like a normal mouse, but smaller so that it's easy to bring with you when you pack a laptop.

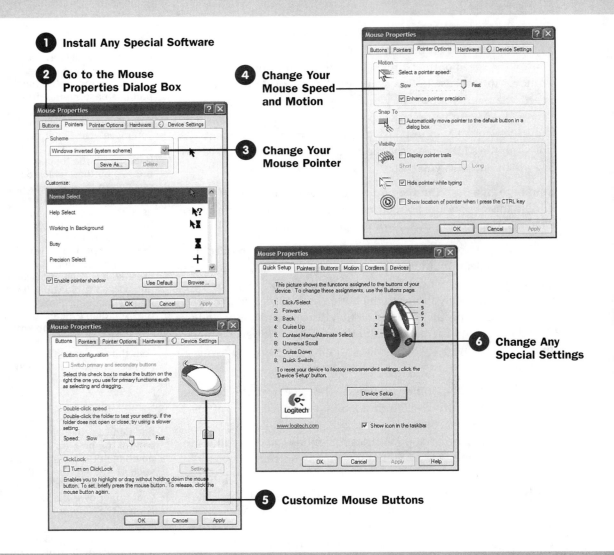

① **Install Any Special Software**

② **Go to the Mouse Properties Dialog Box**

③ **Change Your Mouse Pointer**

④ **Change Your Mouse Speed and Motion**

⑤ **Customize Mouse Buttons**

⑥ **Change Any Special Settings**

⑤ **Customize Mouse Buttons**

You can reassign the way the buttons work on your mouse. To do that, click the **Buttons** tab of the **Mouse Properties** dialog box. The tab you see might differ dramatically from the one shown here, depending on the model of mouse that you use.

The **Button configuration** section lets you change how your mouse buttons work. Again, it will vary according to your model of mouse. In the simplest configuration change, enable the **Switch primary and secondary buttons** check box to change the functions of the left and right mouse buttons. Mice that have more buttons let you change the functions of every button on the mouse.

The **Double-click speed** section lets you control how sensitive the mouse is to your double-clicks—in other words, it changes the speed with which your second click must follow your first for the mouse to recognize the sequence as a double-click. At the slowest speed, your second click can follow the first click slowly, and the mouse will recognize it as a double-click. At the fastest speed, your second click has to follow quickly, or the mouse won't recognize it as a double-click. Drag the slider between **Slow** and **Fast** to determine the best speed for you.

 TIP

Test the double-click speed setting by double-clicking the picture of the folder in the **Double-click speed** section. Watch to see whether the folder opens as you test your double-click speed.

If you have a laptop, you might have a **ClickLock** section. This feature can be useful for laptop owners because it can be difficult to drag items using a touchpad. Dragging requires that you hold down a mouse button while you drag an item. On a touchpad, this sequence normally requires the use of two hands. However, the **ClickLock** feature lets you accomplish it with one hand. When the feature is turned on, when you briefly press the touchpad button (or mouse button), the mouse reacts as if the button is continuing to be held down. You can then drag an object by moving your finger across the touchpad (or moving the mouse). When you're done dragging, click the mouse button again, and the mouse button will be released. To turn on the feature, enable the **Turn on ClickLock** check box.

When you've finished customizing the mouse buttons, click **OK** or choose another tab to further customize your mouse.

6 **Change Any Special Settings**

If you've installed a mouse and special software, there might be many other special settings you can control about the mouse. Click the tabs in the **Mouse Properties** dialog box to find them.

 TIP

The free Microsoft utility TweakUI lets you customize your mouse in other ways as well, such as changing how the wheel of your mouse works if you have a mouse that has a wheel on it. For information about how to download and use TweakUI, turn to **24** **About Customizing Your Desktop with TweakUI**.

28 Create Keyboard Shortcuts to Launch Programs

See Also

→ **15** Change Your Desktop Icons

→ **22** Use the Quick Launch Toolbar

Sometimes, the littlest things are the biggest time-savers. Think of how much time you spend in any week simply launching programs, hunting for them, not finding them, finding them, double-clicking them, and so on. Wouldn't it be nice if you didn't have to do all that, if launching a program was as simple as pressing a key or two on your keyboard?

In fact, it is. You can create keyboard shortcuts that will let you launch programs without having to lift your fingers from the keyboard.

❶ Find the Program for Which You Want to Create a Shortcut

With your desktop visible, click the **Start** button and choose **All Programs**. From the **All Programs** menu, find the program for which you want to create a shortcut and click to select (highlight) it.

KEY TERM

Shortcut—An icon that, when clicked, launches a program or a file. The shortcut is only a pointer to a program or a file and not the file itself. You can delete the shortcut, and the original file or folder will not be deleted.

---

❷ Drag the Program to the Desktop

With the program highlighted in the **All Programs** menu, right-click it and drag the program to the desktop. As you drag it off the **All Programs** menu to the desktop, its icon turns transparent, and a small + sign appears next to it, denoting that it's a *shortcut*.

After you drag the program to the desktop, release the mouse button. An icon for the program is placed on the desktop, along with all your other desktop icons.

Make sure that you right-click the program in the **All Programs** menu and then drag it. If you don't right-click it, you'll drag (move) the actual file itself, and not a shortcut to the file. That means that the program will vanish from the **All Programs** menu, and if you delete its icon from your desktop, you'll actually delete the program itself, and not a shortcut to the program.

❸ Drag the Program to the Desktop from Windows Explorer

Not all programs show up on the **All Programs** menu. If that's the case, you'll have to drag the program to the desktop from Windows Explorer. Open Windows Explorer and then find the program. Typically, it will be found in a folder somewhere in the

---

C:**Program Files** folder, for example, C:**Program Files\AIM95\aim.exe** for the AOL Instant Messenger Program.

Make sure that when you drag the program, you're dragging the file that launches the program and not another file. The program file will end in an **.exe** extension. If you're not sure of the filename and location, check the program's documentation to find the correct filename.

④ Open the Properties Dialog Box

Right-click the icon of the program you've just dragged to the desktop and choose **Properties** from the context menu. Click the **Shortcut** tab of the **Properties** dialog box for the program.

⑤ Choose Your Shortcut Key

Position the mouse pointer in the **Shortcut key** text box. Then press the key combination you want to use to launch the program, for example, **Ctrl+Alt+A**. Make sure that it's a shortcut key you don't use for another program.

In the **Comment** box, place any comments about the program and shortcut, if you have any.

In the **Run** drop-down box, you can choose whether the program should launch maximized, minimized, or in the manner that the program normally launches.

When you're done, click **OK** to close the **Properties** dialog box.

⑥ Try Out the Shortcut

Press the shortcut key combination, and your program should launch. If it doesn't, check the **Shortcut** tab of the **Properties** dialog box for the program to see whether you've made any errors. If you haven't, the problem may be that your shortcut key combination interferes with another shortcut you or XP has created. In that case, go back to the **Shortcut** tab and try setting another combination as explained in step 5.

Keep in mind that it's possible that the shortcut key combination you chose may interfere with a shortcut key used by a specific program, such as Word. In that case, the interference will show up only when you use Word. After you create the shortcut key combination, launch other programs and try out the shortcut key, to make sure that it doesn't interfere with those programs.

TIP

The only combinations you can use are those that start with the **Ctrl+Alt** keys. For example, you can use **Ctrl+Alt+A**, but not **Ctrl+A** or **Alt+A**. In fact, to set the shortcut key, you only need to press the third key in the combination. To set the shortcut key as **Ctrl+Alt+A**, just press the **A** key in the **Shortcut Key** text box.

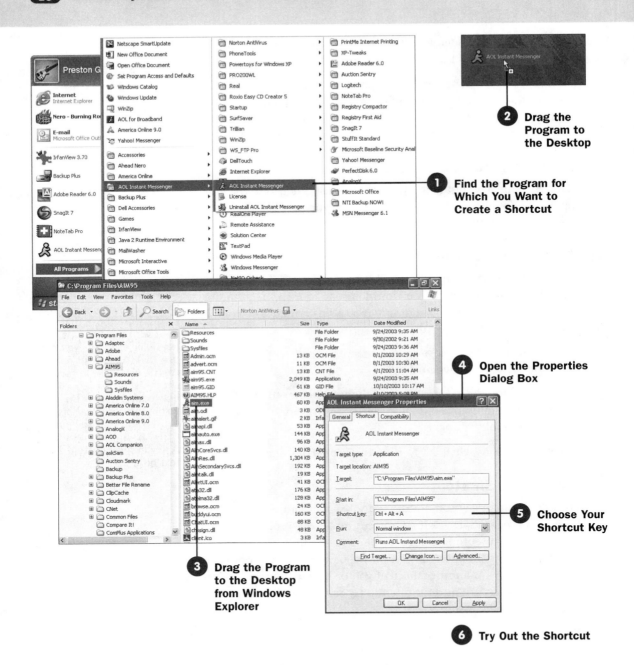

2 Drag the Program to the Desktop

1 Find the Program for Which You Want to Create a Shortcut

4 Open the Properties Dialog Box

5 Choose Your Shortcut Key

3 Drag the Program to the Desktop from Windows Explorer

6 Try Out the Shortcut

29 Start Programs Automatically on Startup

If you're like me, there are certain programs that you start up every time you log on to Windows XP. Whenever I turn on my computer, the first thing I do is check my email, and so I always start off by launching my email program, Outlook. I frequently use Microsoft Word as well, and so that's another one I start whenever XP starts up.

You can save yourself a good deal of time by using XP's ability to run any program whenever you start XP. That way, you won't have to spend the time hunting around for the program; it'll already be running.

You do this by adding programs to the **Startup** folder on your PC. Here's the fastest way to do it.

1 Right-Click the Start Button

When you right-click the **Start** button, a context menu pops up. The menu may vary slightly according to what software you've installed on your PC, but it will include the **Explore** and/or **Explore All Users** options.

2 Choose Explore or Explore All Users

If you want the program to run no matter which account logs into XP, choose **Explore All Users** from the **Start** menu. If you want the program to run for only the account you're currently using, choose **Explore**.

Windows Explorer opens. If you chose **Explore All Users**, you'll be in the C:\Documents and Settings\All Users\Start Menu folder. If you chose **Explore**, you'll be in the C:\Documents and Settings*Your Name*\Start Menu folder, where *Your Name* is the account name under which you're currently logged into Windows.

3 Open the Startup Folder

Navigate to the **C:\Documents and Settings\All Users\Start Menu\Programs\Startup** folder or the **C:\Documents and Settings***Your Name***\Start Menu\Programs\Startup** folder, depending on whether you want the program you choose to run every time XP starts or only when the current account is running XP.

See Also

→ **30** Stop Programs from Running on Startup

→ **119** Turn Off Unneeded Programs and Services

🔋 TIP

If you prefer, you can get to the **C:\Documents and Settings\All Users\ Start Menu** folder or **C:\Documents and Settings***Your Name***\Start Menu** folder without having to right-click the **Start** button. You can instead open Windows Explorer, and navigate to either of those folders, the way you normally go to a folder.

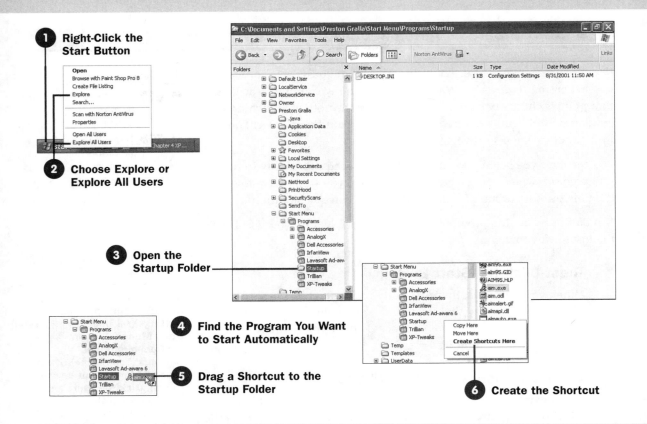

① **Right-Click the Start Button**

② **Choose Explore or Explore All Users**

③ **Open the Startup Folder**

④ **Find the Program You Want to Start Automatically**

⑤ **Drag a Shortcut to the Startup Folder**

⑥ **Create the Shortcut**

Any shortcut you put into this folder will run automatically on startup. There may already be shortcuts in this folder. If there are any, it means that those programs automatically start whenever XP starts.

④ Find the Program You Want to Start Automatically

Leaving the **Startup** folder open, navigate to the program that you want to start automatically. Typically, it will be found in a folder somewhere within the **C:\Program Files** folder: for example, **C:\Program Files\AIM95\aim.exe** for the AOL Instant Messenger program.

⑤ Drag a Shortcut to the Startup Folder

Right-click the file and, while holding down the mouse button, drag the file to the C:\Documents and Settings\All Users\ Start Menu\Programs\Startup or the C:\Documents and Settings*Your Name*\Start Menu\Programs\Startup folder, depending on whether you want the program to run every time XP starts or only when the current account is running XP.

As you drag the program to the **Startup** folder, its icon turns transparent and a small + sign appears next to it, denoting that it's a *shortcut*.

Make sure that you right-click the program and then drag it. If you don't right-click it first, when you drag it, you'll move the actual file itself and not a shortcut to the file. That means that the program will vanish from the **All Programs** menu, and if you delete its icon from your desktop, you'll actually delete the program itself and not a shortcut to the program.

⑥ Create the Shortcut

Release the right mouse button and a context menu appears. Choose **Create Shortcut Here** (it may instead read **Create Shortcuts Here**). A shortcut to the program is placed in the C:\Documents and Settings\All Users\Start Menu\Programs\Startup or C:\ Documents and Settings*Your Name*\Start Menu\Programs\ Startup folder, depending on which you've chosen.

After you log out of XP or turn off your computer, the next time you log into XP, the program will start automatically.

📝 NOTE

Make sure that when you drag the program, you're dragging the file that launches the program and not another file. The file will end in an **.exe** extension. If you're not sure of the program's filename and location, check the program's documentation to find it.

30 Stop Programs from Running on Startup

As you learned in **29** Start Programs Automatically on Startup, you can choose to automatically have programs start up every time you launch Windows XP by using the **Startup** folder.

But you might not realize that there are many other ways that programs might start automatically when you launch XP. There is no single, central location to which you can turn that lists every program that starts up automatically.

Before You Begin

✔ **29** Start Programs Automatically on Startup

See Also

→ **71** Find and Kill Spyware

→ **119** Turn Off Unneeded Programs and Services

TIP

When you run Windows XP, you also run services in the background, which can do tasks such as indexing your hard drive so that it's easier to find a file. But you may not want all those services to run. To find out how to find them and turn them off, see **119** **Turn Off Unneeded Programs and Services**.

Why is this important? Because some programs run in the background, and you might not even know they're running. You might not, in fact, have to run them, and they're taking up precious memory and computer processing power. Additionally, other programs may start up that you don't want to start. For example, some instant messaging programs such as America Online Instant Messenger automatically start up whenever you launch Windows XP, even if you don't want them to.

It's difficult to track down every program that starts up automatically on your system, but in this task, you learn to find most of them and stop them from starting automatically if you want.

① Create a Restore Point

When you delete programs that run on startup, there is a chance that you might delete important ones that help your system function properly. To protect yourself against any damage, use **System Restore**. When you use **System Restore**, you can undo any changes you made to your system, so that if you do it any harm, you can restore your computer to a time when it worked properly. You do this by first creating a *restore point*; if you run into any problems, you can revert your computer to that restore point. To set a restore point, turn to **124** **Protect Your System with System Restore**.

② Identify Any Programs You Don't Want to Start

A good way to find out whether XP is automatically running any programs on startup that you'd prefer not to run is by checking the **Notification Area** (sometimes called the **System Tray**), which is on the far right of the **Taskbar**. It shows icons of programs that are currently running in the background. There may be a left-pointing arrow to the left of the **Notification Area**. If there is, click the arrow to display all the currently running programs.

To see the name of any program in the **Notification Area**, hover your mouse pointer over it. The name of the program appears above the icon in a small box.

TIP

For even more information about a program, run the program itself. To run it, double-click the icon in the **Notification Area**.

After you've done all this, make a note of all the programs you no longer want to run on startup. Keep in mind, though, that the **Notification Area** does not necessarily show you all programs that run on startup. You might find others as you go through the next steps in this task.

1 Create a Restore Point

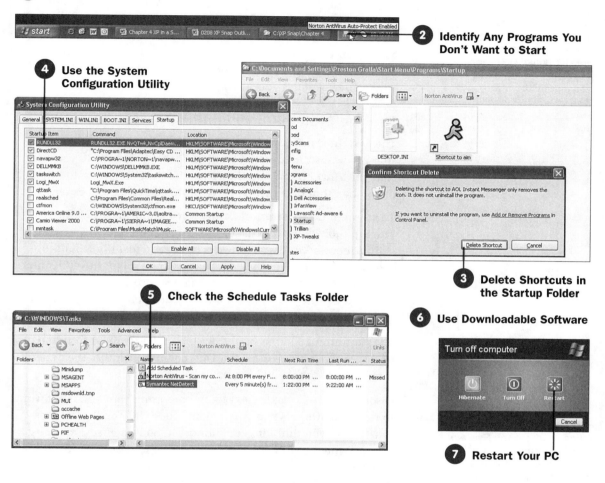

2 Identify Any Programs You Don't Want to Start

4 Use the System Configuration Utility

3 Delete Shortcuts in the Startup Folder

5 Check the Schedule Tasks Folder

6 Use Downloadable Software

7 Restart Your PC

3 Delete Shortcuts in the Startup Folder

In **29** Start Programs Automatically on Startup you learned how to place *shortcuts* in your Startup folders so that the programs will automatically run when Windows XP starts up. To stop those programs from running, delete the shortcuts from those folders by clicking the shortcut and pressing the Delete key. A dialog box appears, reminding you that when you delete a shortcut, you are deleting only the shortcut, not the program itself. Click **Delete Shortcut** and the shortcut will be deleted. Make sure to look in both the C:\Documents and Settings\All Users\Start Menu\Programs\Startup and the C:\Documents and Settings*Your Name*\Start Menu\Programs\Startup folder, where *Your Name* is your account name.

④ Use the System Configuration Utility

The **System Configuration Utility** includes a feature that lets you stop programs that automatically launch on startup. To use it, click the **Start** button and then click the **Run** option. In the **Run** dialog box that appears, type **msconfig.exe** and press **Enter**.

The **System Configuration Utility** screen appears. Click the **Startup** tab. You'll see a list of programs that start whenever you start Windows XP. It won't always be easy to identify what those programs are, or what they do, because they might have filenames such as **qttask** or **realsched**. In some instances, such as the file for **America Online 9.0**, you can readily understand what each program file does.

The **Command** column might give you a better understanding of what the program is and does. That column identifies the folder name and file that will be run.

Disable the check boxes next to any programs that you don't want to run on startup. When you're done, click **OK**. You'll get a message telling you that for your changes to go into effect, you must restart Windows. You don't, however, have to restart Windows now; you can restart it later, and the changes will take effect then. If you're still going to look for programs to kill on startup, don't restart your computer yet.

5 Check the Schedule Tasks Folder

When items are put into the **Scheduled Tasks** folder, they are run at specified times on your PC. These programs don't necessarily run on startup—for example, one might run every Friday at 5 p.m. However, some programs might run every day at a specified time, and that's almost the same as running on startup. Open Windows Explorer and go to **C:\Windows\Tasks**. You'll see a list of tasks, along with information about when each task is to run. Delete any task you don't want to run in the same way that you would delete a file or shortcut, as explained in step 3.

6 Use Downloadable Software

Even doing all the previous steps will not necessarily identify all the programs that run on startup. Some are embedded so deeply in your system that you may not be able to track them down. You can, however, get special software that can help.

The free program AutoRuns, from **http://www.sysinternals.com/ntw2k/freeware/autoruns.shtml**, identifies programs that automatically run on startup. It won't, however, delete them, so you'll have to stop them from running using the steps outlined in this task. Alternatively, you can uninstall the programs themselves using the **Add or Remove Programs** feature of **Control Panel**.

Another free program, Startup Control Panel, available from **http://www.mlin.net/StartupCPL.shtml**, not only identifies programs that run on startup but can disable them as well.

Download and install each program and follow the directions for using them.

7 Restart Your PC

When you're done deleting or disabling programs that you don't want to run, restart your PC. If you experience any problems, use **System Restore** to fix your system, as outlined in ● 124 **Protect Your System with System Restore**.

5

Getting More Out of Windows Explorer and Search

IN THIS CHAPTER:

Hard disks are big. Memories are short. That means that you'll need some way to navigate through your hard disk and find files to work with. That's where **Windows Explorer** and Windows XP's search capabilities come in. They make it easy to take control of XP and all its files and folders, as you'll see in this chapter.

31 About Windows Explorer

See Also

→ **39** About Windows XP Search

KEY TERMS

Windows Explorer—A basic component of Windows XP that lets you browse your hard disk, create folders, and do many system chores.

Task pane—A pane that appears on the left side of Windows Explorer that lets you easily accomplish common tasks such as renaming and moving files and folders, printing pictures, and so on.

TIP

If you're having a hard time finding a way to run Windows Explorer, here's a simple way. Click the **Start** menu then click the **Run** option. In the **Open** box, type **Explorer.exe** and press **Enter**. Internet Explorer will now open.

When you need to find a file, create a new folder, change a folder name, clean up your hard disk, or do any one of a hundred other small tasks, you turn to one tool: *Windows Explorer*.

Windows Explorer lets you easily browse your hard disk and perform a wide variety of tasks. Depending on your setup, you can start Windows Explorer in a variety of ways: By clicking **Start** and then choosing **Windows Explorer** from somewhere on the **Start** menu; or by clicking **Start**, choosing **All Programs**, and then choosing **Windows Explorer** from the list of programs that appears. There's also a shortcut method for launching Windows Explorer: Press the **Windows+E** keys to launch the program. You can find **Windows Explorer** in the **C:\Windows** directory under the filename **Explorer.exe**.

As you browse your hard disk, a + sign next to a folder means that there are subfolders underneath it. Click the + sign to reveal the folders underneath. When you click the + sign, a – sign replaces it. Click the – sign to close the subfolders. When the subfolders close, the + sign reappears.

Perhaps the most confusing aspect of Windows Explorer concerns the basic interface and the use of the *Task pane*. The **Task** pane appears on the left side of the Windows Explorer screen and lets you easily accomplish common tasks such as renaming and moving files and folders, printing pictures, and so on. To perform a task, click the appropriate link.

That doesn't sound very confusing, but the confusions comes in because sometimes the pane appears, and other times it doesn't. Making things more confusing still is that the tasks on the pane sometimes change. When the **Task** pane doesn't appear, Windows Explorer displays a Folder view.

The **Task** pane comes into and out of view depending on whether you've clicked the **Folders** button on the Windows Explorer button bar across the top of the screen. When the **Task** pane is visible, click the **Folders** button to make the **Task** pane disappear and have Windows Explorer show the Folder view. The **Folders** button looks as if it's been pushed in. If you're in Folders view, click the **Folders** button to make the **Task** pane reappear, and the **Folders** button doesn't appear to be pushed in.

The tasks in the **Task** pane change depending on the contents of the folder you're viewing. If you're viewing a folder with pictures in it, you'll see tasks such as printing pictures and ordering prints.

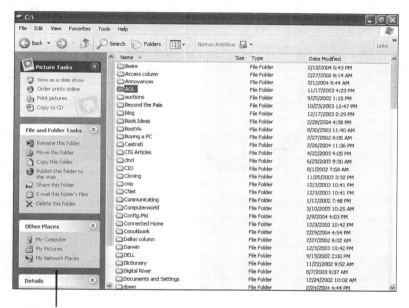

Task Pane

*Here's Windows Explorer, with the **Task** pane visible on the left. Click a link to any of the tasks and follow the directions to accomplish the task. The actual tasks available change according to the contents of the folder. For example, when a folder has pictures in it, new tasks appear, such as **Order Prints Online** and **Print Pictures**.*

You can view your hard disk in many different ways using Windows Explorer; and you'll learn how to do that in this chapter. There are many other things you can do with it as well, such as compressing files so that you gain more hard disk space. Read the following tasks to learn how to do all that and more.

NOTE

Don't confuse Windows Explorer with Internet Explorer. Windows Explorer is used to navigate your hard disk and perform a variety of system functions; Internet Explorer is used to browse the Web.

Folders Button

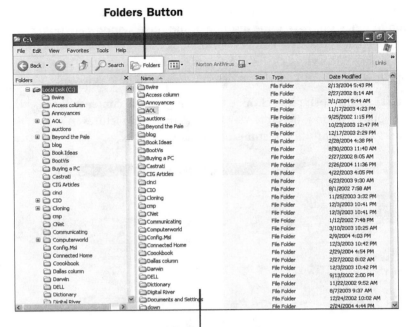

Files Displayed in Folder View

When you click the **Folders** button, the button appears to be pressed in, and Windows Explorer shows the contents of your hard disk in folders.

 **Customize Your Folder View**

Before You Begin

✔ **31** About Windows Explorer

See Also

→ **33** Use the Filmstrip View

Windows Explorer is almost infinitely customizable—you have extraordinary control over the way it looks and works. Here's how to customize Windows Explorer so that it works the way you want.

① Show All Files and Folders

Windows XP doesn't trust you to do the right thing with your computer—it hides certain files and folders from you. It does this in a misguided attempt to save you from yourself. The operating system hides system files and folders—important files that if deleted, altered, or moved, could cause system problems.

Although this might not be a bad idea for absolute beginners, it's a problem for anyone else. If you want to customize Windows XP, you sometimes have to know whether you have certain files on your system, and in some instances, you have to edit those files as well.

You can tell XP to let you see all the files and folders on your system. Open Windows Explorer and, from the **Tools** menu, choose **Folder Options**. The **Folder Options** dialog box appears. Click the **View** tab.

In the **Advanced Settings** list box, enable the **Display the contents of system folders** check box. This option allows you to see all files in *system folders*, folders used by the operating system for its basic functions.

Under the **Hidden files and folders** label, enable the **Show hidden files and folders** radio button. This option tells XP to display other types of hidden files and folders as well.

When you're done, click **OK**.

2 Show Filename Extensions

When you first use Windows Explorer, it hides *filename extensions* from you. But hiding filename extensions is an extremely bad idea—in fact, it can be dangerous, as well. If you can't see a filename extension in Windows Explorer, you won't know what kind of file it is—for example, whether it's a Word file, an Excel file, a graphic file, or a music file.

The danger comes in when you get viruses and worms through email. A virus writer can send a file that looks to you like **familypic.gif**. A **.gif** file can't carry a virus, so you open the file, figuring that you're safe. However, because XP hides filename extensions, you can't see the *real* filename, which is **familypic.gif.exe**. A file that ends in **.exe** is a program, and programs can be and can carry viruses. So you open the file, and set the virus loose on your PC.

To solve these problems, tell XP to show filename extensions. Open Windows Explorer and from the **Tools** menu, choose **Folder Options**. The **Folder Options** dialog box appears. Click the **View** tab. Disable the **Hide file extensions for known file types** check box and click **OK**.

3 Choose Between Task Pane and Folder View

As explained in **31 About Windows Explorer**, you have a choice between the **Task** pane view and the Folders view. To go back and forth between them, click the **Folders** button in the button bar at the top of the Windows Explorer screen.

KEY TERMS

System folders—Folders that contain files used by Windows XP for its basic functions. XP normally hides the contents of system folders, but you can customize Windows Explorer so that those files are displayed.

Filename extension—The letters at the end of a filename, to the right of the period (.). For example, the filename **Firstchapter.doc** has a **.doc** filename extension. Filename extensions commonly have three letters, although they are not limited to three letters.

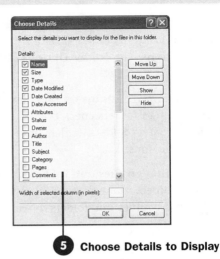

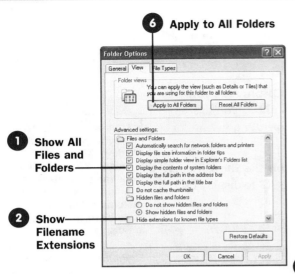

6 Apply to All Folders

1 Show All Files and Folders

2 Show Filename Extensions

5 Choose Details to Display

3 Choose Between Task Pane and Folder View

4 Choose Your View

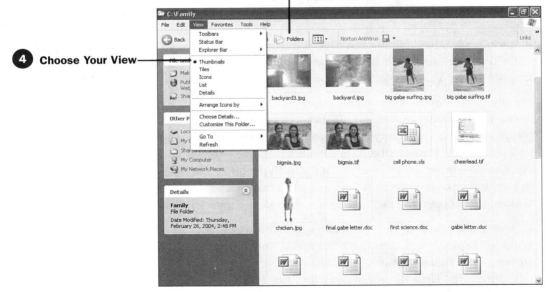

4 Choose Your View

Windows Explorer lets you choose from a variety of different views to best suit how you like to work. You can use different views for different folders, or apply the same view to all folders. You have a choice of the following views:

- **Thumbnails view.** This view shows small thumbnails of all the files in a folder. If there are pictures in the folder, you'll see thumbnails of all the pictures. For more information about using the **Thumbnail** view, see **33** **Use the Filmstrip View**.

- **Tiles view.** This view uses large icons to display different types of files and folders. So all **.doc** files, for example, will have the same icon, all **.xls** files will have an icon different from **.doc** files, and so on.

- **Icons view.** This view is like **Tiles** view except that the icons are small rather than large.

- **List view.** This view lists all the files, one on top of the other, using very small icons.

- **Details view.** This view is similar to **List** view, except that it also lists detailed information about each file, such as the file size, date it was created, and so on.

To choose a view for Windows Explorer, click the **View** menu and choose your view.

5 Choose Details to Display

Windows Explorer's most powerful view is the **Details** view. This view lets you see a great deal of information about each file as you browse, including file size, date of creation, date last modified, who created the file, and much more. This view can also display special information for music and picture files, such as album title and artist, or dimensions of a photo.

NOTE

Another, specialized view is used only in certain folders. The **Filmstrip** view lets you see all files in a folder as if they were a strip of film, and offers special ways to work with pictures. For information how to allow a folder to use the **Filmstrip** view, see **33** Use the **Filmstrip View**.

As explained in step 4, switch to **Details** view by choosing **Details** from the **View** menu. To choose which details to show, right-click one of the column headings on the right side of the Windows Explorer screen, such as **Type**, and choose **More** from the context menu. The **Choose Details** dialog box opens. Enable the check boxes next to those details you want displayed in the **Details** view and click **OK**.

6 Apply to All Folders

You can use the view you've just created only on this individual folder, or instead on every folder in XP. If you want to use these view settings on only this individual folder, you're done.

However, if you want to apply these view settings to all folders, choose **Folder Options** from the **Tools** menu and click the **View** tab. Then click the **Apply to All Folders** button and click **OK**.

33 Use the Filmstrip View

Before You Begin

✔ **31** About Windows Explorer

✔ **32** Customize Your Folder View

See Also

→ **13** Use a Picture from the Web as Your Background/ Wallpaper

KEY TERM

Filmstrip view—A view in Windows Explorer that displays pictures as if they were in a filmstrip and includes links to easy-to-accomplish tasks in the **Task** pane, such as printing pictures, creating a slideshow, or ordering pictures online.

If you have picture or graphic files in a folder, it's best to view that folder in Windows Explorer using the *Filmstrip view*. That view displays pictures as if they were in a filmstrip and includes links to common tasks in the **Task** pane, such as printing pictures, creating a slideshow, and ordering pictures online.

1 Choose Customize This Folder

Open Windows Explorer and open the folder you want to view in the **Filmstrip** view. In the right pane, right-click an empty portion of the screen and choose **Customize This Folder** from the context menu. The folder's **Customize Properties** dialog box appears. Click the **Customize** tab.

2 Choose the Pictures or Photo Album Template

Now you'll choose what kind of *template* to apply to the folder—in other words, how the folder should display its contents. From the drop-down box labeled **Use this folder type as a template** near the top of the tab, choose either **Pictures** or **Photo Album** and click **OK**. These templates are identical to one another, except that when you choose **Photo Album** you're immediately sent into a thumbnail view. But because you're going to change to the **Filmstrip** view, it doesn't really matter which of the two templates you choose. Click **OK**.

3 Choose the Filmstrip View

To view the picture files in the current folder in **Filmstrip** view, choose **View**, **Filmstrip** from the Windows Explorer menu. The right side of the screen changes to the **Filmstrip** view.

4 Browse Using the Filmstrip

Across the bottom of the screen in **Filmstrip** view is a strip of thumbnail pictures of the files in the current folder. Directly above the strip of thumbnails is a larger picture of the currently selected file. To move through the files forward or backward, click the right or left arrow just beneath the large picture. To rotate the large picture, click the small rotation arrows. The leftmost rotation arrow rotates the picture clockwise, and the rightmost arrow rotates it counterclockwise.

5 Display a Slideshow

One of the benefits of the **Filmstrip** view is that you can create a slideshow out of the picture files in any folder. When you do this, each picture in the folder displays against a black background on your screen for several seconds, until it is replaced by the next picture. You can navigate through the slideshow by using buttons that appear in the upper-right portion of the screen, or you can exit the slideshow by clicking the **X** button or pressing the **Esc** key.

To display a slideshow, first make sure that the **Task** pane is visible. If it's not, click the **Folders** button. When the **Task** pane appears, click **View as a slide show** to display the slideshow.

6 Print and Order Pictures

You can also print the pictures in the folder on your local printer and order pictures to be printed by a picture service from the Windows Explorer **Filmstrip** view. To print a picture on your local printer, click **Print this picture** in the **Task** pane. To order prints, click **Order prints online** in the **Task** pane and follow the directions of the wizard that appears.

NOTES

You can also get to the **Customize** tab of the folder's dialog box by choosing **Customize this Folder** from the **View** menu.

You can't customize the view for some system folders, such as **C:** and **C:\Windows**. If you want to view them in **Filmstrip** view, you're out of luck.

TIP

You can set any picture in the current folder as your desktop background. Just click **Set as desktop background** in the **Task** pane.

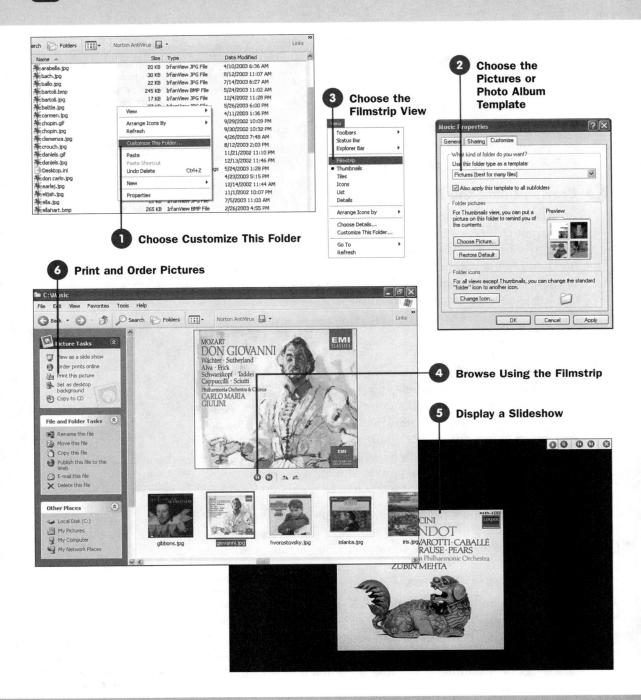

2 Choose the Pictures or Photo Album Template

3 Choose the Filmstrip View

1 Choose Customize This Folder

6 Print and Order Pictures

4 Browse Using the Filmstrip

5 Display a Slideshow

34 About Sharing Files and Folders with Other Accounts

When several people with different accounts share the same computer, confusion may reign. One account might create a file, and then someone else might edit it or delete it, without the first person's knowledge. Entire folders can be created by one account, then deleted by another.

As you'll see in **35 Make Your Files and Folders Private**, there is a way to keep certain folders private. But before you understand how to keep files private, you should understand how to make them public—and how Windows XP distinguishes between public and private folders.

Unless an account uses a password or takes other steps to keep its files private, all folders on the computer can be used by anyone in any other account. So if no account on your computer uses a password, and if no one has gone to the trouble of making any folders private, every file in every folder is up for grabs—anyone can view it and use it. Making a folder public takes no work at all when Windows XP is initially installed—just create a folder.

However, if an account creates a password, certain folders associated with that account can be kept private. Folders in the personal account can be kept private—those in C:\My Documents*Account Name* folder, where *Account Name* is the XP account name, for example, C:\My Documents\Preston Gralla. If someone puts files in that folder or creates folders underneath that folder, those folders and files are kept private. However, all other folders will be public. That means, for example, that if you create a C:**Family** folder, anyone on the computer can view it and use files in it, even if you've created a password for your account.

Just to make things a little bit more confusing, there's another way to share folders and documents with other users of the same computer. Windows XP has a folder called *Shared Documents*, and that folder allows accounts to share files and folders with other accounts on the same computer. To share a file or folder with the **Shared Documents** folder, open Windows Explorer and make sure that the **Task** pane is showing (click the **Folders** button in the button bar to make the pane appear). Then highlight a file or folder in the right pane of Windows Explorer and click the **Share this folder** link in the **Task** pane; that folder can now be shared with others through the **Shared Documents** folder. Any user of the computer will be able to see those documents by going to the **Shared Documents** folder.

Before You Begin

✔ **31** About Windows Explorer

See Also

→ **35** Make Your Files and Folders Private

NOTE

If your account name is **Preston Gralla**, when someone else is logged into the computer, the **C:\My Documents\ Preston Gralla** folder will show up to them as the **Preston Gralla's Documents** folder.

KEY TERM

Shared documents folder—
A folder that contains files and folders that different accounts on the same computer want to share with one another.

The easiest way to get to the **Shared Documents** folder is from **My Computer**. To open **My Computer**, click the **My Computer** icon on your desktop (if there is one; in some instances, it's not there), or click the **Start** menu and choose **My Computer**.

*Open **My Computer** and you'll find the **Shared Documents** folder, which contains documents and folders that different accounts on the same computer want to share with one another.*

---

35 Make Your Files and Folders Private

Before You Begin

✔ **31** About Windows Explorer

✔ **34** About Sharing Files and Folders with Other Accounts

See Also

→ **36** Protect a File or Folder with Encryption

→ **46** Share Files and Folders Across the Network

If you share your computer with others, most likely there are files you'll want to keep private. You'll want to keep them private not only so that others can't read them, but so that the files can't be deleted or edited by someone else.

It's easy to keep files and folders private, as you'll see in the following steps. Keep in mind that you can't designate individual files to be kept private. Instead, you designate entire folders. Every file in the designated folder is kept private; there's no way to make some files in a folder public and some private.

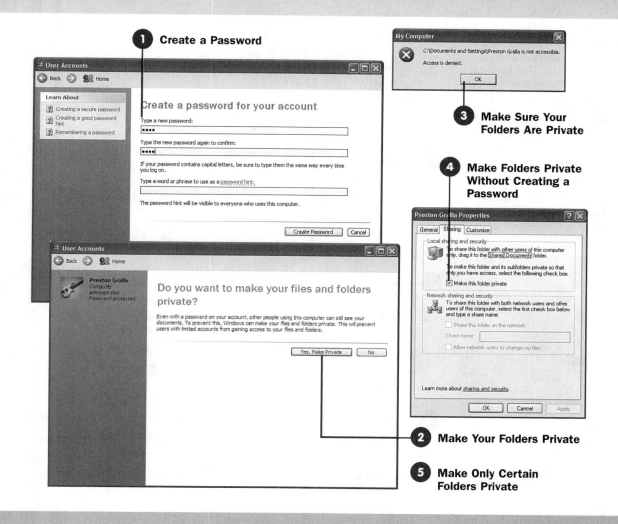

① Create a Password

③ Make Sure Your Folders Are Private

④ Make Folders Private Without Creating a Password

② Make Your Folders Private

⑤ Make Only Certain Folders Private

① Create a Password

If you have an account that requires a password to log on, your files may already be private, depending on how you set up your account. However, when you installed Windows XP, you may have not set up your account so that your files are private.

NOTE

Making folders public and private on an individual computer is different than sharing them with other computers on a network. None of the files and folders on your computer can be shared with other computers on a network unless you specifically allow for that. For details, see **46** **Share Files and Folders Across the Network.**

If your account has no password, you must create a password for the account if you want to protect all the files and folders on your PC. When you create the password, you'll be given the option of keeping all your files and folders private.

Create a password by following the instructions in **4** **Use Passwords for Better Security.**

2 Make Your Folders Private

After you create your password, a screen appears asking **Do You want to make your files and folders private?** Click **Yes, Make Private.** Depending on the size of your hard disk and how many files and folders you have, the screen might display on your computer for several minutes as it makes the files and folders private.

3 Make Sure Your Folders Are Private

To double-check that your folders have been made private, log off Windows XP and have someone else log on using his account. Ask him to open Windows Explorer and go to the **C:\My Documents\Your Name** folder, where **Your Name** is your XP account name. The other user should get an error message denying him access to the folder.

TIP

If you don't password-protect your user account, no folders are truly private, and anyone can log on as you. And after they do, they can view all your private files and folders.

4 Make Folders Private Without Creating a Password

You don't have to create a password if you want to make all your folders private—there's another way to do it. To make all your folders private, open Windows Explorer and go to the **C:\My Documents\Your Name** folder, where **Your Name** is your XP account name. Right-click the folder and choose **Properties.** In the **Properties** dialog box that opens, click the **Sharing** tab. Enable the **Make this folder private** check box and click **OK.** That folder and all the folders beneath it are now private.

5 Make Only Certain Folders Private

You also have the option of keeping some folders private and allowing others to be public. Open Windows Explorer and go to the **C:\My Documents\Your Name** folder, where **Your Name** is your XP account name. Right-click the folder and choose **Properties.** In the **Properties** dialog box that opens, click the **Sharing** tab. Disable the **Make this folder private** check box and click **OK**. That folder (which is your main folder in Windows XP) can now be seen by other users of the computer.

You can, however, make individual folders beneath your main folder private. In Windows Explorer, select any folder you want to be private and follow the instructions in step 4. Keep in mind that when you do this, the selected folder and all folders beneath it are made private. However, you can manually go to any private folder and make it public by disabling the **Make this folder private** check box in the *Folder Name* **Properties** dialog box.

By the way, there's no way to tell whether a folder is private just by looking at it—the icon for a private folder looks just like any other folder icon on your computer. Also, keep in mind that when you move a private folder or file to the **Shared Documents** folder, you're actually *moving* that file or folder there; you are not copying the file or folder.

36 Protect a File or Folder with Encryption

Keeping folders and files private using the techniques described in **35** **Make Your Files and Folders Private** is useful, but this low-level protection of folders leaves something to be desired. You can keep only certain folders private. And when you keep that folder private, every file in it must also be kept private—some files can't be made private and some public.

There's a much more powerful way to keep files and folders private— *encryption*. When a file or folder is encrypted, it is scrambled so that no one can read it except the person who performed the encryption, unless that person wants to share the file or folder with someone else.

Users of Windows XP Home Edition can't use encryption—that version of the operating system doesn't include the feature. Only users of Windows XP Professional Edition can encrypt files and folders.

Encrypted files and folders show up in Windows Explorer as green, so you can tell at a glance which have been encrypted. You can work with encrypted files and folders just as you can with any other file—they're decrypted on the fly as you open them and then encrypted again when you close them. You won't have to do anything special to use them after you've encrypted them.

Before You Begin

✔ **31** About Windows Explorer

See Also

→ **35** Make Your Files and Folders Private

KEY TERM

Encryption—A technique that scrambles data, files, and folders so that the only person who can read them is the person who encrypted them, unless she decides to share them with others.

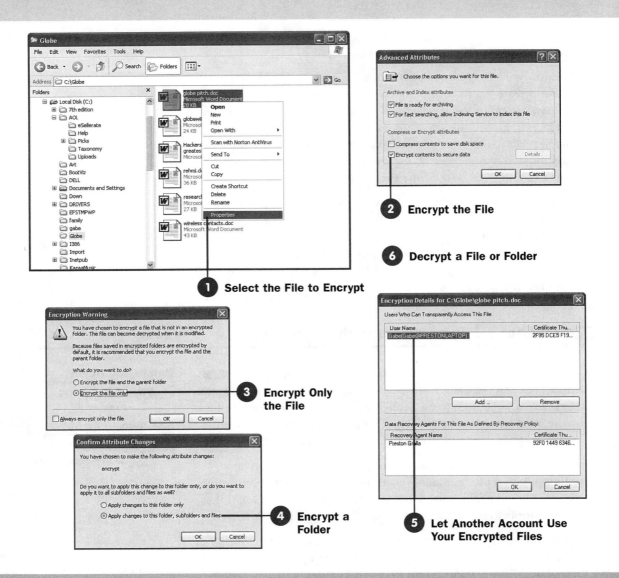

Select the File to Encrypt ①

Encrypt Only the File ③

Encrypt a Folder ④

Encrypt the File ②

Decrypt a File or Folder ⑥

Let Another Account Use Your Encrypted Files ⑤

You're the only person who can read or use files you've encrypted. Even other accounts on the same computer can't read or use them unless you specifically designate certain accounts to be able to read or use them. If you send the encrypted file to someone else on a different computer, for example as an email attachment, the file will be automatically decrypted so that the person can read it.

At any point, you can decrypt files so that anyone who wants can use them normally.

1 Select the File to Encrypt

Open Windows Explorer and navigate to the file you want to encrypt. Right-click the file and choose **Properties** from the context menu. From the **Properties** dialog box that appears, click the **General** tab, then click the **Advanced** button. The **Advanced Attributes** dialog box appears.

2 Encrypt the File

In the **Advanced Attributes** dialog box, enable the **Encrypt contents to secure data** check box and click **OK** twice.

3 Encrypt Only the File

Before the file is actually encrypted, the **Encryption Warning** dialog box appears, asking whether you want to encrypt only the file, or the file and the folder that contains the file. Because we want to encrypt just the file, choose **Encrypt the file only**. If, however, you want to encrypt the file and its folder, choose **Encrypt the file and the parent folder**.

The selected file is now encrypted. It will show up in Windows Explorer in green. No one else can read it or open it, although other users can see that the file exists; because the file is in green, they can see that they cannot use it. On the other hand, you can use the file as you would any other file.

4 Encrypt a Folder

You encrypt a folder in a similar way to how you encrypt a file. In Windows Explorer, right-click the folder you want to encrypt and choose **Properties** from the context menu. From the **General** tab, click the **Advanced** button, enable the **Encrypt contents to secure data** check box, and then click **OK** twice. The **Confirm Attribute Changes** dialog box appears, asking whether you want to encrypt only the current folder, or also all the folders underneath the selected folder and all the files in them.

This may be one of the most misleading dialog boxes in all of XP. If you choose **Apply changes to this folder only**, none of your

NOTE

You can't encrypt a file that you've compressed in order to save disk space. If you try to encrypt a compressed file, you won't be allowed to do it. You also can't compress a file that you've already encrypted. For more information about compressing files, see **37** **Get More Disk Space by Using Compression**.

files will in fact be encrypted. Whenever you create a new file in that folder, however, or copy or move a file into the folder, the new file is automatically encrypted. However, files already in the folder are not encrypted. If you want those old files to be encrypted, you'll have to manually encrypt each one, as outlined in the previous steps.

If you choose **Apply changes to this folder, subfolders, and files**, all the files in the folder and its subfolders are encrypted. Any new files you add to the folder are encrypted as well. In fact, even if the folder doesn't have any subfolders, you might want to make this choice, because then all the files in the folder will be encrypted.

NOTE

Remember, you can't encrypt files and folders unless you have XP Professional Edition.

5 Let Another Account Use Your Encrypted Files

You can allow other accounts on the computer to use your encrypted files if you want. You may want to do this, for example, if you want some accounts to be able to see the files, but not others.

In Windows Explorer, right-click an encrypted file or folder and choose **Properties**. Click the **General** tab and then click the **Advanced** button. From the **Advanced Attributes** dialog box that appears, click the **Details** button to display the **Encryption Details** dialog box for the file. The top part of the dialog box lists the other accounts on the computer. Highlight the account you want to use your encrypted file and click **Add**. The **Select User** dialog box appears, again asking which account you want to use the encrypted files. Click the account name and click **OK**; keep clicking **OK** to close out each dialog box. That user can now use your encrypted files.

WEB RESOURCE

If you're a Windows XP Home Edition user and want to encrypt your files, you're not left out in the cold. Download the free encryption program Cryptainer LE, available from Cypherix.

www.cypherix.co.uk

6 Decrypt a File or Folder

To decrypt a file or folder, open Windows Explorer and right-click the file or folder you want to decrypt. Follow the directions in steps 1 and 2—except that this time you'll disable the **Encrypt contents to secure data** check box. If you're decrypting a file, keep clicking **OK** to close out the dialog boxes. If you're decrypting a folder, you'll be asked whether you want to decrypt just the current folder or all the folders and files underneath it. Make your choice, click **OK**, and keeping clicking **OK** to close out the dialog boxes.

37 Get More Disk Space by Using Compression

No matter how much hard disk space your computer has, it never seems to be enough. However, there's a simple way to get more space without having to pay for an extra hard disk or go to the trouble of installing one—you can use *compression*, which shrinks files and folders so that they take up less hard disk space, and you can fit more on your hard disk.

When you use compression, files are compressed on the fly—that is, the compression and decompression happen invisibly, without your knowledge. You can use compressed files as you would any other file. When you open the file, Windows XP decompresses it, so when you're working with it, the file is no longer compressed. When you save it, the file is compressed again. But you don't have to do any of this manually—once you compress the disk, it all happens automatically.

Because regular compression is so much more useful than ZIP compression, we'll cover only regular compression in this task. When you use Windows XP compression, you don't have to compress the entire hard disk. You can select individual files or folders to compress and leave other files in their normal, decompressed state. Working with compressed files shouldn't slow your system down, or if it does, it should not be very noticeable. However, if you notice a slowdown, decompress the files, and work with them normally.

1 Choose the Files to Compress

Not all files benefit from compression, because certain types of files have already been compressed. If you try to compress these types of files, not only will you not get much (if any) extra disk space, you might slow your system down because it's working hard trying to compress files that have already been compressed.

Don't compress music files in the **.MP3** and **.WMA** formats because those formats are already compressed formats. Graphic files in the **.GIF** and **.JPG** or **.JPEG** formats have also already been compressed, and so shouldn't be compressed with Windows XP compression. However, graphics in most other formats, such as **.TIF** and **.PCX**, can be compressed to an enormous degree. It's not uncommon for those types of files to be compressed 90% and more.

Before You Begin

✔ **31** About Windows Explorer

See Also

→ **36** Protect a File or Folder with Encryption

🔍 KEY TERM

Compression—A technique that shrinks files and folders, so that they take up less hard disk space, and you can fit more on your hard disk.

⚓ TIPS

Don't confuse compression with using the ZIP format and ZIP folders. The ZIP format also compresses files. But as a general rule, you use the ZIP format only for files you are not regularly using or that you're sending to someone with email, because you can't work with files in ZIP format on the fly, as you can with regular compression.

If you've encrypted a file, it can't be compressed, so make sure that any files you want to compress have not been encrypted. If you still want to compress them, you'll first have to decrypt the files.

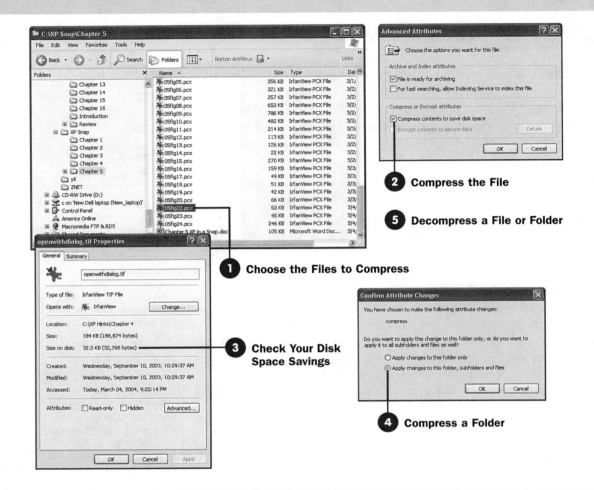

2 Compress the File

5 Decompress a File or Folder

1 Choose the Files to Compress

3 Check Your Disk Space Savings

4 Compress a Folder

2 Compress the File

In Windows Explorer, right-click the file you want to compress and choose **Properties** from the context menu. In the **Properties** dialog box, click the **General** tab and then click the **Advanced** button. In the **Advanced Attributes** dialog box, enable the **Compress contents to save disk space** check box and click **OK**. Click **OK** again to compress the file.

The file will now be compressed and will show up in Internet Explorer in blue. You can work with the file as you would any other file.

③ Check Your Disk Space Savings

When you look at the file details of the file you've just compressed in Windows Explorer, it looks as if you haven't compressed the file—the **Size** column shows that the file is still the same size.

However, if the file appears in blue in Windows Explorer, you have, in fact, compressed it. Windows Explorer reports the original file size, not the compressed file size. To find the true compressed size of the file on the disk, right-click the file in Windows Explorer and choose **Properties** from the context menu. On the **General** tab of the **Properties** dialog box, you'll find two listings of the file size, one that reads **Size** and one that reads **Size on disk**. The **Size** listing tells you the original size of the file; the **Size on disk** listing tells you the size of the file after it's been compressed. In this example, the original file is 184KB, but it compressed to 32KB—a space savings of almost 600 percent!

④ Compress a Folder

You compress a folder in a similar way to how you compress a file. In Windows Explorer, right-click the folder you want to compress and choose **Properties** from the context menu. In the **Properties** dialog box, click the **General** tab and then click the **Advanced** button. In the **Advanced Attributes** dialog box, enable the **Compress contents to save disk space** check box and then click **OK** twice. The **Confirm Attribute Changes** dialog box appears, asking whether you want to compress only the current folder or all folders underneath the folder and all files in them.

As with the similar dialog box for encrypting files, this may be one of the most misleading dialog boxes in all of Windows XP. If you choose **Apply changes to this folder only**, none of your files will in fact be compressed. Whenever you create a new file in that folder, however, or copy or move a file into the folder, the new file is automatically compressed. However, files already in the folder are not compressed. If you want those existing files to be compressed, you must manually compress each one, as outlined in steps 1 and 2.

If you choose **Apply changes to this folder, subfolders, and files**, all the files in the folder and its subfolders are compressed. And any new files you add to the folder are compressed as well. In fact, even if the folder doesn't have any subfolders, you might want to make this choice because then all the files in the folder will be compressed.

NOTE

If you can't compress a file, it may be that your hard disk does not use something called the NT File System (NTFS). As a general rule, all XP computers in the last several years use this filesystem, but if you can't compress a file, perhaps your hard disk doesn't use it. To find out if it does, right-click the **My Computer** icon on the desktop, choose **Properties**, and click the **General** tab. Look at the **File System** entry. If your computer uses NTFS, it will say so there.

NOTE

You aren't allowed to compress a file that you've encrypted to keep private. You also can't encrypt compressed files. For more information about encrypting files, see **36** **Protect a File or Folder with Encryption.**

When you compress the folder, no matter which option you choose, you can continue to work with the files as if they were not compressed.

5 **Decompress a File or Folder**

If you decide that you want to decompress a file or folder, simply reverse the process you used to compress it. Repeat step 2, except this time disable the **Compress contents to save disk space** check box and click **OK**. If you're decompressing a file, keep clicking **OK** to close out the dialog boxes. If you're decompressing a folder, you'll first be asked whether you want to decompress just the current folder or all the folders underneath it. Make your choice, click **OK**, and keeping clicking **OK** to close out the dialog boxes.

38 **Change What Program Opens a File (File Association)**

Before You Begin

✔ **31** **About Windows Explorer**

Whenever you double-click a file in XP, a program launches and opens the file. Windows XP determines which program should run and open the file based on the *filename extension*, the three letters at the end of the filename. In the filename **newpicture.tif**, **.tif** is the filename extension.

Sometimes, when you install a new program, it hijacks filename extensions. The installation may warn you that it will do so, but you didn't really take note of the warning; alternatively, the new program might take over the extension without telling you. Or perhaps you let one program take over the file extension but have now decided that you'd prefer a different program to open that file type.

It's easy to change what program should open files with a particular filename extension. Here's how to do it.

1 **Run Windows Explorer**

Locate and run Windows Explorer. You'll find it in a variety of places, such as the **All Programs** menu (access from the **Start** menu), or on the left side of the **Start** menu. You can also launch it by pressing the **Windows+E** key combination.

1 Run Windows Explorer

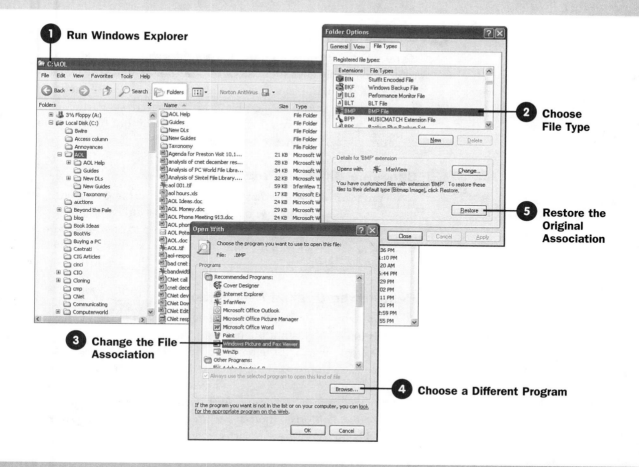

2 Choose File Type

5 Restore the Original Association

3 Change the File Association

4 Choose a Different Program

2 Choose File Type

From the Windows Explorer menu bar, choose **Tools, Folder Options**. The **File Types** tab of the **Folder Options** dialog box appears. From this tab, you can see and change what programs open which file types.

In the **Registered file types** list box, scroll to the file type you want to change and click to select (highlight) it. In the **Details** section, look at the **Opens with** line, which tells you what program will open files with this extension when you double-click them. If you want to leave the association as is (that is, you want the named program to open files with this extension), don't take any further action.

③ Change the File Association

If you want a different program to open files with this extension when you double-click them, click the **Change** button. The **Open With** dialog box appears. From the **Programs** list, choose the program you want to use to open files with the selected extension and click **OK** twice. When you double-click any file of that file type, the program you've just chosen will open it.

④ Choose a Different Program

If the program you want to use doesn't appear in the **Open With** dialog box, click the **Browse** button. In the new dialog box that opens, navigate to the program you want to use to open files with this extension. When you find the program, click **Open**. Then click **OK** twice.

⑤ Restore the Original Association

If the file association shown on the **File Types** tab of the **Folder Options** dialog box is not the one that Windows XP originally used—in other words, if the program named to open files with that filename extension was changed by some program from when XP was first installed—you can easily revert the file association to the original program. In the **Opens with** section of the **Files Type** tab of the **Folder Options** dialog box, click the **Restore** button. The file type will be automatically associated with the original program.

39 About Windows XP Search

Before You Begin

✔ **31** About Windows Explorer

See Also

→ **40** Kill the Search Dog

→ **41** Find Files and Folders Faster

Hard disks are big. Human memory is short. Hence the need for Windows XP's **Search** feature.

Search does exactly what it says—it helps you find files when you don't recall their names or where they are. You can search in a variety of different ways, including by filename, by file type, by words in the file, and so on.

When you launch search, the *Search Companion* appears, which includes an animated dog named Rover. Many people find this canine exceedingly annoying. To learn how to turn him off (or change Rover to some other character), see **40** Kill the Search Dog.

The Search Companion presents you with options for four types of searches. When you click any of them, you perform the search in a wizard-like interface. Here are the four search types:

- Pictures, music, or video

- Documents (word processing, spreadsheet, and so on)

- All files and folders

- Computers or people

Although the wizard approach works well for people who haven't used **Search** before, it's a slow way for more advanced users to search. You can customize **Search** so that you can find what you want much more quickly. To see how, turn to **41** **Find Files and Folders Faster**.

KEY TERM

Search Companion— Windows XP's search feature, that includes step-by-step wizards to help you search; you can also bypass the wizards and more directly type search terms.

40 Kill the Search Dog

Before You Begin

✔ **39** About Windows XP Search

See Also

➔ **41** Find Files and Folders Faster

Rover, the search dog, is one of the most reviled characters in all of computerdom. Launch search and he walks out toward you, then sits there, every once in a while blinking his eyes, or wagging his tail, rolling his eyes occasionally, or pulling out a book and leafing through the pages. He serves absolutely no purpose, however.

If you want, you can kill the dog entirely or replace him with another animated character—although there are some who find the other animated search characters just as annoying as Rover.

1 Launch a Search

You can launch the Windows XP **Search** feature in a variety of different ways: Click the **Start** button and choose **Search** from the **Start** menu. Alternatively, press the **Windows+F** key combination. If you're in a Windows Explorer window, you can press **F3** or click the **Search** button at the top of the screen.

2 Click Change Preferences

From the **Search Companion** area on the left side of the **Search** window, click the **Change preferences** link. A screen appears, asking how you want to use the **Search Companion**. You can use the links in this list of options to customize it in a variety of ways, including killing the search dog.

1 Launch a Search

3 Click Without an
Animated Character

5 Browse for a
New Animated
Character

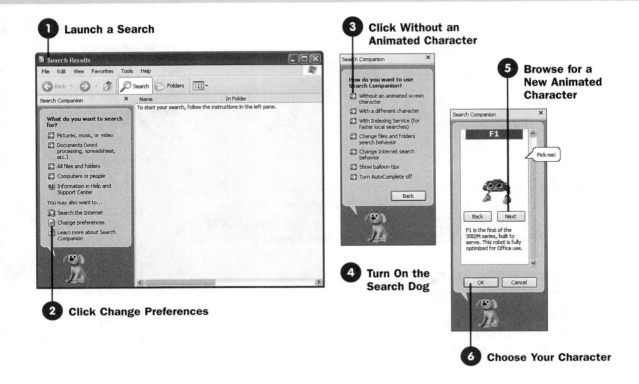

2 Click Change Preferences

4 Turn On the
Search Dog

6 Choose Your Character

NOTE

Turning off the search dog
has no effect on how you'll
search using Windows XP,
or the results you'll get
when you search.

3 **Click Without an Animated Character**

In the **Search Companion** area on the left side of the **Search** window, click the **Without an animated screen character** link. When you do this, the search dog turns on his heel, and slowly walks away from you, off the screen and into the sunset. The **Search Companion** pane stays on the screen, the same except that the dog is gone.

4 **Turn On the Search Dog**

If you get lonely for the search dog, you can easily turn it back on again. Display the **Search** window as described in step 1. Click the **Change Preferences** link on the left side of the screen and then click the **With an animated screen character** link. Rover hops back on the screen.

⑤ Browse for a New Animated Character

Windows XP includes a variety of other animated characters you can use in place of the search dog. To browse for another character, display the **Search** window as described in step 1. Click the **Change Preferences** link and, from the screen that appears, click the **With a different character** link.

A new screen appears with a picture of Rover the search dog. To see another character, click the **Next** button. Keep clicking the **Next** button until you find a character you want to use.

⑥ Choose Your Character

Click **OK**. The search dog will walk away, and the new character you selected appears in his place.

41 Find Files and Folders Faster

Rover, the search dog, isn't the only problem with Windows XP's **Search Companion**. Using the **Search Companion** in its default configuration can slow you down, and might even prevent you from finding all the files you want. There are ways, however, to speed up your search and make it more accurate as well.

① Turn On Advanced Search

To more finely tune your searches and find what you want faster, you need to use the **Advanced Search** feature. To turn it on, launch the **Search Companion** and then click the **Change Preferences** link. From the screen that appears, asking how you want to use the **Search Companion**, choose **Change files and folders search behavior**. You'll then come to a screen with two choices: **Standard** search and **Advanced** search. Choose the **Advanced** option and click **OK**. The **Search** screen returns, but using the advanced search screen.

② Perform an Advanced Search

The advanced search screen gives you many more options than the basic **Search Companion** does. You can search for a file based on the text it contains, by the file size, file type, when the file was

Before You Begin

✔ **39** About Windows XP Search

See Also

→ **40** Kill the Search Dog

TIP

Launch the **Search** feature by clicking the **Start** button and choosing **Search** or pressing the **Windows+F** key combination. If you're in a Windows Explorer window, you can press **F3** or click the **Search** button in the button bar at the top of the window.

NOTE

When you're searching for text in a file, you can have the search only match words when they are the exact case of the words you type into the **A word or phrase in the file** box. To do that, enable the **Case sensitive** check box at the bottom of the **Search Companion** pane. Now when you search, you'll only match the case of words you type in the search box. For example, if you type the search term "**Family**," you wouldn't find any files that contained the word "**fami-ly**"—you'd only find files that contained the word "**Family**."

last changed, and more. To use all the options, on the advanced search screen, click **More Advance Options**. Then you can search using these advanced options:

- To search by a filename, type the name of the file in the **All or part of the file name** text box.

- To search by a word or phrase contained in the text of the file, type the word or words in the **A word or phrase in the file** text box.

- To search in a specific folder, choose **Browse** from the **Look in** drop-down list, and navigate to the folder in which you want to search.

- To search by the date the file was modified, click **When was it modified?** and fill in the information about when the file was modified.

- To search by file size, click **What size is it?** and fill in the information about the file size.

- If you want to search through system folders and through hidden files and folders, enable the **Search system folders** and **Search hidden files and folders** check boxes. (For more information about system folders and hidden files and fold-ers, see **32 Customize Your Folder View**.)

When you're done specifying your search criteria, click the **Search** button, and XP will perform the search for you. You'll see the results in a Windows Explorer interface, so you can open files just as you would using Windows Explorer.

KEY TERM

Metadata—Information that XP stores about every file on your hard disk. The type of metadata stored about each file varies according to what type of file it is. For example, digital music may have meta-data including the genre of music, the artist, and the album title.

3 Search Using Metadata

It's easy to search for a file based on the text in it. But what if you're searching for a picture file or a music file? Those files con-tain no text, and so you might think that there's no way to search through them. However, there *is* a way to do it, using what's called *metadata*. Metadata is information that XP stores about every file on your hard disk. The type of metadata stored about each file varies according to the type of file.

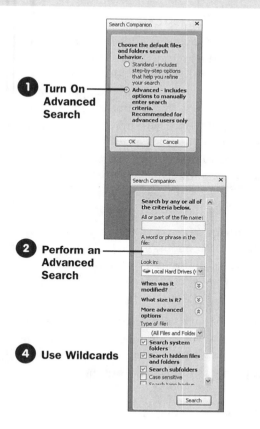

1 Turn On Advanced Search

2 Perform an Advanced Search

4 Use Wildcards

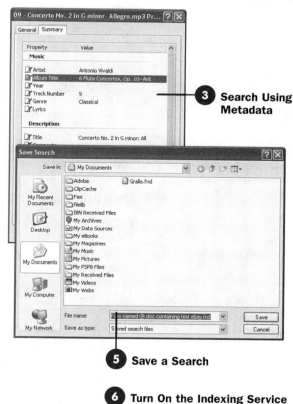

3 Search Using Metadata

5 Save a Search

6 Turn On the Indexing Service

The metadata for music files in **.WMA** and **.MP3** formats can include a great deal of descriptive information, including the artist name, the album title, the year the song was recorded, the musical genre, comments inserted by you or the person who recorded the track, and even the lyrics. The metadata is inserted into the music file when the file is created. Metadata for graphics files doesn't contain as much descriptive information, but it does include basic information such as the resolution of the file. Some metadata such as the resolution of a graphics file is automatically gathered by Windows XP when a file is created.

TIP

To see metadata information for a media file, right-click the file and choose **Properties** from the context menu. Click the **Summary** tab in the **Properties** dialog box to see the metadata. (Sometimes after you click the **Summary** tab, you'll have to click the **Advanced** button to see metadata.)

You don't have to do anything special to search through metadata for files; you just have to know that you *can* search through it. To search through metadata, type the information for which you want to search in the **A word or phrase in the file** text box. For example, type **Classical** to find all your classical music files; type a musical artist's or composer's name to find all music written or recorded by that artist or composer on your hard disk. For graphics files, you can type the resolution of the file. When you want to find all files with an 800 by 600 resolution, for example, type **800 × 600**. Then click **Search** to perform the search.

4 Use Wildcards

Often, when you're searching for a filename, you might not remember the entire filename. You might, however, recall part of the filename. Windows XP lets you use wildcards that allow you to search for files when you only know part of their names.

You can use the two wildcards characters * and ?. If you type **snap*.doc**, the * wildcard searches for all filenames that start with *snap*, end in *.doc*, and have zero or more numbers or letters in the filename after the letters *snap*. Searching for **snap*.doc** will find these files: **snap.doc**, **snapa.doc**, **snappy.doc**, **snappiest.doc**, and **snap8.doc**.

If you type **snap?.doc**, the ? wildcard searches for all files that start with *snap*, end in *.doc*, and have only one letter or number after the letters *snap*. Searching for **snap?.doc** will find these files: **snapa.doc** and **snap8.doc**.

Type your search term using wildcards in the **All or part of a file name** box and click the **Search** button. You can use wildcards only in that text box, and not in the **A word or phrase in the file** box.

5 Save a Search

You might frequently do the same search over and over again. Particularly if the search is a complex one, you might want to save that search so that you don't have to type it in each time you want to do it.

To save a search, first enter the criteria you're going to search on and do the search. You can't save a search until you run it. After you've run it, choose **Save Search** from the **File** menu in the **Search Results** dialog box. The **Save Search** dialog box appears. Type a name for the search in the **File name** field at the bottom of the dialog box and choose where you want to save the search. Your best bet is to save it on the desktop. That way, you'll only have to double-click the search file icon to run it again.

TIP

By default, your saved searches are saved in your **My Documents** folder. They look something like this: **Files named @.doc.fnd**.

6 **Turn On the Indexing Service**

If you have a big hard disk with a lot of files on it, it can take a long time to do a search. There's a way to significantly speed up searching—use the *Indexing Service*. The Indexing Service creates an index of every file on your hard disk. When you perform a search through your hard disk, you actually search through the index, rather than the entire hard disk. That way, searching goes much more quickly.

There are some pros and cons to using the Indexing Service, so before deciding to use it, consider these points:

- **The Indexing Service takes up a good deal of disk space.** The index requires a substantial amount of disk space—anywhere from 15% to 30% of the space currently used by your files and folders, according to Microsoft. That means giving up gigabytes of hard disk space to the index.

- **The Indexing Service doesn't search by case.** If it's important for you to be able to search by case (uppercase or lowercase letters), don't use the index.

- **The Indexing Service searches only through certain file types.** It searches through HTML files, text files, and documents created by Microsoft Office. If you want to search effectively through other file types, you'll have to get a non-Microsoft-supplied filter on the Internet (search Google to find them), and there aren't filters for all file types.

- **There are times you won't be able to use the Indexing Service.** When the service is in the process of indexing your hard drive, either initially or when it's updating, you can't use the Indexing Service to search. You can, however, still use the **Search Companion**.

KEY TERM

Indexing Service—A feature that lets you speed up your searches by indexing your hard disk. When you do a search, you search through the index, which is much faster than searching the entire hard disk.

TIP

When searching through Google for filters, try a variety of combinations to find your filter, such as **xp indexing service filters**.

When you activate the **Indexing Service**, it won't immediately be available. It first has to build the index, which can take a substantial amount of time, depending on the number of files on your hard disk and your processor speed. It's best to start the **Indexing Service** and leave your computer on overnight so that it can complete indexing. When the indexing is done, you submit a search to the **Indexing Service** in the same way you do to the **Search Companion**.

The bottom line? If you can spare the hard disk space and can live with its limitations, it'll be worth your while to use the **Indexing Service**—speed is a major benefit.

To turn on the **Indexing Service**, start from the **Search Companion** pane and choose **Change preferences**. Then choose **With Indexing Service**. If the **With Indexing Service** option isn't available, and instead you see **Without Indexing Service**, it means that the Indexing Service is already turned on.

To turn off the indexing service from the **Search Companion**, choose **Change preferences** and then click **Without Indexing Service**. When you do that, the service is shut off. The index remains intact; when you do a search, you just won't search through it. You can always turn the index back on whenever you want.

42 Change the Default Folder for Saving Files

Before You Begin

✔ **31** About Windows Explorer

Whenever you save a file in Windows XP, the **Save** or **Save As** dialog box opens to a specific location—your **My Documents** folder, which is in the **C:\My Documents***Account Name* folder, where *Account Name* is your XP account name; for example, **C:\My Documents\Preston Gralla**.

But perhaps you don't use that folder and you want to save files to a different folder. It's easy to set up Windows XP to use whatever folder you prefer.

Find the My Documents Icon

Depending on how you've set up Windows XP, the **My Documents** icon can be in one of a number of locations—for example, on the desktop or on the **Start** menu. It will most likely be on the **Start** menu unless you've changed the **Start** menu in some way.

Right-click the **My Documents** icon and choose **Properties** from the context menu. The **My Documents Properties** dialog box appears. Click the **Target** tab.

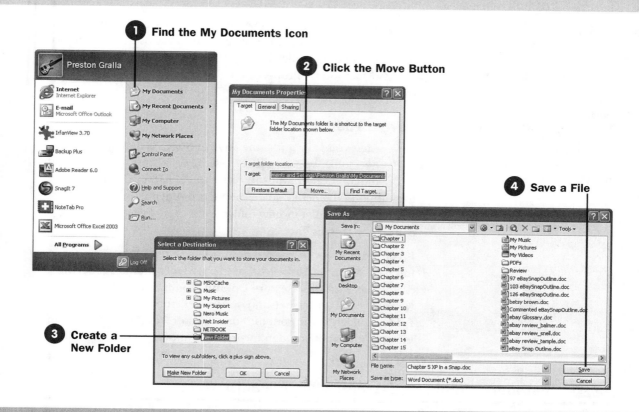

1 **Find the My Documents Icon**

2 **Click the Move Button**

4 **Save a File**

3 **Create a New Folder**

2 **Click the Move Button**

Notice the folder named in the **Target** text box in the middle of the dialog box. To change this folder, click the **Move** button. The **Select a Destination** dialog box appears. Navigate to the folder you want to use as your new default folder for saving files.

3 **Create a New Folder**

If you want to create a new folder to be the default folder for saving files, click the **Make New Folder** button. A new folder called **New Folder** is created in the list of folders shown in the screen in the middle of the dialog box. The cursor will be next to the folder name, allowing you to type a different name for the folder. Give it a new, meaningful name.

Whether you've created a new folder or navigated to an existing one, when you find the folder you want to use as the default location for saving files, click **OK**. You'll be back at the **Target** tab of the **My Documents Properties** dialog box. The new folder is now the **Target** location for your files. Click **OK**.

❹ Save a File

Now, when you save a file, the **Save** or **Save As** dialog box opens to the new folder you specified in step 2 or 3. Note, however, that in the dialog box, XP will still call it the **My Documents** folder, even though the actual folder name is a different one. You'll be saving the files to your new folder, even though the dialog box calls it **My Documents**.

If you want to revert back to your original default location for saving files, open the **Target** tab of the **My Documents Properties** dialog box and click **Restore Default**. You'll be asked whether you want to move all the existing documents from your new **My Folders** folder to your original one. Choose **Yes** if you want them moved, and **No** if you don't want them moved.

Customize Windows Explorer with TweakUI

Before You Begin

✔ About Windows Explorer

See Also

➜ ㉔ About Customizing Your Desktop with TweakUI

Perhaps the best way to customize how Windows Explorer works is to use Microsoft's great free utility TweakUI. It lets you change Windows Explorer so that it works in ways not otherwise readily possible, and lets you do it quickly and easily.

To use it, you must first download it. Refer to ㉔ **About Customizing Your Desktop with TweakUI** for information on locating, downloading, and installing this utility. After you've installed TweakUI, find the file or icon for the file (the file is named **tweakui.exe**) and either double-click the file or single-click the icon. TweakUI will run.

❶ Click the Explorer Folder

The **Explorer** folder of TweakUI, and the subfolders beneath it, lets you customize how Windows Explorer works. Click the **Explorer** folder in the left pane of the TweakUI window; in the **Settings** list in the right pane, you can change a wide variety of Windows

Explorer settings. You can, for example, determine whether to include the **Recent Documents** link on the **Start** menu or leave it off, whether to include the **Help** link on the **Start** menu or leave it off, and several other settings. To enable a setting, enable the check box next to the option. To turn the setting off, disable the check box.

② Customize How Shortcuts Look

When you create a shortcut on your desktop or anywhere else, the icon shows it's a shortcut by displaying an arrow in the lower-left corner. You can change how and whether to display the arrow. Click the **Shortcut** folder under the **Explorer** folder. You can choose to use a light arrow, no arrow, or use an entirely new icon. Choose the option you want from the list on the right side of the screen.

If you choose the **Custom** button, click the **Change** button so that you can browse to choose a different icon for displaying shortcuts.

③ Change the Colors

Windows Explorer uses colors to denote special files and folders. It shows compressed files and folders as blue, encrypted files as green, and "hot-tracking" files and folders as a very dark blue.

You can change any of those colors. Click the **Colors** folder under the **Explorer** folder and click the color bar next to the file type whose color you want to change. A color-picking dialog box appears. Click the new color you want to use for the specified type of file and click **OK**.

④ Change the Thumbnail Display

TweakUI lets you change how thumbnail files are displayed in a folder. (For details about the **Thumbnail** view, see **Customize Your Folder View**.) Click the **Thumbnails** folder under the **Explorer** folder. To change the image quality of the thumbnails, move the **Image Quality** slider between **High** and **Low**. A **High** setting displays higher-quality thumbnails but the thumbnails will take up more disk space, while a **Low** setting displays lower-quality thumbnails that take up less disk space.

NOTE

The **Explorer** folder and subfolders beneath it in TweakUI control not only how Windows Explorer works, but how Internet Explorer works as well. You'll also find options there for controlling Internet Explorer.

TIP

When you hover your mouse pointer over a file or a folder, the file or folder changes to the very dark blue—this is what Microsoft calls *hot-tracking*.

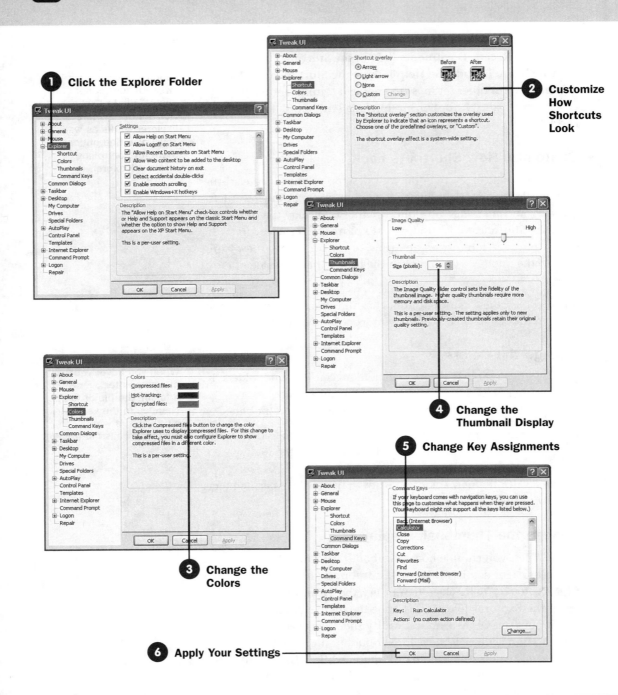

1 Click the Explorer Folder

2 Customize How Shortcuts Look

4 Change the Thumbnail Display

5 Change Key Assignments

3 Change the Colors

6 Apply Your Settings

To change the size of the thumbnails, choose a new number from the **Size (pixels)** box. The default size is 96 pixels. You can make the thumbnails larger or smaller by typing a larger or smaller number here.

When you change the thumbnail display, you only change how new thumbnails are displayed. Your old thumbnails will keep displaying the way they have been.

⑤ Change Key Assignments

Many special keyboards come with special navigation keys that let you perform certain tasks by pressing the key—for example, closing a window, launching the **Search Companion**, and so on. You can use the TweakUI utility to change what those keys do. Click the **Command Keys** folder under the **Explorer** folder. Then click the key whose assignment you want to change and click the **Change** button. A dialog box appears, asking whether you want to leave the key to perform its default action, want the key to do nothing when pressed, or want the key to run a specific program.

If you want the key you've selected to run a program, click **Run a custom program when the key is pressed**, and in the **Target** box, type the filename and location of the program, for example, **C:\Windows\System32\calc.exe** to run the Windows Calculator.

⑥ Apply Your Settings

When you've made all your changes to the **Explorer** folder and subfolders, click the **OK** button. If Windows Explorer is open, close it and then restart it. Your settings will be applied.

NOTE

You can force XP to display your old thumbnails using your new settings. Folders that display thumbnails contain a small file named **Thumbs.db**. Delete that file in any folder that displays thumbnails. The next time you choose the **Thumbnail** view for that folder, the thumbnails will be re-created, using your new settings.

PART II

Networking and the Internet

IN THIS PART:

6

Networking Your PC

IN THIS CHAPTER:

A PC by itself is a lonely thing. It's most useful when it's networked with other computers. When you have a network, you can share files and folders, printers, and even an Internet connection.

A network is made up of a number of computers connected to a *router*, which is a device that allows computers to communicate with one another and to share an Internet connection. Many people think that setting up a network is a technically complex task beyond their capabilities, but it's not particularly hard to do. In this chapter, you'll learn how to set up and use a home network.

44 Install a Home Router

See Also

→ **45** Create a New Network Installation

→ **60** Install a Wi-Fi Router

KEY TERM

Router—A piece of hardware that connects computers to one another and that lets them all share an Internet connection.

TIP

Some wireless routers include Ethernet "wired" connections. If you have desktop PCs that you want to connect using Ethernet connections, and laptops or desktop PCs that you want to connect wirelessly, you can buy a wireless router than has both types of connections. If you also think that at some point in the future you might want to buy computers that connect wirelessly, consider buying a wireless router that has Ethernet connections.

The first step in setting up your network is to set up a *router*, the hardware that connects all your computers, and that connects the computers to the Internet.

Routers are inexpensive, and typically cost $50 or less. That will buy you a wired router, one to which you'll have to physically connect your computers to create the network. If you want a wireless router, they cost $20 to $50 more than wired ones.

❶ Choose Your Router

The most basic decision you have to make is whether to buy a wired or wireless router. If all your computers are located in the same room near one another, and you do not expect to use any in another room in your house, a wired router is a good idea. If, however, you have computers in the house far away from where the router will be located, a wireless router is a better idea. For more information about how to choose and install a wireless router, see **60** Install a Wi-Fi Router.

❷ Connect the Router to Your High-Speed Internet Connection

When you install a home network, the point is not only to connect your computers to one another, but to also let them all share a single high-speed Internet connection. The first step in setup is to connect the router to your Internet connection (for example, to a cable modem or DSL modem).

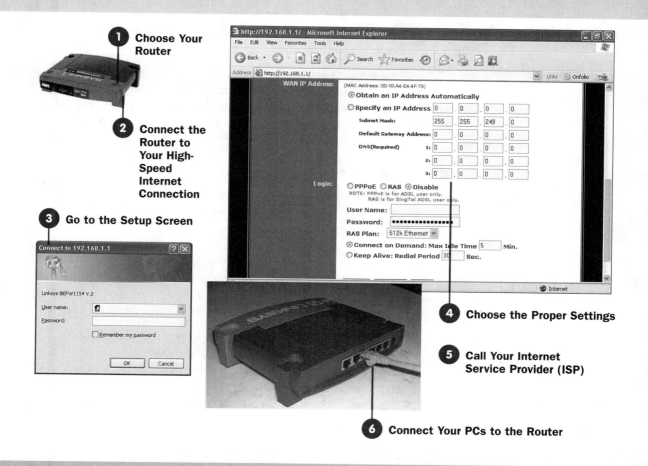

1 Choose Your Router

2 Connect the Router to Your High-Speed Internet Connection

3 Go to the Setup Screen

4 Choose the Proper Settings

5 Call Your Internet Service Provider (ISP)

6 Connect Your PCs to the Router

Unpack the router but don't plug it into a power outlet yet. Then connect one end of an Ethernet cable to your cable model or DSL modem, and the other end to your router. When you connect the cable to the router, make sure that you connect it to the correct port. Look for the connection labeled **WAN**. (This connection is often by itself, away from any other ports.) Check your router's documentation for details if there is no connection labeled **WAN**— different manufacturers use different terminologies, and so you should check for the right one.

After you connect the Ethernet cables, turn off your cable modem or DSL modem for five minutes. Then turn it back on again, plug in your router's power cord, and turn on the power switch if your router has a power switch.

After several minutes, you should see green lights flashing on your router, depending on the manufacturer. That means that the router is working and making a connection to the Internet through your cable modem or DSL modem. Check your router's documentation for more details.

③ Go to the Setup Screen

Your router is now connected physically to the Internet, but you still have to configure it to work properly. You'll do this using a setup screen that you access from your PC. Every router manufacturer has a different setup screen, and the way you get to that screen varies by manufacturer. In this task, you'll see how to do it with the most popular type of router, a Linksys router. The directions given here are similar, but not identical, to those you'll follow for other routers, so check your router's documentation for details.

To get to the setup screen of a Linksys router, first connect your computer to the router using the Ethernet cables. Then open Internet Explorer, type the location **http://192.168.1.1** in the address bar, and press **Enter**. A login screen appears. Leave the **User name** box blank, type **admin** in the **Password** box, and press **Enter**. The setup screen appears.

④ Choose the Proper Settings

The router's settings most likely don't have to be changed because they're usually set properly when you unpack the box. However, they may not be set properly, and you also may need to get information from the setup screen to give to your high-speed ISP such as your cable company or DSL company.

Make sure that your router is set to **Obtain an IP Address Automatically**. For the Linksys router used in this example, this option is a simple radio button that you select. An *IP address* is a number such as **136.87.23.45** that uniquely identifies your router on the Internet. Every computer and device on the Internet must have its own unique IP address.

KEY TERM

IP address—A number such as **136.87.23.45** that uniquely identifies any computer or device connected to the Internet. To be connected to the Internet, computers and other equipment must have an IP address.

Your high-speed ISP will automatically give your router its IP address when it is connected to your cable modem or DSL modem. In fact, when you plugged your router into the Internet, your ISP gave the router an IP address, as long as your router was set to **Obtain an IP Address Automatically**. If the router wasn't set to **Obtain an IP Address Automatically**, choose that option now and restart your router.

5 Call Your Internet Service Provider (ISP)

Your router still might not be ready to use (depending on your Internet service provider, you might have to call to enable it). Some ISPs require that you give them the router's *MAC address*, which is a number, such as 00-90-4B-0E-3F-BD, that uniquely identifies a piece of hardware, such as a router or a network card. You'll find the Mac address displayed on the setup screen.

Check with your ISP. If it requires the Mac address, call the technical support line and read it to them. After a few minutes, your router will be connected to the Internet.

6 Connect Your PCs to the Router

Now you're ready to connect the rest of your computers to your router. Each of your computers will have an Ethernet connection at its back, front, or side. Check your computer's documentation for details. Plug one end of the Ethernet cable into your computer and the other end into your router for each PC.

NOTE

If you have a DSL modem, you may require special settings. Often, DSL modems use a way to communicate called PPoE, although cable modems do not. Check with your ISP whether you need to use PPoE. If you do, choose PPoE in the appropriate section. In the Linksys router setup screen, enable the **PPoE** radio button next to the **Login** section. You might also need a username and password, and may require more special settings as well. Check with your ISP for details.

NOTE

To check whether your network is working properly, look at the lights on the router. Each connection should have a green light.

45 Create a New Network Installation

After you've set up your router and connected your PCs to it, you're ready to set up an Internet connection so that each PC can get onto the Internet through your router. Here's how to do it. Keep in mind that you have to do this for each computer you want to access the Internet—you can't do it from one master computer for all the computers on your network.

Before You Begin

✔ 44 Install a Home Router

See Also

→ 67 Protect Yourself with the Windows Firewall

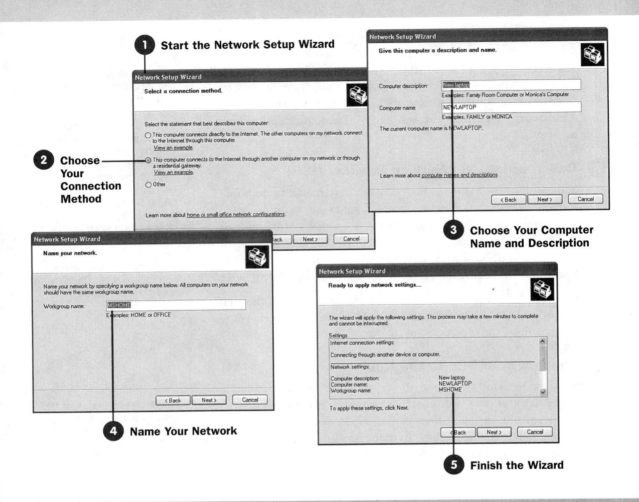

① **Start the Network Setup Wizard**

② **Choose Your Connection Method**

③ **Choose Your Computer Name and Description**

④ **Name Your Network**

⑤ **Finish the Wizard**

① Start the Network Setup Wizard

The simplest way to connect your computer to the Internet through your router is to use the **Network Setup Wizard**. To start it, click the **Start** button, choose **Control Panel** from the **Start** menu, click the **Network and Internet Connections** icon, and from the screen that appears, click **Network Connections**. In the **Network Tasks** pane, click **Set up a home or small office network**. The **Network Setup Wizard** launches. Click the **Next** button to pass the opening screen. The wizard reminds you to connect all the cables to the network. Because you did that in **44 Install a Home Router**, click **Next**.

② Choose Your Connection Method

The wizard asks how you'll connect to the network. In this instance, you're connecting through a router, also called a *gateway*, so choose the option that says you'll be connecting through a residential gateway. Click **Next**.

③ Choose Your Computer Name and Description

Each computer on the network should have a name and description so that it can be easily identified by other computers on the network. In the next wizard screen that appears, type a name for the computer you're currently using; also type a description for the computer and click **Next**.

④ Name Your Network

Your new network will need a name, so in the next screen that appears, type a name for the network you are creating and click **Next**.

⑤ Finish the Wizard

You'll next review your settings, including your computer name, description, and network name. If you want to change any of these names, click the **Back** button and change them. If not, click **Next**. Your settings will be applied, and your network will be set up.

Repeat steps 1 though 5 for each computer connected to the router to link each computer to the network.

> **NOTE**
>
> When you name your computers and your network, give them names that describe them so that it's easy to know at a glance what they are—for example, **Mia's computer**, **Gabe's laptop**, or **My Home Network**. They're the names that you'll see when you browse your network, so make them clear and easy to distinguish from one another.

㊻ Share Files and Folders Across the Network

Now that you've set up a network, what will you do with it? Obviously, all the computers on it can now connect to the Internet, but that's just the beginning. The computers can also share files and folders with one another, as you'll see how to do in this task.

When you share a folder, anyone on the network can use it, just as if it were on their own computer. However, as you'll see, you can set options so that the other users can only view the files in the folder, and not change them.

Before You Begin

✔ **44** Install a Home Router

✔ **45** Create a New Network Installation

See Also

→ **47** Share a Printer

→ **48** Browse the Network with My Network Places

→ **49** Map a Network Drive

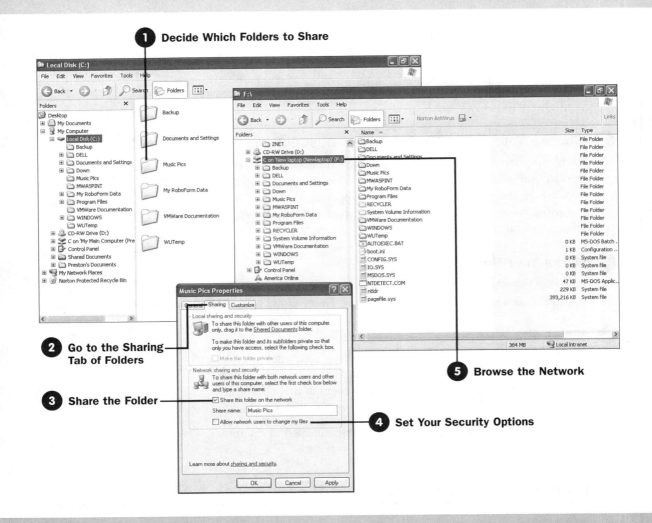

1 Decide Which Folders to Share

2 Go to the Sharing Tab of Folders

3 Share the Folder

4 Set Your Security Options

5 Browse the Network

① Decide Which Folders to Share

Before you tell Windows XP which folders you want to share, you should first decide which folders you want to share and which you want to keep private. There will necessarily be some folders that you want to keep private, and others that you'll be willing to share. So launch Windows Explorer (press the **Windows+E** keys), and examine your files and folders and decide which you want to share.

② Go to the Sharing Tab of Folders

Locate a folder you want to share, right-click it, and choose **Sharing and Security** from the context menu that opens. The **Properties** dialog box for that folder opens, with the **Sharing** tab selected. From this tab, you can set options to share the folder on the network.

③ Share the Folder

To share the folder named in the dialog box title bar, enable the **Share this folder on the network** check box. When you check that box, the folder is automatically given a *share name*, the name that other people on the network will see when they connect to it. You can change the folder name if you want people on the network to see a folder name that's different than the one actually on your computer.

④ Set Your Security Options

You can either let others change your files in the shared folder or only let them view the files. If you let others change the files (by enabling the **Allow network users to change my files** check box), they'll have full access to the files, just as if they were sitting at their own computer, so be careful if you choose this option. (This is called giving them *rights* to the folder.) After you set the option, click **OK** to close the dialog box. The folder will now be available over the network.

Repeat steps 2 through 4 for each folder you want to share with other computer users on the network.

⑤ Browse the Network

Now that you've set up folders that can be shared, you can browse to them from another computer. To learn how to do it, see **48** **Browse the Network with My Network Places**.

TIP

Be wary about sharing the **C:** folder, also called the *root* folder, of your hard drive with others on the network. If you do that, other users will have access to your *entire computer*, which could be dangerous. It's better to set sharing options on a folder-by-folder basis. However, if you have several computers—for example, a PC and a laptop—that only you use, it's a good idea to share the **C:** folder because then you'll have access to both computers when you're seated at either of them.

KEY TERMS

Share name—The name that other users on the network will see when they view a shared folder on your PC.

Rights—When someone is given access to a folder on another computer on a network.

47 Share a Printer

Before You Begin

✔ **44** Install a Home Router

✔ **45** Create a New Network Installation

See Also

→ **46** Share Files and Folders Across the Network

NOTE

The first screen of the **Add Printer Wizard** implies that if you have a certain type of printer, you don't need to use the wizard to add a printer. In fact, though, that's not true. You must run the wizard to install a network printer. If you install a printer on a single PC, in some instances you don't have to run the wizard.

TIP

If you know the exact location and name of the network printer, such as **\\PrestonPC\HP Printer**, you can enable the **Connect to this printer** radio button, type the printer name in the text box, and click **Next**.

One of the great benefits of a network is that it allows multiple computers to share a printer. You can have one printer serve the entire network—each computer doesn't have to have its own printer.

Or perhaps you have more than one printer and want to use different ones for different purposes. For example, you might want to use a laser printer when you need sharp black text printed out at high speed, but an inkjet printer when you need color printing. In this task, you'll learn how to share printers on the network.

1 **Launch the Add a Printer Wizard**

If you want to use a printer on the network, you use the **Add a Printer Wizard**. To get to it, click the **Start** button and choose **Control Panel** from the **Start** menu. Then choose **Printers and Other Hardware** and click **Add a printer**. The **Add Printer Wizard** appears. Click the **Next** button to advance to the first screen of options.

2 **Choose to Add a Network Printer**

The wizard asks whether you're setting up a local or a network printer. Enable the **A network printer, or a printer attached to another computer** radio button and click **Next**.

3 **Specify a Printer**

The **Specify a Printer** page of the wizard appears. To find your printer on the network, enable the **Browse for a printer** radio button and click **Next**.

4 **Browse for the Printer**

The **Browse for Printer** page of the wizard appears, with a list of all the printers on your network. Choose the printer to which you want to connect and click **Next**.

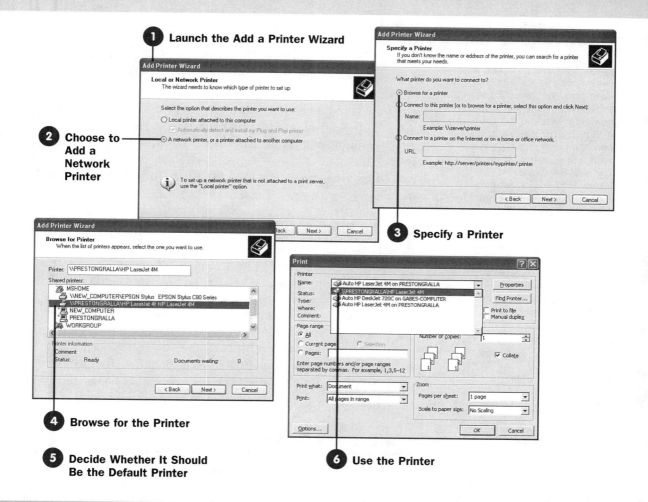

1 Launch the Add a Printer Wizard

2 Choose to Add a Network Printer

3 Specify a Printer

4 Browse for the Printer

5 Decide Whether It Should Be the Default Printer

6 Use the Printer

If you don't immediately see the printer listed, double-click the + next to the computer on the network to which the printer is attached. The printer will appear. Choose it and click **Next**. You'll get a warning that when you connect to the printer, a printer driver will be installed on your computer. You need that driver to use the printer, so click **Yes** to allow the driver to be copied to your computer. After a short amount of time, the driver will be installed.

NOTE

You must repeat this process for every computer you want to use the printer. Note that Windows XP uses some very confusing terminology: When you run the **Add a Printer Wizard** to let one computer use a printer on another computer on the network, Windows insists that you're installing a printer on that PC, even though the printer is attached to ("installed on") another PC. That's why it tells you that the printer is installed on your computer, even though it's actually physically connected to another machine.

5 Decide Whether It Should Be the Default Printer

After the driver is installed, you'll be asked whether you want to make the printer your default printer—the printer that you will automatically print to when you choose the **Print** command in a program. If you do not use this printer as your default, you can still print to it; it will just take an extra step. If you want the printer to be your default printer, click **Yes**; if you do not want this to be your default printer, click **No**. Then click **Next**. You'll get a confirmation that the printer was installed. Click **Finish** to complete the wizard.

6 Use the Printer

Now that the printer is installed, you can use it, just as if it were connected to your computer. Issue the print command from within a program as you would to a printer connected to your PC. If you've selected the network printer as your default printer, there's nothing else you have to do. But if it's not your default printer and you want to print to it, when the **Print** dialog box appears, click the **Name** box to see a list of all the printers to which you can print—any printer connected to your computer, as well as any printers you've set up to print to on your network. Choose the printer you want to use and click **OK** to print to that printer.

48 Browse the Network with My Network Places

Before You Begin

✔ 46 Share Files and Folders Across the Network

✔ 47 Share a Printer

See Also

→ 49 Map a Network Drive

After you have a network set up, you can use it for more than just printing. One of the most useful features of a network is its capability to share files and folders.

But how can you even know what files and folders are available on your network? And if you know that, how can you get to them? The best way to do both is to use **My Network Places**, which gives you instant access to your network and all its resources. Here's how to use it.

1 Go to My Network Places

Click the **Start** button and then click **My Network Places**. Windows Explorer opens, and it will display all the available resources on your network. You'll be able to use Windows Explorer to navigate through your network in the same general way you can use it to navigate through your hard disk.

② Go to a Network Place

To go to one of the locations represented by the resources in the list, double-click an icon. That resource (usually a folder) will open in Windows Explorer. Depending on the *rights* you've been given to that location, you'll be able to edit or view the files there. If there are folders inside that network place, you can navigate to them, and use those folders and the files in them, depending on the rights that you've been given.

The lower-left section of Windows Explorer shows you where you are on the network, for example, \\NEWLAPTOP\Shared Docs.

③ Add a Network Place

You can add a Network Place to your network. Network Places you add to your network can be locations on your network or on the Internet, although if it's an Internet location, it has to be a site to which you have special access, such your own personal Web site.

To add a Network Place, go back to the main **My Network Places** screen. Click the **Add a network place** link in the **Network Tasks** list on the left side of the screen. The **Add Network Place Wizard** appears. Click **Next** to advance past the welcome screen. From the next screen that appears, select **Choose another network location**. You'll come to a screen that will let you type an Internet address (such as **http://www.sams.com**), a network location (such as \\NEWLAPTOP\Shared Docs), or browse through your network for a network location. Click **Next**.

You'll come to a screen that asks what name you want to give the new location. You can give it any name you want. For example, if the network location is \\NEWLAPTOP\Books, you can call it **Newest Books**. After you've provided a name for the location, click **Next**. You'll come to a screen that confirms all the details about the new network location. If it's what you want, click **Finish**. If it's not, click **Back** and go back through the wizard to change your options.

When you're done, the new location will be added to **My Network Places**.

TIP

If you want to see the exact network name and location of any resource, hover your mouse over the resource icon. You'll see its name and location in a balloon tip, such as **NEWLAPTOP\Shared Docs**. In this example, **NEWLAPTOP** is the name of the computer and **Shared Docs** is the name of the folder.

TIP

If you've chosen an Internet location to which you have special access, you may be asked for your user name and password. Type it in and press **Enter**. If you typed a network location on your own network, you won't be asked for that information.

1 Go to My Network Places

6 Find a Computer on Your Network

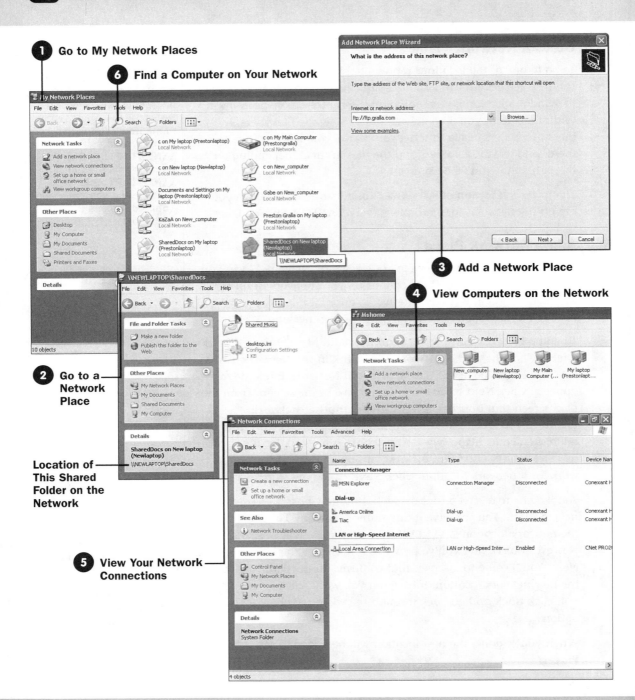

3 Add a Network Place

4 View Computers on the Network

2 Go to a Network Place

Location of This Shared Folder on the Network

5 View Your Network Connections

4 View Computers on the Network

My Network Places shows you locations on the network, such as specific folders on specific computers on the network. For example, you might see three folders listed from one computer and no folders from another computer, if that other computer did not create any folders to be shared.

Because of this, it can be difficult to see exactly what computers are on the network. To see a simple list of all the computers on your network, click the **View workgroup computers** link in the **Network Tasks** list on the left side of the main **My Network Places** screen. You'll see a list of all the computers on your network. You may or may not have access to all the resources in each of these computers, and all the computers might not be currently on the network. Double-click any computer to which you want to connect; if they're offline, or if you haven't been given access to that computer's **C:** drive, you'll get an error message telling you so.

5 View Your Network Connections

Windows XP terminology when it comes to networks can be confusing. XP calls the Internet a *network* (which it is), a term it also uses to describe your home network. You have many ways to connect to these networks. For example, for your home network you have a local area network connection. But you might have network connections in addition to that, for example to connect to the Internet using America Online or a dial-up ISP.

To see all the ways you can connect to a network, click the **View network connections** link in the **Network Tasks** list on the left side of the main **My Network Places** screen. You'll see all of your available network connections. For each connection, you'll see whether it's currently enabled or disconnected. To enable a connection, double-click it and follow the normal connection routine for that specific connection (for example, logging into America Online or your ISP).

6 Find a Computer on Your Network

To find a computer on your network, from the main **My Network Places** screen, click the **Search** button at the top of the screen. The **Search Companion** appears, asking you what computer you are looking for. Type the computer name (or any part of the computer name) and you'll see a list of all the computers on the network that match the name or part of the name you typed. Double-click any resource in the list to connect to it. (For more information about using the **Search Companion**, see **39** **About Windows XP Search**.)

49 Map a Network Drive

Before You Begin

✔ **46** Share Files and Folders Across the Network

✔ **48** Browse the Network with My Network Places

EY TERM

Map a network drive—To make it appear as if a network resource, such as a folder, is actually on your own computer. You make it look just like another disk drive on your own PC, such as **E:**.

TIP

When choosing your drive letter, make sure that it won't interfere with any additions you plan to make to your computer. If you are considering adding an additional hard drive, DVD drive, or CD drive, don't use the letter you would plan to use for any of those pieces of hardware. Also, if you have a removable hard drive that is not currently attached to your computer, don't use the letter that the drive normally uses. It's usually safe to start assigning drives with the letter **G**.

Using **My Network Places** is a great way to browse your network. But what if you frequently use a specific folder on another computer on the network? Rather than going through **My Network Places**, wouldn't it be nice to be able to go straight to that folder?

There is a way to do it, by *mapping a network drive* to your local computer. When you map a network drive, you make it appear as if the network resource, such as a folder, is actually on your own computer. You make it look just like another disk drive, such as **E:**. It's actually quite simple to do, as you'll see in this task.

1 Open Windows Explorer

To map a network drive, you'll have to open Windows Explorer, so open it now. For a faster way to open the program, press the **Windows+E** keys.

2 Open the Map Network Drive Dialog Box

From the Windows Explorer menu, choose **Tools, Map Network Drive**. The **Map Network Drive** dialog box appears.

3 Choose Your Drive Letter

In the **Drive** drop-down box, choose a letter for the network resource you want to map to your hard disk (the drive letter you want the other resource to be known as on your computer). You'll be shown only those letters that are available. So, for example, if you have a hard disk called **C:** and a DVD drive called **D:**, those letters won't show up as available drive letters.

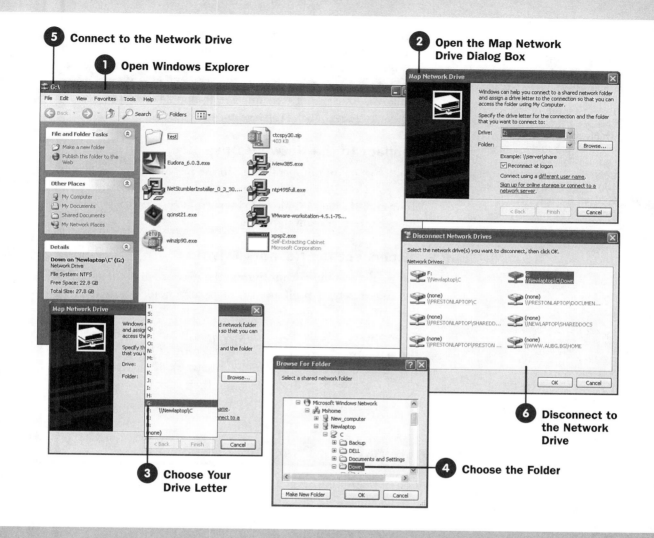

5 Connect to the Network Drive

1 Open Windows Explorer

2 Open the Map Network Drive Dialog Box

3 Choose Your Drive Letter

4 Choose the Folder

6 Disconnect to the Network Drive

4 Choose the Folder

Choose the network resource (the folder) to which you want to map. If you know the network location of the folder, such as **Newlaptop\Music**, type the location name in the **Folder** text box in the **Map Network Drive** dialog box. If you don't know the location, click the **Browse** button and browse to the network location to which you want to map. Highlight the location and click **OK**.

NOTE

Make sure that you have access to the folder to which you're mapping—in other words, that it can be shared on the network. Check on the computer to which you plan to connect whether the folder can be shared. For information about how to share folders, see **46** Share Files and Folders Across the Network.

If you want this network resource to be automatically available whenever you log into Windows XP, make sure that the **Reconnect at logon** check box is enabled. If it's not, you'll have to manually connect whenever you log on to Windows XP to make the drive available. To manually reconnect to it, double-click it in **My Network Places**. Click **Finish** when you're done.

5 Connect to the Network Drive

You'll now be automatically sent to the network drive and can use it as you would any other drive. In the future, when you want to connect to it, open Windows Explorer and click the drive letter for the resource you want to access.

6 Disconnect the Network Drive

You might no longer want to map the network drive to your PC— you may rarely, if at all, use the drive any more, it may have been deleted, or you no longer have *rights* to it.

To disconnect the network drive, launch Windows Explorer (press the **Windows+E** keys) and choose **Disconnect Network Drive** from the **Tools** menu. The list of all your network drives appears. Click the one you want to disconnect and then click **OK**. The drive will no longer be mapped to your computer.

50 About Troubleshooting Network Problems

Before You Begin

✔ **44** Install a Home Router

✔ **45** Create a New Network Installation

See Also

→ **65** About Solving Wi-Fi Connection Problems

Count on it: Use a network long enough and you'll run into a network problem. It's inevitable. Tracking down and fixing a network problem can be exceedingly frustrating and difficult, and even network pros can have problems fixing them.

That being said, there *are* common ways to fix network problems, which we'll cover in this task. If you have a wireless network, there's a whole layer of problems on top of normal network woes, so to fix them, see **65** About Solving Wi-Fi Connection Problems. Here's what to do when you run into network problems:

• **Check your router and modem lights.** The problem with your network might be caused by problems with your router or your cable modem or DSL modem, so that's the first place to turn. Are the lights lit on both the router and the modem, and if so, are they green? Check your router documentation to see what color the lights should be, and what problems there might be if they are not that color. For example, flashing green lights may be fine, and an indication of network usage, while orange lights might mean trouble.

- **Check the cable and power connections.** A surprisingly high number of times, the problem is a physical one—cables have come loose or the power cord isn't plugged in. Check all the physical connections—including the Ethernet cables and power cords—and make sure that the power is turned on to all the devices.

- **Check with your ISP.** If you can use your network to share files and folders and print, but you can't get Internet access, or if Internet access is slow, the problem might be with your ISP, which might be having problems of its own. Call technical support, or check the ISP's website.

- **Restart your modem and router.** Often, simply restarting the router or modem will solve your problems. If you turn off your cable modem or DSL modem, leave it off for at least five minutes before turning it back on. You don't have to turn your router off for that long, however—a few moments will do the trick for the router.

- **Try repairing the connection.** Windows XP has a great built-in feature that will automatically repair network connections that have been broken for some reason. For each computer experiencing network problems, right-click **My Network Places** on the **Start** menu and choose **Properties** from the context menu. You'll come to the **Network Connections** folder. Right-click the connection that is broken and choose **Repair**. In most cases, Windows XP will automatically fix the problem.

- **Run the Network Troubleshooters.** If none of the preceding tips fixes the network problem, run any one of a variety of Network Troubleshooters, a wizard-like feature that asks a series of questions about your problem and then fixes it. To run the troubleshooter, click the **Start** button and choose **Help and Support**. Then click **Networking and the Web** and then **Fixing networking or Web problems**. You'll see a variety of problems you might be having, such as **File and Printer Troubleshooter** or **Home and Small Office Network Troubleshooter**. Click whichever troubleshooter title best describes your problem and follow its instructions.

 TIP

If you're having problems with your router, sometimes updating the router's "firmware" can help. *Firmware* is software built directly into a piece of hardware. Router firmware can easily be updated. Check your router's documentation and its manufacturer's website for details.

CHAPTER 6: Networking Your PC

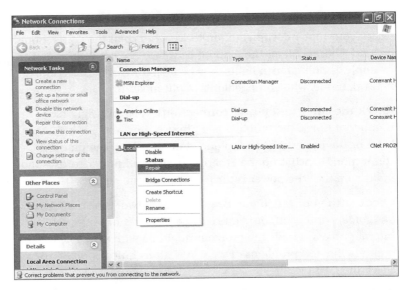

For a simple but effective fix to many network problems, right-click the connection in the Network Connections folder and choose Repair. This command solves a wide variety of network problems.

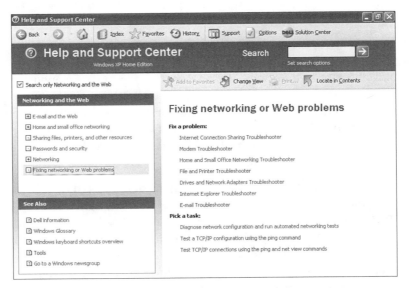

These Network Troubleshooters can help you solve a wide variety of common and not-so-common network problems.

7

Surfing the Web

IN THIS CHAPTER:

Is there a person on the planet who uses Windows XP and *doesn't* use the Internet? Perhaps someone somewhere doesn't, but as a practical matter, we all do.

And that's a good thing, because Windows XP was built from the ground up assuming that anyone using it would be using the Internet. One of the first tasks that XP automates after you install it is creating an Internet connection for you.

Windows XP's built-in browser, Internet Explorer, is the most popular browser on the planet and has become the *de facto* standard in the browsing world. In this chapter, we'll mainly look at ways to make the most out of Internet Explorer.

51 Take Control of Your Favorites

See Also

→ **52** Control Your History List

→ **56** Rearrange Your Internet Explorer Toolbar

🔍 KEY TERM

Favorites—A collection of Internet sites that you store in Internet Explorer so that you can easily revisit them without having to remember their URLs.

💡 TIP

If you want to add the website that you're visiting to the bottom of the **Favorites** menu, you can use a shortcut. Press **Ctrl+D** to add the current website as a favorite. You won't see the **Add Favorite** dialog box— the site will simply be added to the bottom of your **Favorites** menu.

The Internet is a vast place, and there are no roadmaps. Yet frequently, you'll come across sites you want to revisit, but you know that you won't remember the URL (Universal Resource Locator). When that happens, you can make a website a *favorite* that you add to Internet Explorer so that you can more easily return to the site.

There's more to using favorites than you realize—follow these steps to get the most out of them.

① Add a Favorite

When you come to a website that you want to add to your favorites, choose **Add to Favorites** from the **Favorites** menu. The **Add Favorite** dialog box appears. Look in the **Name** text box— does it describe the URL well enough so that you'll remember it when you read it on your **Favorites** menu? Frequently, the name will be at least partially incomprehensible, so type or edit the name so that it adequately describes the URL.

If you want to save the favorite to the bottom of your **Favorites** menu list, and not place it in any particular folder, click **OK** to close the dialog box. However, if you've created folders for your favorite websites, you might want to store a favorite in an existing folder. In that case, in the **Create in** list box, scroll to the folder where you want to save the current website and click **OK**. If the **Create in** box is not displayed, click the **Create in** button.

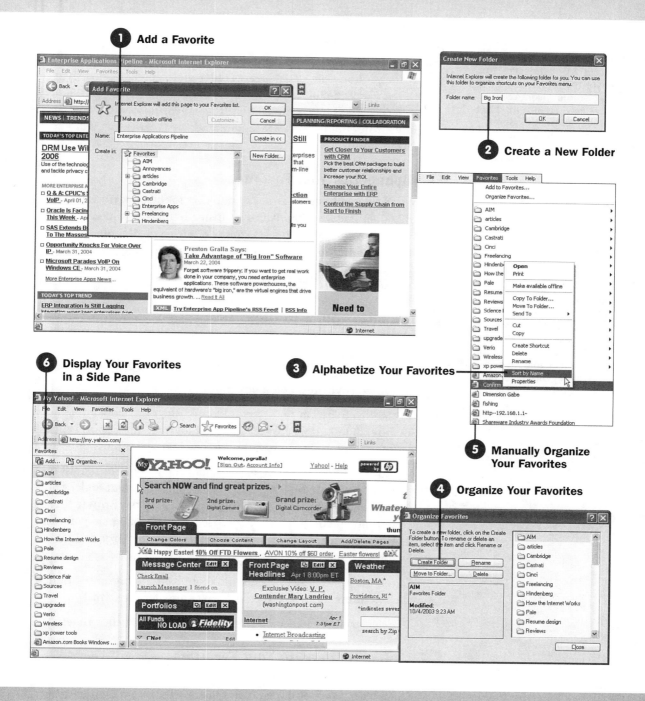

1 Add a Favorite

2 Create a New Folder

6 Display Your Favorites in a Side Pane

3 Alphabetize Your Favorites

5 Manually Organize Your Favorites

4 Organize Your Favorites

❷ Create a New Folder

If you want to store the favorite in a new folder, click the **New Folder** button. The **Create New Folder** dialog box appears. Type the name of the folder you want to create in the **Favorites** menu and click **OK**. The new folder will be created. To save the favorite in your new folder, click **OK** again, and the favorite you're adding is added to that new folder.

❸ Alphabetize Your Favorites

When you add new favorites and folders to the **Favorites** menu, they aren't added alphabetically. Instead, they are added to the bottom of your **Favorites** list. You can, however, alphabetize the items automatically. Click to open the **Favorites** menu, then right-click any favorite or folder in the list. From the context menu that appears, choose **Sort by Name**. Your favorites will be alphabetized.

❹ Organize Your Favorites

If you want to move favorites between folders, create and delete folders, delete and rename favorites, and organize your favorites in almost any way, choose **Favorites, Organize Favorites**. The **Organize Favorites** dialog box appears.

To create a folder, in the list of folders on the right side of the dialog box, highlight where you want the folder to appear and click **Create folder**. Type a name for the new folder and press **Enter**.

To move a favorite to a folder, highlight the favorite in the list on the right (if the favorite is in another folder, open that folder and select the favorite) and click **Move to Folder**. In the **Browse for Folder** dialog box that opens, browse to the folder where you want to move the favorite and click **OK** to return to the **Organize Favorites** dialog box.

To rename a favorite or folder, highlight it in the list on the right, click **Rename**, and then type the new name for the item.

To delete a file or folder, highlight it in the list and click **Delete**.

❺ Manually Organize Your Favorites

You can also organize your favorites without having to use the **Organize Favorites** dialog box. Click the **Favorites** item in the menu bar to display a list of favorites. To move a folder or favorite, simply drag it to its new location on the **Favorites** list. To delete a favorite or folder, right-click it and choose **Delete** from the context menu. To rename a favorite or folder, right-click it, choose **Rename** from the context menu, and then type the new name.

6 Display Your Favorites in a Side Pane

If you want your favorites always visible when Internet Explorer is open, you can display the **Favorites** list in a big pane on the left side of the Internet Explorer window. In the Internet Explorer toolbar, click the **Favorites** button (the one with a big graphic of a star). Your favorites will now take up the left side of your screen. You can add favorites to it as explained in step 1, although you can also click the **Add** button at the top of the list to add them. You can organize your favorites by clicking the **Organize** button at the top of the list to open the **Organize Favorites** dialog box.

TIP

You can also organize items in your **Favorites** list on the left side of the Internet Explorer screen by dragging them around in the list, just as you did with the items in the **Favorites** menu in step 5.

52 Control Your History List

When you browse the Internet, it's often as important to know where you've been as where you're going. You frequently visit many websites but put very few of them onto your **Favorites** list, yet you'll often want to revisit a site, and won't recall how to get there.

That's where Internet Explorer's *history list* comes in. It makes it easy for you to revisit websites you've already been to. Here's how to make the most of it.

1 Use the History List from the Address Bar

As you type a URL in the Internet Explorer **Address** bar, Internet Explorer looks in its history list for matches and displays matches when it finds them. For example, if you had recently visited **www.yahoo.com** and **www.yellow.com**, when you type in **www.y**, Internet Explorer displays a drop-down list with both **www.yahoo.com** and **www.yellow.com** in it. To visit one of the sites, select it and press **Enter**.

See Also

→ **51** Take Control of Your Favorites

EY TERM

History list—A list of sites you've recently visited. Internet Explorer remembers them so that you can visit them again.

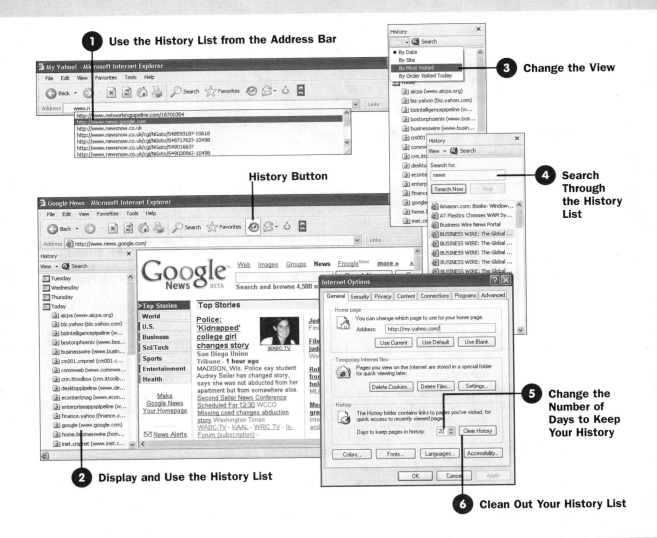

Use the History List from the Address Bar

History Button

Change the View

Search Through the History List

Display and Use the History List

Change the Number of Days to Keep Your History

Clean Out Your History List

② Display and Use the History List

If you want to easily navigate through pages you've recently visited—and see all those pages—click the **History** button on the Internet Explorer toolbar (the one that looks like a circular arrow with a clock inside it).

When you click the **History** button, the **History** list displays in a pane on the left side of the screen. It's organized by day; within each day, the websites you've visited are arranged alphabetically. For example, to find a site you visited today, click **Today** and then look for the site in the alphabetized list. To revisit that site, click it.

3 **Change the View**

You might not remember which day you visited a site, and so you can change the way the **History** list displays sites. To do that, you change the view. Click the **View** button at the top of the **History** list to see a menu of four choices:

- **By Date.** This is the view you normally see—websites organized by day, and then alphabetically within each day.

- **By Site.** This view displays all the sites in an alphabetical list, regardless of which day you visited them.

- **By Most Visited.** This view displays the sites by the number of times you visited them, with the most frequent at the top and the least frequent at the bottom.

- **By Order Visited Today.** This view displays only the sites you've visited today, and displays them in the order in which you visited them.

After you change the display, you can visit sites by clicking them in the list.

4 **Search Through the History List**

The **History** list can get extremely long, and so it can take a good deal of time to scroll through it. To find sites faster, you can search through it: Click the **Search** button at the top of the **History** list, type a word, and click **Search Now**. A list of sites will appear whose title includes your search term. Use the search results list as you normally use the **History** list.

To go back to a normal display, click the **View** button and choose the view you want to use.

TIP

To make the History list go away, click the **History** button again or click the **X** to the right of the **History** list title.

NOTE

In the **By Most Visited** view, when you've visited more than one site the same number of times (for example, if you've visited four sites two times each), they'll be listed in alphabetical order.

TIP

Be careful when choosing the number of days to keep your history. If you keep sites in your **History** list for too many days, it becomes extremely difficult to find them later because you'll have so many days and sites to scroll through. Too many sites also makes searching more difficult. On the other hand, if you don't keep sites long enough, you might lose track of some sites you want to visit later.

5 **Change the Number of Days to Keep Your History**

A site normally stays in the **History** list for 20 days, but you can change the number of days that each site stays in your **History** list. To change the number of days, choose **Tools, Internet Options** from the menu; the **Internet Options** dialog box opens. Click the **General** tab. In the **Days to keep pages in history** field, choose the number of days you want to keep each site in your history list and click **OK**.

6 **Clean Out Your History List**

There might come a time when you want a fresh start—you want to start over with a new **History** list. To do that, choose **Tools, Internet Options** from the menu; the **Internet Options** dialog box opens. On the **General** tab, click the **Clear History** button and then click **OK**. Your **History** list will be wiped clean.

53 Power Up Internet Explorer Search

See Also

→ **39** About Windows XP Search

→ **55** Find Information Faster with the Google Toolbar

The Internet has such vast amounts of information that it overwhelms most people. Where do you even begin to find the needle in the global haystack?

You use Internet Search. Search is built directly into Internet Explorer, although that might not be immediately obvious. Here's how to get the most out of Internet Search.

1 **Display the Search Companion**

The best way to search the Internet from Internet Explorer is to display the **Search Companion**. Click the **Search** button (the one that looks like a magnifying glass) on the Internet Explorer toolbar.

TIP

For more information about how to use and customize the **Search Companion** in general, and specifically about searching for information on your computer, turn to **39** About Windows XP Search.

2 **Do a Search**

Type your search term or terms into the search box and press **Enter**. Internet Explorer will search the Internet using the MSN search engine and bring back a list of web pages that most closely match your search. The results list fills the right side of the screen. For each web page, MSN provides a link and title with a description under it. To visit any page, click the link.

1 Display the Search Companion

Search Button

2 Do a Search

3 Automatically Try Your Search on Another Search Engine

4 Highlight Your Search Terms

5 Change Your Search Engine

6 Search from the Address Bar

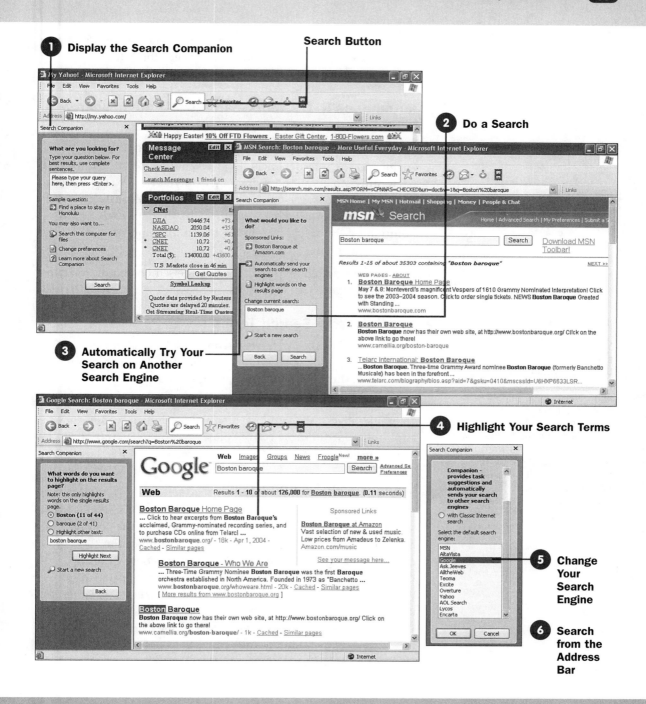

If you want to hide the **Search Companion** after you've done your search, click the **Search** button again or click the **X** to the right of the **Search Companion** title.

③ Automatically Try Your Search on Another Search Engine

The MSN search engine is only one of many popular search engines on the Internet, including **www.google.com**, **www.altavista.com**, and many others. If you want to see search results from another search engine, click the **Automatically send your search to other search engines** link in the **Search Companion** list of tasks. From the screen that appears, choose your search engine.

You can now search the Internet using the search engine you chose and will be able to see the results.

④ Highlight Your Search Terms

It can be very confusing to view search results, and at times difficult to filter out the good results from the bad. One way to more easily weed through the results is to have your search terms highlighted on the page and to jump to them.

To highlight your search terms after you've done a search, click the **Highlight words on the results page** link in the **Search Companion** list of tasks.

⑤ Change Your Search Engine

If you like a particular search engine better than the default MSN search engine, you can use that search engine as the default engine when you search. From the **Search Companion** task list, click the **Change preferences** link and then choose **Change Internet search behavior**. From the screen that appears, choose your search engine from the bottom pane and click **OK**. From now on, the specified search engine will be used whenever you search. If the **Search Companion** doesn't display the **Change Preferences** link, click the **Back** button until you get to the **Search Companion**'s main screen.

✎ NOTE

You can highlight only a single search term at a time. And when you highlight a term, it doesn't highlight every single instance of it on the page. Instead, when you click the term, your cursor jumps to the first instance of the word, where it is highlighted. To jump to the next instance of the word and highlight it on the page, click **Highlight Next**.

6 Search from the Address Bar

If you want to do a quick search, there's no need to use the **Search Companion**. Simply type your search term into Internet Explorer's **Address** bar (the place where you type URLs) and press **Enter**, and Internet Explorer will conduct a search using your default search engine.

54 Clean Up Cookies and Delete Temporary Files

When you browse the Web, the websites you visit leave traces of themselves behind on your PC. When you visit a website, the site frequently places a *cookie* on your computer—a small bit of data the website uses to track your use of the site, or to provide services such as customized views or automatic logins.

Cookies are controversial because they can be used to invade people's privacy. But they can also be helpful, because they can help you customize how you use a site (for example, telling it to always display information about your specific interests), or can automatically log you in to a site. You can learn more about how to handle cookies in **73** **Protect Your Privacy by Managing Your Cookies**.

When you visit websites, you also download pictures, sounds, videos, and text to your computer—that's how you view web pages. Those files are not immediately deleted from your hard disk, and are temporarily stored on your computer. Obviously, all this "temporary" information can chew up quite a bit of your hard disk space. To regain disk space, one of the first places you can look for files to delete is the **Temporary Internet Files** folder.

1 Delete Cookies

If you want, you can delete all the cookies on your hard disk. You might want to do this if you're very worried about privacy. However, if you delete all your cookies, you might not be able to automatically log into some websites, and some websites that use customization might not work without cookies.

However, if you want to delete all of the cookies on your PC, choose **Tools, Internet Options** from the menu. When the **Internet Options** dialog box opens, click the **General** tab. Then click the **Delete Cookies** button. Click **OK** to close the dialog box.

See Also
→ **73** Protect Your Privacy by Managing Your Cookies

KEY TERM
Cookie—A small bit of data that a website puts on a PC so that it can track the person's use of the site or to provide services such as customized views or automatic logins.

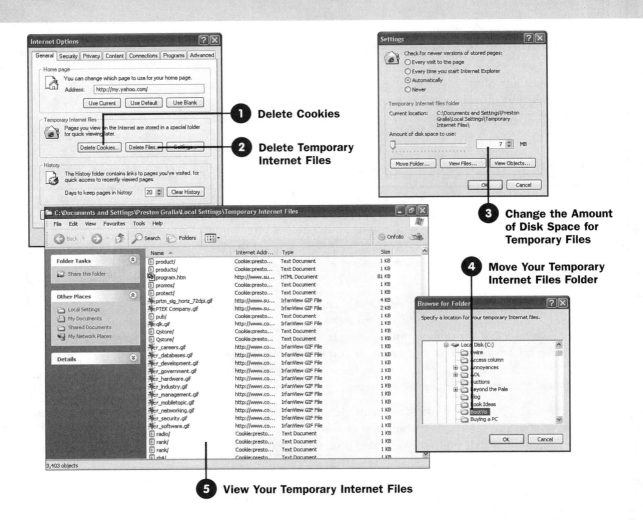

1 Delete Cookies

2 Delete Temporary Internet Files

3 Change the Amount of Disk Space for Temporary Files

4 Move Your Temporary Internet Files Folder

5 View Your Temporary Internet Files

 TIP

If you surf the Web a lot, you can easily accumulate a substantial number of temporary Internet files that can take up a great deal of hard disk space— dozens or even hundreds of megabytes. That's space you otherwise can't use.

2 Delete Temporary Internet Files

If you want to get back the hard disk space used by temporary Internet files, you can delete them. To do it, choose **Tools, Internet Options** from the menu. When the **Internet Options** dialog box opens, click the **General** tab. Click the **Delete Files** button and then click **OK** to close the dialog box.

③ Change the Amount of Disk Space for Temporary Files

You can put a cap on the amount of disk space your computer will use to store temporary Internet files. That way, you won't have to continually delete them—just determine the maximum amount of space you want to devote to the storage of these files, and Windows XP will then automatically delete files—the oldest first— when it reaches that maximum.

To specify the amount of disk space you want to use for the files, choose **Internet Options** from the **Tools** menu and click **Settings**. From the **Settings** dialog box that appears, move the slider in either direction to increase or decrease the amount of disk space devoted to temporary files. If you want to more finely control the amount of disk space, click the up or down arrows or type a number directly into the box. When you're done, click **OK** three times.

④ Move Your Temporary Internet Files Folder

Your temporary Internet files are stored in **C:\Documents** and **Settings***Your Name***\Local Settings\Temporary Internet Files**, where ***Your Name*** is your XP account name.

However, you can move that folder if you'd like. You might be running out of hard disk space on your primary hard disk, for example, and want to move it to another hard disk. Alternatively, you might simply want it located in a folder whose name you can more easily remember.

To move the folder, in the **Settings** dialog box, click **Move Folder**, then navigate to the location where you want the folder moved and click **OK** twice.

⑤ View Your Temporary Internet Files

You can also view the Internet files that have been temporarily stored on your hard disk. There might have been a picture on a website that was downloaded to your computer that you want to see, for example.

To see the list of all the files in your temporary folder, in the **Settings** dialog box, click **View Files**. You'll see a list of all the files in your temporary folder. Mostly these files won't make much sense and will have incomprehensible names. However, if you see a file that ends in **.gif** or **.jpg**, those are graphics files, and you can view them.

To view a graphics file, double-click it. You'll get a warning that **Running a system command on this item might be unsafe. Do you wish to continue?** Click **Yes**, because viewing the file will not damage your system in any way. The graphics file will open in Internet Explorer.

55 Find Information Faster with the Google Toolbar

Before You Begin

✔ **53** Power Up Internet Explorer Search

See Also

→ **39** About Windows XP Search

→ **56** Rearrange Your Internet Explorer Toolbar

Using Internet Explorer Search (see **53** **Power Up Internet Explorer Search**) is convenient, but the best search on the Internet can be found at Google (**www.google.com**). Google searches are the fastest, simplest, and most accurate.

However, it can quickly become irritating having to head to Google every time you want to do a search. Wouldn't it be easier to be able to search Google no matter where you are on the Internet?

That's exactly what the Google toolbar will do for you. It installs within Internet Explorer, and when you use it, you can search Google from any-where on the Internet. It has a lot of other useful features, too, as you'll see in this task.

① Install the Google Toolbar

You install the Google toolbar from the Web. It's free; you won't have to pay for it. Note that you'll only be able to install it if you have Internet Explorer—it doesn't work with other browsers.

To install it, go to **http://toolbar.google.com** and click the **Download Google Toolbar** link. Follow the instructions. It will only take a short time to install.

② Display the Google Toolbar

After you install the Google toolbar, it should automatically show up somewhere on the Internet Explorer interface as its own toolbar. However, it will not always automatically show up.

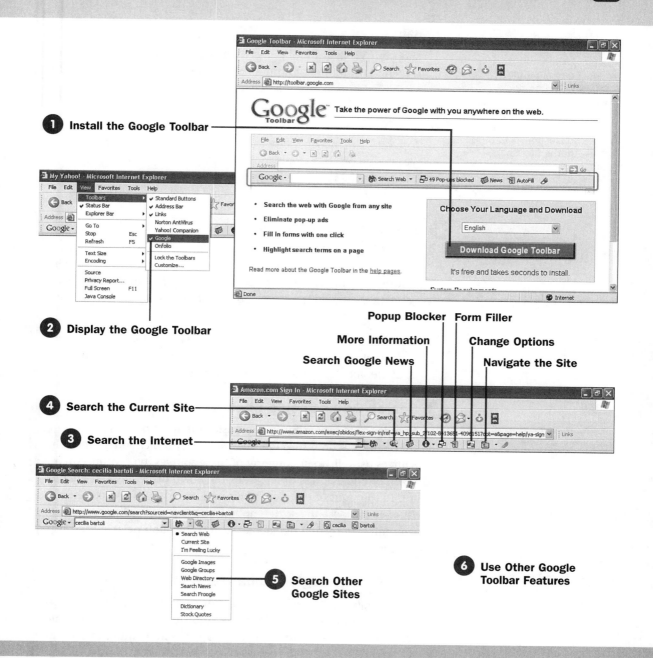

① Install the Google Toolbar

② Display the Google Toolbar

Popup Blocker   Form Filler

More Information   Change Options

Search Google News   Navigate the Site

④ Search the Current Site

③ Search the Internet

⑤ Search Other Google Sites

⑥ Use Other Google Toolbar Features

NOTE

For inexplicable reasons, when you choose **View**, **Toolbars**, **Google** doesn't always appear. Instead, you might see two entries labeled **Radio**. If that happens, choose the *second* entry—that is the **Google** toolbar.

If it doesn't automatically appear, you can make it appear by choosing **View**, **Toolbars**, and then choosing **Google** so that there is a check mark next to that toolbar name. When you do that, the toolbar will appear on the screen.

③ Search the Internet

To search the Internet, type your search term or terms into the search box on the Google toolbar and press **Enter** or click the button just to the right of the toolbar. You'll search the Internet just as if you were searching from the Google site.

④ Search the Current Site

One of the Google toolbar's most useful features is its capability to search the current site you're on. Many sites don't have a search feature, and many sites that do have a search feature don't have a good one. You can use the Google toolbar to search through any site you're visiting.

Type your search term or terms into the Google toolbar, but instead of pressing **Enter**, click the button two buttons to the right of the toolbar. You'll search the current site.

⑤ Search Other Google Sites

Google offers more than just a basic search—it also lets you search for pictures, search through news stories or a dictionary, and other sources as well. To choose any of these sources, type your search term, but don't press **Enter**. Click the down arrow next to the button to the right of the search box and choose your search option. After you choose the search option, the Google toolbar searches through that section of Google, such as through news stories, using the search term in the search box.

⑥ Use Other Google Toolbar Features

The Google toolbar offers other features, such as blocking popup ads, automatically filling in forms, and showing you pages related to the one you're visiting. Click the appropriate button to use those features. For more information about the features, go to **http://toolbar.google.com/help.html**.

56 Rearrange Your Internet Explorer Toolbar

The Internet Explorer toolbar is one of the browser's most useful features. With a click on one of its buttons, you can check your email, display your history list, display the search pane, go to your home page, refresh your current page, and more.

But using the Internet is not a one-size-fits-all proposition. You might never use the history list, but might want to use your toolbar to launch the instant messaging program Windows Messenger, for example.

The good news: It's easy to customize Internet Explorer's toolbar. You can add and take away buttons, move around the buttons you have, and change the way they're displayed.

See Also

→ **55** Find Information Faster with the Google Toolbar

1 Right-Click the Toolbar and Choose Customize

To customize the toolbar, you must display the **Customize Toolbar** dialog box. Right-click an empty area of the toolbar and choose **Customize** from the context menu.

2 Add and Remove Buttons

To add a button to the toolbar, choose it from the list of available buttons on the left side of the **Available toolbar buttons** and then click the **Add** button. The selected button is added to the **Current toolbar buttons** list, which means that the button will be displayed on your toolbar.

To remove a button from the toolbar, choose it from the list of available buttons on the right side of the **Current toolbar buttons** list and then click the **Remove** button.

TIP

The **Reset** button in the **Customize Toolbar** dialog box serves a mysterious function—it resets your toolbar so that all available buttons are displayed. If you want to display all your buttons, click it; otherwise stay away from the **Reset** button.

3 Change the Order of the Buttons

You can change the order of the buttons on your toolbar by moving them toward the right or the left. To move a button to the left along the toolbar, highlight it in the **Current toolbar buttons** list and click the **Move Up** button repeatedly until you have it in the location you want. To move a button to the right, highlight it and click **Move Down** repeatedly until you have it in the location you want.

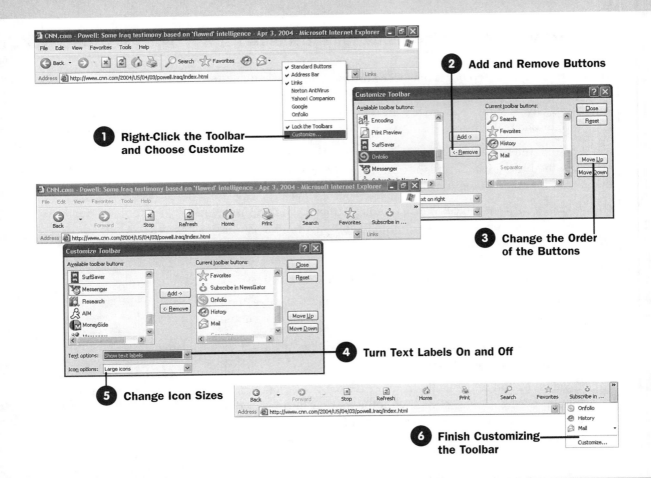

1 **Right-Click the Toolbar and Choose Customize**

2 **Add and Remove Buttons**

3 **Change the Order of the Buttons**

4 **Turn Text Labels On and Off**

5 **Change Icon Sizes**

6 **Finish Customizing the Toolbar**

④ Turn Text Labels On and Off

You can have your toolbar display text labels near the buttons, or not display labels at all. When you're displaying text labels, you'll always be able to see at a glance the purpose of each button, but you'll also take up screen real estate, leaving room for fewer buttons.

To turn text labels on or off, click on the **Text options** drop-down box and choose one of these three options:

- **Show text labels.** This option displays the text for each button directly below each button.

- **Selective text on right.** This option displays the text for only selected important buttons, such as **Search** and **Favorites** to the right of buttons.

- **No text labels.** With this option, no text appears with the buttons on the toolbar.

As you make your choices, the toolbar will change so that you can see which option is best for you.

5 **Change Icon Sizes**

You can use either large or small icons on the toolbar. To make your selection, click the **Icon options** button and choose either large or small icons.

6 **Finish Customizing the Toolbar**

When you're done making choices, click the **Close** button. The **Customize Toolbar** dialog box closes, and the toolbar reflects the changes you've made. If you've changed the toolbar so that all the buttons can't fit on it, a small double-sided arrow appears on the right side of the toolbar. Click this arrow to display the extra buttons; click any of those buttons to use them, as you would the other toolbar buttons.

---

57 **Create a Custom Toolbar for Internet Explorer**

The background for Internet Explorer's toolbar is, to put it mildly, dull—a plain gray. However, it doesn't have to stay that way. You can change that toolbar so that the background is any picture of your choosing.

To change it, you'll need a few things—a picture you want to use as the background, and a piece of software that will let you make the change to the toolbar.

1 **Download and Install TweakUI**

The software you need is called **TweakUI**, and it is available free from Microsoft. To use it, you'll first have to download it. Go to **www.microsoft.com/windowsxp/pro/downloads/powertoys.asp** and click the **TweakUI.exe** link on the right side of the screen and save the file to a folder on your computer. The file will be called

Before You Begin

✔ **56** Rearrange Your Internet Explorer Toolbar

✔ **24** About Customizing Your Desktop with TweakUI

✔ **39** About Windows XP Search

See Also

→ **55** Find Information Faster with the Google Toolbar

TweakUiPowertoySetup.exe, or something similar. After it downloads, go to the folder where you downloaded it, double-click the file, and follow the installation instructions. (For more information about installing and using TweakUI, see **24** About Customizing Your Desktop with TweakUI.)

TIP

If you have a graphic in a format on your hard disk other than **.bmp**, it's easy to convert that graphic to the **.bmp** format so that you can use it as the background for your toolbar. To see how, turn to **107** Convert Between Image Formats.

2 **Find a .BMP File on Your Hard Disk**

For your picture, you need a graphic in **.bmp** format. Windows XP ships with many pictures in **.bmp** format, many of which are suitable for use as a toolbar background. To find all the **.bmp** files on your hard disk, launch the **Search Companion** by pressing the **Windows+F** key combination. In the search box, type ***.bmp** and click the **Search** button. (For more information about using Search, turn to **39** About Windows XP Search.) You can also look in the **C:\Windows** folder, which has many files in the **.bmp** format.

Make sure that the image you plan to use is small. Don't worry if it's very small—Internet Explorer will "tile" the image by making it a repeating pattern if it's smaller than the toolbar. Particularly useful are patterns and textures, so look for those.

3 **Search the Web for a Picture**

You can also find many free graphics on the Web to use as your background. The best place to find images is at the Google Images search at **www.google.com/imghp**. If you want to fine-tune your search, click the **Advanced** link and you'll get a variety of options, such as selecting the size of the graphics you're looking for. It's a good idea to go to the **Advanced** search page, and from the **Size** drop-down list, select **small**.

After you do a search, you'll see a list of results. Scroll through them until you find one you think might be suitable. Click the link. A page with the graphic appears. Right-click the graphic and choose **Save Picture As** from the context menu. From the **Save Picture** dialog box that appears, name the file, and from the **Save as type** drop-down list, choose **Bitmap (.bmp)**. Then navigate to the folder where you want to save the picture and click the **Save** button.

2 Find a .BMP File on Your Hard Disk

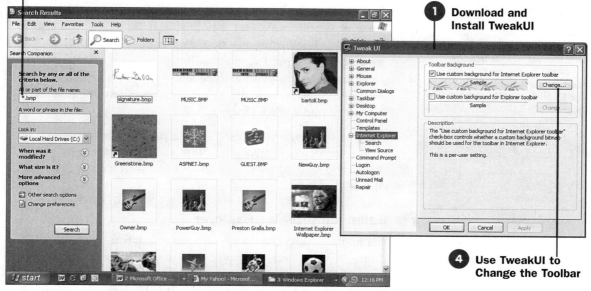

1 Download and Install TweakUI

4 Use TweakUI to Change the Toolbar

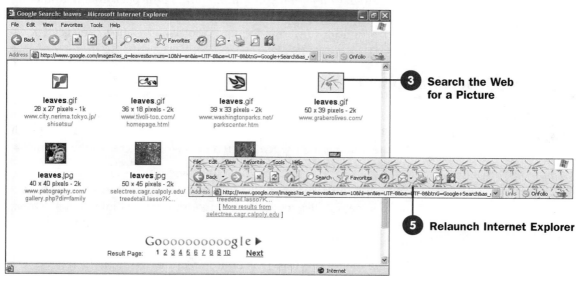

3 Search the Web for a Picture

5 Relaunch Internet Explorer

TIP

You can also change the background for the Windows Explorer toolbar using TweakUI. To do it, follow the same instructions as here, except enable the **Use custom background for Explorer toolbar** check box.

4 **Use TweakUI to Change the Toolbar**

After you've found the graphic you want, launch TweakUI. Click **Internet Explorer** and on the right side of the screen, you'll see the **Toolbar background** section. Enable the **Use custom background for Internet Explorer toolbar** check box and then click the **Change** button and navigate to the folder where you've stored the graphic you want to use as the background for the toolbar. When you find it, click **Open**.

You'll be sent back to TweakUI, and in the **Sample** area you'll see what your toolbar will look like. If the text is hard to read, you should choose a different background image. If it's what you want, click **OK**.

5 **Relaunch Internet Explorer**

You might have to close down and restart Internet Explorer for the change to take effect. Close it down and then restart it. You'll now have a background for your toolbar. If you want to change it, use TweakUI again. If you want to turn off the background, in the **Internet Explorer** section of TweakUI, disable the **Use custom background for Internet Explorer toolbar** check box and click **OK**.

58 Read Websites Offline

Before You Begin

✔ **51** Take Control of Your Favorites

There are times when you find a website that you want to read, but you don't have time at the moment. You'd like to be able to read it at your leisure, and perhaps when you're not even connected to the Internet—on a laptop on a train, for example.

You might also want to save that website permanently on your hard disk. Some websites might be so important to you that you'd like them to automatically be downloaded to your hard disk so that you can read them whenever and wherever you want.

You can do all this using the built-in features of Internet Explorer.

1 **Visit the Site You Want to Save**

You have to be on the site you want to save before you can save it, so head to that website in Internet Explorer.

1 Visit the Site You Want to Save

2 Choose Save As from the File Menu

3 Save the Web Page to Your Computer

4 Open the Web Page

5 Automatically Update a Web Page

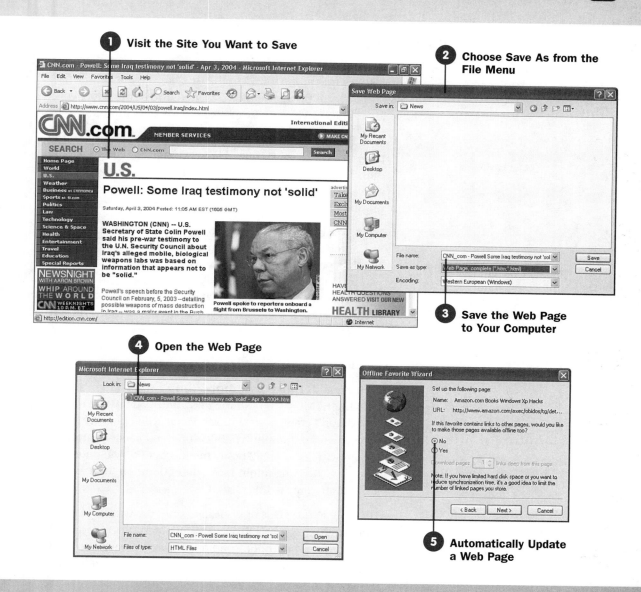

2 **Choose Save As from the File Menu**

With the website displayed, choose **File, Save As** from the menu. The **Save Web Page** dialog box appears. Browse to the folder where you want to save the page.

❸ Save the Web Page to Your Computer

Give the page a new name or keep its default name. The default name is the same name found in the title bar of your browser, which is put there by the website. When you save the page, you have four choices available from the **Save as type** drop-down list:

- **Web Page, complete (*.htm, *.html).** This option saves the page in its normal HTML (Hypertext Markup Language) format. This option creates a folder underneath the folder in which you save the page, and stores all the web page's graphics there.

- **Web Archive, single file (*.mht).** This option saves the page in a single file in a special compressed format known as Multipurpose Internet Mail Extension (MIME) HTML. When you use this option, no folders are created, and all the graphics are saved in the single file. If you don't have any plans to use the HTML, it's better to save the file in the **.mht** format than in the **Web Page, complete (*htm, *html)** format, because the **.mht** format keeps all the files in a single, tidy location.

- **Web Page, HTML only (*.htm, *.html).** This option saves only the HTML portion of the page and none of the graphics, so it doesn't create a new folder. When you open the saved page, though, it might be difficult to read because graphics are sometimes used to "hold" the pieces of a web page together. The page might look odd in addition to lacking graphics if you use this format.

- **Text File (*.txt).** This option saves only the text from the page, and doesn't create a separate folder. When you open the web page, you might find a lot of extraneous text you'll want to delete; for example, advertisements placed in the middle of articles.

❹ Open the Web Page

After you've saved the web page, when you want to open it, launch Internet Explorer, then choose **File**, **Open** from the menu. Browse to the folder and file you want to open and click **Open**; the website opens in Internet Explorer. You don't have to be online to do this because the website is saved on your computer.

TIP

If you plan to send the web page to someone using email, save it in the **.mht** format. That way, you can attach the single file to an email message, and the web page will be sent on its merry way.

⑤ Automatically Update a Web Page

If you want, Internet Explorer can automatically go out and grab a web page you want on your PC and save it so that you can read it when you're not connected to the Internet. You'd do this for a page that is updated frequently; for example, a news site.

First, go to the website you want to have automatically updated and save it in your **Favorites** list. (See **51 Take Control of Your Favorites** for details.) Then right-click the site in your **Favorites** list and choose **Make Available Offline**. The **Offline Favorite Wizard** appears. Click **Next** to start the wizard. From the page that appears, you have a choice of whether to save only the page or to also save all the pages linked to this page. If you want to save only the page itself, click **No**. If you want to save pages linked from it, click **Yes** and then choose the number of links you want to save. Click **Next** when you're done.

On the next page that appears, choose whether to synchronize the page only when you tell it to synchronize or to do so automatically on a schedule.

If you choose to synchronize only when you tell it to, you'll have to choose **Tools**, **Synchronize** from the menu when you want to get the latest copy of the page. If you have it synchronized on a schedule, Windows XP will synchronize on whatever schedule you choose. Click **Next**.

If you choose to synchronize on a schedule, a new screen appears, letting you choose the frequency and time of the synchronization.

You also have the option of having your PC connect to the Internet automatically at the time of synchronization if you're not online. To have it connect automatically, enable the check box at the bottom of the screen. If you don't check the box and your computer isn't connected at that time, it won't be able to synchronize.

Finally, complete the wizard by clicking **Finish**. To view the page on your PC after you've synchronized and when you're not connected to the Internet, choose **File**, **Work Offline** and then click the site in your **Favorites** list that you want to view.

NOTE

If you want to save links from the current page, you must decide how many links you want to save—in other words, do you want to save not only pages that are linked from the main page, but also pages linked from each of those pages, and so on. Be very careful if you choose to save linked pages because your hard disk can very quickly fill up with all those unnecessary pages.

8

Going Wireless

IN THIS CHAPTER:

When most people think about the Internet, they think of wires—telephone wires, cable wires, network wires…wires, wires, and more wires. But wires are so twentieth century. They entangle you, they limit where you can put your computer, they impede your freedom.

It needn't be that way, though. Millions of people are getting onto the Internet without wires—at home, in coffee shops, in airports, and beyond. You can do it, too. As you'll see in this chapter, it's easy to set up a wireless network at home, or get onto the Internet wirelessly when you travel. Read on to see how.

59 About Wireless (Wi-Fi) Computing

Before You Begin

✔ **44** Install a Home Router

KEY TERMS

Wi-Fi—A technology, also known as standard 802.11, that allows computers to access the Internet without wires. It requires that a wireless network card be used on a laptop or desktop computer, and that there be a wireless router nearby that the computer can communicate with. Wi-Fi is used in home networks, corporate networks, and wireless HotSpots in public locations such as coffee shops and airports.

Wireless router—A wireless device that connects computers to one another and to the Internet. Computers connected to a wireless router can share files with one another and can each access the Internet.

The easiest way to network all the PCs in your house and to give them all access to a single Internet connection is to install a wireless network (also called *Wi-Fi*). You won't need to drill holes or string wires; you just install a piece of equipment called a *wireless router* (or wireless access point) and wireless network adapters in each PC, and you'll be ready to go.

Wireless networks work similarly to wired networks, so for more details about networking, turn to **45** Create a New Network Installation. To build a wireless network, you'll need a wireless router, which you can commonly buy for from about $50 to $100, depending on its capabilities. You'll also need a wireless network adapter for each computer, which can either be a PC card for a laptop, or a USB adapter or internal wireless network card for a desktop. Prices typically run from about $30 to $100 for each.

Many wireless routers also have ports into which you can plug regular Ethernet cables. If you have a PC with an Ethernet connection (which almost, if not all, do), you won't have to buy a wireless network adapter for it. You can locate the PC near your wireless router, and connect an Ethernet cable between the PC and the router. Laptops or other PCs can still access the network wirelessly.

Another big part of the wireless world are *HotSpots*, public locations that let you get onto the Internet if you have a wireless-equipped laptop. Some HotSpots are free and others are for-pay. For more information about connecting to HotSpots, see **63** Connect to a HotSpot or Wi-Fi Network.

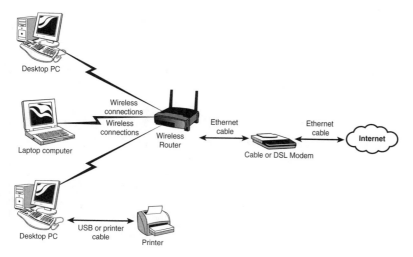

In a wireless network, PCs and laptops communicate with a wireless router without wires, but the router is connected with a physical Ethernet cable to your cable modem or DSL modem, which in turn is connected to the Internet by wires.

KEY TERM

HotSpot—A public location, such as a coffee shop, hotel, or an airport, that lets you access the Internet wirelessly if you have a laptop with a wireless card. Some HotSpots are free, although for many, you'll have to pay a fee.

Wireless technologies are grouped together under a single name called *Wi-Fi*. The technologies are based on a group of standards called 802.11. There are a number of different 802.11 standards, but the most important are these two:

- **802.11b.** This standard lets computers communicate with each other at a theoretical top speed of 11Mbps, and it operates in the 2.4GHz spectrum—the same spectrum that cordless phones use, so there is a chance that they could interfere with it.

- **802.11g.** This standard lets computers communicate with each other at a theoretical top speed of 54Mbps, and it also operates in the 2.4GHz spectrum. It's a newer standard than 802.11b.

Hardware that uses one standard only partially works with hardware that uses the other standard. It can be rather confusing to keep straight, but here's the rundown on what you need to know:

- An 802.11b-equipped PC can communicate with either an 802.11b or an 802.11g router, but it will work at the slower 802.11b speed, not the 802.11g speed.

TIP

You most likely won't be able to reach the top speeds for either network; as a practical matter, don't expect to get speeds of more than half their rated speeds, and possibly less.

- An 802.11g-equipped PC can communicate with either an 802.11b or an 802.11g router. When it communicates with an 802.11g router, it communicates at the faster 802.11g speed. When it communicates with the 802.11b router, it communicates at the slower 802.11b speed.

Keep in mind that if you mix and match 802.11b and 802.11g hardware on a network, the entire network will generally slow down to the slower 802.11b speed. (Manufacturers are working to change that, so by the time you read this, it may have changed.) That means that if you have a network with an 802.11g router, and it has three PCs with 802.11g adapters and one with an 802.11b adapter, the entire network will communicate at the slower 802.11b speed.

60 Install a Wi-Fi Router

Before You Begin

✔ **44** Install a Home Router

✔ **59** About Wireless (Wi-Fi) Computing

See Also

→ **61** Install a Wi-Fi Network Adapter

→ **65** About Solving Wi-Fi Connection Problems

The first step in building a wireless network at home is to install the *router*—the device to which all of your computers will connect. The router will not only let the computers communicate with each other, but will also let each of the computers connect to the Internet.

One of the main reasons that most people install a wireless network at home is to share a high-speed Internet connection, such as a cable modem or DSL connection. These instructions show how to install a wireless router that will let you share a high-speed Internet connection.

1 Buy the Right Router

As described in **59** **About Wireless (Wi-Fi) Computing**, there are several *Wi-Fi* standards from which to choose, notably 802.11.b and 802.11g, so make sure that you buy the routers and wireless adapters that use the same standard. An 802.11g router is higher speed than 802.11b, but costs more as well. If you want to take advantage of 802.11g's higher speed, however, all your Wi-Fi network cards should be 802.11g as well.

2 Choose the Right Location

Where you place your router will have a major impact on the effectiveness of the network, notably the speed with which computers can connect to one another. You'll have to take into account the locations of where Wi-Fi-equipped PCs will be most likely located in your house. **65** About Solving Wi-Fi Connection Problems can give you more advice about troubleshooting Wi-Fi connection problems, but follow these general rules for placing your router:

- **Put your router in a central location.** If you locate your router in a central location in the house, all of your PCs will be able to connect. If you put your router in a far corner of the house, PCs near it may get a high-speed connection, but others may get a weak connection or fail to connect at all.

- **Locate the router near your Internet connection.** You're going to need to physically connect your router to your cable modem or DSL modem, so make sure that the router is close enough to the cable modem or the phone jack so that you can run an Ethernet cable between the router and the Internet access device.

- **Don't place your router next to an outside wall.** If you put the router next to an outside wall, you will be broadcasting signals to the outside, not the inside of the house.

NOTE

Don't put your access point or PCs near microwave ovens or cordless phones. Many microwave ovens and cordless phones operate in the same 2.4GHz part of the spectrum as does 802.11b or 802.11g Wi-Fi equipment. Cordless phones often cause more problems than microwaves.

❸ Connect the Router

To allow all your computers to connect to the Internet, you'll have to connect your wireless router to your cable modem or DSL modem. Connect one end of your Ethernet cable to your cable modem or DSL modem, and the other end to your router. When you connect the cable to the router, make sure that you connect it to the right port. Some wireless routers allow you to connect PCs to them using Ethernet cables as well as wirelessly, and so there may be multiple Ethernet connections on the router. If there are, connect the cable or DSL modem to the router using the connection labeled **WAN**. Check your router's documentation for details if there is no connection labeled **WAN**—different manufacturers may use different terminologies, so you should check for the right connection port.

After you connect the Ethernet cable, turn off your cable modem or DSL modem for five minutes. Then turn it back on again, plug in your router's power cord, and turn on the power switch if your router has a power switch.

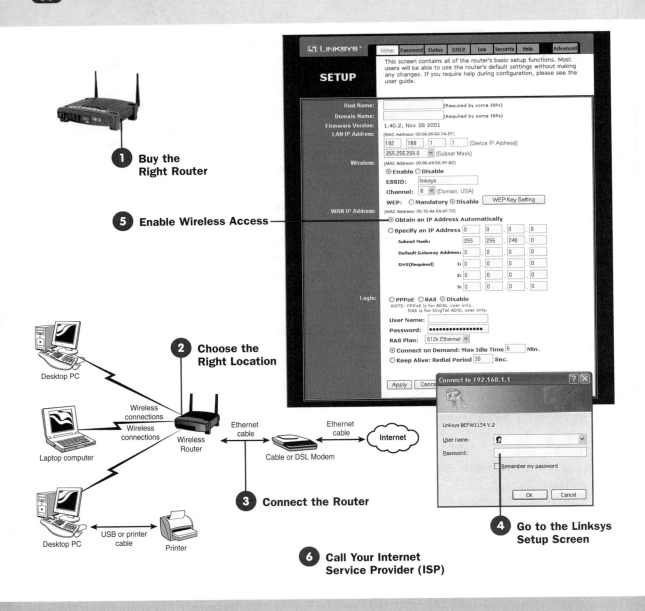

1 Buy the Right Router

5 Enable Wireless Access

2 Choose the Right Location

Desktop PC

Wireless connections
Wireless connections

Laptop computer

Wireless Router

Ethernet cable

Cable or DSL Modem

Ethernet cable

Internet

3 Connect the Router

Desktop PC

USB or printer cable

Printer

4 Go to the Linksys Setup Screen

6 Call Your Internet Service Provider (ISP)

After several minutes, you should see green lights flashing on your router, depending on the manufacturer. Check your router's documentation for details of how your router looks when it is properly connected to the cable or DSL modem.

④ Go to the Linksys Setup Screen

Your router is now connected to the Internet, but you need to con-figure it to work properly. Every manufacturer has a different setup screen, and the way that you get to that screen varies by manufac-turer. In this task, you'll see how to set up the most popular type of Wi-Fi router, a Linksys router. The directions for Linksys routers are similar, but not identical, to other routers, so check your router's documentation for details.

Go to a computer that is connected to the router. (You'll have to install a network card in the computer so that the computer can communicate with the router; see **61 Install a Wi-Fi Network Adapter**.) Then, to get to the setup screen of a Linksys router, open Internet Explorer, type the location **http://192.168.1.1** in the address bar, and press **Enter**. A login screen appears. Leave the **User name** field blank; in the **Password** field, type **admin** and press **Enter**.

⑤ Enable Wireless Access

You'll now have to tell your router to work wirelessly. Some routers do this without any setup required, but if you have a router that includes both wires and wireless connections, you may have to tell it to use its wireless capabilities.

On the Linksys **Setup** screen, go to the section marked **Wireless** and click the **Enable** radio button. That action enables wireless capabilities for your router. Then click the **Apply** button.

⑥ Call Your Internet Service Provider (ISP)

Your router still may not be ready to use; depending on your Internet service provider, you might have to call your ISP to enable the wireless router. Some ISPs require that you give them the router's *MAC address*, which is a number, such as **00-90-4B-0E-3F-BD**, that uniquely identifies a piece of hardware such as a router or a network card.

Check with your ISP. If it requires that number, call the technical support line and read it to them. After a few minutes, your router will be connected to the Internet.

To test whether your router is communicating successfully with the Internet, you'll have to connect your PCs to the router wirelessly, as you'll see how to do in **61 Install a Wi-Fi Network Adapter**.

NOTE

Even though you're using a browser and a URL location to set up your browser, you're not actually going out to the Internet to set it up. The URL is the location of the router on the home network you're setting up at home—you're only visit-ing it inside your own net-work. No one out on the Internet can get to it.

KEY TERM

MAC address—A number, such as 00-90-4B-0E-3F-BD, that uniquely identifies a piece of hardware such as a router or a network card.

61 Install a Wi-Fi Network Adapter

NOTE

A USB wireless adapter plugs into the USB port on your PC, and then sits on your desktop, using a small antenna to communicate with your wireless router.

Each computer that you want to connect to your wireless network must have a wireless network adapter installed before it can connect to the *Wi-Fi* network. Installation is a three-step process—first physically install the adapter, run the setup software, and finally configure the adapter to connect to your network.

1 Choose the Right Wireless Adapter

When buying a Wi-Fi network adapter for your computer, consider several factors. The first is to match the Wi-Fi network adapter to your Wi-Fi network—especially the *router*. As explained in **59** **About Wireless (Wi-Fi) Computing**, there are two Wi-Fi standards, 802.11b and 802.11g, so make sure that you choose a network adapter that matches the standard used by your router.

When you've determined which standard to buy for your adapter, you must decide whether to buy an adapter that connects to your PC using a USB port or as a PC card (if you have a laptop). USB devices tend to be slightly more expensive than PC cards. And if you're going to travel with your laptop, USB devices are not as easy to carry around and use as PC cards. If you have a laptop, it's generally a better idea to buy a PC card wireless adapter. For desktops, buy a USB adapter because desktops don't usually have slots to accept PC cards. Although you *can* buy internal wireless cards for a desktop computer, that's not a good idea as well. An internal wireless network card is more difficult to install than a USB adapter, it can't be repositioned for the best reception, and if you want to use it for a different computer, it's very difficult to do.

2 Connect the Adapter to Your PC

When you have purchased the appropriate Wi-Fi network card for your computer and your wireless access point (or router), you must physically connect the network card to your PC. If you're installing a PC card adapter, slip it into the empty slot until it's firmly seated. If you're installing a USB adapter, connect the USB cable to the USB port on the PC or laptop. USB ports can be in many different locations, depending on your computer, and so may be on the front or the back of the computer. Check your system's documentation for more details.

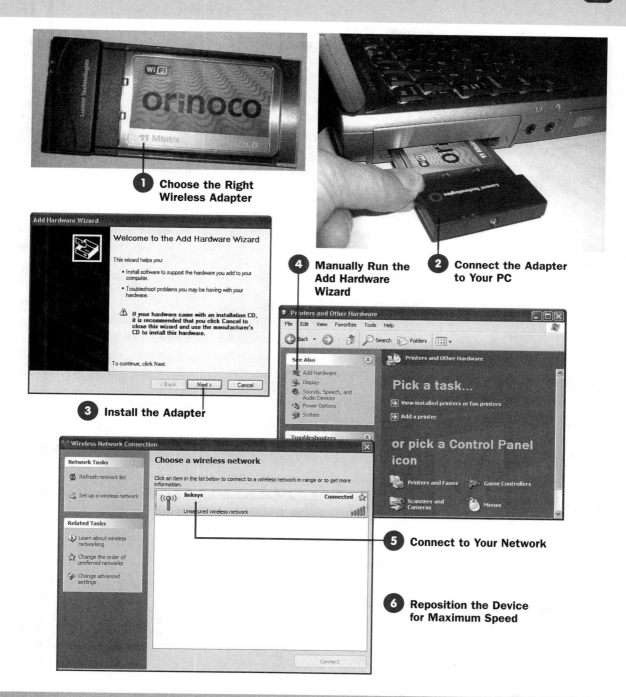

1 Choose the Right Wireless Adapter

2 Connect the Adapter to Your PC

3 Install the Adapter

4 Manually Run the Add Hardware Wizard

5 Connect to Your Network

6 Reposition the Device for Maximum Speed

③ Install the Adapter

When you connect the adapter, depending on the adapter, it may be automatically recognized by Windows XP and need no configuration. If that happens, you will get a message in the **Notification Area** (the lower-right corner of the desktop) telling you that the adapter is installed and ready to work.

If the adapter is not automatically recognized by Windows XP, the **Add Hardware Wizard** appears. Click the **Next** button and follow the simple instructions for installation.

If your adapter came with an installation disk, you should click the **Cancel** button on the first page of the **Add Hardware Wizard**, insert the installation disk in your PC, and install the hardware using that disk.

You might also have received a disk with your network adapter that does not have installation software, but does include a *driver*, a small piece of software that hardware needs to work properly with Windows XP. If that's the case, when the **Add Hardware Wizard** asks for the location of your driver, make sure to insert the disk in your PC and tell the wizard to use the driver from that disk.

④ Manually Run the Add Hardware Wizard

There's a chance that your hardware won't install, and that the **Add Hardware Wizard** may not automatically appear. If that's the case, click the **Start** button and choose **Control Panel** from the **Start** menu. Choose **Printers and Other Hardware** and from the **See Also** area, choose **Add Hardware**. The **Add Hardware Wizard** will appear, allowing you to install the hardware. If you still have trouble, see **113 Install New Hardware**.

⑤ Connect to Your Network

Your wireless adapter is now set up and running. If the device has an external light, the light will now be green, indicating that it recognizes your wireless router. You will also notice a small network icon appearing in Windows XP's **Notification Area** in the lower-right corner of the desktop.

However, even though the network card is communicating with the wireless router, your computer cannot yet connect to the

---

NOTE

The way in which you connect to a wireless network can differ slightly in Windows XP, depending on the exact version of XP you have. In the middle of 2004, Microsoft released an update to XP, called XP SP-2 (Service Pack 2). It made a number of changes to the interface you use for connecting to and using wireless networks. If you bought a PC sometime after the middle of 2004, or if you upgraded to SP-2, you'll see the new way of connecting to wireless networks pictured here. The old way is very similar, however, and in general the steps are much the same—primarily, only the screens look different.

Internet or the other computers on the network. You must configure the adapter to recognize your network. Right-click the small
network icon in the **Notification Area** and choose **View Available
Wireless Networks**. The **Choose a wireless network** dialog box
appears. You'll see your network listed. Double-click it, and from
the dialog box that appears, click **Connect**. You'll be connected to
the network. If you turn off your PC or router in the future, whenever you turn it back on, you are automatically reconnected.

6 ## Reposition the Device for Maximum Speed

The exact position of the computer's adapter and its antenna
might have a major effect on your connection speed to the router.
You can check the quality and speed of your connection by double-
clicking the network icon in the **Notification Area** on that computer's desktop and looking on the **General** tab of the **Wireless
Network Connection Status** dialog box. Look for the green bars
next to **Signal Strength**. Ideally, all the bars should be lit because
that means that the signal is the strongest.

If you've installed a USB adapter, make sure that the antenna on it
is pointed vertically, because that's the best position for receiving
and transmitting. Move the position of the network adapter to see
whether that has any effect on the signal strength. For PC cards,
move your laptop to different locations until you find the location
with the best signal strength.

NOTE

If you have the pre-SP-2
version of XP, here's how to
connect to your wireless
network: Double-click the
small network icon in the
Notification Area. The
**Wireless Network
Connection Status** dialog
box appears. On the
General tab, click the
Properties button; when
the next dialog box opens,
click the **Wireless
Networks** tab. The network
your router has created
should show up in the
Available Networks area.
To connect this computer
to that network, click the
Configure button and then
click **OK** twice to close both
dialog boxes. Even though
you click a **Configure** button, you don't actually have
to manually configure the
adapter to work. Windows
XP, working behind the
scenes, does that for you
automatically.

62 ## About Wireless Printing

As with any other kind of network, one of the great benefits of a wireless
network is how easily it lets you share a printer. Instead of every person
in the house having her own printer, a single printer can be shared by
everyone on the network. You set up a printer on a wireless network in
exactly the same way you set up a printer on a wired network. (For
details on how to do it, see **47** **Share a Printer**.)

One of the problems with sharing a printer on a network, however, is
that the printer must be plugged into a computer to print, and that
computer must be running and connected to the network.

Before You Begin

✔ **47** Share a Printer

See Also

→ **59** About Wireless
(Wi-Fi) Computing

NOTE

Because you can use your laptop to connect to a *HotSpot* in a coffee shop or if you use your laptop when you travel, there may be days at a time when no one else in your home network will be able to use the printer because it's not connected to your laptop.

In a wired network, this is only a minor annoyance. To print, you make sure that the computer to which the printer is connected is running, but you at least know that the computer is always in a location next to the printer.

That's often not the case with a wireless network, though. One of the major reasons for installing a wireless network, after all, is that you can take your laptop with you anywhere around the house and still be connected to the network, its printer, and the Internet. Let's say you have a laptop that you normally use in a home office, and you have a printer connected to it. Other people in the house print to that printer. But when you decide to use your laptop in your living room or your back porch, the printer will no longer be connected to your laptop. That means no one else in the house will be able to print until you connect the printer back up to your laptop.

There is a solution to the problem, however. You can directly attach your printer to the wireless network—it won't have to be connected to a PC. Because it won't be connected to a computer, it's available to anyone at any time, even when your laptop is turned off or isn't near the printer.

You connect your printer to the network using a special device that plugs into your printer's USB port. The device then sits next to the printer, using its antenna to wirelessly connect to the network, so that anyone can use the printer by printing to it the same way they print to any network printer. (Again, see **47** **Share a Printer** for details.)

Connect a printer to your wireless network using a special device that plugs into the printer and communicates with the computers through its antenna.

Several manufacturers make these wireless printer devices, including D-Link and Linksys. Prices vary, but were in the $120 to $140 range when this book went to press.

Even if you don't have a printer with a USB port, you can still wirelessly connect your printer to a network. Some wireless devices made by manufacturers such as Linksys and D-Link can connect to your printer's parallel port instead of a USB port, and prices are the same as for those that connect to a USB port.

63 Connect to a HotSpot or Wi-Fi Network

Wireless networking is great not just because it's so easy to set up a network at home. It's also useful because you can connect to the Internet easily when you're away from home, for example in a coffee shop, at a hotel, or at an airport. Here's how to connect to wireless networks around the world.

Before You Begin

✔ **60** Install a Wi-Fi Router

✔ **61** Install a Wi-Fi Network Adapter

See Also

→ **64** About Wi-Fi Security

→ **65** About Solving Wi-Fi Connection Problems

1 Locate a HotSpot Before You Travel

One of the biggest problems with connecting to a *HotSpot* is simply finding one before you travel. Before you leave home, search for a HotSpot in a location where you'll be traveling.

There are two types of HotSpots—free HotSpots that are provided by stores, individuals, and some local municipalities; and for-pay HotSpots provided by HotSpot providers. As you might imagine, there are many more for-pay HotSpots than there are free HotSpots. The four largest for-pay HotSpot providers are Boingo, T-Mobile, Wayport, and Surf and Sip.

WEB RESOURCE

http://locations.hotspot.t-mobile.com/

http://www.boingo.com/search.html

http://www.wayport.net/locations

http://www.surfandsip.com/location.htm

Visit these websites to find the locations of the T-Mobile, Boingo, Wayport, or Surf and Sip HotSpots nearest where you plan to travel.

Pricing plans for HotSpots vary according to the provider, but as a general rule, you'd be best off starting out with a pay-per-day plan rather than a monthly plan. That way, you can find out whether you'll use any plan enough to justify paying by the month.

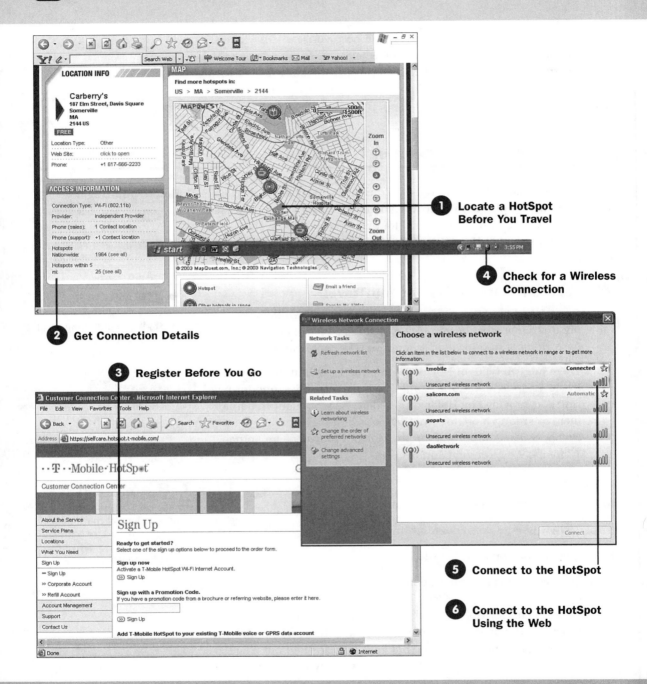

1 Locate a HotSpot Before You Travel

4 Check for a Wireless Connection

2 Get Connection Details

3 Register Before You Go

5 Connect to the HotSpot

6 Connect to the HotSpot Using the Web

An even better way to find out a HotSpot location before you travel is to go to one of a number of websites that let you search any area for nearby HotSpots (both free and for-pay):

- www.wi-fihotspotlist.com

- www.wifinder.com

- www.wifimaps.com

- www.jiwire.com

TIP

If you're looking only for free HotSpots, go to **www.wififreespot.com**.

2 Get Connection Details

After you find a HotSpot location, get details about how you'll connect—information such as pricing and any special connection instructions. If it's a for-pay provider, check the previous step for website locations. If it's a free HotSpot, the HotSpot search sites listed in the previous step will include phone numbers, websites, and (when available) any special connection information.

3 Register Before You Go

If you're going to travel and connect to a for-pay HotSpot, it's a good idea to register with the provider before you leave on your trip. There may not be an easy way to sign up for the HotSpot when you're at the location itself. Typically, the people who work at a location where a HotSpot is located have very little, if any, information about the HotSpot. For example, cafe employees might know how to make a latte, but not how to troubleshoot a Wi-Fi connection.

4 Check for a Wireless Connection

When you travel to the HotSpot, make sure that you have a Wi-Fi network card in your PC. Turn on your PC. If a HotSpot is available, you will see green lights flashing on your Wi-Fi card (if the card is equipped with lights). You will also see a network icon in the **Notification Area** in the lower-right corner of the desktop. If you don't see the icon and don't see green lights flashing, it means that no HotSpot is nearby.

NOTE

If you find yourself on an unexpected layover at an airport and are wondering if there's a HotSpot nearby, ask at the information desk—they may be able to help you. You can also head for the nearest Starbucks coffee shop if there's one there, because many Starbucks have HotSpots. The simplest way of all is to follow step 4 of this task—turn on your laptop with your wireless card already in it. If there's a nearby HotSpot, you'll see the lights flashing on your card.

NOTE

If you have a pre-SP-2 version of XP, you connect in a slightly different way to a free HotSpot. Double-click the network icon in the **Notification Area**; in the dialog box that opens, click the **Properties** button. In the **Wireless Network Connection Properties** dialog box, click the **Wireless Networks** tab. Look in the **Available networks** list. You will see one or more networks listed there. Look for any whose icon has a small circle on top of it—that means that the connection is strong enough to connect to. Highlight that icon, click the **Configure** button, and make sure that there is no check mark next to the **Data Encryption (WEP Enabled)** option or next to the **This is a computer-to-computer (ad hoc) network; wireless access points are not used** option.

5 Connect to the HotSpot

How you connect to a HotSpot varies from location to location. One way to connect, particularly if you're connecting to a free HotSpot, is to right-click the network icon in the **Notification Area** and choose **View Available Wireless Networks**. You'll see a list of all the nearby wireless networks. If you're in a congested urban area with many HotSpots, the list might show more than one. Double-click the one to which you want to connect. You'll get a notification screen. Click the **Connect** button to connect to the HotSpot.

When you're done, click **OK** twice to close both dialog boxes. You should now be able to use the HotSpot connection.

6 Connect to the HotSpot Using the Web

Many HotSpots, notably for-pay ones, require that you visit a website to connect to the service. When you see the network icon in your **Notification Area**, and so know a HotSpot is within connection distance, go to the website that the HotSpot provider requires you to visit (you must find this out ahead of time, before you travel, as explained in step 1). Then provide your registration information (typically a username and password), and you can connect. In some instances, all you'll have to do is launch your browser, and the website will immediately appear on your screen.

---

64 About Wi-Fi Security

Wireless computing offers many benefits, but there are some accompanying dangers as well. Any network should be protected (for more details, see **66** **About Firewalls and Routers**). Wireless networks are especially vulnerable. Unless you take some basic steps, there's nothing to prevent any passerby from connecting to your network in the same way that you can connect to it—wirelessly. After all, if you can connect to your network from your backyard, someone passing by can just as easily connect to it from your front yard or from the street.

But those network protections are only a starting point for wireless networks. There's a lot more you should do to protect yourself on your Wi-Fi:

- **Disable broadcasting your network name (also called an SSID).**
When you broadcast your network name, it's easier for people outside your network to find it and connect to it. Check your router documentation for instructions on how to disable this information. Not all *routers* can do it, and even different models from the same manufacturer may differ on how to do it. On some Linksys wireless routers that allow you to disable SSID broadcast, go to your setup screen as outlined in **60 Install a Wi-Fi Router**, click the **Disable** button next to **SSID Broadcast** and click **Apply**.

NOTE

Not all Linksys wireless routers let you disable SSID broadcast, so if you don't see the option on the setup screen, it means you can't disable broadcast on yours.

- **Change your SSID name.** Each manufacturer ships its routers to have the same SSID name, for example, Linksys routers have the SSID name **Linksys**. Those who want to break into networks know that they should look for networks named **Linksys**, and they'll be likely to find such wireless networks, even if the names aren't being broadcast. How you change the name varies from manufacturer to manufacturer and model to model, so check the documentation. In a Linksys router, go to your setup screen as outlined in **60 Install a Wi-Fi Router**; in the **ESSID** box, type a new name and click **Apply**.

- **Use WEP.** WEP is a method of encrypting data so that it can't be read by anyone outside your network. How you do this varies from router manufacturer to manufacturer, and from model to model. For a Linksys router, access the setup screen, and enable the **Mandatory** radio button next to **WEP**. Then click the **WEP Key Setting** button and follow the directions for creating a "key," a kind of password that each PC that wants to connect to the network must use. Write down the key and then click **Apply**. For each PC that you want to connect to the network, double-click the network icon in the **Notification Area** and click the **Properties** button. On the **Wireless Networks** tab of the **Wireless Networks Connection Properties** dialog box, select your network from the **Available networks** list and click the **Configure** button. Enable the **Data encryption (WEP enabled)** check box and in the **Network key** box, type the key. Type the key again in the **Confirm network key** box and click **OK** twice.

NOTE

There's an even stronger encryption method than WEP—WPA. However, WPA is more difficult to configure than WEP and works with only some hardware. You also have to download and install special software to use it. Eventually it will become the main encryption standard, but right now it isn't as frequently used as WEP.

65 About Solving Wi-Fi Connection Problems

Before You Begin

✔ **59** About Wireless (Wi-Fi) Computing

✔ **60** Install a Wi-Fi Router

✔ **61** Install a Wi-Fi Network Adapter

See Also

→ **50** About Troubleshooting Network Problems

 TIP

Wi-Fi PC cards usually don't have an external antenna, so you might have trouble figuring out its antenna orientation. Usually, though, the antenna is located at the edge of the card itself, so point that at the router.

When you use wireless networking, sooner or later you're going to run into connection problems. It might happen at home or on the road, but it's going to happen to you. The signal will be so weak that you can't connect to it, or it will drop all together, or you will have any one of a number of other problems.

So what to do? Although there can be many different types and causes for wireless problems, these tips will help you out in most situations:

• Move your *router* or *Wi-Fi*-enabled PCs away from microwave ovens or cordless phones. Many microwave ovens and cordless phones operate in the same 2.4GHz part of the spectrum as does 802.11b and 802.11g Wi-Fi equipment. Cordless phones are often more problematic than microwaves.

• Make sure that the router's antenna and network adapter antennas are pointed vertically. Usually, transmission is better when antennas are vertically oriented rather than horizontally. However, unique circumstances in your house may change that, so experiment.

• Point the antennas of your wireless PCs in the direction of the router—doing this usually makes for a better connection. If you are using USB wireless adapters, point their antennas toward your router.

• Don't place the antennas of routers or wireless adapters near filing cabinets and other large metal objects. Metal structures often cause significant interference and can cut throughput dramatically.

• As a last resort, consider using external and booster antennas. Some routers can accept booster antennas that can increase throughput. Check the manufacturer's website for details; if booster antennas are available, they'll be listed there.

9

Keeping Yourself Safe Online

IN THIS CHAPTER:

The Internet is a great place to visit. It's also a dangerous and sometimes annoying one. Pop-up ads can appear out of nowhere, taking over your screen, spyware can report on your web visits, cookies can invade your privacy, and worms and viruses can attack your computer.

But you can fight back. As you'll see in this chapter, it's easy to protect yourself when you go online.

66 About Firewalls

(K)EY TERM

Firewall—Software (and sometimes hardware) that protects you from hackers by not allowing them to get onto your PC.

A *firewall* is the best protection you can get for protecting yourself online. It puts up a wall of sorts between you and the Internet so that only the information and software you want gets onto your computer.

In particular, a firewall blocks hackers from using what are called *Internet ports* to sneak into your computer. A port isn't a physical device of any kind. Rather, a port is a kind of virtual, invisible connection between your PC and the Internet. There are thousands of these incoming virtual ports that can be used to make a connection, and you need many of them. For example, whenever you connect to a web page, you're making a connection through port 80. Certain ports are well-known for being used by hackers to sneak in. Firewalls close down ports and make sure that only the required ports are open.

Firewalls protect you in another way as well. You might get a kind of program called a Trojan horse planted on your PC. When that happens, the Trojan horse makes an outbound connection from your computer and announces that the computer is available to hackers. Hackers can then take control of your PC, even if a firewall blocks the incoming virtual ports. To minimize the damage done by Trojan horse programs, a firewall can block any outbound connection being made from your PC—in other words, connections made by a program without your knowledge.

Windows XP includes a built-in firewall to help protect you when you're on the Internet. But there's a better one you can get for free, and you'll see how to use it in **69** **Protect Yourself with a Better Free Firewall**.

67 Protect Yourself with the Windows Firewall

Windows XP's built-in firewall offers good basic protection. But depending on your exact version of XP, that firewall may or may not be automatically turned on. If you have what is called the SP-2 (Service Pack 2) version of Windows XP, XP's firewall is automatically turned on. That version of XP was released in the middle of 2004; if you bought a computer some time after that, you most likely are running SP-2. You might also have upgraded to SP-2, however, and forgotten that you did. And depending on your exact version of Windows XP, how you use the firewall can vary somewhat.

In this task, you'll learn how to turn on the firewall in both the SP-2 version of XP, and the non-SP-2 version of XP.

1 Check Whether You Have SP-2

Before you turn on your firewall, you should know which version of Windows XP you have. To know whether you have SP-2, right-click the **My Computer** icon on the desktop and choose **Properties** from the context menu. In the **System Properties** dialog box that opens, click the **General** tab. On that screen, at the bottom of the **System** area, you'll see a notation about what version of Windows XP you have. If you have SP-2, it will say so right there.

2 Run the Security Center

If you're running SP-2, you turn on and control the firewall from the **Security Center**. There are two ways to get to the **Security Center**. Look in your **System Tray**. If you see a small icon of a red shield there, click it and the **Security Center** will run.

If you're running SP-2 and there's no icon of a red shield in the **System Tray**, click the **Start** button and then click **Control Panel**. From the **Control Panel**, click the **Security Center** icon.

3 Turn On the Firewall

Look at the **Firewall** section near the top of the screen. If there is a red button that says **Off**, it means that your firewall is turned off. To turn it on, click the **Windows Firewall** picture at the bottom of the screen. The **Windows Firewall** dialog box appears. Click the **On** radio button and then click **OK** to turn on your firewall.

Before You Begin

✔ **66** About Firewalls

See Also

→ **68** Customize the Windows Firewall for Maximum Protection

→ **69** Protect Yourself with a Better Free Firewall

💡 TIP

Another way to open the **System Properties** dialog box is to click the **Start** button, choose the **Control Panel** option, click the **Performance and Maintenance** icon, and then click the **System** option. If you don't see the **Performance and Maintenance** icon in the **Control Panel** list, choose the **System** icon to launch the **System Properties** dialog box.

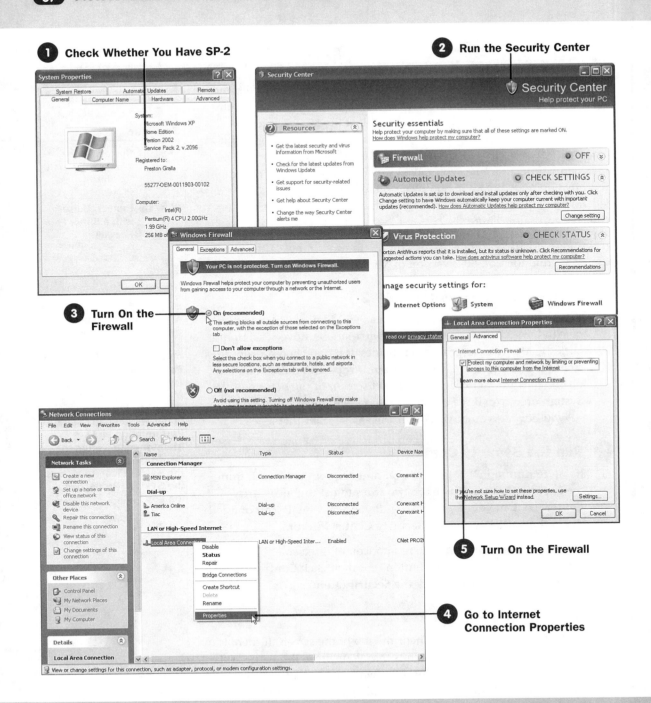

1 Check Whether You Have SP-2

2 Run the Security Center

3 Turn On the Firewall

4 Go to Internet Connection Properties

5 Turn On the Firewall

4 Go to Internet Connection Properties

If you don't have SP-2, you turn on your firewall by using the **Internet Connection Properties** dialog box. To get there, click the **Start** button and then click **Control Panel**. Click the **Network and Internet Connections** link and then click **Network Connections**. Right-click your Internet connection and choose **Properties** from the context menu. When the **Properties** dialog box opens, select the **Advanced** tab.

5 Turn On the Firewall

Enable the check box in the **Internet Connection Firewall** section of the dialog box and click **OK**. The firewall is now turned on.

68 Customize the Windows Firewall for Maximum Protection

To make the most out of the Windows *firewall*, you should customize how it works. When it's first turned on, it blocks almost every program from accessing the Internet, only letting a handful through, including Internet Explorer, email software, and Windows Messenger. You'll be able to tell it to let certain programs use the Internet (such as instant messaging programs) that it normally blocks. You can also configure it so that it is in use for some of your Internet connections, but not for others. These instructions are for the SP-2 version of the Windows firewall; it works somewhat differently in earlier versions of Windows.

Before You Begin

✔ **66** About Firewalls
✔ **67** Protect Yourself with the Windows Firewall

See Also

→ **69** Protect Yourself with a Better Free Firewall

1 Unblock a Program

When you launch a program that needs to access the Internet, such as America Online Instant Messenger, a **Security Alert** screen launches, asking whether you want to allow the program to use the Internet. If you want to let it use the Internet, click **Unblock this program** and click **OK**. From now on, that program can access the Internet without asking your permission. If you don't want the program to ever access the Internet, click **Keep blocking this program**. If you think that you might want the program to access the Internet at some later point, click **Keep blocking this program, but ask me again later**. When you choose this third option, the next time you launch the program, the **Security Alert** screen launches again, giving you the option of allowing the program through.

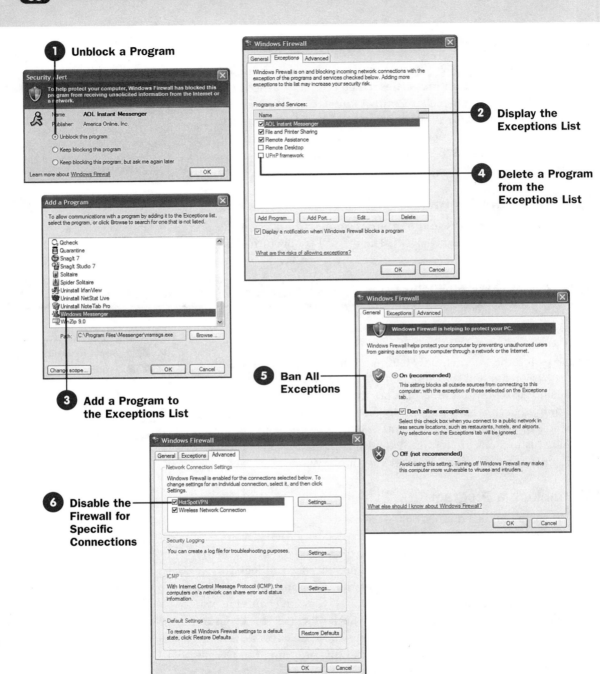

1 Unblock a Program

2 Display the Exceptions List

4 Delete a Program from the Exceptions List

3 Add a Program to the Exceptions List

5 Ban All Exceptions

6 Disable the Firewall for Specific Connections

2 Display the Exceptions List

The **Windows Firewall Exceptions** list shows you all the programs you've said should be allowed through the firewall. By default, it also allows **File and Printer Sharing** services and **Remote Assistance**. (The **File and Printer Sharing** services allow computers on your network to share files with each other and to use printers connected to other PCs.)

When you let a program through the firewall, as outlined in step 1 of this task, the program shows up on the **Exceptions** list with its check box enabled.

To display the **Exceptions** list, double-click the **Security Center** icon in the **System Tray** (the red shield), click the **Windows Firewall** icon at the bottom of the **Security Center** screen, and then click the **Exceptions** tab in the **Windows Firewall** dialog box.

From this screen, you can manually add programs you want to allow through the firewall and block programs you have previously decided to let through the firewall.

3 Add a Program to the Exceptions List

To add a program to the **Exceptions** list—and so allow it to access the Internet—click the **Add Program** button at the bottom of the **Exceptions** page of the **Windows Firewall** dialog box. The **Add a Program** dialog box appears. Scroll until you find the program you want to allow to access the Internet and click **OK**.

You'll return to the **Exceptions** page of the **Windows Firewall** dialog box. The program you selected is added to the list, but its check box is not enabled, and so the firewall will still block it. To allow the program through the firewall to use the Internet, enable the check box next to the program and click **OK**.

4 Delete a Program from the Exceptions List

If there's a program you no longer want to access the Internet, disable its check box and click **OK**. That program is no longer allowed to access the Internet—when the program next launches, the **Security Alert** dialog box appears.

NOTE

One of the biggest problems with using a firewall is deciding which programs to let through and which to block. When you have to decide whether to block a program, the Windows Firewall doesn't offer any advice. A better solution is to get the ZoneAlarm firewall. For information about how to install and use ZoneAlarm, see **69** Protect Yourself with a Better Free Firewall.

NOTE

For more information about how to use wireless HotSpots, turn to **63** **Connect to a HotSpot or Wi-Fi Network.**

5 Ban All Exceptions

For maximum security, you can tell the firewall not to allow *any* of your exceptions to access the Internet. You might want to do this when you're using a public network that is less secure than your own home network—for example, at a public wireless *HotSpot*. To ban all exceptions, open the **Security Center**, click the **Windows Firewall** icon at the bottom of the screen, and click the **General** tab of the **Windows Firewall** dialog box. Enable the **Don't allow exceptions** check box and click **OK**.

6 Disable the Firewall for Specific Connections

You might have more than one Internet connection on your PC— for example, one for your home network and one for wireless networks. You can turn on the firewall for some connections and turn it off for others. To do it, open the **Security Center**, click the **Windows Firewall** icon at the bottom of the screen, and click the **Advanced** tab of the **Windows Firewall** dialog box. Disable the check box next to the connection you don't want to use the firewall and click **OK**.

 **Protect Yourself with a Better Free Firewall**

Before You Begin

✔ **66** About Firewalls

✔ **67** Protect Yourself with the Windows Firewall

See Also

→ **68** Customize the Windows Firewall for Maximum Protection

Windows XP's firewall is good, but it sometimes will not catch every program on your computer that tries to make a connection to the Internet. That means that it might miss some Trojan horses.

There are a number of firewalls that are better than XP's firewall, including Norton Firewall, the McAfee Personal Firewall, and ZoneAlarm. All these options do a very good job, but ZoneAlarm is the only firewall that is free. You can download it, install it, and use it without paying. If you want, you can buy a version that includes more advanced features, such as finding the source of anyone who might be trying to attack your PC. But the basic version does as good a job as any of them in blocking Trojan horses and similar dangers.

1 Download and Install ZoneAlarm

To get the free ZoneAlarm firewall, go to **www.zonelabs.com**. Scroll toward the bottom of the page and click **Our checklist will help you decide**. Click the red **Download** button underneath the

ZoneAlarm product. From the screen that appears, click the **Download free ZoneAlarm** link and follow the instructions for downloading and installing the program.

When you first install ZoneAlarm, a screen appears asking you to choose ZoneAlarm Pro or ZoneAlarm. If you choose ZoneAlarm Pro, you can try it out for 15 days. After 15 days, you can either pay for it or switch to ZoneAlarm for free.

Whichever product you choose, the basic firewall works the same. Choose the product you want to install and click **Next**; then click **Finish**. The ZoneAlarm firewall is now installed on your computer.

2 Set Firewall Alerts

When ZoneAlarm launches, you're asked whether ZoneAlarm should alert you whenever it blocks any inbound traffic—that is, attempts to connect to your computer—or only the traffic that appears to be hacker-like activity. Choose **Alert me whenever ZoneAlarm blocks traffic** if you want to get all alerts; choose **Don't alert me at all – protect my computer silently** if you don't want to be notified of the firewall's activity. Click **Finish**.

3 Configure ZoneAlarm for Your Browser

The next screen that appears asks whether ZoneAlarm should allow your browser to access the Web. It checks your system to determine your default browser and automatically configures ZoneAlarm to allow it to access the Internet, if you tell it to do so. Choose **Yes** if you want ZoneAlarm to allow the named browser to access the Internet; choose **No** if you want to be alerted every time your browser and its components try to access the Internet. You can also choose **Advanced** to fine-tune the way the browser accesses the Internet. After you've made your choice, click **Finish**.

4 Configure eBay Fraud Protection

The next screen that appears helps protect eBay users from fraud. If you want ZoneAlarm to check that whenever you send an eBay password, it's only to a true eBay site, click **Yes**, enter your eBay password, confirm the password, and click **Next**.

The next several screens give you a basic ZoneAlarm tutorial. Click **Next** to move from screen to screen until you get to the final screen. Then click **Finish**. ZoneAlarm launches and begins protecting you.

TIP

If you want a free firewall, don't download the **ZoneAlarm Pro** or **ZoneAlarm Pro and PestPatrol Special** products, because those two require that you pay for them.

NOTE

eBay users are often the targets of fraud attacks called "phishing" in which a scam email is sent, claiming that eBay needs to verify your personal information, including your eBay password. The mail seems to be from eBay, and when you visit the site the mail sends you to, the site appears to be an eBay site. But, in fact, the site is fraudulent and is used to collect eBay passwords.

① Download and Install ZoneAlarm

③ Configure ZoneAlarm for Your Browser

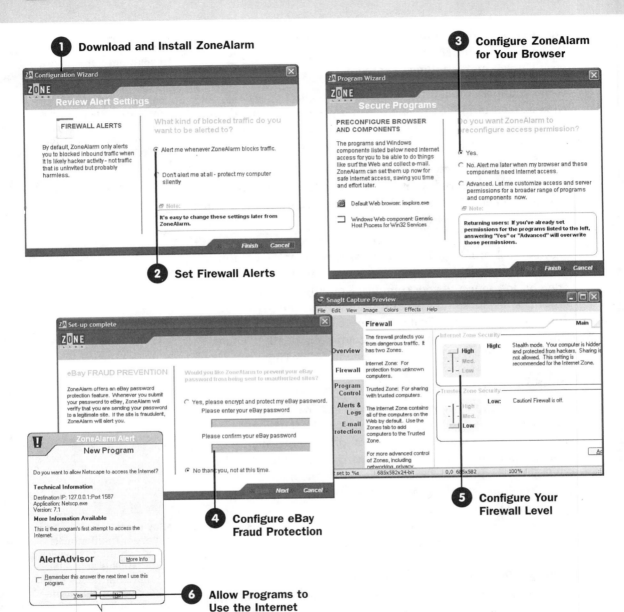

② Set Firewall Alerts

④ Configure eBay Fraud Protection

⑤ Configure Your Firewall Level

⑥ Allow Programs to Use the Internet

5 **Configure Your Firewall Level**

ZoneAlarm's main screen appears. You can customize your level of protection with it. Click the **Firewall** tab on the left side of the screen. You'll find two "zones" that the firewall can use—the **Internet Zone** and the **Trusted Zone**. The **Internet Zone Security** section contains settings for when you use the Internet. The **Trusted Zone Security** section has settings for use on a network, such as a home network. You can change the settings in each section.

The zones have three levels of security: **Low**, **Medium**, and **High**. The **Low** setting actually provides no protection at all—the firewall is turned off. The **Medium** setting allows your computer to be seen by others, but its resources are blocked from external access. On the **High** setting, the firewall blocks access to your PC, and so in essence your computer is invisible on the Internet. You should choose **High** for the **Internet Zone**, and **Low** for the **Trusted Zone** if you're on a network.

6 **Allow Programs to Use the Internet**

As with Windows XP's default firewall, ZoneAlarm blocks programs from accessing the Internet unless you tell it to let them through. Whenever you launch a program that attempts to contact the Internet, ZoneAlarm pops up an alert asking whether you want to let the program access the Internet. If you click **Yes**, the program is allowed to access the Internet; if you click **No**, the program won't be allowed to access the Internet. When you click **No**, the program is put on a blocked list of programs, and cannot connect to the Internet. When you click **Yes**, the program can access the Internet *only this once*, and the same alert pops up the next time you use the program. However, if you want the program to always be able to use the Internet, enable the **Remember this answer the next time I use this computer** check box before clicking **Yes**, and the program is put on a list of programs that are allowed to access the Internet.

Even after programs have been allowed to use the Internet or have been banned from using the Internet, you can change their settings. For example, if you banned an instant messaging program, but later decide you want to allow it, you can do that. You can also ban programs from using the Internet that you've already allowed.

To do both, first click the ZoneAlarm icon in the Windows XP taskbar (the icon looks like a small Zone logo) to launch the program's main screen. Click the **Program Control** tab on the left side of the screen, and then click the **Programs** tab. You'll see a list of programs you've stopped from using the Internet and those programs you've allowed to use the Internet. Green check marks appear next to programs you've allowed to use the Internet; red **X**s appear next to programs you've banned from using the Internet; and question marks appear next to programs you've said should ask before using the Internet. Click the check mark, **X**, or question mark to display a pop-up list with a check mark, **X**, and question mark on it. Choose from that pop-up list how you want ZoneAlarm to treat the program, and then minimize ZoneAlarm. The new settings go into immediate effect.

70 Stop Pop-Ups

See Also

→ **72** About Internet Security Levels

→ **73** Protect Your Privacy by Managing Your Cookies

What frustrates you the most out of browsing the Web? If you're like most people, the answer is a simple one: ads that pop up over your browser when you visit websites. It's not uncommon to encounter many dozens of these ads a day, and some websites by themselves might pop up a dozen of them.

The version of Internet Explorer in the Service Pack 2 (SP-2) version of Windows XP includes a built-in pop-up blocker that lets you block these ads, and you'll learn how do that in this task. To find out whether you have SP-2 installed on your system, see **67** **Protect Yourself with the Windows Firewall**.

➊ Turn On Pop-Up Blocking

Pop-up blocking is turned on in Internet Explorer automatically, but there is a chance that for some reason yours has been turned off. To check, choose **Tools**, **Pop-Up Blocker** from the menu. If it is turned off, you will see a check mark next to **Turn off Pop-Up Blocker**. To turn on the pop-up blocker, click the check mark to disable it. Pop-ups will now be blocked.

➋ Watch for Blocked Pop-Ups

When Internet Explorer blocks a pop-up, you'll hear a small popping sound, and a message appears in the **Information** bar, just below the Address bar, reading **A pop-up was blocked. To see this pop-up or additional options, click here.**

If you want to see the pop-up that was blocked, click the message and choose **Show Blocked Pop-up**.

③ Allow Pop-Ups from a Site

There are some sites on which you'll want to allow pop-ups. For example, some sites use pop-ups to launch a log-in screen or an extra, smaller browser window with information you want to view. To allow pop-ups on just the site you're visiting, but not on other sites, when you're on the site, click the **Information** bar and choose **Allow Pop-ups from this Site**. A confirmation screen appears, asking whether you want to allow pop-ups from the site. Click **OK**, and the pop-ups will be allowed, but only on this site, and not on all sites. The **Information** bar also disappears.

If you later want to block pop-ups from this site, choose **Tools, Pop-up Blocker** from the menu and choose **Block Pop-ups from this Site**.

④ Display Pop-Up Blocker Settings

You can further customize the way that the pop-up blocker works. To do it, open the **Pop-up Blocker Settings** dialog box by clicking the **Information** bar and choosing **Pop-up Blocker Settings**. If the **Information** bar isn't displayed, you can open the dialog box by choosing **Tools, Pop-up Blocker Settings** from the menu.

⑤ Customize Pop-Up Blocker Settings

From the **Pop-up Blocker Settings** dialog box, you can add new sites from which you want to allow pop-ups, stop pop-ups from sites you previously said to allow pop-ups from, and set several other options.

To add a site from which you want to allow pop-ups, type its URL into the **Address of Web site to allow** text box near the top of the screen and click the **Add** button. The specified site is added to the **Allowed sites** list. To stop allowing pop-ups from a site, click its URL in the **Allowed sites** list and click the **Remove** button.

If you don't want to hear the small popping sound when a pop-up is blocked, disable the **Play a sound when a pop-up is blocked** check box.

NOTE

The bar that appears under the Address bar when a pop-up is blocked is called the **Information** bar.

2 Watch for Blocked Pop-Ups

1 Turn On Pop-Up Blocking

5 Customize Pop-Up Blocker Settings

4 Display Pop-Up Blocker Settings

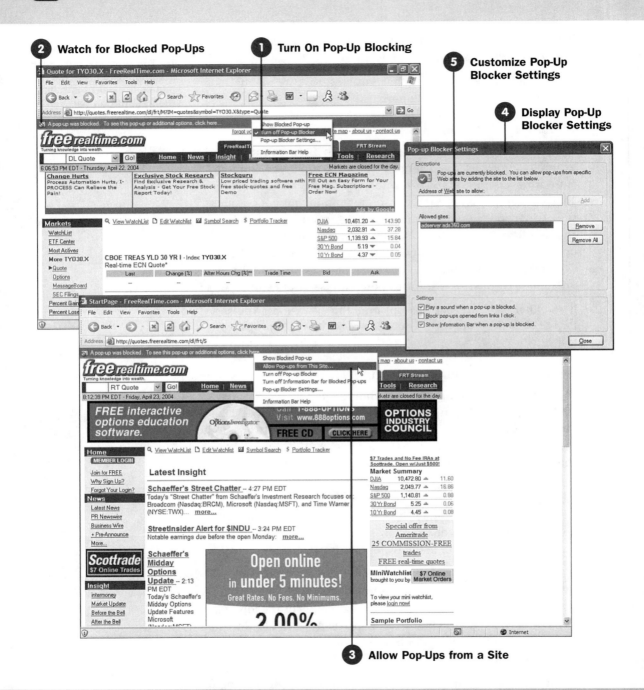

3 Allow Pop-Ups from a Site

On some websites, when you click a link, a new browser window opens up, and sends you to the linked location. The pop-up blocker will block these kinds of links from opening, but in many instances, you want them to open, because the pop-ups are frequently not ads, but instead websites you want to visit. To allow these kinds of pop-ups, disable the **Block pop-ups opened from links I click** check box.

If you don't want the **Information** bar to appear when a pop-up is blocked, disable the **Show Information Bar when a pop-up is blocked** check box.

 TIP

If you don't have the SP-2 version of Windows XP, you can still block pop-up ads by downloading a free pop-up blocker. The Google toolbar blocks pop-up ads, in addition to letting you get more out of Google. Get it from **http://toolbar.google.com**.

71 Find and Kill Spyware

The latest threat to using computers on the Internet is so-called *spyware*, software that silently watches what you do and reports that information to a computer or person somewhere across the Internet. Some spyware can even hijack your computer.

There is a great debate about exactly what spyware is, and whether particular pieces of software should even be called spyware. As a general rule, though, these are the basic kinds of spyware:

- **Software that watches your surfing habits and reports those habits to an Internet server.** (This kind of spyware is sometimes called adware.) The server then examines your surfing habits, and sends you advertising in pop-up windows based on where you surf. This kind of spyware is often installed on your computer when you download a separate free piece of software. For example, the Kazaa music-sharing software carries a spyware payload along with it. The ads delivered to your computer when you use Kazaa are delivered through the spyware. This kind of spyware is not malicious and does not actually harm your computer, but it can invade your privacy and is very intrusive.

- **Software called "drive-by downloads" or "hijackers."** This kind of software can, in essence, hijack your browser so that you're forced to visit a certain home page every time you open your browser. It causes browser windows to constantly pop up, and can even alter your search results when you visit a site such as Google. This kind of software is malicious and can harm your computer.

See Also

→ **74** Protect Yourself Against Viruses

→ **75** Protect Yourself Against Email Worms

KEY TERM

Spyware—Software that watches your Internet habits or computer use and then reports that information to a person or a computer on the Internet. There are many different kinds of spyware; some is used for relatively benign purposes such as delivering targeted advertising; others serve malicious purposes such as damaging your computer or reporting every keystroke you make.

- **"Key-loggers" that record every keystroke you make on your computer and then send that information to someone on the Internet.** By recording your keystrokes, the spyware can see everything you do on your computer. This kind of spyware is exceedingly rare. It has sometimes been used by law enforcement agencies in criminal investigations—the key-logger is put on a suspect's computer, and the investigators can then watch what the person does at his computer.

TIP

Even if someone you do know sends you a link or program, contact that person first before installing the program or clicking the link, because a piece of spyware could have taken over their email software or instant messaging program, and could be trying to spread itself.

➊ Protect Yourself from Downloading Spyware

In computing, as in football, the best offense is a good defense. It's better not to get spyware in the first place than to clean it out after you've gotten it. Don't download any software sent to you from people you don't know, and don't click any links sent to you in email messages or from instant messaging programs from people you don't know.

Also avoid clicking links in pop-up ads. A common ploy for installing spyware is to automatically install software when you click a link. (For more information about blocking pop-ups, see **70** Stop Pop-Ups.)

➋ Install Anti-Spyware Software

You might have spyware on your system without knowing it. To make sure that you're spyware-free, install anti-spyware software. There are many different programs available, some free and some for pay. A very good free one is Ad-aware. To download it, go to **www.lavasoftusa.com**. Click the **Ad-aware** link on the left side of the screen. There are also links to **Ad-aware Plus** and **Ad-aware Professional**, but those are the for-pay versions of the software, and you only need the free version.

NOTE

The primary benefit of the Plus edition of Ad-aware is that it monitors your system, warns you if any spyware is being installed, and lets you stop the installation; it costs $26.95. The Professional version includes the features of the Plus edition as well as tools for protecting networks from spyware; it costs $39.95.

From the page that appears, go to the **Download** section and click the **Our Software** link. Scroll to the bottom of the next page that appears, click the **Full Install** link, and then follow the directions for downloading and installing the software.

After you've installed the Ad-aware software, double-click the **Ad-aware** icon on your desktop. Alternatively, click the **Start** button and choose **Ad-aware** from the **All Programs** menu. The Ad-aware program launches.

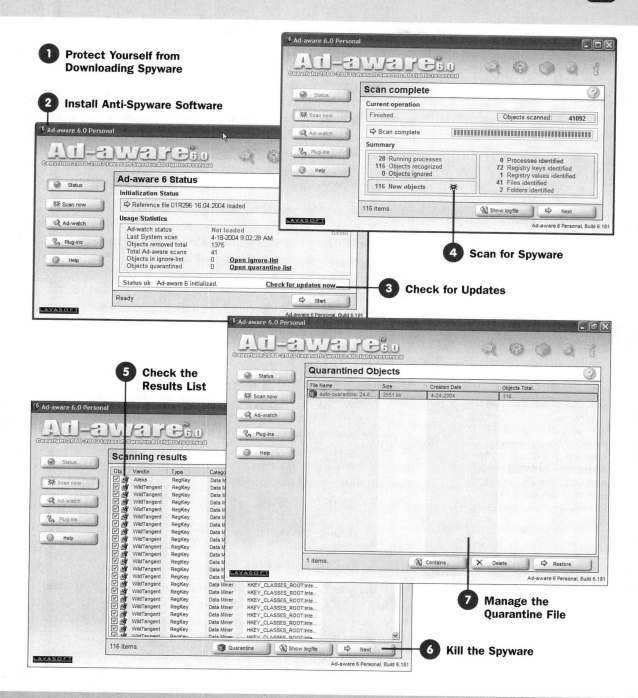

1 Protect Yourself from Downloading Spyware

2 Install Anti-Spyware Software

4 Scan for Spyware

3 Check for Updates

5 Check the Results List

7 Manage the Quarantine File

6 Kill the Spyware

③ Check for Updates

New spyware is constantly being released, and to detect and kill these new programs, Ad-aware must continually update its reference file, which contains information about the newest spyware. Even though you've just downloaded the program, new reference files might be available. Before you scan your system for spyware, check for the newest reference file by clicking the **Check for updates now** link on the opening screen. You must be connected to the Internet to check for updates, so make sure that you're connected.

From the screen that appears, click **Connect**. Ad-aware checks whether there is a newer reference file available. If a new reference file is available, a screen appears, asking whether you want to download and install the file. Click **OK**. Ad-aware downloads the file, showing you the download progress. When it's done, the screen tells you that the update is complete. Click **Finish**. You'll be sent back to the main Ad-aware screen that appears when you first launch the program.

④ Scan for Spyware

TIP

Spyware objects can be programs, folders that contain potential spyware, Registry keys (Registry keys control much of the operations of Windows XP, and software can install its own Registry keys in Windows XP), or files.

To check your system for spyware, click the **Start** button at the bottom of the main Ad-aware screen. From the screen that appears, choose **Perform smart system-scan** and click **Next**. Ad-aware begins scanning your computer's hard disk for spyware. The scan takes several minutes; the time depends on how many files you have on your hard disk and how fast your processor is. As it scans, the program reports its progress to you, including how many potential spyware "objects" it has identified and of what type they are. When the program has finished scanning, it gives you a summary of its findings.

⑤ Check the Results List

From the screen summarizing Ad-aware's findings, click the **Next** button. You'll see a screen that shows the exact results of the scan. It lists every object that it identifies as being spyware, and a description of each object. A check mark is placed next to every object. The program will delete all objects with check marks next to them. Examine the list of objects, to see whether any appear not to be spyware. It might be hard for you to determine whether any objects are not spyware, but look to see if you find anything famil-iar that you know is not spyware, and disable the check box next to it. Leave the other check boxes enabled.

6 Kill the Spyware

When you're done checking the results list, click **Next**. You'll get a message asking whether the spyware should be removed. Click **OK**. Ad-aware will show its progress as it removes the spyware from your computer's hard disk. Actually, it puts the spyware into "quarantine." This means that it removes the spyware, but puts it in a special location, so that if for some reason the removal has damaged your system, you can restore everything that Ad-aware removed.

7 Manage the Quarantine File

When the spyware has been quarantined, you return to Ad-aware's main screen. You can now exit the program; the spyware has been removed. If you notice problems with your PC, you can restore everything that Ad-aware removed: Run Ad-aware, and from the main screen, click the **Open Quarantine list** link. You'll see a file that contains all the items that Ad-aware removed. Highlight it and click **Restore** to put the items back onto your system.

However, if you know that your computer runs correctly after the spyware has been quarantined, you can remove the quarantined items. To do that, run Ad-aware, click the **Open Quarantine list** link on the main screen, highlight the quarantine file, and click **Delete**.

72 About Internet Security Levels

It can be dangerous to surf the Web—malicious but safe-appearing web-sites may try to damage your PC without your knowledge. When you're in the real world, it's easy to know how to keep away from the more dangerous parts of town, but it's not so easy to do that on the Web. A friendly appearing, friendly looking Web front door might disguise a site that wants to do you harm.

See Also

→ **73** Protect Your Privacy by Managing Your Cookies

KEY TERM

ActiveX control—A small piece of software that downloads from a website to your PC and runs inside your browser. ActiveX controls often add interactivity to websites. Most are safe, but some are malicious.

KEY TERM

Java applet—A small piece of software that downloads from a website to your PC and runs inside your browser. Written with the Java language, they frequently add interactivity to websites. Most are safe, but some are malicious.

There are several dangers in particular you need to be wary of:

- **ActiveX controls.** This is a kind of small program that can be downloaded from the Internet to your PC. It runs inside a browser and often adds some kind of interactivity to a website. For example, some security-related websites include *ActiveX controls* that can scan your computer for viruses. However, ActiveX controls have the potential to do damage to your computer as well.

  There are two types of ActiveX controls: signed and unsigned. A signed control is one that has been submitted to what's called a certificate authority, and that authority guarantees that the ActiveX control is from the company that claims created it. In other words, if you run a signed ActiveX control that claims it's from Microsoft, it's guaranteed that the control is actually from Microsoft. If you trust the company that created the signed control, you can trust the control. An unsigned ActiveX control is one that has not been sent to a certificate authority. That means that there's no way for you to know who actually created the control. It's potentially dangerous to run unsigned ActiveX controls.

- **Java applets.** Like types of ActiveX controls, *Java applets* are small programs that download from a website to your PC and run inside your browser to add interactivity to a website. They use the Java programming language. Most are safe, but the applets can be malicious as well.

- **Downloadable software.** As you browse the Web, you'll come across many programs you can download. For example, as outlined in **69 Protect Yourself with a Better Free Firewall**, you can download the free personal firewall ZoneAlarm. But some software you download can be malicious.

To help protect you from malicious software downloads, Internet Explorer includes a variety of security controls over ActiveX controls, Java applets, and downloadable software. Internet Explorer has several different security levels that treat all of these categories slightly differently: **Low**, **Medium-Low**, **Medium**, and **High**. The **Low** option offers the lowest level of security and offers the most freedom to run ActiveX controls and Java applets and to download software. The **High** option offers the highest level of security and restricts how you can run ActiveX controls and Java applets, and download software.

You must decide which level of security is best for you by balancing your need for security against the freedom to use the Web. Most people use the **Medium** setting. If you generally visit popular, well-known websites, this setting should work well. However, if you're very worried about security, you should use the **High** setting. (It's not a good idea to use the **Low** setting. That one is generally best if you visit only the sites inside a safe network, for example, visiting web locations inside your corporate network.)

The following chart explains how each level handles security:

Security Zone Setting	How the Setting Affects Security
High	Disables most features, including ActiveX controls and Java applets, and won't let you download software.
Medium	Asks before running signed ActiveX controls; disables running unsigned ActiveX controls and certain other ActiveX controls; allows downloads and Java applets; prompts before letting you download potentially unsafe content.
Medium-Low	Most settings are the same as **Medium**, except that this setting will run certain controls and applets without first asking you.
Low	Runs all active content; has the minimum number of safeguards and prompts.

TIP

As a default, Internet Explorer is set to **Medium**. If you want to change the setting, choose **Tools**, **Internet Options** from the menu to open the **Security Settings** dialog box and click the **Security** tab. Click the **Internet** icon and then click **Custom Level**. From the **Reset to** drop-down list at the bottom of the screen, choose the level you want and click **OK**. Then click **OK** again. You don't have to restart Internet Explorer; the new setting goes into immediate effect.

*From this screen, change your Internet security level by choosing the level you want to use from the **Reset to** drop-down list box.*

73 Protect Your Privacy by Managing Your Cookies

Before You Begin

✔ **54** Clean Up Cookies and Delete Temporary Files

See Also

→ **72** About Internet Security Levels

Cookies are bits of data that Internet sites put on your PC as you browse the Web so that sites can track your use of the site or provide services to you such as customized views or automatic logins.

Cookies are controversial because they can be used to invade your privacy. But they're useful as well, because they can help you customize how you use a site (for example, telling it to always display information about your specific interests or automatically logging you into the site).

Ideally, you'd like to accept only those cookies that are helpful, and ban those that invade your privacy. Windows XP's Internet Explorer gives you ways to do that, as you'll see in this task.

❶ Understand Cookie Jargon

Before you can learn how to control your cookies, you must learn a bit of cookie jargon. In particular, you should understand these three cookie-related terms:

- **First-party cookie.** This cookie is created by the site you're currently visiting. It is often used to let you log on automatically without having to type your user name and password, or to customize how you use the site. These kinds of cookies do not usually invade your privacy and are generally considered safe.

- **Third-party cookie.** This cookie is created by a site other than the one you're currently visiting. It is often used by advertisers or advertising networks to identify you and track your surfing activities. Some people consider these kinds of cookies invasive.

- **Compact Privacy Statement.** This policy describes how cookies are used on a site, for example, explaining why and how cookies are used on the site and how long they will stay on your PC. (Some cookies are automatically deleted when you leave a website, while others stay alive until a specified date.)

You also need to know the difference between *implicit consent* and *explicit consent*. Explicit consent means that you have specifically told a site that it can use personally identifying information about you. Implicit consent means that you haven't specifically told a site not to use personally identifiable information.

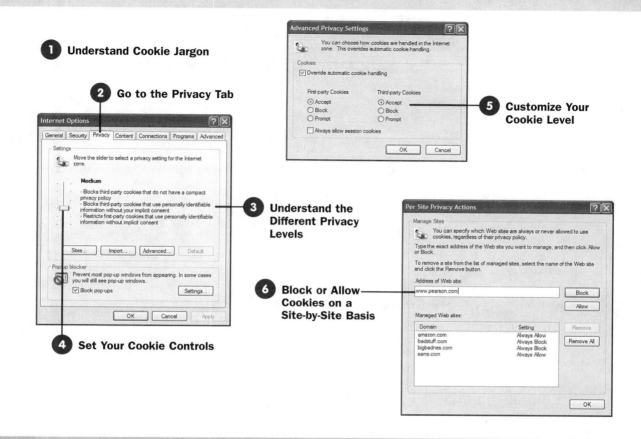

1 Understand Cookie Jargon

2 Go to the Privacy Tab

3 Understand the Different Privacy Levels

4 Set Your Cookie Controls

5 Customize Your Cookie Level

6 Block or Allow Cookies on a Site-by-Site Basis

2 **Go to the Privacy Tab**

You control how you want to treat cookies from the **Privacy** tab of the **Internet Options** dialog box. Choose **Tools, Internet Options** from the menu and click the **Privacy** tab.

3 **Understand the Different Privacy Levels**

The **Privacy** tab lets you control how you want to handle your cookies by choosing from several settings: **Accept All Cookies**, **Low**, **Medium**, **Medium-High**, **High**, and **Block All Cookies**. The following chart explains how each level controls cookies.

Setting	How the Setting Affects Cookies
Block All Cookies	Blocks all cookies, without exception.
	Does not allow websites to read existing cookies.
High	Blocks cookies from all websites that don't have a compact privacy policy.
	Blocks all cookies that use personally identifying information without your explicit consent.
Medium High	Blocks third-party cookies from sites that don't have a compact privacy policy.
	Blocks third-party cookies that use personally identifying information without your explicit consent.
	Blocks first-party cookies that use personally identifying information without your implicit consent.
Medium (Default)	Blocks third-party cookies from sites that don't have a compact privacy policy.
	Blocks third-party cookies that use personally identifying information without your implicit consent.
	Accepts first-party cookies that use personally identifying information without your implicit consent, but deletes them when you close Internet Explorer.
Low	Blocks third-party cookies from sites that don't have a compact privacy policy.
	Accepts third-party cookies that use personally identifying information without your implicit consent, but deletes them when you close Internet Explorer.
Accept All Cookies	Accepts all cookies, without exception.
	Allows websites to read existing cookies.

4 Set Your Cookie Controls

The default setting for handling cookies is **Medium**. To change how Internet Explorer handles cookies, move the slider to another level and click **OK**. The setting goes into immediate effect. Most people find that **Medium** or **Medium-High** is a good setting because they protect your privacy but still allow cookies that help you get the most out of the Web.

5 Customize Your Cookie Level

You can customize the way Internet Explorer handles cookies to be exactly the way you want. For example, perhaps you want to use the **Low** setting, but want slightly stricter settings. To do that, on the **Privacy** tab of the **Internet Options** dialog box, click the **Advanced** button. The **Advanced Privacy Settings** dialog box appears. Enable the **Override automatic cookie handling** check box and then select how you want to handle first-party cookies and third-party cookies. Click **OK** and then click **OK** again. The settings go into immediate effect.

6 Block or Allow Cookies on a Site-by-Site Basis

You can set cookie controls on a site-by-site basis. So no matter what your cookie settings, you can decide to always allow cookies from some sites and always block them from another site. For example, you might have a **High** cookie control setting, but want to allow cookies from certain sites so that you can always sign into them automatically and use their customization features. Or you might have a **Low** setting and want to ban cookies from certain sites that you know invade your privacy.

From the **Privacy** tab of the **Internet Options** dialog box, click the **Sites** button. The **Per Site Privacy Actions** dialog box appears. Type the address of the website you want to block or allow into the **Address of Web site** text box. Click the **Block** button if you want the cookies blocked from this site; click the **Allow** button if you want the cookies allowed from the site. Each site you choose to block or allow is listed in the **Managed Web sites** area.

When you're done, click **OK** and then click **OK** again. The settings go into immediate effect.

 TIP

If you change your security level to a higher level than it currently is, you might find that you can't use some websites or that you might not be automatically logged into them. If that happens to you, change your security level back to the way it was before those problems occurred.

74 Protect Yourself Against Viruses

NOTE

Even if someone you know has sent you a file, you still shouldn't open it unless she's told you that she's sending it to you, or unless you contact her and ask whether she's sent the file. Some viruses take over a person's email program and send out copies of itself in that person's name. If that happens, you could get a file from your friend, but that file could be infected with a virus.

TIP

Norton Anti-Virus and McAfee Anti-Virus are the two most popular antivirus programs, and both are excellent. Get them at retail stores or at **www.symantec.com** or **www.mcafee.com**.

Like it or not, computer viruses are a danger we all live with. When a virus infects your PC, it might do as much damage as deleting all the important files from your hard disk, or it might do no damage at all, perhaps just displaying an annoying pop-up screen.

Although viruses are dangerous, they are also very easy to avoid. As you'll see in this task, if you take the right steps, it is incredibly unlikely that your PC will ever be infected by one.

1 Take Basic Precautions

The first and most important step you can take to protect yourself against viruses is to learn when you should open files and when you shouldn't.

Cardinal rule number one is to never open a file that someone you don't know has sent to you over email or with an instant messaging program. There's simply no way to know whether the file contains a virus or not.

2 Install Antivirus Software

Every computer should run antivirus software. Antivirus software checks programs as they run to see whether they contain viruses. If the programs do contain viruses, the antivirus program warns you and then gets rid of the virus.

Install antivirus software according to the instructions and then run the program. In this task, you'll see how to use Norton Anti-Virus to protect your PC, but McAfee works in a similar manner.

3 Check for Updates

New viruses are released all the time. Antivirus software can keep you protected from new viruses only if you get new virus definitions—information that tells the antivirus software how to detect the new viruses. Virus definitions are constantly being released, and so when you first install your antivirus software, it won't contain the most up-to-date virus definitions.

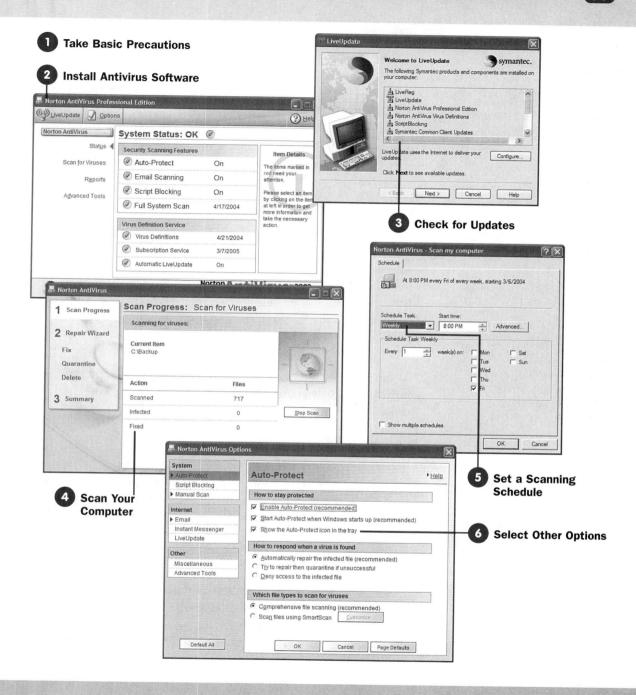

1 Take Basic Precautions

2 Install Antivirus Software

3 Check for Updates

4 Scan Your Computer

5 Set a Scanning Schedule

6 Select Other Options

NOTE

You must be connected to the Internet for the antivirus software to check for updates, so make sure to connect to the Internet before checking for updates.

To check for new virus definitions with Norton, click the **Live Update** button near the top of the main screen. A screen appears, welcoming you to **Live Update**. Click the **Next** button. The program checks for new virus definitions and also checks whether there are any updates to the antivirus program itself.

Live Update shows you its progress in searching for updates and then shows you if there are any updates or new virus definitions to install. If there are, click the **Next** button and follow the installation instructions. If you're only installing new virus definitions, you won't have to restart your computer at the end. But if you're updating the program itself, you might have to restart your computer.

❹ Scan Your Computer

After the most recent virus definitions are in place, you should scan your PC for viruses. From the main screen, click the **Scan for Viruses** link on the left side of the screen. From the screen that appears, click the **Scan my computer** option. The software scans your PC for viruses. You can use your computer while it does this, although it will slow down your system as it scans.

At the end of scanning, Norton reports what it found. If there are no viruses, it tells you so. If it finds viruses, it asks whether it should fix the problem. Tell it to fix the problem, and then follow any prompts it gives you.

❺ Set a Scanning Schedule

It can be easy to forget to scan your computer regularly for viruses, and so you should have the antivirus software scan for viruses on its own, automatically. Antivirus developers recommend a once-a-week schedule. Pick a time and day of the week when you know your computer will be turned on, but when you are not likely to be using it.

To set a schedule, from the left side of the main screen, click the **Scan for Viruses** link. On the right side of the **Scan my computer** line, under the **Task Schedule** heading, click the icon of a clock. In the dialog box that opens, choose the schedule (weekly, monthly, and so on) from the **Schedule Task** drop-down list and then choose a start time, day of the week, and so on. Click **OK** when you're done. The antivirus software will now scan your PC for viruses on the schedule you set for it.

⑥ Select Other Options

For maximum protection, there are several options you should configure correctly. Go back to the main screen and then make sure that you have these settings turned on:

- **Enable Auto-Protect.** Make sure that this option is enabled. When it is, the program scans for viruses in every program and potentially dangerous file as you open it—that way, a virus can't infect your PC.

- **Enable Email Scanning.** Make sure that this option is enabled. When it is, Norton scans incoming and outgoing email for viruses.

- **Script Blocking.** Make sure that this option is enabled. Scripts are mini-programs that can be run from email and from websites and that can damage your computer.

- **Automatic LiveUpdate.** Make sure that this option is enabled. Your antivirus software will automatically check for new virus definitions and keep itself up to date without you having to do anything.

TIP

If any are of these options are disabled, click the **Options** button at the top of the main screen. The **Norton Anti-Virus Options** screen appears. From here you can change your options to keep yourself protected. Follow the onscreen instructions for doing so.

75 Protect Yourself Against Email Worms

An *email worm* is a special kind of virus designed to infect network email programs, notably Outlook and Outlook Express. You get a worm by opening a file sent to you by someone as an email attachment, and often the person who sent you the file appears to be someone you know. In fact, however, the email containing the worm was sent out without your friend's knowledge, because your friend's computer was infected by the worm, and the worm sent out the email.

Different worms work differently, but as a general rule, when you open a file containing one, it infects your PC, looks through your address book, and then mails copies of itself to many or all the people in your address book. It mails itself out as an email attachment, but it disguises itself in the attachment, often appearing to be a picture or some other innocuous file. The subject line might sound like a personal message—for example, "**Check this out!**" or "**Thought you might like to see this <g>**".

Before You Begin

✔ **74** Protect Yourself Against Viruses

See Also

→ **82** About Dealing with Attachments

KEY TERM

Email worm—A malicious program that takes over your email program and mails copies of itself to people in your address book without your knowledge. Those people's computers in turn are infected, and infect others. The worm can also do damage to your computer.

1 **Don't Open Files You Aren't Expecting**

2 **Install Antivirus Software**

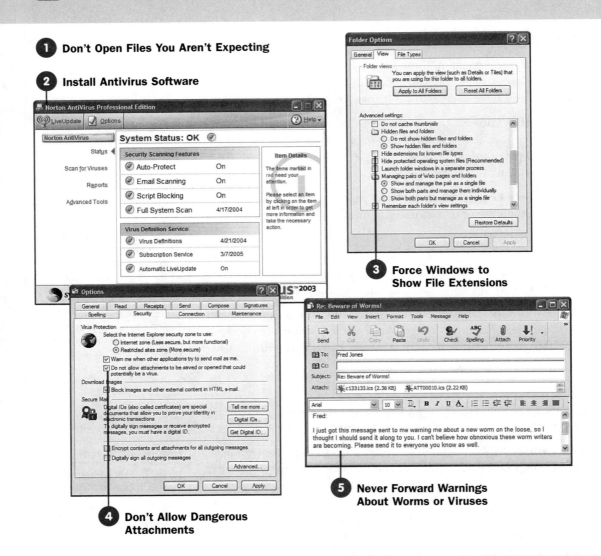

3 **Force Windows to Show File Extensions**

5 **Never Forward Warnings About Worms or Viruses**

4 **Don't Allow Dangerous Attachments**

When your friend opens the attachment, her computer is infected without her knowledge, and then the worm mails itself out to others. Sometimes the worm can also do damage to the computers it infects. But it's easy to protect yourself against worms, as you'll see in this task.

1 Don't Open Files You Aren't Expecting

Because worms are contained in files that appear to be from friends or acquaintances, and appear to contain personal messages, you will be caught off-guard when one is sent to you. If you're not expecting a file from someone, don't open it. And even if you are expecting a file, contact your friend and ask whether he sent you a file recently. If he didn't, delete the email.

2 Install Antivirus Software

Antivirus software such as that from Norton or Symantec can scan all your incoming email and tell you whether any messages contain worms. If the antivirus software finds a worm, it deletes the worm. Follow the steps in **74** **Protect Yourself Against Viruses** to install antivirus software and turn on its email protection.

3 Force Windows to Show File Extensions

Worm-writers are very tricky, and go to great lengths to disguise the fact that a worm is being sent over email. Frequently, the file being sent looks as if it is a graphics file, ending in a **.jpg** or **.gif** extension. However, it really isn't that kind of file, it only appears to be that way. The file might look to you to be **mypics.jpg**, but in reality might be named **mypics.jpg.exe**—and a file that ends in **.exe** is a program file and can contain a virus.

There's a way you can see the real name of any file sent to you as an email attachment, however. Run Windows Explorer, then select **Tools, Folder Options** from the menu. When the **Folder Options** dialog box appears, click the **View** tab. Disable the **Hide File Extensions for Known File Types** check box. Click **OK**. From now on, whenever a file is sent to you over email, you'll be able to see its true extension. The following are potentially dangerous file extensions, so be wary about opening any files with these extensions:

.ade, .adp, .asx, .bas, .bat, .chm, .cmd, .com, .cpl, .crt, .exe, .hlp, .hta, .inf, .ins, .isp, .js, .jse, .lnk, .mda, .mdb, .mde, .mdt, .mdw, .mdz, .msc, .msi, .msp, .mst, .ops, .pcs, .pif, .prf, .reg, .scf, .scr, .sct, .shb, .shs, .url, .vb, .vbs, .wsc, .wsf, .wsh

NOTE

Some *firewalls*, such as ZoneAlarm, also scan incoming email for worms, so if you have a personal firewall, turn on its email protection as well. See **69** **Protect Yourself with a Better Free Firewall** for more information about installing a firewall.

4 Don't Allow Dangerous Attachments

To be even safer, you can tell Outlook Express not to let through any attachments that could be potentially dangerous. Outlook Express doesn't actually examine the contents of each attachment (as does antivirus software). Instead, it blocks all files that have an extension indicating a program that could potentially infect your computer, such as those extensions listed in step 3.

To tell Outlook Express not to accept dangerous attachments, first launch Outlook Express. Choose **Tools**, **Options** from the menu; when the **Options** dialog box opens, click the **Security** tab. Then enable the **Do not allow attachments to be saved or opened that could potentially be a virus** check box. Click **OK**. From now on, email attachments with potentially harmful contents will be blocked.

5 Never Forward Warnings About Worms or Viruses

Frequently, virus and worm writers use a confidence trick to help spread their viruses. They'll create a worm and attach it to a message that warns people to watch out for worms or viruses—but the attachment is a worm itself! Never forward these kinds of messages.

10

Email and Instant Messaging

IN THIS CHAPTER:

Probably more than any other part of the Internet, email has changed how we live. It may be entertaining or informative to visit a web page, but sending and receiving email is about something far more important—communicating with others.

Email isn't the only way that people communicate over the Internet. Increasingly popular is *instant messaging*, which isn't just for teens and kids anymore: It's for parents, to keep in touch with kids in college and at home; for friends, to keep in touch with each other; and is increasingly even for co-workers as a productivity booster. Instant messaging is great when people need information instantly, but don't want to have to spend the time on a phone call.

Windows XP ships with free software for using email and instant messaging. Outlook Express, even though it's free, is a surprisingly useful and powerful piece of email software. As you'll see in this chapter, there are a lot of ways you can use Outlook Express to make your life easier. Read on to see how to get more out of Outlook Express and how to teach it some new tricks.

For instant messaging, the Windows Messenger instant messenger program comes pre-installed with Windows XP. In this chapter, you'll learn how to get the most out of it as well.

76 Customize Outlook Express

See Also

→ **77** Create a Personal Signature

→ **78** Create an Email Business Card

→ **79** Use Multiple Email Accounts

→ **80** Organize Your Mailboxes

→ **81** Automate Your Mail Handling by Creating Mail Rules

→ **82** About Dealing with Attachments

Outlook Express, email software that ships with every version of Windows XP, takes some getting used to—you can use it in many different ways, with its many different views and features. That's both its strength and its weakness.

It can be confusing to figure out how to bend the email software to your will, though. If you follow these steps, you'll have it working exactly the way you want it.

❶ Choose the Bars to Display

When you run Outlook Express for the first time, it practically bristles with bars and buttons. It's unlikely that you'll want to use all of them, but you'll certainly want to use some.

You can easily change the basic view you use whenever you run Outlook Express—in other words, which bars you want to be displayed. To do that, run Outlook Express and choose **View, Layout** from the menu. The **Window Layout Properties** dialog box appears.

In the **Basic** section, you have a choice of turning on or off seven parts of the Outlook Express interface. To turn a part on, put a check mark in the box next to the option name; to turn it off, remove the check mark.

The **Contacts** option shows your list of contacts (your address book in which are listed all the addresses to whom you send email). If this option is enabled, you can double-click a contact to create an email message to him. If you have many contacts, displaying the Contacts list can take up a good portion of your screen.

The **Folder Bar** option shows you what folder you're currently in. However, you can also see what folder you're in by looking in the **Folders** list—the folder you're in is highlighted. If you want more screen real estate, you don't need to display this bar.

The **Folder List** option shows you the list of folders in Outlook Express and lets you easily navigate among them. It's the easiest way to get around Outlook Express, so it's a good idea to always display this list.

The **Outlook Bar** is an easy way to jump from folder to folder because it has your favorite locations on it. But it takes up a lot of screen real estate, is distracting, and isn't that much easier to use than the **Folders** list. Consider not displaying it, because it doesn't serve an especially useful function.

The **Status Bar** is the strip along the bottom of Outlook Express that displays some messages such as whether you're online or offline and the number of messages you have. It doesn't take up extra space and is often useful, so leave this option enabled.

The **Toolbar** option controls the display of the main toolbar across the top of Outlook Express.

The **Views Bar** option controls the display of a drop-down list that lets you choose different views of Outlook Express, such as showing only the messages you've read or messages you haven't read. Some people love this bar; others can't wait to get rid of it.

NOTE

If you don't display your Contacts list, it's still easy to get to it—just click the **Addresses** button on the Outlook Express toolbar at the top of the screen.

TIP

The toolbar gives you easy access to many Outlook Express functions and features, so you should display it.

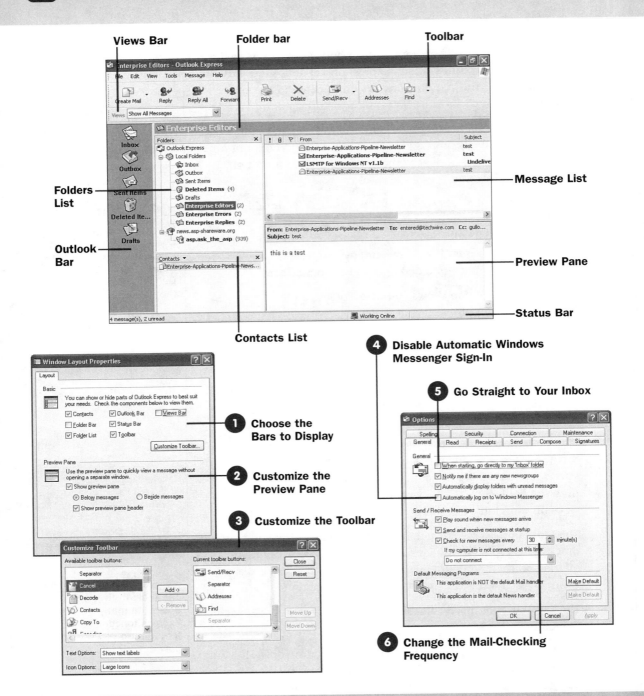

Views Bar   Folder bar   Toolbar

Message List

Folders List

Outlook Bar

Preview Pane

Status Bar

Contacts List

4 Disable Automatic Windows Messenger Sign-In

5 Go Straight to Your Inbox

1 Choose the Bars to Display

2 Customize the Preview Pane

3 Customize the Toolbar

6 Change the Mail-Checking Frequency

When you've made all your layout selections, click **OK** to close the dialog box and effect the changes.

2 Customize the Preview Pane

The **Preview** pane is a window that appears when you've highlighted an email message; it lets you see a preview of the message before opening the entire message. The **Preview** pane appears on the bottom part of the Outlook Express screen.

You can choose to turn the **Preview** pane off or leave it on; if you choose to display it, you can customize where it appears. Click the **Inbox** option in the **Folders** list and then choose **View**, **Layout** to open the **Window Layout Properties** dialog box. To turn the **Preview** pane off, disable the **Show preview pane** check box. To turn it on, enable the check box. If you want the pane to appear below the **Message** list, enable the **Below messages** radio button, and if you want the pane to appear to the right of the **Message** list, enable the **Besides messages** radio button.

When you've made all your layout selections, click **OK** to close the dialog box and effect the changes.

3 Customize the Toolbar

The Outlook Express toolbar gives you instant access to functions and features such as sending and receiving messages, opening your address book, creating new mail messages, and more. You can customize it by adding buttons to it or deleting buttons from it.

Choose **View**, **Layout** to open the **Window Layout Properties** dialog box and then click the **Customize Toolbar** button. The **Customize Toolbar** dialog box appears. The **Available toolbar buttons** list, on the left side of the dialog box, shows what buttons are available to you, and has a text label next to each button. The **Current toolbar buttons** list, on the right side of the dialog box, shows what buttons are currently on the toolbar, and has a text label next to each button. To add a new button to the toolbar, highlight it in the **Available toolbar buttons** list and click the **Add** button. To remove a button, highlight it in the **Current toolbar buttons** list and click the **Remove** button.

To move the location of a button in the toolbar, highlight it in the **Current toolbar buttons** list and click either the **Move up** or

TIP

You can also decide whether to display the **Preview** pane header, which is the information at the top of the pane that tells you who the message is from, the subject line, and similar information. To display the header, enable the **Show preview pane header** check box. To hide the header, disable the check box.

NOTE

If you choose to add more buttons to your toolbar than can fit on it, the ones that are furthest to the right are not displayed. You will see a small double-sided arrow at the right end of the toolbar; when you click the arrow, you will see the buttons that are hidden.

Move down button. When you click **Move up**, the selected button moves the button further to the left along the toolbar; when you click **Move down**, the selected button moves further to the right on the toolbar.

You can also choose whether to display large or small icons on the toolbar by choosing either one from the **Icon Options** drop-down list. Use the options in the **Text Options** drop-down list to determine whether to display text along with the buttons, and if so, how to display it.

When you're done customizing the toolbar, click **OK** to close the dialog box and effect the changes.

4 **Disable Automatic Windows Messenger Sign-In**

When you launch Outlook Express, the Windows Messenger instant messenger program automatically launches. For most people, this is not a particularly useful feature, and many find it annoying because there is no reason that someone will want to use the instant messenger program just because they want to check email. To stop Windows Messenger from launching every time you run Outlook Express, choose **Tools, Options** from menu and click the **General** tab in the **Options** dialog box. Then disable the **Automatically log on to Windows Messenger** check box.

5 **Go Straight to Your Inbox**

When you launch Outlook Express, it opens to a page that includes links to many sections of the program and gives an overall view of the program. But many people, when they open Outlook Express, want to go straight to their email inbox. To do that, on the **General** tab of the **Options** dialog box, enable the **When starting, go directly to my 'Inbox' folder** check box.

NOTE

On the **General** tab of the **Options** dialog box, disable the **Check for new messages every _ minutes** check box if you don't want Outlook Express to automatically check for new mail.

6 **Change the Mail-Checking Frequency**

Outlook Express automatically checks for new mail every 30 minutes if you have it open. You can turn off automatic email checking, or change the interval at which it will check for email. On the **General** tab of the **Options** dialog box, enable the **Check for new messages every _ minutes** check box and choose a new interval from the box if you want to change the interval. Then click **OK** to close the **Options** dialog box.

77 Create a Personal Signature

Many people like their email messages to have a personal touch—a *signature* at the bottom of it, text that can include contact information, a favorite saying, or literally any text you want.

It can take a good deal of time to type all that text into every message you create. You can instead have Outlook Express automatically put a signature at the bottom of all of your messages. Here's how to do it.

1 Open the Signatures Tab of the Options Dialog Box

You create signatures using the **Signatures** tab of the **Options** dialog box. To get there, choose **Tools, Options** from the menu and then click the **Signatures** tab.

2 Name the Signature

Click the **New** button. A name will be given to your signature: **Signature #1** and it will be listed as the **Default signature** in the **Signatures** list box.

You should give your signature a descriptive name, which will be particularly useful if you create more than one signature. To rename it, select the signature you want to rename from the **Signatures** list, click the **Rename** button, and type the new name.

3 Create Your Signature

Now that your signature has a name, you should create the actual signature by typing the text that you want to appear at the bottom of your emails. Click the **Text** radio button in the **Edit Signature** portion of the dialog box and type the text you want to appear in your signature block.

4 Choose the Account for the Signature

If you have more than one email account, you can tie your signature to a specific account—in other words, the signature will be used for only one specific account and not for any others.

KEY TERM

Signature—Text at the bottom of email messages you send that can include contact information, a favorite saying, or literally any text you want.

TIP

It's a good idea to set off your signature in some way from the rest of the message so that it's easy for people to see your signature and not mistake it for the body of the message. Consider putting a row of asterisks (*******************) above and below it. Do it by typing the asterisks into the **Edit Signature** text box as shown in the example.

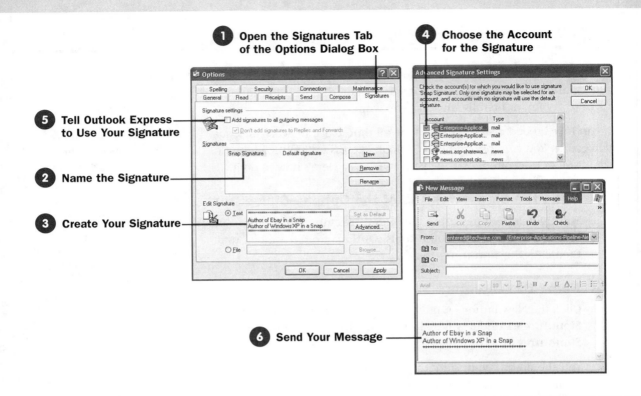

1 Open the Signatures Tab of the Options Dialog Box

4 Choose the Account for the Signature

5 Tell Outlook Express to Use Your Signature

2 Name the Signature

3 Create Your Signature

6 Send Your Message

TIP

Instead of typing your signature into the **Edit Signature** box, you can create your signature in a text file, and have Outlook Express automatically use the text from it in your messages. First create a text file using Notepad. After creating a signature name as described in step 2, enable the **File** radio button in the **Edit Signature** section, then click the **Browse** button and navigate to the folder where you created the text file. Select the text file, click **Open**, and then click **OK**. Text from the file will be used as your signature.

To choose the account for the signature, click the **Advanced** button. The **Advanced Signature Settings** dialog box appears. Enable the check boxes next to each of the accounts that you want to use the signature. Then click **OK** to close the **Advanced Signature Settings** dialog box and return to the **Signatures** tab of the **Options** dialog box.

5 Tell Outlook Express to Use Your Signature

To tell Outlook Express to use your signature, enable the **Add signatures to all outgoing messages** check box. If you don't want messages that you reply to or forward to have your signature on them, disable the **Don't add signatures to Replies and Forwards** check box.

When you're done selecting signature options, click **OK** to close the **Options** dialog box.

6 ## Send Your Message

Create an email message as you would normally. When you create the message, your signature is automatically included at the bottom of the message.

78 Create an Email Business Card

When you meet someone in person and you want them to have your contact information, you give them your business card. When you want someone you've met through email to have your business card, there's nothing physical you can give them.

However, you *can* create an electronic business card, sometimes called a *vCard*, that you attach to your email messages. It's an electronic file you can attach to your outgoing email messages that, when clicked by the recipient, automatically puts your contact information into their Address Book.

1 ### Create a New Contact

To create an electronic business card, you first must create the information you want to include in it. You do that by creating a new contact in the address book. From the **File** menu, choose **New** and then choose **Contact**.

A multi-tabbed dialog box will appear, with tabs for all your contact information, including name, phone number, email address, work and business addresses, instant messaging IDs, and more. Fill in just the information you want others to have.

There's only one portion of this dialog box that might be confusing. To add an email address, go to the **Name** tab, type the email address in the **E-Mail Addresses** text box, then click the **Add** button. If you don't click **Add**, the email address isn't added to the contact information. When you're done, click **OK**.

2 ### Open the Address Book

After you've created a contact entry in your Address Book for yourself, you have to open the Address Book to see it. To open the Address Book, click the **Addresses** icon on the toolbar.

See Also

→ **77** Create a Personal Signature

KEY TERM

vCard—An electronic file you can attach to your outgoing email messages that automatically puts your contact information into the recipient's Address Book.

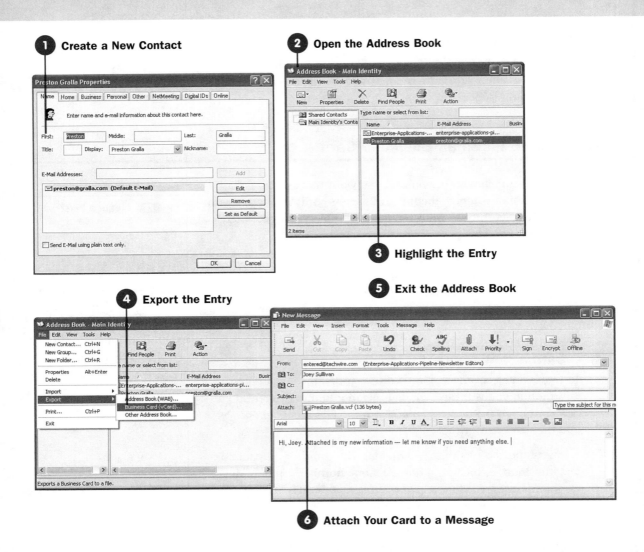

1 Create a New Contact

2 Open the Address Book

3 Highlight the Entry

4 Export the Entry

5 Exit the Address Book

6 Attach Your Card to a Message

3 Highlight the Entry

Find the entry you just created and click to highlight it.

4 Export the Entry

To attach your vCard to email messages, you must create a file out of your contact entry in the **.vcd** format. With the entry highlighted in the Address Book, choose **File, Export** and then choose **Business Card (vCard)**.

When the **Export** dialog box appears, choose a location where you want to save the vCard file and click **Save**.

5 Exit the Address Book

When you've exported the Address Book entry as a vCard, exit the Address Book by clicking the **X** button in the upper-right corner of the dialog box.

6 Attach Your Card to a Message

When you want to attach a vCard to a message, first create the message. Then click the **Attach** button in the toolbar in the **New Message** window, navigate to the folder where the vCard is stored, highlight the vCard file, and click the **Attach** button.

Then send your email as you would normally (click the **Send** button). When someone receives the message, he can double-click the attached vCard, and the information in the attached vCard will be automatically added to his Address Book.

TIP

When you double-click a vCard in most email software, the contact is added to the Address Book; the recipient doesn't necessarily have to have Outlook Express for the vCard to work. The only way to know for sure is to ask the person to whom you've sent the message whether it worked.

79 Use Multiple Email Accounts

If you're like a growing number of people, you might have more than one email account. At a minimum, you might have one for home and one for work. You also might have others as well: For example, if you use more than one Internet service provider (ISP), you'll have an email address for each service.

It's easy to set up and use multiple email accounts with Outlook Express. First you have to sign up with your ISP or an email provider. After you do that, follow these steps to use multiple email accounts with Outlook Express.

Before You Begin

✔ **76** Customize Outlook Express

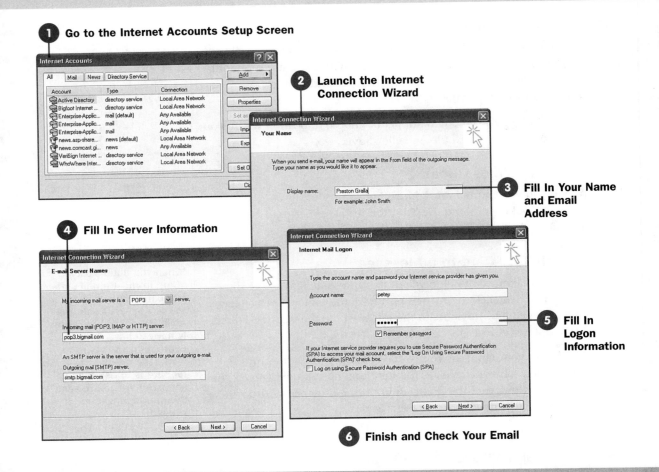

① **Go to the Internet Accounts Setup Screen**

② **Launch the Internet Connection Wizard**

③ **Fill In Your Name and Email Address**

④ **Fill In Server Information**

⑤ **Fill In Logon Information**

⑥ **Finish and Check Your Email**

① Go to the Internet Accounts Setup Screen

Choose **Tools, Accounts** from the menu to open the **Internet Accounts** setup screen. This is where you add new email accounts to Outlook Express.

② Launch the Internet Connection Wizard

To set up a new mailbox in Outlook Express, you need to launch the **Internet Connection Wizard**. To launch it, click the **Add** button on the **Internet Accounts** setup screen and choose **Mail**.

3 Fill In Your Name and Email Address

On the first screen of the **Internet Connection Wizard**, type your name. This is the name people will see when they receive email from you. You can use spaces if you want. Click the **Next** button at the bottom of the wizard. On the next screen that appears, type your email address. It should be the address for the new email account that you're creating, not for an older account. Click **Next** again to advance to the next wizard screen.

4 Fill In Server Information

To send and receive mail with this email account, Outlook Express uses special computers called *servers* that do the work of sending and receiving mail. A *POP3* or *IMAP server* lets you receive mail, and an *SMTP server* lets you send mail.

The wizard asks for the names of the servers that will send and receive email for the account you are creating. If the email service you're adding requires that you use email software rather than use the Web (Hotmail accounts, for example, use the Web), choose **POP3** from the **My incoming mail server is a _ server** drop-down list box. In the **Incoming mail** text box, type the name of the server, such as **POP3.myisp.net**. Get the server information from your ISP or mail service. Call its tech support line, or you might be able to find the information on the Web. This is the server that will let you receive mail.

You must also specify the email server that will let you send mail, the SMTP server. Type the name of this server in the **Outgoing mail (SMTP server)** text box, such as **smtp.myisp.net**. Get this server information from your ISP or mail service. Call its tech support line, or you might be able to find the information on the Web. This is the server that will let you send mail.

When you're done providing server information, click **Next**.

5 Fill In Logon Information

The next wizard screen that appears asks for your logon information, including your name and password. You'll get this information from your ISP or email provider. Type the information into the **Account name** and **Password** boxes.

KEY TERMS

POP3 server—A computer that receives email from people who send it to you, and then lets you retrieve the mail using your email software.

IMAP server—A computer that receives email from people who send it to you, and then lets you retrieve the mail using your email software. IMAP servers offer more capabilities than do POP3 servers—for example, with them, it's easier to synchronize your email among different computers.

SMTP server—A computer that sends mail for you when you send it from your email program.

NOTE

If you use a Web-based email service such as Yahoo! Mail, you may or may not be able to use Outlook Express to send and receive email through it, depending on the service. You can use Outlook Express to send and receive mail through the Microsoft mail services Hotmail and MSN. For Yahoo!, you won't be able to send and receive with Outlook Express if you use the free service, but you can send email with Outlook Express if you use the Yahoo! pay service. If you have another Web-based mail account, check its website for details.

Enable the **Remember password** check box so that Outlook Express can automatically log on to the mail servers and send and receive mail. If you don't check that box, every time Outlook Express sends or receives mail for this account, you'll have to type your name and password.

Check with your ISP or email provider about whether you need to enable the **Log on using Secure Password Authentication (SPA)** check box. Most ISPs and email providers do not require this option, so if you're not sure, do not enable the check box. When you're done, click **Next**.

6 Finish and Check Your Email

When you're done providing the information for the new email account, click the **Finish** button. The wizard finishes, and you'll be back at the **Internet Accounts** dialog box. Click the **Close** button. You can now use your new account in the same way as you use any other account; when Outlook Express checks mail, it will check your new account as well as your existing account.

You won't actually see different accounts when you use Outlook Express, however. Outlook Express automatically checks all your email accounts and puts all your messages into your existing folders—so your email from all accounts will come into your **Inbox**.

You view all the information about your accounts by choosing **Accounts** from the **Tools** menu and clicking the **Mail** tab.

 Organize Your Mailboxes

Before You Begin

✔ Customize Outlook Express

See Also

→ **81** Automate Your Mail Handling by Creating Mail Rules

Email boxes have a way of turning into chaos. The world lives by email these days, and that means that just about everyone who uses email suffers from email and information overload.

There are ways you can get your email under control, however, as you'll see in this task. You'll be able to create new folders to organize your mail, move your mail between folders, flag important messages for follow-up, search for messages, and more.

① Make a New Folder

When you first run Outlook Express, you have a basic set of folders, including an **Inbox**, an **Outbox**, a **Sent Items** folder for mail you've sent, and a **Drafts** folder for mail you've composed and saved but haven't yet sent. If you use only those folders, you'll soon be inundated by hundreds or more messages in your **Inbox**, and it'll quickly become impossible to find any specific message.

The best way to handle the overload is to create new folders to hold your mail, for example, one for family, one for a specific project you're working on, and so on. To create a new folder, right-click anywhere in the **Folders** list area and choose **New Folder** from the context menu. In the **Create Folder** dialog box that opens, click the folder *underneath which* you want your new folder to live, type the name of your new folder in the **Folder name** text box, and click **OK**. Your new folder will be created.

Create as many folders as you want. You can even create folders underneath folders: For example, you can create a folder called **Work**, and have underneath it a folder for each different work project.

NOTE

If you want a folder to live on the same level as **Inbox**, **Outbox**, and so on, choose to create a new folder underneath the **Local Folders** folder.

② Move Your Mail into the New Folders

To move mail between folders, double-click a folder in the **Folders** list to open the contents of that folder in the **Message** list on the right side of the screen. Highlight the mail you want to move and drag it from the **Message** list to another folder in the **Folders** list. Release the mouse button to drop the selected mail into the new folder. You can drag multiple messages between folders. To select multiple contiguous messages, click the first one, hold down the **Shift** key, and click the last message. To select multiple noncontiguous messages, select one, hold down the **Ctrl** key, and click the other messages you want to select. You can then drag them all in a group from one folder to another.

NOTE

You can have incoming mail automatically routed into folders by using mail rules. See **Automate Your Mail Handling by Creating Mail Rules** for information on how to do it.

③ Flag a Message for Follow-Up

Even when you organize your mail into folders, it can be difficult to track it all. There may be messages in various folders that you later want to follow up on, but don't have time to do so now.

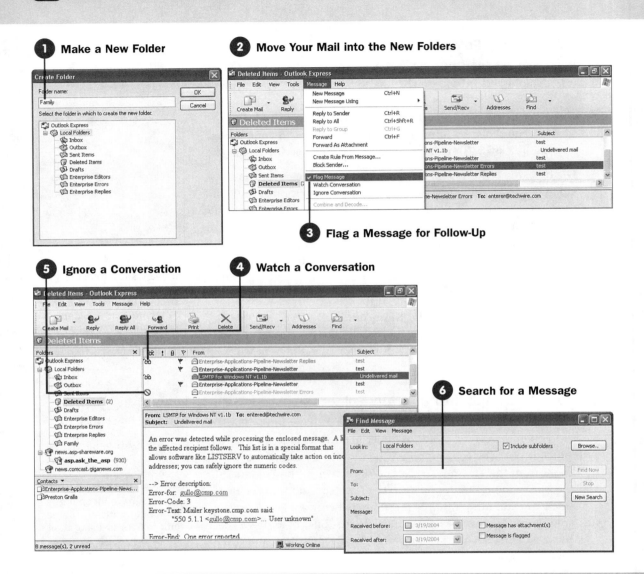

1 Make a New Folder

2 Move Your Mail into the New Folders

3 Flag a Message for Follow-Up

5 Ignore a Conversation

4 Watch a Conversation

6 Search for a Message

You can place red flags next to important messages. That way, you can see at a glance which messages need your attention. To flag a message, highlight it in the **Message** list and choose **Message**, **Flag Message** from the menu. The message will have a red flag next to it in the **Message** list, and a check mark shows up next to the **Flag Message** option on the **Message** menu for that message. To take the flag away, highlight the message and choose **Message, Flag Message** again. The message will no longer have the red flag next to it and the check mark is removed from the menu option for that message.

④ Watch a Conversation

You can tell Outlook Express to "watch" a conversation—that is, to highlight any email that comes in response to an email you've sent or received. Highlight the original message in the **Message** list and choose **Message, Watch Conversation** from the menu. You'll get a warning that you must first create a column in the **Messages** list that will contain the icon (a pair of glasses) for watched messages. Click the **Yes** button when you get the warning to create the new column. Now an icon of a pair of glasses will appear next to every email in that conversation, including new emails that come in.

⑤ Ignore a Conversation

You can also tell Outlook Express to ignore conversations that you don't care about. Although you might not be able to stop people from sending you messages on topics you're not interested in, you can have Outlook Express filter those messages. Highlight one of the messages you want to ignore and then choose **Message, Ignore Conversation** from the menu. All the emails related to the message you selected will have an icon of a circle with a line through it next to them.

⑥ Search for a Message

Especially if your email folders are bursting at the seams with messages, sometimes the best way to find a particular email message is to search for it. You can fine-tune your search in a variety of ways, such as searching within a folder, by date, by the sender, receiver, subject line, and text in the message. In the **Folders** list, click the folder through which you want to search, then click the **Find** button. In the **Find Message** dialog box that opens, fill in the information you know about the email message you're hoping to find and then click **Find Now**.

NOTE

If you haven't watched or ignored a conversation before, you'll get a warning that you must first create a column in the **Message** list that will contain the icon for an ignored message (this column is actually shared by icons for watched conversations). Click the **Yes** button when you get the warning to create the new column.

TIP

If you want to search through all your email, search through the **Local Folders** folder, because that is the "parent" folder for all your Outlook email folders. Make sure that you enable the **Include subfolders** check box on the **Find Message** dialog box.

81 Automate Your Mail Handling by Creating Mail Rules

Before You Begin

✔ **80** Organize Your
Mailboxes

Creating new mail folders, as outlined in **80** Organize Your Mailboxes, goes a long way towards helping you keep your mail under control. However, it only goes part way to helping because it still forces you to manually move your mail around.

A much better way to handle your mail is to have Outlook Express automatically route mail into the right folders, based on rules you set up. For example, you could have all mail from your boss go into your **Work** folder, and all mail from your mother go into your **Family** folder. A rule is essentially just a condition that a message must meet for Outlook Express to take some kind of action—for example, moving an incoming email into a specific folder.

1 Choose a Message for Creating a Rule

The best way to create a new rule is to choose a message that you would normally want to be handled automatically by a rule—for example, an email from your boss. Find the mail message and highlight it.

2 Choose to Create a Rule

With the mail message highlighted, choose **Message, Create Rule from Message** from the menu. The **New Mail Rule** dialog box appears.

3 Select the Condition for the Rule

In the **Select the Condition for your rule** section, choose what conditions must be met by an email message in order to have the rule applied to it. You can choose from a variety of conditions, such as where the **From** line has the name of a specific person, where the **Subject** line has specific words in it, and so on. You can apply more than one condition—for example, you can create a rule that would apply when a message comes from a specific person *and* the **Subject** line contains a specific word. To choose a condition, enable the check box next to the condition. In step 5, you'll specify the names or words for the conditions.

2 Choose to Create a Rule   **1** Choose a Message for Creating a Rule

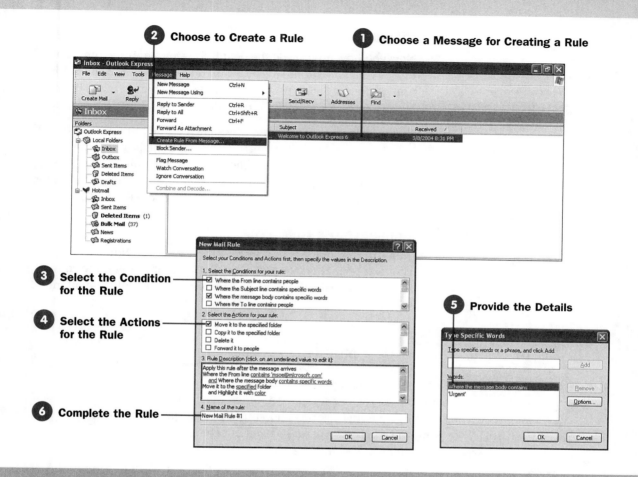

3 Select the Condition for the Rule

4 Select the Actions for the Rule

5 Provide the Details

6 Complete the Rule

4 Select the Actions for the Rule

Choose what action you want this Outlook Express rule to take. In the **Select the Actions for your rule** section, you can choose a variety of actions that the rule will take when the conditions are met. For example, you can have the mail routed to a specific folder, have the mail highlighted in a color, have the mail deleted, have the mail automatically forwarded to someone, and so on. You can take more than one action—for example, having a piece of mail moved to a folder, flagged, and automatically forwarded to someone. To choose an action, enable the check box next to the action.

⑤ Provide the Details

Now you have to provide the details for the rule. For example, if one of your conditions was based on a specific word in the **Subject** line, you must define that word; if the action was to move the message to a specific folder, you must define that folder.

In the **Rule Description** area, click each of the links and fill in the details to complete the rule. For example, if the link says **contains**, it means you'll type a word. Click the link, type the word in the dialog box that appears, and click the **Add** button. If the link is for a folder, a dialog box appears letting you choose the folder.

⑥ Complete the Rule

To finish the rule, type a name for the rule in the **Name of the rule** text box. Then click **OK**. You'll get a confirmation that the rule was created. From now on, the rule will be applied to all mail you receive.

82 About Dealing with Attachments

Before You Begin

✔ **76** Customize Outlook Express

See Also

→ **74** Protect Yourself Against Viruses

→ **75** Protect Yourself Against Email Worms

One of the biggest problems facing anyone who uses email is the possibility of having her computer infected by a dangerous virus or worm set loose by an email. Worms and viruses can be spread by attachments. Someone can send you an infected attachment, and if you open it, your computer will become infected.

In **74** **Protect Yourself Against Viruses** and **75** **Protect Yourself Against Email Worms**, you learned how to protect yourself against these dangers. But certain versions of Outlook Express take protection to the extreme—they block certain attachments from even reaching you—you simply won't be able to open them because Outlook Express won't let you. Among the file types Outlook Express won't let you see are **.exe**, **.com**, **.pif**, and many others.

🌐 WEB RESOURCE

Visit this page for a list of all the file types that Outlook Express won't let you view.

http://support.microsoft.com/?kbid=291369

If you have an older version of Windows XP, Outlook Express won't block these attachments. Versions of Windows XP that have **Service Pack 1** or **Service Pack 2** on them will block the attachments. To see whether your version of XP is one of these, right-click the **My Computer** icon on your desktop, choose **Properties** from the context menu to open the **System Properties** dialog box, and click the **General** tab. At the bottom of the **System** area, look to see whether **Service Pack 1** or **Service Pack 2** appears; if it does, your version of Outlook Express blocks attachments.

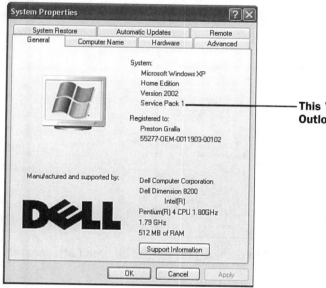

This Version of Windows Blocks Outlook Express Attachments

If you see Service Pack 1 or Service Pack 2 here, Outlook Express blocks attachments.

If you receive an attachment that Outlook Express has blocked, at the top of the email message, you'll see this alert, followed by the name of the file that was blocked:

> **Outlook Express removed access to the following unsafe attachments in your mail:**

Many people think that completely blocking attachments like this is overkill, that as long as people are educated about how to handle attachments (as you were in **74** **Protect Yourself Against Viruses** and **75** **Protect Yourself Against Email Worms**), you'll be perfectly safe.

There is a way, however, to tell Outlook Express to let those attachments through. Open Internet Explorer and choose **Tools, Options** from the menu to open the **Options** dialog box; click the **Security** tab. Disable the **Do not allow attachments to be saved or opened that could potentially be a virus** check box. Click **OK**, and all the attachments will make it through.

Disable This Check Box to Allow Attachments ————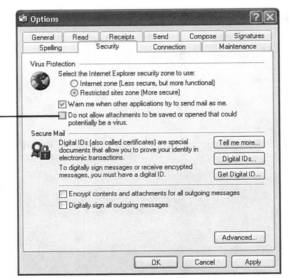

From this tab, you can tell Outlook Express to let all email attachments through.

TIPS

If you need to send a large file, you can always compress it before you send it with Zip compression technology. Windows XP includes Zip technology. To compress a file, you must first create a Zip folder for it. In Windows Explorer, double-click a drive or folder; on the **File** menu, point to **New**, and then click **Compressed (zipped) Folder**. Type a name for the new folder and press **Enter**. To add a file to the folder, drag a file onto the folder; as the file is copied to the folder, it is compressed (zipped). Then mail the folder as an attachment.

A better way to compress files is to use the shareware program WinZip, available from **www.winzip.com**. It's free to try, but if you want to keep using it, you're supposed to pay $29.

You can also use Outlook Express to easily send attachments. When you compose an email message, click the **Attach** button, navigate to the file you want to send, and click **Attach**. Then send your mail as you would normally.

You should be careful about sending attachments that are too large because they can tie up people's Internet connections when they're using email. There's no generally accepted rule for attachment size limits, but you should be careful before sending attachments over 250KB. However, if you know someone has a high-speed connection, such as a cable modem or DSL connection, you can send much larger files. Often, though, it's a good idea to send an email ahead of time to the person, asking whether you can send a large attachment.

83 About Spam

Perhaps the most unfortunate fact of life on the Internet is the existence of *spam*—email you didn't ask to be sent to you that offers to sell you services or goods, often fraudulent. Spam can sometimes be pornographic in nature, as well.

Spam started as a mere nuisance years ago, but it has long ago passed beyond a nuisance. It costs people and businesses many millions of dollars a year. Because of the onslaught of spam, Internet service providers (ISPs), for example, have to buy many more servers and software to handle the extra flood of email, as well as hire extra staff to support all that extra hardware and software. Spammers typically don't send spam from their own servers; instead, they piggyback onto other people's servers, such as those from unsuspecting businesses, so that businesses pay more as well. Individuals, both at home and at work, spend many hours a week weeding through spam, which means lost productivity. And because spam often sells fraudulent goods and services, a great deal of money is lost to fraud as well.

The numbers of spam messages involved are truly staggering. The anti-spam software maker Brightmail claims that 62 percent of all email sent over the Internet is spam, and that Brightmail software products filter out billions of spam messages a month—91 billion spam messages in a single month.

You might think that spammers are small mom-and-pop operations—shady individuals trying to make a quick buck by sending out a few thousand spams a month. Nothing could be further from the truth. In fact, most spam is from companies that send out many tens of millions of pieces of spam in a month. For example, Yahoo! claims that a single spamming operation sent out 91 million emails to those with Yahoo! email accounts over a two-month period—of course, the spammer didn't send email only to those with Yahoo! accounts, so the total number sent by the spammer is, in fact, much higher.

According to the anti-spam organization known as the Spamhaus project (**www.spamhaus.org/rokso**), only 200 spamming organizations are responsible for 90 percent of all the spam sent out.

Spammers frequently *spoof* their return email addresses—that is, they hide their true email addresses so that they can't be tracked down.

See Also

→ **84** Slam Spam

KEY TERM

Spam—Unsolicited email offering to sell you services or goods, often fraudulent.

NOTE

Perhaps the worst thing about spam is the sheer annoyance factor of having to wade through dozens, or even hundreds of unwanted email messages a day, almost all of which are offensive (for example, offering to enlarge certain exceedingly private body parts). Worse than that is pornographic spam that contains not only invitations to pornography sites but also pornographic photos.

KEY TERM

Spoof—To hide the true address of a sender of email. Spammers frequently spoof their email addresses so that they can't be tracked down.

WEB RESOURCE

http://www.brightmail.com/spamstats.html

The federal government has tried to get into the act of protecting people against spam, passing the so-called Can Spam Act of 2003. However, that legislation has been widely derided as being toothless, and statistics show that spam actually *increased* after the legislation was passed. The legislation doesn't actually outlaw spam, but instead tries to regulate it by requiring marketers to include real, unspoofed email addresses in their spam, and that information be included in all spam that allows recipients to *opt out*—that is, ask not to receive future mailings from the marketer.

The law, however, applies only to American-based companies. It also overrides stricter laws that a number of states had passed, some of which completely banned spam.

KEY TERM

Opt out—To ask not to receive any more email from the marketer sending the unsolicited email.

Still, some large companies are trying to use the law to combat spam. America Online, Earthlink, Yahoo!, and Microsoft filed six lawsuits against big spammers using the law. At press time, the suits had not yet come to court.

The upshot, though, is that spam will be an unfortunate way of life on the Internet for years to come. As you'll see in **84** Slam Spam, though, there are ways you can fight back, even if you can't completely eliminate the problem.

84 Slam Spam

Before You Begin

✔ **81** Automate Your Mail Handling by Creating Mail Rules

✔ **83** About Spam

As you learned in **83** About Spam, spam has become ubiquitous, and there's no real way you can avoid it. However, if you follow these steps, you'll be able to cut down on the spam you receive, and to more easily manage the spam you do get.

1 Be Wary of Signing Up for Email Newsletters

Many websites ask whether you want to sign up for their email newsletters. Be very careful of signing up for these; if you do, you might be deluged by spam. Not only might the site itself send you spam, but the site might sell your email address to spammers and you could be deluged by even more spam.

Before signing up for any email newsletter, check the site's rules about privacy. Find out whether it will share your information with other sites or business partners. There should be a link somewhere on the email signup page about the site's privacy policy. If there isn't such a link, be wary of signing up.

Some sites such as shopping sites require that you provide an email address to register. In those cases, consider getting a free email address from a site such as Yahoo! or Hotmail, and use that email address when registering at shopping sites. That way, if you do get spam as a result of registering, it will go to your free address rather than your normal address.

TIP

Even if a site says it won't share your email address, be careful. If it is a big, well-known site, it's likely to follow its published rules, but smaller, less well-known sites might not.

WEB RESOURCE

www.hotmail.com

www.yahoo.com

Click the Mail link on either of these sites to get a free email account from Hotmail or Yahoo!.

❷ Try to Opt Out

The Can Spam Law of 2003 requires that spammers include instructions at the bottom of their emails that let you *opt out*— that is, ask to be removed from future mailings.

Many spammers, however, do not include opt-out information in their email. And the law only covers spammers who are based in the United States.

There is a great debate whether you should opt out if a spammer includes opt-out information or an opt-out link in a piece of spam. Some people say that attempting to opt out only confirms to spammers that your email address is valid, and so they will increase the amount of spam they send to you. Others say that many spammers feel pressured to follow the Can Spam Act, so it may help reduce spam.

To opt out of a piece of spam, go to the bottom of the spam message. There you'll find information about how to opt out—for example, by clicking a link which will bring you to a website that will let you opt out.

NOTE

If there is no contact information or opt-out information, don't try to opt out of a spam. If the contact information is for a foreign country, don't try to opt out. I have opted out from many spammers (only those based in the United States), and doing so seemed to have reduced the spam I received from those companies. Over time, however, spam increased again.

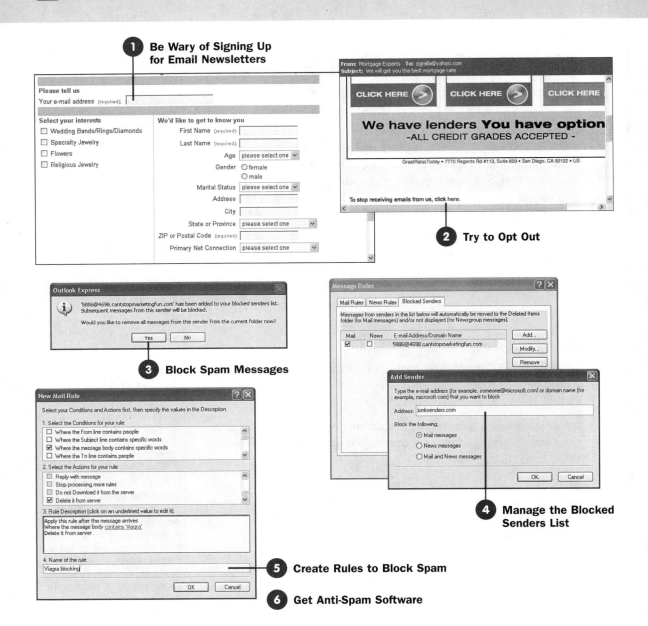

① Be Wary of Signing Up for Email Newsletters

② Try to Opt Out

③ Block Spam Messages

④ Manage the Blocked Senders List

⑤ Create Rules to Block Spam

⑥ Get Anti-Spam Software

③ Block Spam Messages

Outlook Express lets you block spam on a message-by-message basis. When you come across a piece of spam, you can tell Outlook Express to always block messages from that sender or from that domain. (The *domain* is to the right of the @ sign in an email address. For example, in the email address **ispamyou@big-giantspammer.com**, **biggiantspammer.com** is the domain.)

To do it, highlight the spam message and choose **Message, Block Sender** from the menu. You'll get a confirmation that the sender has been added to your blocked senders list, so that you will not receive email from that sender again—such messages will be automatically deleted. You'll also be asked whether you want to remove all the messages from that sender from the current folder. If you click **Yes**, messages from that sender are immediately deleted. If you click **No**, they are not deleted.

④ Manage the Blocked Senders List

You can manually add or delete email addresses to and from the blocked senders list. Choose **Tools, Message Rules** from the menu and click **Blocked Senders List**. The **Blocked Senders List** dialog box appears, showing you all the senders whose mail you've already blocked. If you want to add a new sender to the list, click the **Add** button and type the email address or domain you want to block. For example, if you want to block only a single email address, you might type the address **5886@cantstopmarketing-fun.com**. But if you did that, you would block only that single email address from the spammer; if the spammer sent you an email with the address **5887@cantstopmarketingfun.com**, the new spam would get through. You are often better off blocking the entire domain—in this instance, **cantstopmarketingfun.com**.

When you add a blocked sender to the list, you'll have the option of blocking the domain from News messages as well. News messages have nothing to do with news. They are messages in *newsgroups*, which are Internet-based discussion groups, like bulletin boards, that let you participate in discussions about topics of interest to you.

TIP

Some ISPs, such as AT&T, offer free spam-blocking software. Check with your ISP to see whether it offers this feature.

NOTE

You can only block spam messages in an email account that uses POP3 or IMAP servers; you can't block spam messages if you use an HTTP-based mail account such as Hotmail.

KEY TERM

Newsgroups—Internet discussion groups that let you discuss topics of interest to you with others in public online bulletin boards.

After you add the domain or email address to the blocked senders list and block it for mail, news, or both, click **OK** twice to close both dialog boxes.

If you want to remove a blocked sender, highlight the sender's name on the **Blocked Senders** tab of the **Message Rules** dialog box, click **Remove**, and then click **Yes**. You can also edit any blocked sender—for example, by changing its email address—by highlighting the sender's name on the **Blocked Senders** tab of the **Message Rules** dialog box, clicking **Modify**, making your changes in the dialog box that opens, and then clicking **OK** twice.

⑤ Create Rules to Block Spam

You can create email rules that automatically handle spam. (For details on how to create rules, see **81** **Automate Your Mail Handling by Creating Mail Rules**.) These rules can often be more effective than adding senders to the blocked senders list. Spammers frequently change their email addresses, so blocking email from one address or domain doesn't do a great deal to cut down on spam. However, you can create rules that can cut down on spam from senders of *any* domain. For example, a common spam concerns selling Viagra; you can create a rule that automatically deletes all mail that contains the word *Viagra*. You can also create rules that route spam to a specific folder so that you can check whether the messages are spam, or even delete the spam from your email server so that it's never even delivered to you.

Examine incoming spam for common words in the **Subject** line or in the message body and then create rules that filter those words. This goes a long way toward canning spam.

 WEB RESOURCE

This site offers news about spam and advice about how you can combat it—you *can* help stamp out spam.

http://spam.abuse.net/

⑥ Get Anti-Spam Software

Outlook Express can help kill spam, but it's not nearly as effective as software you can download or buy. There are many different programs you can try for free before buying, or even use for free.

PART II: Networking and the Internet

Norton AntiSpam, available for $39.95, does an excellent job of killing spam. In addition to buying it online or from retail stores, you can try it out for free at **www.symantec.com/antispam**, and pay for it only if you decide to keep using it. If you want a free product, try All in One Secret Maker at **www.secretmaker.com**.

85 Import Messages from Another Email Program

Perhaps you were using another email program before you began using Outlook Express. If so, you don't want to lose those messages when you begin using Outlook Express—you'd probably like to view them in Outlook Express as well.

It's easy to get those messages into Outlook Express. You just have to import them. Note that you won't be able to import mail from every email program. You can, however, import from Eudora, Netscape, previous versions of Outlook Express, and Outlook.

1 Start the Outlook Express Import Wizard

You import messages from another email program using an Outlook Express wizard. To launch it, choose **File**, **Import**, **Messages** from the menu. The **Outlook Express Import** wizard launches.

2 Choose the Email Program Whose Messages You Want to Import

From the screen that appears, choose the email program from which you want to import messages and click **Next**. Make sure that you choose the right version of the email software, if more than one version is listed.

3 Choose a Profile

Some email programs let you create separate profiles for each person who uses the software. If you're importing from a program that uses a profile, the **Choose Profile** screen appears. Choose the profile you want to import from and click **OK**.

Before You Begin

✔ **76** Customize Outlook Express

See Also

→ **79** Use Multiple Email Accounts

→ **80** Organize Your Mailboxes

NOTE

You can also import contacts from an existing email program or account information—the information you need to check an email account, such as the POP3 and SMTP servers. Choose **File, Import, Mail Account Settings** to important account information, and **File, Import, Address Book** to import contacts. You'll be able to import address books from Outlook, Outlook Express, Eudora, and Netscape.

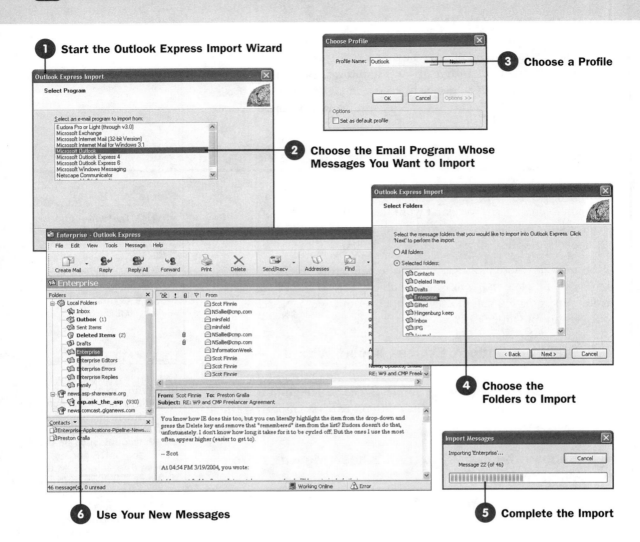

1 Start the Outlook Express Import Wizard

3 Choose a Profile

2 Choose the Email Program Whose Messages You Want to Import

4 Choose the Folders to Import

5 Complete the Import

6 Use Your New Messages

4 Choose the Folders to Import

The **Select Folders** screen appears. This screen gives you the option of importing all mail from all folders, or importing only individual folders. To import all messages from all folders, choose the **All folders** option. To import messages from only certain folders, choose the **Selected folders** option and then choose one or more folders to import. Click to highlight or select a folder. To select multiple contiguous folders, select one, hold down the **Shift** key, and select the last folder in the group; all the folders in between will be selected. To select multiple noncontiguous folders, highlight one, hold down the **Ctrl** key, and click the other folders whose messages you want to import. When you're done selecting the folders, click **Next**.

5 **Complete the Import**

Outlook Express begins importing your messages. You'll see a screen showing the progress of the import, including the total number of messages being imported, and how many have been currently imported.

When Outlook Express is done importing, a screen appears, telling you that you've completed importing the messages. Click **Finish**.

6 **Use Your New Messages**

Your new messages will now be in Outlook Express, and can be used like any other messages. The messages will be in the same folders they were in in your original email program. Here you can see that the **Enterprise** folder that I selected for import from an older version of Outlook in step 4 is now located in its entirety in Outlook Express.

86 Sign Up for Windows Messenger

The first step in using Windows Messenger is signing up for the service. However, it's a little more complicated to sign up for Windows Messenger than it is for other instant messaging programs. You'll have to get a *.NET Passport*, a technology that confirms your identity. After you get the Passport, you can sign up for Windows Messenger, as you'll see in this task.

1 **Launch Windows Messenger**

There are several places where you might find the Windows Messenger program on your computer. On the **Start** menu, check above the **All Programs** link; it might be one of the programs listed there. If not, you can find it in the **All Programs** list, either on its own, or in the **Accessories** area. When you find the program, double-click to launch it.

See Also

→ **87** Customize Your Buddy List

KEY TERM

.NET Passport—A Microsoft technology that uniquely identifies you, and that you'll need to use Windows Messenger. With the Passport, you can sign into multiple Microsoft sites and features, such as Hotmail.

1 Launch Windows Messenger

2 Launch the .NET Passport Wizard

3 Start .NET Registration

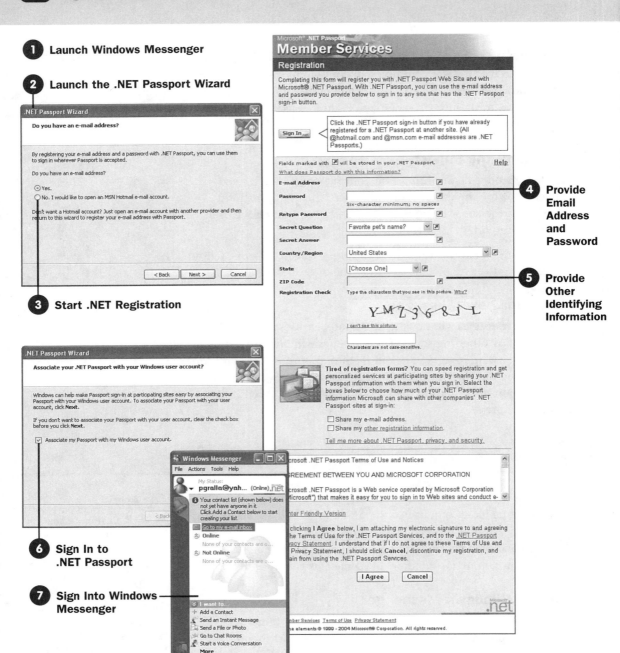

4 Provide Email Address and Password

5 Provide Other Identifying Information

6 Sign In to .NET Passport

7 Sign Into Windows Messenger

Windows Messenger opens with a mainly blank screen with an icon and a link in the middle of it reading **Click here to sign in**.

2 Launch the .NET Passport Wizard

Click the **Click here to sign in** link. Because this is your first time using Windows Messenger, the **.NET Passport Wizard** appears. You'll have to get a .NET Passport before you can use Windows Messenger. Click the **Next** button to start the process of getting a .NET Passport.

3 Start .NET Registration

The wizard asks whether you have an email address. You'll use your email address as your username when you log into .NET Passport (and into Windows Messenger). If you have an email address and want to use that, choose **Yes**. If you don't have an email address, or you want to get a free email address on Hotmail, choose **No. I would like to open an MSN Hotmail e-mail account**.

Click **Next**. If you choose to open a Hotmail account, you'll be brought to a page that will let you open an account. If you choose to use your own email address, after a few moments a screen will appear asking whether you've already registered your email address with .NET Passport. Because this is the first time you are creating a .NET Passport, click **No. I want to register my e-mail address with Passport now**. Then click the **Next** button.

4 Provide Email Address and Password

A screen appears telling you that if you want to register your email address with Passport, you should click **Next**. Click **Next**; your web browser will launch, and you'll be sent to a page that will start the actual registration process. Click **Next** again.

A registration page appears, asking that you enter your email address and type a password. You'll also get to choose a "secret question" and a "secret answer" you can use to get your password if you forget it.

5 Provide Other Identifying Information

You'll be asked other information, such as your country/region and state of residence. For security reasons, you'll be asked to type a series of graphic characters you see on your screen.

NOTE

You need to be online to get a .NET Passport and to sign into Windows Messenger, so make sure that you connect to the Internet before launching Windows Messenger or signing up for a .NET Passport.

TIP

Like many online services, .NET Passport uses a secret question to help you if you forget your password. If you do, you'll be asked the question, and if you answer it correctly, the service will email you your password so that you can use the service. The question should have an answer to which only you know the answer.

Toward the bottom of your screen, you'll be asked whether you want Microsoft to share your email address and other registration information with other sites that use .NET Passport. If you choose to allow that information to be shared, any other .NET Passport sites will be able to get that information. If you're worried about privacy, don't enable these check boxes.

Read the terms of use at the bottom of the screen when you're done filling out the form. Then click **I agree** to register. Another page may appear, asking that you type a series of graphic characters you see on the screen. Type them and click **I agree**.

NOTE

When you finish registering for .NET Passport, you'll see a large graphic that reads **Sign In .NET**. Don't click that graphic—it won't do anything. It's there only as a confirmation that you've registered and serves no useful purpose.

⑥ Sign In to .NET Passport

Your registration is now complete. Click **Continue**. A screen appears asking whether you want to associate your .NET Passport with your Windows XP user account. If you do that, whenever you visit a site or use a service that uses a .NET Passport (such as Hotmail or Windows Messenger), you can sign in automatically. If you want to sign in automatically, enable the **Associate my Passport with my Windows user account** check box. If you're worried that someone would be able to gain access to your computer and then use your .NET Passport to gain access to your mail or Windows Messenger account, disable the check box. Whichever option you choose, click **Next**, and then click **Finish** on the screen that appears.

At some point after you register with .NET, an email will be sent to the email address you used to register. Follow the instructions in the email message to confirm your registration. If you don't confirm your registration, you can still use Windows Messenger, but people will see **E-mail address not verified** next to your name on their contact list.

TIP

Microsoft has another instant messaging product called MSN Messenger. MSN Messenger does not come as part of Windows XP; you must download it separately. MSN Messenger looks and works very much like Windows Messenger. You can use the same .NET Passport to sign into MSN Messenger that you use to sign into Windows Messenger.

⑦ Sign Into Windows Messenger

You'll now be returned to Windows Messenger. Your .NET Passport email address will appear in the middle of the program window, along with a link that reads **Click here to sign in**. Click the link, and you'll be signed into Windows Messenger.

 Customize Your Buddy List

The *buddy list* is at the heart of instant messaging. When you set one up, it will alert you whenever any of your buddies comes online. Although it's easy to set up a basic buddy list, there are a lot of hidden features of the list you can use, as you'll see in this task. You can customize the list so that it works precisely the way that you want.

When you add someone to your buddy list, you'll get an alert when they sign into Windows Messenger, but you won't get an alert when they're online but not signed into Windows Messenger.

 Add a Contact

When you first start Windows Messenger, your buddy list, also called a *contact list*, will be empty, so you should start by adding contacts to it.

To add a contact, click **Add a Contact** in the main screen that appears. The **Add a Contact** dialog box appears. If you know the person's email address or sign-in name for Windows Messenger or MSN Messenger, select **By e-mail address or sign-in name** and click **Next**. On the next screen that appears, type the person's complete email address and click **Next**. The contact will be added to your buddy list.

Whenever that person logs into Windows Messenger, you'll get a notification, and they'll also show up in the **Online** area of your buddy list.

If you want to tell the person that you've added her to your buddy list, click the **Send E-mail** button on the confirmation screen that appears when you've successfully added a contact. Follow the instructions for sending an email.

If the person does not have a .NET Passport, she can't be added to your buddy list. In that case, you'll get a warning message that she doesn't have a .NET Passport account. Click the **Next** button to send an email to her explaining how to get a .NET Passport and how to install Windows Messenger.

Before You Begin

✔ **86** Sign Up for Windows Messenger

See Also

→ **88** About Sending Instant Messages

KEY TERM

Buddy list—The list of people in Windows Messenger (or another instant messaging program) with whom you frequently communicate, and about whom you want to be notified when they log on to their instant messenger program. Also called a *contact list*.

 TIP

You don't necessarily have to send an email message to your new contact, because when you add someone to your buddy list, she'll get a notification that she's been added to your list. She can then add you to her buddy list, and she also has the option of blocking you from seeing her when she logs in.

1 Add a Contact

2 Search to Add a Contact

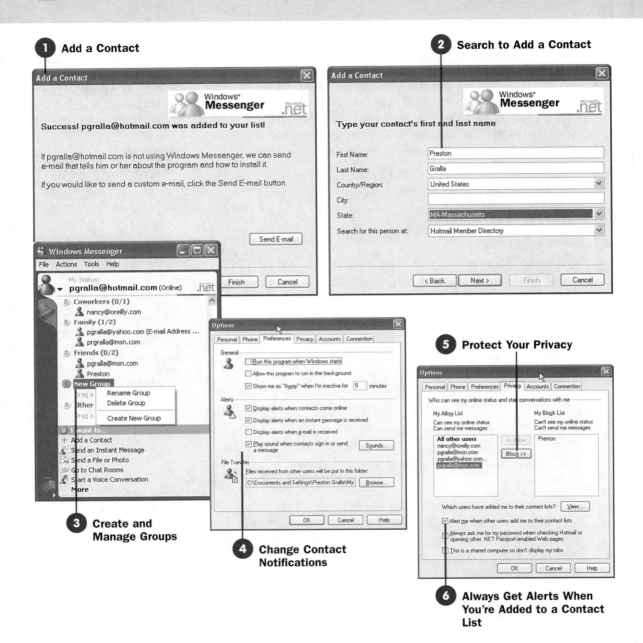

3 Create and Manage Groups

4 Change Contact Notifications

5 Protect Your Privacy

6 Always Get Alerts When You're Added to a Contact List

② Search to Add a Contact

You might not know the email address of the person you want to add to your buddy list. In that event, you can search for him. Click the **Add a Contact** link at the bottom of the main screen, and in the screen that appears, select **Search for a Contact**. A search screen will appear. Type the person's name and address (if you know it) and from the **Search for this person at** drop-down list, choose whether you want to search through Microsoft's Hotmail directory, or through your own Address Book. Then click **Next**. The next screen shows a list of matches; add any or all to your contact list.

Sometimes the search feature of Windows Messenger does not work, and so you'll have to come back later to use it.

③ Create and Manage Groups

If you add a lot of contacts to your buddy list, it could soon become unmanageable. It's a good idea to create *groups* that organize contacts for you. For example, you might want one group for friends, another for family, another for people in your department at work, and so on.

To create a group, choose **Tools, Manage Groups** from the menu and then choose **Add a Group**. You'll get a notification that your contact list must first be sorted into groups, which is confusing because you have yet to create a group. (If you haven't created a group, how can you sort your contacts into groups?) But yours is not to reason why, so click **Yes** when asked whether to sort your contacts into groups.

When you answer **Yes**, a series of groups is automatically created for you: **Coworkers**, **Family**, **Friends**, **New Group**, and **Other Contacts**. Your existing contacts are all put into the **Other Contacts** group. If you want to use only the groups automatically created for you, you don't have to create any other groups. To move contacts from **Other Contacts** to one of the other groups, simply drag the contact from one group to the other group.

If you want to delete a group, rename a group, or add a group, right-click the group you want to delete or rename. A context

NOTE

Windows Messenger allows you to communicate only with others who use Windows Messenger or MSN Messenger. You can't use it to communicate with people who use AOL Instant Messenger or Yahoo! Messenger, and you can't add contacts from people who use those programs or other instant messenger programs.

menu appears that will let you rename or delete the selected group or add a new group. Choose **Rename** or **Delete** to rename or delete the group. Choose **Create New Group** to create a new group. When you choose to create a new group, it will be called **New Group** (if you've deleted the **New Group** that Windows XP automatically created) or **New Group 1** (if you haven't deleted the **New Group** that XP automatically created). Type the name that you want the new group to have.

④ Change Contact Notifications

As you know, whenever a contact in your buddy list signs onto Windows Messenger, you'll get a notification that they've signed in. A sound will also play on your PC.

If you want, you can disable the notification Windows XP sends you when a contact signs in, and you can also disable the sound that plays when a contact signs in. Choose **Tools, Options** from the menu and click the **Preferences** tab. In the **Alerts** section, if you don't want to receive a notification when a contact comes online, disable the **Display alerts when contacts come online** check box. If you don't want a sound to play when a contact comes online, disable the **Play sound when contacts sign in or send a message** check box.

⑤ Protect Your Privacy

There may be Windows Messenger users with whom you prefer not to correspond, and whom you prefer not know when you come online. You can block them from sending you messages or seeing when you're online.

Choose **Tools, Options** from the menu to open the **Options** dialog box and click the **Privacy** tab. On the left side is your **My Allow List**. Anyone in your **My Allow List** can see when you come online and can send you instant messages. To block a contact from seeing when you're online or sending you messages, highlight the contact in the **My Allow List** and click the **Block** button. That contact is moved to your **My Block List** and can't see when you come online or send you messages. To move a contact off the **My Block List**, highlight the name in that list and click **Allow**.

TIP

Whenever you start Windows Messenger, the contact list appears. You can switch between the messaging window and contact list by using the normal Windows **Alt+Tab** key combination.

6 **Always Get Alerts When You're Added to a Contact List**

If you always want to get alerts when you're added to someone's contact list, on the **Privacy** tab make sure to check the **Alert me when other users add me to their contact list** check box. If you don't want those alerts, disable the check box.

88 About Sending Instant Messages

After you have placed someone on your buddy list, it's exceptionally easy to send him an instant message. Double-click his name in the buddy list, and a box pops up with two panes on the left. Type your message in the bottom pane, press **Enter** or click **Send**, and your message is instantly sent to your contact.

Your contact will receive a notification in the **Notification Area** on his desktop, with the first several lines of the message, alerting him that he's received a message. The Windows Messenger instant message area—the same one you used to send the message—also appears on his desktop, in a separate window, containing your complete message. Your contact can then respond to you in the same way that you originally sent the message: by typing a response in the bottom-left pane and pressing **Enter**.

When you send an instant message to someone, he gets this notification; the Windows Messenger instant messaging window also opens, allowing him to see and respond to your message.

You can send "emoticons"—small graphics of smiling faces, angry faces, or similar graphics—in your instant messages. Emoticons dress up your message and also make your intentions clearer. To send an emoticon, click the **Emoticon** button in the bar that divides the two panes on the left side of the window, choose the one you want to use, and press **Enter**.

Before You Begin

✔ **86** Sign Up for Windows Messenger

✔ **87** Customize Your Buddy List

See Also

→ **89** Send a File or Photo

→ **90** Have a Voice or Video Conversation

TIP

You can dress up your messages by using special fonts. Click the **Font** button in the bar that divides the two panes and choose a font—including its size, color, and effects such as bold and strikethrough. You can format your entire message in the selected font, or only single letters or words. To format an entire message, first choose your font and then type your message. To format a word, highlight it and choose the font before you send the message.

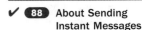
When you're done with the conversation, close the window as you would any other window in Windows XP: Click the close button (the **X**) in the upper-right corner of the title bar.

There are times, particularly if you're using instant messaging at work, when you might want to save an instant messaging conversation as a text file. To save a conversation, before you close the window, choose **File, Save As** from the menu. Then navigate to the folder where you want to save the conversation, give the file a name, and click **Save**.

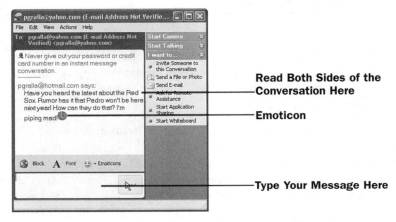

When you send an instant message in Windows Messenger, consider using emoticons if you think that your meaning might be misunderstood.

89 Send a File or Photo

Before You Begin

✔ **88** About Sending Instant Messages

See Also

→ **90** Have a Voice or Video Conversation

One of the more useful features of Windows Messenger is rarely used—the capability to send files and pictures. For friends and family, it's the quickest way to send pictures. For those at work, it's a particular boon because it allows important files to be sent instantly, arriving faster than through email. Another benefit is that some ISPs and businesses block files over a certain size from being sent or received with email, and attaching files to an instant message is a way around that. In addition, some email programs, such as Outlook and Outlook Express, block certain attachments from being received, and so if you need to send these blocked files to people, you can do it using Windows Messenger. (For details, see **82** About Dealing with Attachments.)

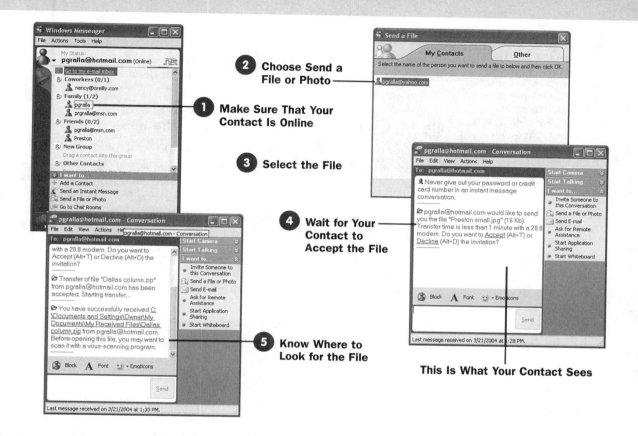

2 **Choose Send a File or Photo**

1 **Make Sure That Your Contact Is Online**

3 **Select the File**

4 **Wait for Your Contact to Accept the File**

5 **Know Where to Look for the File**

This Is What Your Contact Sees

1 Make Sure That Your Contact Is Online

Start Windows Messenger. If your contact isn't online, you won't be able to send her a file or a photo. Check your buddy list to be sure that she's online. The name of anyone who is online is highlighted in green.

2 Choose Send a File or Photo

When you're sure that the person is online, choose **Actions, Send a File or Photo** from the menu. (You might also see a **Send a File or Photo** link at the bottom or side of the Windows Messenger screen.) The **Send a File** dialog box appears. Select the contact to whom you want to send a file and click **OK**.

TIP

Make sure that the file you're sending does not contain a virus. To be safe, use your antivirus software to scan the file before sending it. For details, see **74** Protect Yourself Against Viruses.

3 Select the File

A dialog box opens, allowing you to navigate to the folder that contains the file you want to send. Highlight the file you want to send and click **Open**.

4 Wait for Your Contact to Accept the File

Your contact is sent an alert that you want to send him a file. Additionally, an instant messaging window opens on his screen, with details about the file you're sending, including its name, size, and amount of time it might take to transfer the file. The contact can accept or decline the invitation. If he declines the invitation, you'll get a notification that the invitation was declined.

If he accepts the invitation, you'll be notified that the invitation was accepted. You'll then be shown the status of the file transfer, and will be notified when the transfer is complete.

5 Know Where to Look for the File

If you're on the receiving end of a file transfer, you must click the **Accept** link (or press **Alt+T**) to receive a file. After you do, you'll be shown the transfer status, and be told when the transfer is complete.

TIP

Only accept file transfers from people you know. And after receiving any file, even from someone you know, scan it for viruses before opening it.

You'll also be shown a link to where the file is located. To open the file, click the link in the message window. If you want to find the file at some later point, you'll find it in **C:\Documents and Settings***Your Name***\\My Documents\\My Received Files**, where ***Your Name*** is your Windows XP account name.

---

90 Have a Voice or Video Conversation

Before You Begin

✔ **88** About Sending Instant Messages

See Also

→ **89** Send a File or Photo

The world has gone multimedia, and instant messaging is no different. No longer do you have to chat by typing words on your keyboard. You can have voice conversations and even video chats using Windows Messenger.

1 Make Sure That You Have the Right Hardware

You can have a voice conversation or video chat only if your hardware, and the hardware of the person with whom you want to communicate, supports talking by either voice or by video.

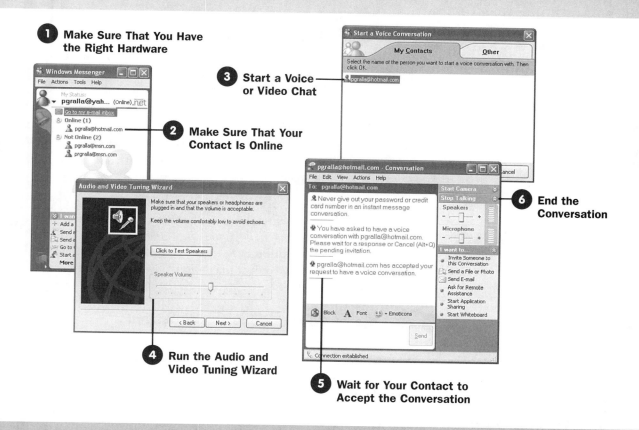

1 Make Sure That You Have the Right Hardware

2 Make Sure That Your Contact Is Online

3 Start a Voice or Video Chat

4 Run the Audio and Video Tuning Wizard

5 Wait for Your Contact to Accept the Conversation

6 End the Conversation

For video conversations, you'll need a digital video camera or a webcam connected to your PC. These rarely come with computers, so you'll have to buy and install the hardware yourself.

For voice conversations, you'll only need a microphone, because all computers come with speakers and a sound card. Some computers ship with microphones you can attach to the computer. Many computers also include built-in microphones. Check your documentation to see if yours has a built-in microphone; if not, you'll have to buy one and plug it into the microphone jack. You can usually find the jack near or next to the jack where you plug in your speakers.

Make sure that the person with whom you want to communicate is outfitted properly as well.

 TIP

For information about how to install hardware, see **113** Install New Hardware.

② Make Sure That Your Contact Is Online

If your contact isn't online, you won't be able to have a video or voice chat. Check your buddy list to be sure he's online. The name of anyone who is online is highlighted in green in your buddy list.

③ Start a Voice or Video Chat

From the **Actions** menu, choose **Start a Voice Conversation** if you want to talk; choose **Start a Video Conversation** if you want to have a video conversation.

You might also be able to choose **Start a Voice Conversation** or **Start a Video Conversation** from the bottom or side of the Windows Messenger screen, depending on how it is set up. The **Start a Voice Conversation** or **Start a Video Conversation** dialog box appears. Select the contact to whom you want to have a conversation and click **OK**.

④ Run the Audio and Video Tuning Wizard

NOTE

The first screen provides recommendations on how to orient your microphone and speakers—put the microphone within three to five inches of your mouth, and point the microphone away from your speakers (or use headphones), so that you don't hear echoes.

Before you can actually have the conversation, the **Audio and Video Tuning Wizard** will appear. The wizard checks that your computer is capable of having a voice or video chat. When the wizard appears, close down any programs that use audio or video and then click **Next**. Click **Next** again after you read the recommendations on the first screen.

You'll then be walked through a series of screens that confirms and tests the hardware you're using. If you're using headphones, make sure to enable the **I am using headphones** check box.

You will be asked to test your microphone and speakers by clicking boxes. When you test your speakers, you'll hear the volume. Adjust the volume using the sliders until the sound is the way you want it. When you test your microphone, you'll see a voice indicator, indicating volume. Adjust the microphone volume. You'll also test your video camera if you have one attached.

When you're done working through the pages of the wizard, click **Finish**.

5 Wait for Your Contact to Accept the Conversation

Your contact will be sent an alert that you want to contact him. Additionally, an instant messaging window will open up on his desktop, telling him you want to have a voice or video conversation. The contact can accept or decline the invitation. If he declines the invitation, you'll get a notification that the invitation was declined. If he accepts the invitation, you'll be notified that the invitation was accepted.

NOTE

On the right side of your screen are **Speakers** and **Microphone** sliders you can use to change the volume. If you've initiated a video conversation, you'll see a video of your friend as you both speak.

6 End the Conversation

Keep speaking until you both no longer want to talk. When you want to end the conversation, click the **Stop Talking** button at the top-right of the screen. The **Speakers** and **Microphone** sliders will disappear, and you will be disconnected from the conversation.

91 Customize Your Messenger Settings

Windows Messenger might appear to be a straightforward program, but there are many ways in which you can customize how it looks and works. For example, you can hide or show panes and tabs, and change color schemes and fonts. You can also change the startup behavior of Windows Messenger.

Before You Begin

✔ 86 Sign Up for Windows Messenger

See Also

→ 87 Customize Your Buddy List

1 Show or Hide the Action Pane

The **Action** pane is the section at the bottom of the Windows Messenger screen that gives you quick access to many of Messenger's functions, such as adding a contact, sending an instant message, and starting a voice conversation. Click any of the links or icons there to perform an action.

You can either hide or display the **Action** pane. You might hide it if you have a great many contacts and you can't see them all because the **Action** pane takes up too much screen real estate. You might display it if you don't have a great many contacts, or you always want Messenger's most common functions within easy reach.

To hide the pane, choose **Tools, Show Actions Pane** to remove the check mark from the option. To display the pane, choose **Tools, Show Actions Pane** again to enable the option.

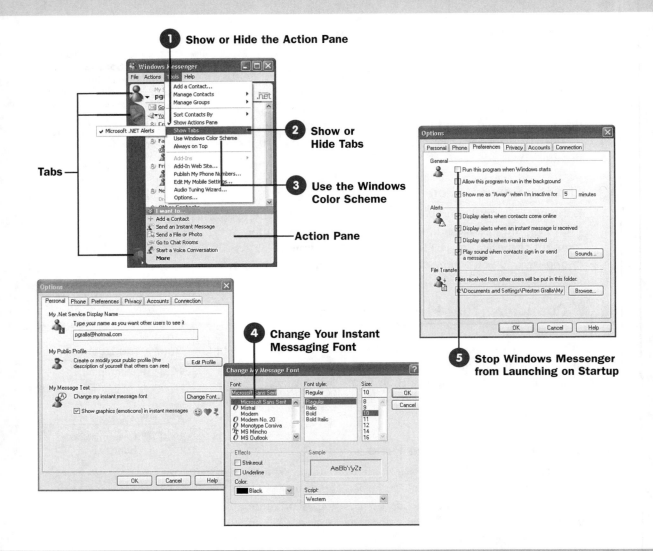

1 Show or Hide the Action Pane

2 Show or Hide Tabs

3 Use the Windows Color Scheme

Tabs

Action Pane

4 Change Your Instant Messaging Font

5 Stop Windows Messenger from Launching on Startup

2 Show or Hide Tabs

Windows Messenger can either display or hide tabs on the left side of the screen. The tabs let you quickly navigate to items such as .NET Alerts, which are alerts such as news briefs and weather reports. (For more information about .NET Alerts and how to set them up, see **92** Get .NET Alerts.)

If you don't use .NET Alerts, there's no reason to display the tabs because they take up useful screen real estate. If, however, you use .NET Alerts, the tabs are a useful navigational device.

To hide the tabs, choose **Tools, Show Tabs**; from the submenu that opens, uncheck any option whose tab you don't want displayed. Check any option whose tab you do want displayed.

③ Use the Windows Color Scheme

Windows Messenger uses its own color scheme, which may or may not match the color scheme you're currently using for Windows XP. If you customized your Windows XP color scheme, the Messenger color scheme might clash with it. Or you simply might prefer that Messenger use the same color scheme you've set up for Windows XP.

To use the Windows XP color scheme you've created, choose **Tools, Use Windows Color Scheme** from the Windows Messenger menu and make sure that the option is checked. To use the Windows Messenger color scheme, choose **Tools, Use Windows Color Scheme** again and make sure that the option does not have a check mark.

④ Change Your Instant Messaging Font

The default font that Windows Messenger uses for messages is the very plain and unadorned Microsoft Sans Serif 10-point font. You can, however, use any font on your system for your messages.

To change the font for your messages, choose **Tools, Options** from the menu and click the **Personal** tab in the **Options** dialog box. Click the **Change Font** button to open the **Change My Message Font** dialog box. Select the font, font style, size, and color you want to use and click **OK** twice to close the dialog boxes.

⑤ Stop Windows Messenger from Launching on Startup

After you register for Windows Messenger, every time you start up Windows XP, Messenger also launches and logs you in automatically. However, you might not want Windows Messenger to always start up, because there might be times—many times for some people—when you don't want to be bothered by instant messages.

TIP

Even though Windows Messenger says that you can display multiple tabs, at this point there's only one tab you can display—the .NET Alerts tab (the bell). At some point there may be more options, but at the moment, that's the only one you can display or hide.

TIP

For information about how to change your Windows XP color scheme, see ⑪ **Change Your Desktop's Appearance.**

TIP

If you are not a fan of emoticons, you can turn them off in Windows Messenger. On the **Personal** tab of the **Options** dialog box, disable the **Show graphics (emoticons) in instant messages** check box.

You can tell Windows Messenger not to run automatically when you launch Windows XP. Choose **Tools, Options** to open the **Options** dialog box and click the **Preferences** tab. Disable the **Run this program when Windows starts** check box and click **OK**.

92 Get .NET Alerts

Before You Begin

✔ **86** Sign Up for Windows Messenger

See Also

→ **91** Customize Your Messenger Settings

Windows Messenger is more than just an instant messaging program. It can also deliver news alerts, weather alerts, and other kinds of information straight to your desktop, without you having to visit a web page. You'll get a summary of the alert, and if you want more information about it, you can click it to visit a website with more details. These notifications are called .NET Alerts. Here's how to set them up.

1 Go to the Microsoft .NET Alerts Site

You don't set up .NET Alerts from within Windows Messenger—you instead set them up from the Microsoft .NET Alerts page at **www.microsoft.com/net/services/alerts/signup.asp**.

2 Choose the Alert You Want to Receive

NOTE

The Microsoft .NET Alters site lists "content providers" that offer .NET Alerts. Content providers include news sites, financial sites, sports sites, weather sites, auction sites, and others.

Read through the list of content providers and click the icon of the content provider whose alerts you want to receive. You'll be brought to a page that includes information about the alerts you'll be receiving, as well as information about how to sign up. Look for a link or button to sign up for the alert (some sites call it signing *in*). Click the link or button. When you sign in to that content provider, you'll be asked for your email address and password; if you've set up your .NET Passport to sign you in automatically, you'll be signed in to the content provider automatically.

3 Choose Your Alerts

Some sites have multiple alerts from which you can choose. Read through the alerts and sign up for those that interest you. Then click the **Submit** button (or whatever other button the sites ask you to click). You might be sent to a page that asks you to read the terms of service for using the alerts. Read the terms of service and click the **Accept** button if you agree to the terms.

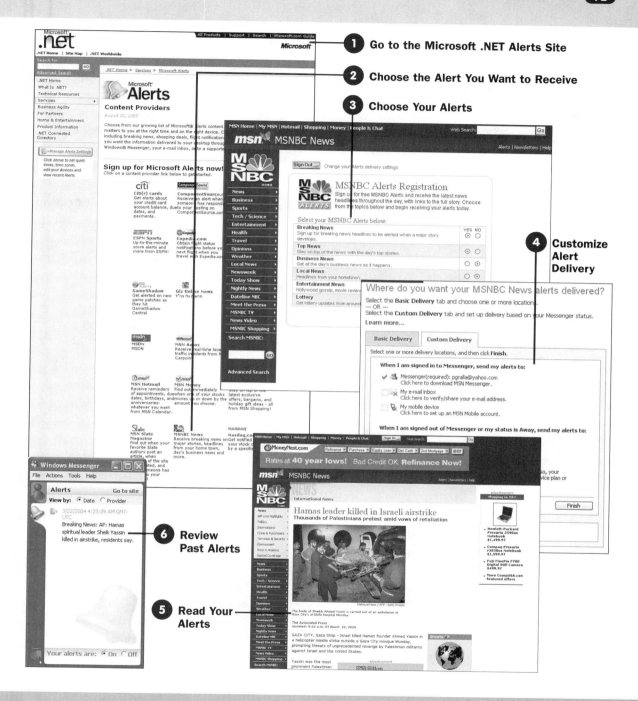

1 Go to the Microsoft .NET Alerts Site

2 Choose the Alert You Want to Receive

3 Choose Your Alerts

4 Customize Alert Delivery

6 Review Past Alerts

5 Read Your Alerts

NOTE

If you want to receive messages on your cell phone, you'll have to sign up for an MSN Mobile Account. From the **Tools** menu, choose **Options**, click the **Phone** tab, and then click **Mobile Settings**. You'll be sent to a website where you can sign up.

NOTE

For information about how to turn the .NET Alert tab on and off, see **91** Customize Your Messenger Settings.

4 Customize Alert Delivery

You'll next be sent to a page that lets you customize how you want the alerts delivered—for example, you might be able to have them sent to your email box in addition to, or in place of, Windows Messenger. You might also have the alerts delivered to your cell phone, and so on. When you're done selecting the delivery methods you want, click **Finish**.

5 Read Your Alerts

Whenever an alert is sent to you, it will appear in the **Notification Area** in the lower-right corner of your desktop. You'll get a brief summary of the alert in that area; click the alert to get more details.

6 Review Past Alerts

You can also review past alerts that you've received. To review them in Windows Messenger, click the **.NET Alert** tab (the one that looks like a bell). You'll see a list of your previous alerts. Click any alert to read the full alert. To go back to the main Windows Messenger screen, click the **Windows Messenger** tab (the one that looks like a person).

PART III

Entertainment, Digital Pictures, and Graphics

IN THIS PART:

11

That's Entertainment: Music and Video

IN THIS CHAPTER:

Windows XP is the first version of Windows designed from the ground up with entertainment—including audio and video—in mind. It makes it extremely easy to listen to music on your PC, copy music to your PC, make your own CDs, and watch DVDs on your PC.

It does all this using the free Windows Media Player. In this chapter, you'll learn how to use this software to play CDs and DVDs, copy music to your PC, manage that music, and even make your own CDs. You'll also find out how you can share your music with others and buy music online.

93 About Windows Media Player

KEY TERM

Burn—To make a music CD by copying digital music from your PC to a blank CD. You'll have to have a CD or DVD drive that can write to CDs in order to burn CDs.

If you're interested in listening to music or watching animations and videos, or if you want to copy digital music to your PC and *burn* CDs, you'll use Windows XP's built-in Windows Media Player. This software is simple, colorful, and puts digital entertainment at your fingertips.

To use the Windows Media Player, click the **Start** button, choose **All Programs**, choose **Accessories**, **Entertainment**, and then choose **Windows Media Player**.

Media central for Windows XP: The Windows Media Player can play music, videos, DVDs, and even Internet radio stations.

Using it is straightforward, although it does have a few quirks. At first, it's difficult to find its menu; there simply doesn't appear to be one. But if you move your mouse pointer over the top of the Windows Media Player screen, the menu appears. If you want the menu to be always visible, click the small double-sided arrow in the upper-left corner of the Windows Media Player screen.

There is one main drawback to the Windows Media Player—it does not do a good job of working with *MP3 files*, which are the most popular digital music files. (For more information about MP3 files and other digital music files, see **98 About Audio File Formats**.) Windows Media Player can play MP3 files, but it can't record them at a high quality, so if you listen to MP3 files you recorded using Windows Media Player, they'll sound muddy. You can, however, record digital music in high quality using other formats, notably WMA (Windows Media Audio) files. If you want to record high-quality MP3 files, you can get free software that does it, such as MusicMatch Jukebox from **www.musicmatch.com**. Or you can pay for extra software that will let Windows Media Player record high-quality MP3s. For details, run Windows Media Player, choose **Tools**, **Options** from the menu, click the **Copy Music** tab and click the **Learn more about MP3 formats** link.

KEY TERM

MP3 files—Digital music files you can play on your PC. MP3 files are the most popular form of digital music.

94 Play a CD or DVD

The most basic thing you can do with Windows Media Player is to play a music CD or a DVD. You'll most likely find yourself playing CDs a great deal, because if you have a good pair of speakers, the sound is every bit as good as what you get from a normal CD player and your stereo music system. But you most likely won't want to watch many DVDs with it, because it's uncomfortable to sit at your PC and watch a full-length movie on the small screen.

In this task, you'll see how to play CDs, but the steps for playing DVDs is the same.

Before You Begin

✔ **93** About Windows Media Player

See Also

→ **95** Customize How Your Music Sounds

1 Run Windows Media Player

Click the **Start** button, choose **All Programs**, choose **Accessories**, **Entertainment**, and then choose **Windows Media Player**. The Windows Media Player will launch.

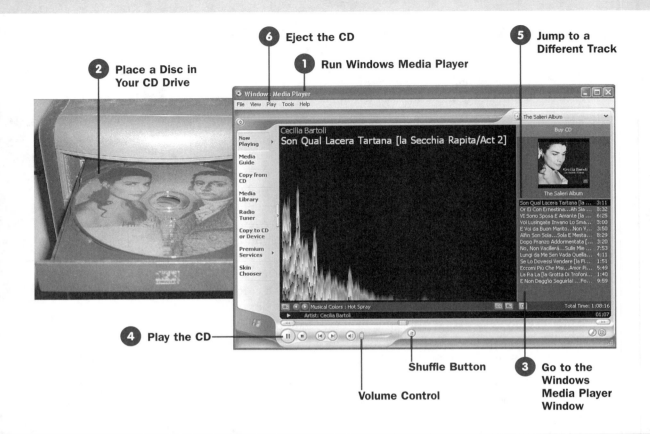

6 Eject the CD

5 Jump to a Different Track

1 Run Windows Media Player

2 Place a Disc in Your CD Drive

4 Play the CD

Shuffle Button

3 Go to the Windows Media Player Window

Volume Control

---

2 **Place a Disc in Your CD Drive**

Press the eject button (located on the front of your PC, probably under the face of the disc tray) to open the CD tray, place the CD or DVD into the tray, and then press the eject button again. The CD tray will retract into the PC.

3 **Go to the Windows Media Player Window**

Windows Media Player will automatically go out to the Internet and download information about the CD that you've put into your PC. It will display the CD's album cover art and list every track on the CD, including each track's time. It will also tell you the total

NOTE

You must be connected to the Internet if you want Windows Media Player to automatically find out what CD you're playing, and display information about the CD, including its cover art and tracks.

playing time of the entire CD. Similarly, when you insert a DVD, it will download the information about the DVD and display vital information about the DVD.

4 Play the CD

The Windows Media Player controls are found at the bottom-left of the screen. They are the exact same controls that you find on a CD player, including buttons for **Play**, **Pause**, **Stop**, **Previous Track**, **Next Track**, and **Mute**.

To play the CD, click the **Play** button. To control the volume, drag the volume control to either the right or the left. (You can also use your speaker's volume controls to control the volume.)

5 Jump to a Different Track

To play a different track on the CD, double-click the track title in the track listing on the right side of the screen. Windows Media Player immediately jumps to that track.

You can also shuffle the tracks so that they plan in a random order, not in the order they appear on the CD. To do that, click the small **Shuffle** button, directly to the right of the volume control.

6 Eject the CD

When you're done playing the CD or DVD and want to eject it, choose **Play**, **Eject** from the menu. Alternatively, press **Ctrl+E**.

95 Customize How Your Music Sounds

One of the great benefits of the Windows Media Player is that it lets you easily change how your music sounds—not just the loudness or softness, but the mix of tones, treble, and bass. Opera was meant to be heard differently than rock music, for example, and so the player lets you change settings for each CD you play.

In addition, Windows Media Player will also play 3D surround sound, so that the music will sound as if it surrounds you, rather than just coming at you from one direction.

NOTE

When you play a DVD instead of a CD, instead of a track list you'll get a set of menu options for playing the DVD. Those menu options are the same as those you see when you play a DVD on a DVD player: You can skip to a specific section of the DVD, see additional material, turn captions on and off, and so on, in the same way you use the remote control on a DVD player.

Before You Begin

✔ **93** About Windows Media Player

✔ **94** Play a CD or DVD

See Also

→ **96** Customize Windows Media Player's Appearance

1 Display the
Graphics Equalizer

3 Choose the SRS
WOW Effects

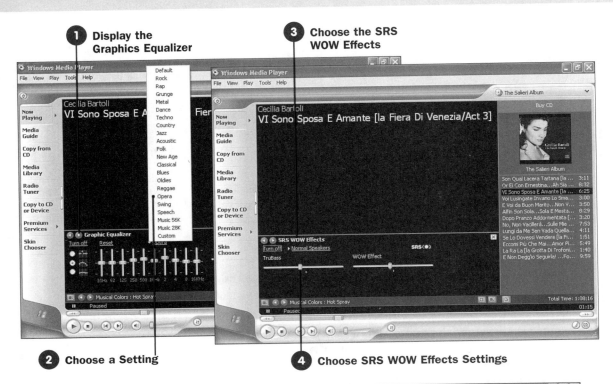

2 Choose a Setting

4 Choose SRS WOW Effects Settings

5 Use Quiet Mode

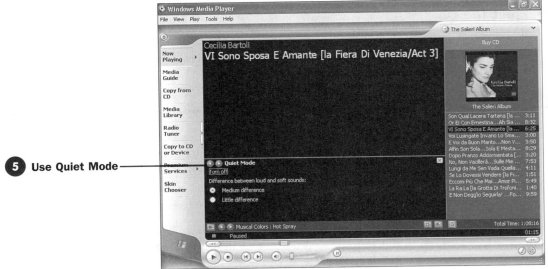

① Display the Graphics Equalizer

The Graphics Equalizer has premade settings you can choose to adjust the way that your music sounds so that it is best suited to the kind of music you're listening to. There are over a dozen different settings you can choose from, from **Rock** to **Rap** to **Grunge**, **Jazz**, **Acoustic**, **Opera**, **Folk**, **Blues**, **Classical**, and others.

To use the Graphics Equalizer, select **View**, **Enhancements** from the Windows Media Player menu and then choose **Graphics Equalizer**.

② Choose a Setting

The Graphics Equalizer appears on the lower-left portion of your screen. To turn on the Graphics Equalizer, click **Turn On** at the left side of the screen. (If the Graphics Equalizer is already on, the words **Turn Off** will instead appear.)

Click the right-most link with a downward pointing triangle—which initially reads **Rock**, **Opera**, **Grunge**, or any of the Graphics Equalizer's settings. A pop-up list appears. Choose the setting you want to use for the CD you are currently playing and then release the mouse. When you play music now, the Media Player will use the selected setting. The setting you select adjusts the tone, bass, treble, and a variety of other options best-suited for that type of music.

③ Choose the SRS WOW Effects

SRS WOW Effects can make it sound as if you are surrounded by sound, rather than having the sound come at you from a single direction. To use the SRS WOW Effects, select **View**, **Enhancements** from the menu and choose **SRS WOW Effects**.

④ Choose SRS WOW Effects Settings

The SRS WOW Effects settings replace the Graphics Equalizer on the lower-left portion of your screen. To turn on SRS WOW Effects, click **Turn On** at the left side of the screen. (If the SRS WOW Effects are already on, the words **Turn Off** instead appear.)

NOTE

The term Graphics Equalizer is somewhat confusing—the term makes it sound as though it changes the graphics on Windows Media Player. In fact, it has nothing to do with graphics. It's called the Graphics Equalizer because it contains sliders you can move, so it's a *visual* way of changing the way Windows Media Player sounds.

NOTE

You can also manually customize your Graphics Equalizer settings by moving the sliders on it. But the settings are almost incomprehensible; unless you're extremely experienced with sound and settings, you won't really know what you're doing.

TIP

You can also change the settings so that they sound best for how you'll be listening to the music—with normal speakers, large speakers, or headphones. To choose from these options, click the link to the right of the **Turn On/Turn Off** link. This link initially reads **Normal Speakers, Large Speakers,** or **Headphones.** Keep clicking the link until you choose the way you'll be listening to music. From now on, you'll be using the SRS WOW Effects in the way you customized.

To change the bass effect, move the TruBass slider (drag to the left to make the bass weaker, drag to the right to make it stronger). To change the SRS WOW Effect (which gives the effect of sound surrounding you), move its slider (drag to the left to make surround sound weaker, drag to the right to make it stronger).

⑤ Use Quiet Mode

If you're listening to quiet music quietly, you might experience problems: If the music gets too loud, you'll want to turn it down, but when it gets soft, you might not be able to hear it. You can adjust the way Windows Media Player plays music when you listen to quiet music so that the difference in loudness between the loudest and softest sounds is not that great. That way, you'll be able to hear all sounds equally well.

To listen in Quiet Mode, select **View, Enhancements** from the menu and choose **Quiet Mode.** The Quiet Mode controls appear in the lower-left portion of the window. To turn on Quiet Mode, click **Turn On** at the left side of the screen. (If Quiet Mode is already on, the words **Turn Off** will instead appear.) You can also change whether there should be a small amount of difference between the largest and smallest sounds by clicking the appropriate radio button.

Customize Windows Media Player's Appearance

Before You Begin

✔ **93** About Windows Media Player

See Also

→ **95** Customize How Your Music Sounds

Don't like the way Windows Media Player looks? No problem—you can change it. The program is almost infinitely customizable. You can change the information it displays, what kinds of special effects show as your music plays, and whether to display toolbars.

Better yet, you can *skin* the program—that is, thoroughly alter its appearance—and you can use the program in a stripped-down mode or full screen.

① Display or Hide the Taskbar

The Taskbar is the bar on the left side of Windows Media Player screen that displays the buttons **Now Playing, Media Guide, Copy from CD,** and so on. You can either display or hide those buttons. When you're playing music, for example, you'll most likely want to hide the Taskbar because it takes space away from the special effects (called *visualizations*) that play when you listen to music.

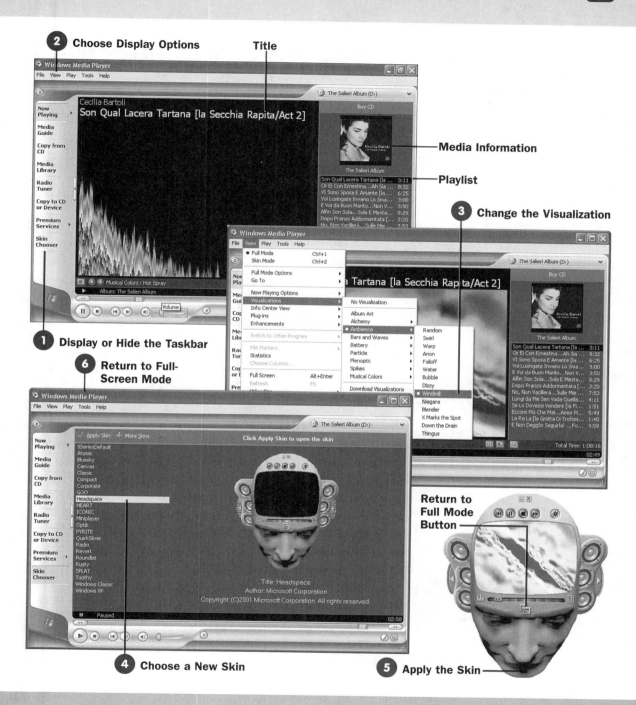

2 Choose Display Options

Title

Media Information

Playlist

3 Change the Visualization

1 Display or Hide the Taskbar

6 Return to Full-Screen Mode

Return to Full Mode Button

4 Choose a New Skin

5 Apply the Skin

To turn the Taskbar back on, choose View, Full Mode Options from the menu and choose Hide Taskbar so that the check mark goes away.

To hide the Taskbar, choose **View**, **Full Mode Options** from the menu and choose **Hide Taskbar**. A check mark appears next to **Hide Taskbar** in the menu and the Taskbar goes away.

2 Choose Display Options

You can customize what information should appear when you play music. These are the options you can turn on or off:

- **Title.** This is the title of the current song, displayed at the top of the middle of the Windows Media Player.

- **Media Information.** This is the picture of the CD (its cover art), along with the CD title, played at the top-right side of the screen, just above the playlist.

- **Playlist.** This is the list of the songs on the CD, along with the duration in minutes:seconds format displayed on the right side of the screen.

By default, all these options are displayed. To turn any off, select **View**, **Now Playing Options** from the menu and disable (remove the check mark from) the options you don't want to be displayed. To turn them on again, select **View**, **Now Playing Options** from the menu and select the options you want to be displayed.

3 Change the Visualization

Visualizations are the animations that take up most of the screen as you play music; the graphics change according to the volume, rhythm, and intensity of the music currently being played. To change a visualization, choose **View**, **Visualizations** from the menu and choose the category of visualization you want to use, such as **Bars and Waves** or **Spikes**. Then choose the specific visualization that you want to use.

KEY TERM

Skin—A kind of wrapper around a program that can give it a completely different look and feel, including different colors, fonts, graphics, sizes, and even where buttons are located.

4 Choose a New Skin

Windows Media Player can use *skins*—an easy way to apply different looks to the program so that the window appears completely different.

To choose a new skin, click the **Skin Chooser** button in the Taskbar. A list of skins appears. As you scroll through the list, click a skin option to see what the skin looks like on the right side of the screen.

To choose a skin, click to highlight it. When you choose the skin, you won't apply it yet. Skins work only when you switch to "skins mode," and you haven't yet put Windows Media Player into skins mode. If you don't yet want to go into skins mode, go back to what you were doing before you chose the skin (for example, listening to music). To go back to listening to music, click the **Now Playing** button in the Taskbar.

5 Apply the Skin

To use the skin you selected in step 4, you must switch to skins mode: Choose **View, Skins Mode** from the menu or press **Ctrl+2**. Windows Media Player now uses the new skin. The window will get much smaller, and look much different. It might take you a while to learn where the controls are, because their locations might be different from where they are when Windows Media Player is full-screen, and the controls even differ from skin to skin.

6 Return to Full-Screen Mode

To return to full-screen mode, press **Ctrl+1**. You can also click the **Return to Full Mode** button, which looks like two overlapping squares. It is not always easy to find that button, however, and so **Ctrl+1** is usually an easier solution.

97 Listen to Internet Radio Stations

One of the quietest revolutions in radio broadcasting is the advent of Internet radio stations. These radio stations don't broadcast in the traditional sense, by using the airwaves. Rather, they send their signals over the Internet, and you can tune into them using Windows Media Player. Note that in an increasing number of instances, traditional radio stations broadcast over the Internet as well as over the airways.

The radio stations you'll find on the Internet are even more varied than the ones you'll find on your radio dial. That's because your radio limits you to listening in a relatively small geographic region. Internet radio, on the other hand, covers the entire world.

Before You Begin

✔ **93** About Windows Media Player

1 Go to the Radio Tuner

2 Play a Radio Station

4 Browse for Stations

3 Add Your Favorite Stations to My Stations List

5 Search for Stations

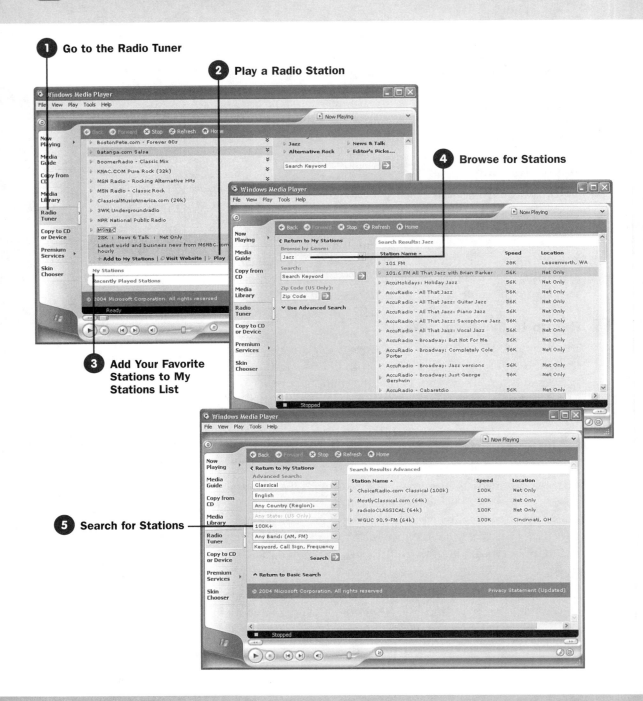

❶ Go to the Radio Tuner

To find an Internet radio station, click the **Radio Tuner** button in the Windows Media Player Taskbar. You'll see a list of individual stations you can listen to, categories of stations, and a way to search for stations.

❷ Play a Radio Station

To play a station, click its title in the list. A description of the station is displayed, as well as several links, including a **Visit Website** link and possibly a **Play** link. If there is a **Play** link, click it; after Windows Media Player contacts the station, the station begins playing. If there is no **Play** link, click the **Visit Website** link. A browser window opens, asking whether you want to play the station inside Internet Explorer or inside Windows Media Player. After Windows Media Player contacts the station, the station begins playing.

❸ Add Your Favorite Stations to My Stations List

There are so many radio stations on the Internet that it can be difficult to keep track of them all and remember where you found the ones you like. You can add your favorite stations to a **My Stations** list to make it easy to get back to them. For any station you want to add to the list, click the **Add to My Stations** link underneath it.

To visit your **My Stations** list, click the **My Stations** link, and you'll see the list of all your favorite stations. Play them as you would play any other station. To get back to the main screen of the Radio Tuner, click the **Back** button near the top of the screen.

❹ Browse for Stations

The right side of the main screen of the Radio Tuner includes a list of main categories of radio stations, such as **Top 40**, **Country**, **Jazz**, and so on. To browse through a category, click the category title in this list. A list of stations in that category appears on the left side of the window. Play any of them as you would normally play a station.

TIP

Generally, it's a better idea to play the radio station inside Windows Media Player rather than in a browser window because you can more easily control how many windows are open and which stations you are listening to.

NOTE

When you're in a category, click the **Browse by Genre** drop-down menu to move to another category. Note that this menu has a much more comprehensive list of categories than does the main Radio Tuner screen, so it's a better way to browse categories.

5 **Search for Stations**

The best way to find a specific station is to use the Windows Media Player search feature. The feature is hidden, though, so you can't get to it right away. From the main Radio Tuner screen, click the **Find More Stations** link just above the category listing. From the screen that appears, click the **Use Advanced Search** button. A screen appears that lets you search by genre, language, country, keywords, and so on. After you fill in your search criteria, click the green **Search** button. You'll get a list of stations that match your search terms. Play these stations as you would any other stations.

98 About Audio File Formats

Before You Begin

✓ **93** About Windows Media Player

See Also

→ **99** Copy Music from an Audio CD

(K)EY TERM

Ripping—To record music from a CD and put it on your PC in a digital format.

When it comes to music, Windows Media player can do more than play music CDs, DVDs, and Internet radio stations. It can also record music from CDs to your PC (a process called *ripping*), and it can play digital music you get from other people. You can also create CDs from digital music on your PC (a process called *burning*).

You can use several digital music file formats when recording music to your PC, but the two most important, and most used, are MP3 and WMA (Windows Media Audio). The most popular format is MP3, but Windows Media Player, as explained earlier, cannot *record* music in MP3 format (unless you buy an add-in), although it can *play* music in the MP3 format.

There are several good add-ins that will let you record music in MP3 format in Windows Media Player, including MP3 PowerEncoder, MP3 XPack, and CinePlayer MP3 Creation Pack. For more details, and to buy them, connect to the Internet and launch Windows Media Player. Then choose **Tools**, **Options** from the menu, click the **Copy Music** tab, and click the **Learn more about MP3 formats** link.

The MP3 and WMA formats compress music using different methods, so some of the quality of the music is lost when it is recorded in either format. But you have a choice of how much the music should be compressed. You have to balance file size and the music quality when doing this—the larger the file, the better the quality.

When you record digital music, you record at a specific *bit rate*, as measured in kilobytes per second (Kbps). The bit rate measures how many bytes of data should be recorded per second. The higher the bit rate, the higher the quality of the music and the larger the file. The lower the bit rate, the lower the quality of the music, and the smaller the file. Also, the higher the bit rate, the longer it takes to record a song; the lower the bit rate, the less time it takes to record a song.

When you record music in Windows Media Player, you can record music at rates between 48Kbps and 192Kbps. At 48Kbps, music sounds very muddy and fuzzy; you should never record music at that low rate. Usually, you should record at 96Kbps or higher. Music recorded at 128Kbps is generally considered near-CD quality; when recorded at 192Kbps, music is considered CD quality.

KEY TERM

Bit rate—The rate at which digital music is recorded, measured in kilobytes per second. The higher the bit rate, the higher the quality of the recorded music, and the larger the file.

99 Copy Music from an Audio CD

Perhaps the best thing about Windows Media Player is its capability to *rip* music from a CD—that is, record it to your hard disk. After you have the music on your PC, you can do a variety of different things with it. You can build your own music library so that you can listen to music on your PC whenever you want; you can share that music library with others; and you can *burn* CDs from your music. For example, you might want to make a compilation CD of different tracks from different CDs in your music collection to play in your car CD player.

Before You Begin

✔ **98** About Audio File Formats

See Also

→ **100** Manage Your Music and Media Library

→ **101** Create a Playlist

→ **102** Burn an Audio CD

1 Run Windows Media Player and Place a CD in Your CD Drive

Click the **Start** button, choose **All Programs, Accessories, Entertainment**, and then choose **Windows Media Player**. The Windows Media Player launches. Press the eject button on the face of your computer to open the CD tray, place the CD into the tray, and then press the eject button again. The CD tray retracts into the PC. The CD will start playing, so click the **Stop** button.

2 Open the Copy Music Tab in the Options Dialog Box

Before you record music, you must set your recording options. To get to them, choose **Tools, Options** from the menu and click the **Copy Music** tab.

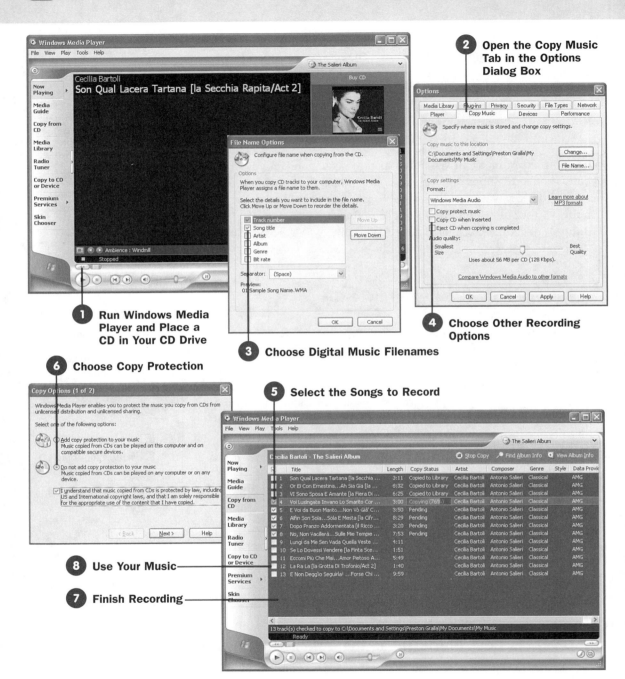

2 Open the Copy Music Tab in the Options Dialog Box

1 Run Windows Media Player and Place a CD in Your CD Drive

3 Choose Digital Music Filenames

4 Choose Other Recording Options

6 Choose Copy Protection

5 Select the Songs to Record

8 Use Your Music

7 Finish Recording

③ Choose Digital Music Filenames

Windows Media Player automatically names files as it records them. It chooses filenames that help you determine the contents of each file by extracting information about the file and using it in the filename. For example, you can choose to use the song name, track number, artist name, album name, music genre, and bit rate in the filename.

To make your choice, click the **File Name** button on the **Copy Music** tab. The **File Name Options** dialog box appears. Enable the check boxes for the attributes you want Windows Media Player to use in the filenames for the songs you are about to record. When you're done, click **OK**.

④ Choose Other Recording Options

On the **Copy Music** tab of the **Options** dialog box, select the remaining options for how you want to record music. Choose your audio quality by moving the slider in the **Audio quality** section to select your bit rate. Leave the **Format** option set to **Windows Media Audio** unless you've paid for an add-in that lets you record MP3 files. If you want Windows Media Player to automatically start recording from a CD whenever you insert a CD into your PC, enable the **Copy CD when inserted** check box. If you want the CD to be ejected when you've finished copying the CD, enable the **Eject CD when copying is complete** check box.

The **Copy protect music** check box is largely useless. If you enable that check box, people on other computers won't be able to listen to the music you record, and if you try to listen to the music on another computer, you might not be able to access it if the owner of that computer has enabled this option. In addition, you might not be able to listen to the music on a portable audio device if you enable the option. So, there's no reason to check the box.

When you've selected your recording options, click **OK**. You'll be brought back to the main screen of the Windows Media Player.

TIP

You can also tell Windows Media Player in which order to use the attribute in the filename. For example, you might want the filename to start off with the album name rather than the track number, and so on. To rearrange the order, after you enable the attributes you want to use, highlight each attribute, and click the **Move Up** or **Move Down** button until the attributes are in the order you want them used in the filenames.

NOTE

The **Copy protect music** check box exists in large part for copyright reasons. Music companies contend that it violates copyright law for you to record music and then share it with others. If you check the box, you won't be able to share the music you record with others, but you'll make the music companies happy.

5 Select the Songs to Record

Now you're ready to record your music. To start recording, click the **Copy from CD** button on the Taskbar. A list of all the tracks on the CD appears, including song title, length, artist, composer, and so on. All the tracks are selected (that is, all their check boxes are enabled). Disable the check boxes for the songs you don't want to record; leave check marks next to those songs you do want to record.

6 Choose Copy Protection

When you're done making your song selections, click the **Copy Music** button at the top of the screen. If, on the **Copy Music** tab of the **Options** dialog box, you did not enable the **Copy protect music** check box, a warning box appears, asking whether you want to copy protect the music you record. If you choose not to copy protect the music, you'll also have to check a box that says you understand the copyright law about copying music. After you make your selection, click **Next**.

Another dialog box will appear, telling you about your current bit rate settings and asking whether you want to change them. If you want to change them, click the **Change my current format settings** button and then click **Next** to be sent back to the **Copy Music** tab of the **Options** dialog box. If you don't want to change bit rate settings, click the **Keep my current format settings** button and click **Finish**.

7 Finish Recording

Windows Media Player begins copying your tracks, one by one. You'll see the progress for each track. After each track is copied, the check mark disappears next to the track title.

When the copying is done, you'll remain on the **Copy from CD** screen, with all the music copied.

8 Use Your Music

Now that you've recorded your music, you're ready to use it. For more information, see **100** **Manage Your Music and Media Library** and **101** **Create a Playlist**.

100 Manage Your Music and Media Library

After you learn how to *rip* music from CDs, you'll most likely start putting a sizable part of your music collection into Windows Media Player. You'll find that having your music close at hand is a great convenience, particularly because—unlike with CDs—you can play individual tracks easily.

But how to manage it all? Windows Media Player offers excellent tools for organizing your library and lets you view your media collection in many different ways: by CD, by genre, and even by the bit rate at which the music was recorded. It's a far better way to see all your music than rummaging through CDs.

Before You Begin

✔ **99** Copy Music from an Audio CD

See Also

→ **101** Create a Playlist
→ **102** Burn an Audio CD
→ **103** Copy Music to an MP3 Player

1 Open the Media Library

Launch Windows Media Player and then click the **Media Library** button in the Taskbar. On the left side of the screen you'll see a list of folders, and on the right side of the screen are the contents of the current folder.

Each song track has information about the song's title, artist, album, genre, length, bit rate, format, and other relevant information. Not all of that information is immediately visible. To see more information than is currently visible in the right side of the screen, move the scroll box at the bottom of the window to the right.

2 Browse by Folder

Open the **All Music** folder in the list on the left side of the screen to see the folders underneath it titled **Artist**, **Album**, and **Genre**. Your music collection will be visible in each of those folders, sorted in different views. The **Artist** folder lists all your songs by artist, for example. This means if you have an artist who sings three songs on one CD and four songs on another, all of that artist's songs are in a separate **Artist** subfolder, regardless of what CD they are found on. The same organizational logic holds for the **Album** and **Genre** folders and subfolders.

TIP

Folders work in Windows Media Player the same way they do in Windows Explorer. When a folder has folders inside of it, there is a + sign next to the folder. Click the + sign to reveal folders underneath. When a folder is open, click the – sign to close it back up.

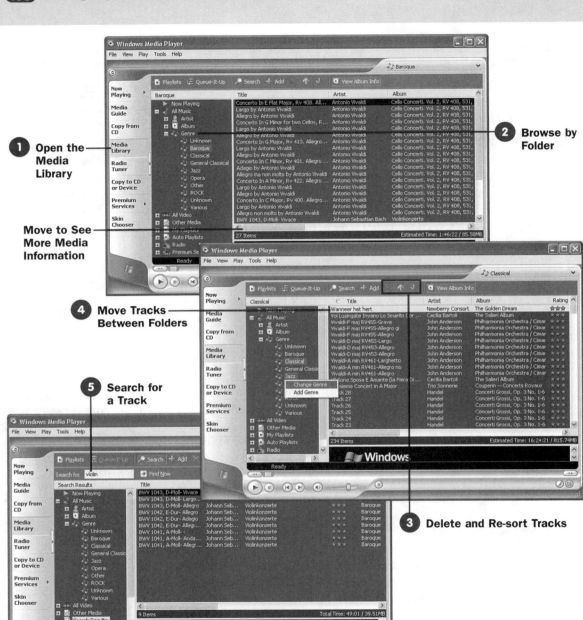

1 Open the Media Library

Move to See More Media Information

2 Browse by Folder

4 Move Tracks Between Folders

5 Search for a Track

3 Delete and Re-sort Tracks

③ Delete and Re-sort Tracks

You can delete tracks from your library and re-sort them. To delete a track, right-click the track title and choose **Delete from Library** from the context menu. To move a track up or down in the order it's listed, right-click the track title and choose either **Move Up** or **Move Down** from the context menu.

④ Move Tracks Between Folders

You can move your tracks between folders. For example, if there is a track in the **Classical** folder that you would rather have in the **Jazz** folder, drag the track from the **Classical** folder to the **Jazz** folder. Keep in mind, though, that when you do this, you'll change the actual attributes of the file. In other words, when you move the track from the **Classical** folder to the **Jazz** folder, the **Genre** information for that track is changed to **Jazz** (rather than its original **Classical** designation).

To move a track from one folder to another, drag it from its current folder to the folder where you want it to be. When you drop the track onto its new folder, a dialog box appears, offering the choice **Change genre** or **Add genre**. If you choose **Change genre**, a dialog box appears asking whether you want to change the genre. Click **Yes** and the track will be moved.

If you instead choose **Add genre**, you can keep the track in its original folder and *also add it* to the new folder—it will show up in both folders. The track will have more than one genre. When you make this choice, a second dialog box appears asking whether you want to add the new genre to the file. Click **Yes**; the file will appear in both folders and will have two genres.

⑤ Search for a Track

If you have a large music collection, it can be difficult to find the track you want, even when you browse through folders, so you can also search for a particular track. Type a search term in the **Search** box at the top of the screen and click the green **Search** button. Your results appear in the windows. If there is no **Search** box at the top of the screen, there will be a **Search** button. Click the **Search** button to make the **Search** box appear.

 TIP

You can also delete tracks and move them up and down in the list using the buttons at the top of Windows Media Player. Click a track; to delete it, click the button with a red **X**. To move the track up in the list, click the blue up arrow; to move it down the list, click the blue down arrow.

101 Create a Playlist

Before You Begin

✔ **100** Manage Your Music and Media Library

See Also

→ **102** Burn an Audio CD

KEY TERM

Playlist—A collection of digital music tracks that Windows Media Player will play, one after another, in the order you put them in. You also use playlists to burn music to CDs.

TIP

The difference between an auto playlist and a playlist is that in an auto playlist, Windows Media Player automatically updates the playlist, adding tracks to it based on criteria you specify. For example, you can create an auto playlist that contains WMA files recorded at 128Kbps or above from a specific artist. Whenever you copy music into Windows Media Player that meets that criteria, the songs are automatically put into the specified playlist. A normal playlist, by contrast, contains only the tracks you put in there; it never automatically updates itself.

Playing music on your PC by clicking individual tracks in Windows Media Player is not a particularly effective way to play your music. Instead, you can create *playlists*, collections of tracks that you tell Windows Media Player to play, one after another. The great benefit of playlists is that you can also use them to *burn* music to a CD or copy them to an MP3 player.

① Click the Playlists Button

Launch Windows Media Player and click the **Playlists** button at the top-left of the screen. You'll have three choices: **New Playlist**, **New Auto Playlist**, and **Copy to CD or Device**.

For more information about the third option, **Copy to CD or Device**, see **102** Burn an Audio CD and **103** About Copying Music to an MP3 Player.

For now, we're going to create a playlist, so select **New Playlist**. The **New Playlist** dialog box appears.

② Name the Playlist

Type the name of your playlist in the **Playlist Name** text box. Make sure to give it a unique, descriptive name, because you might end up creating many playlists, and you want to be able to easily distinguish among them.

③ Select Songs for the Playlist

From the **View Media Library by** drop-down list, select the view of the Media Library you want to use to select your tracks for the playlist. You can view them by a wide variety of criteria, including **Album**, **Genre**, **Artist**, and so on.

When you've selected how you want to view your library, scroll through the list looking for songs to add to the playlist. Click each song you want to add to move it to the playlist in the right side of the screen. As you move tracks into it, you'll be told how many items there are in the playlist and how long the playlist will take to play.

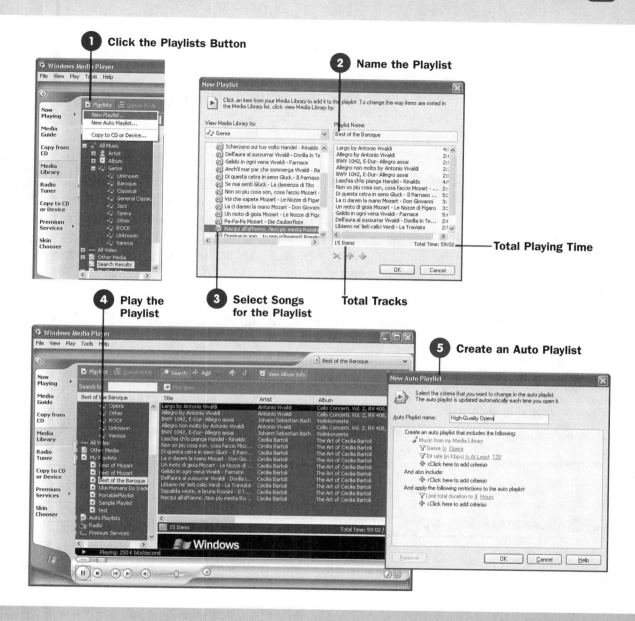

1 Click the Playlists Button

2 Name the Playlist

Total Playing Time

4 Play the Playlist

3 Select Songs for the Playlist

Total Tracks

5 Create an Auto Playlist

When you're done adding songs to the playlist, click **OK** to close the **New Playlist** dialog box. The playlist is added to the **My Playlists** folder, which you can see in the Media Library. (To get to the Media Library, click the **Media Library** button on the Taskbar.)

4 **Play the Playlist**

If it's not already displayed, click the **Media Library** button on the Taskbar. Click the **My Playlists** link in the list of folders in the left window of the screen. To play the playlist you just created, double-click it. The tracks in the playlist now play, starting with the first song and continuing until the final song in the playlist, after which it will stop.

5 **Create an Auto Playlist**

To create an auto playlist, click the **Playlists** button at the top-right of the main Windows Media Player screen and choose **New Auto Playlist** from the menu that opens. The **New Auto Playlist** dialog box appears. Name the auto playlist you are about to create and then select the criteria to use to create the playlist. Click the + button underneath the **Music from my Media Library** listing and then choose the various criteria you want to use—for example, by **Genre**, **Artist**, **Bit rate**, and so on. You can choose multiple criteria—keep clicking the + button to add more criteria.

When you're done specifying the criteria for your auto playlist, click **OK**. Open the playlist as explained in step 4 and view the track list it contains. If the filtering criteria you established in the **New Auto Playlist** dialog box didn't return the results you wanted, edit the criteria by right-clicking the playlist and choosing **Edit** from the context menu. Repeat step 5 to change your criteria.

The auto playlist can now be used like any other playlist.

> **TIP**
>
> One problem with auto playlists is that they can get very long, because Windows Media Player continually adds new tracks to them as you copy music into your library. You can restrict size of the playlist; by limiting it to a certain playing time, number of tracks, and so on, for example. To do that, click the + button underneath **And apply the following restrictions to the auto playlist** and choose your restrictions.

102 Burn an Audio CD

Before You Begin

✔ **100** Manage Your Music and Media Library

✔ **101** Create a Playlist

See Also

→ **103** About Copying Music to an MP3 Player

Windows Media Player can do more than record music and let you listen to music on your PC. It can also let you create, or *burn*, CDs so that you can listen to music on a CD player.

Before you can understand how to copy music to CDs, you must understand the two different ways music can be copied to CDs. Songs on a CD that you buy from a music store are not in the WMA, MP3, or similar digital format. Instead, the music is in a special format designed for CD players, a format that existed before MP3, WMA, and similar digital music formats were created. Such a disc is called an *audio CD*.

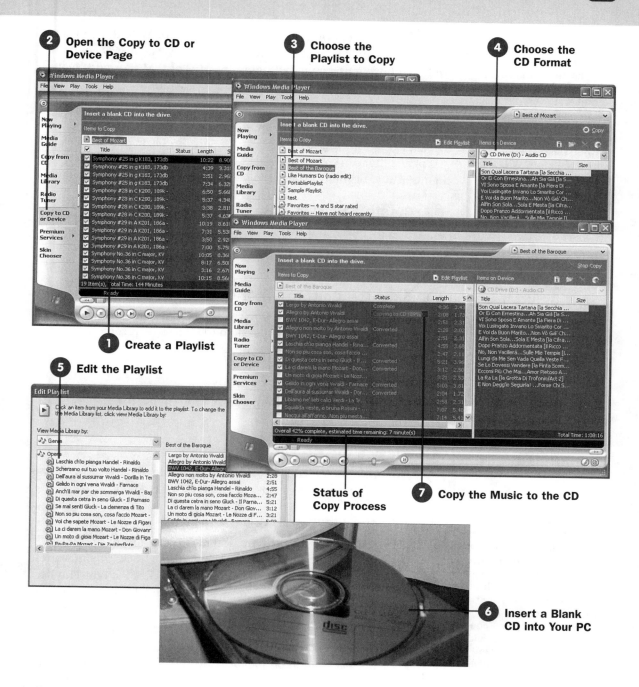

2 Open the Copy to CD or Device Page

3 Choose the Playlist to Copy

4 Choose the CD Format

1 Create a Playlist

5 Edit the Playlist

Status of Copy Process

7 Copy the Music to the CD

6 Insert a Blank CD into Your PC

NOTE

Making things even more complicated is that when you burn a CD in audio CD format, not every CD player will be able to play those burned CDs. This is primarily a problem with older CD players. Older CD players will be able to play CDs manufactured by music companies, but some can't play those burned by PCs.

NOTE

If you want to copy files to an MP3 player, you must first obtain a device driver for your MP3 player. When the driver is installed, select the device name from the drop-down list on the right side of the screen instead of the audio or data CD format. See **103** About Copying Music to an MP3 Player.

NOTE

You can copy music to CDs only if you have a CD drive that can write to CDs. Such a drive is called a CD-R or CD-RW drive. Check your computer's manual to make sure that yours does. Almost all computers sold in the last several years have CD-R or CD-RW drives. If you have a DVD-R or DVD-RW drive, it can write to CDs, as well.

One way you can burn a CD is to turn the WMA or MP3 files on your PC into the proper format for playing on CD players. The CD you burn will then have music on it, but not in the MP3 or WMA formats—you can copy your music to the CD in the audio CD format.

The other way to copy music to a CD is to simply copy the WMA or MP3 files themselves to the CD. This approach is called copying them in a *data format*. If you copy music this way, you'll only be able to play the CD on a CD player that can specifically play MP3 or WMA files. Check with the manufacturer of your CD player to see whether your player can do this.

1 **Create a Playlist**

To copy music to a CD, you must first create a *playlist* containing the music you want to burn to the disc. Follow the instructions in **101** Create a Playlist.

2 **Open the Copy to CD or Device Page**

Click the **Copy to CD or Device** button on the Taskbar to open the page you'll use to copy music to a CD. The screen contains the contents of the last playlist you used.

3 **Choose the Playlist to Copy**

From the **Items to Copy** drop-down box, choose the playlist you want to copy to the CD.

4 **Choose the CD Format**

From the drop-down list box on the right side of the screen, choose whether you want to create an audio CD or a data CD.

5 **Edit the Playlist**

If there are tracks on the playlist that you don't want to copy to the CD, disable the check boxes next to those tracks. If you want to add tracks to the playlist to copy to the CD, click the **Edit Playlist** button near the top of the screen, select the tracks you want to add, and click **OK**.

6 **Insert a Blank CD into Your PC**

Press the eject button on the face of your computer to eject the CD tray, place the CD into the tray, and then press the eject button again so that the CD is taken into your computer.

7 Copy the Music to the CD

Click the **Copy** button at the top-right of the Windows Media Player screen. Windows Media Player first examines each track in the selected playlist and then converts each track to the proper format for playing on a music CD. After it does that, it will copy each of the tracks to the CD. You'll be shown the progress of the overall copying, at the bottom of the screen. When the CD copying is complete, Windows Media Player ejects the CD.

103 About Copying Music to an MP3 Player

One of the most popular ways to listen to music is to use MP3 players, portable gadgets that can in some cases hold up to thousands of files. The most well-known of these is the iPod, but there are many others as well.

Windows Media Player can be used to copy music to MP3 players, but the truth is, it's not the best piece of software for doing it. One issue is that Windows Media Player can record music only in the WMA format, and not all MP3 players can play WMA files. (For example, the iPod does not play WMA files.)

Another issue is that Windows Media Player won't work with every MP3 player. To make it work with any MP3 player at all, you must first download special software called a *device driver* specific for that MP3 player.

To find a driver for your MP3 player, choose **Tools**, **Download** from the menu, and then choose **Portable Device SPs**. You'll be sent to a website that has a list of MP3 players that can work with Windows Media Player. Follow the directions for downloading and installing the device driver and making it work with Windows Media Player. (The directions vary from device to device.)

When the device driver is installed, you're ready to copy files to your MP3 player. Run Windows Media Player, click the **CD or Device** tab, and then follow the directions outlined in **102** **Burn an Audio CD**. The steps are the same, except in step 4, from the right side of the screen, choose your device name instead of an audio CD or data CD format.

Before You Begin

✔ **102** Burn an Audio CD

104 About Finding, Sharing, and Buying Music Online

Before You Begin

✔ **98** About Audio File Formats

✔ **99** Copy Music from an Audio CD

NOTE

Be wary when using this type of software, particularly the Kazaa software. Kazaa comes with what some people consider spyware that might track your movements across the Internet and send you pop-up advertising. (For information about how to kill spyware, see **71** Find and Kill Spyware.)

Windows Media Player makes it easy to copy music from a CD to your PC. After that music is on your PC, you can easily share it with others, and others can share their music with you.

Of course, just because you can share something with others doesn't make it legal. Copyrights cover most music that you buy, and the record industry contends that it violates copyright law for you to share your music with others, and for others to share their music with you. They have even used well-publicized prosecutions as a way to try to stop people from sharing music.

That hasn't stopped music sharers, of course. Countless people share countless songs with others every hour of every day of the year. You can share music with others using file-sharing software such as Kazaa, available from **www.kazaa.com**; iMesh, available from **www.imesh.com**; and Limewire, available from **www.limewire.com**.

When you use music-sharing software, you put your music in a special folder that other users of the software (and who are on your network) can download. You in turn can download from their folders. You don't have to know exactly where the music is located. You search for a piece of music, and the software searches the hard disks of everyone connected to the file-sharing network, then downloads it from that person's hard disk to your hard disk.

The quality of what you'll find is variable. Increasingly, the recording industry puts files on the file-sharing networks that appear to be music files when you search for them, but turn out to be worthless junk when you download them.

For all these reasons, services that let you buy music online have become increasingly popular. The best-known and most successful is iTunes at **www.itunes.com**. You can choose from thousands of digital music tracks and pay only 99 cents per track. To use iTunes, download the free iTunes software, which performs similar functions to the Windows Media Player—it lets you listen to your digital music, organize your digital music, and make CDs from your music, for example. The software ties directly into the iTunes Music Store, so you must use the iTunes software to buy music, as well. If you're an AOL user, you can try AOL's MusicNet music service; use the keyword **Musicnet**.

12

Using Photos and Graphics

IN THIS CHAPTER:

Windows XP makes it a breeze to use pictures of any kind. Whether you want to take pictures with a digital camera and import them into XP or use a scanner to get your prints into XP, it's easy to do.

There are also great tools for using those pictures once they're available in Windows XP. You'll be able to manipulate them in many ways, create online photo albums, use them as your desktop background, and more, as you'll see in this chapter.

105 Import Photos from a Digital Camera

Before You Begin

✔ **113** Install New Hardware

See Also

→ **107** Convert Between Image Formats

→ **108** Change Photo Resolution and Size

→ **111** Create an Online Photo Album

→ **112** Put Any Picture on Your Desktop

Windows XP makes it extremely easy to import photos from a digital camera into your PC. Before you can import the photos, of course, you must first install the camera so that it works with your PC, and install the camera's software, if it has any. To do that, follow the camera's instructions. You can also turn to **113** **Install New Hardware** for more details about how to install hardware.

In this task, you'll learn how to import photos into your PC using XP's built-in software. Many digital cameras also include software that lets you import photos, so you can instead use that software to do it. The quality of the camera's software varies widely, though, so you might want to use XP's built-in software instead of the software that ships with your camera.

1 Connect the Camera to Your Computer

Before you can transfer pictures to your PC, you must connect the camera to your computer. Unless you have a very old digital camera, connect it to the USB port and install it as explained in **113** **Install New Hardware**. After you've installed the camera, even after you disconnect it from the USB port, XP will automatically recognize the camera the next time you plug it in.

2 Run the Scanner and Camera Wizard

When you plug your camera into the USB port of your PC, the **Scanner and Camera Wizard** might start up automatically. If it doesn't, you can force the wizard to run by clicking the **Start** button, choosing **Control Panel**, choosing **Printers and Other Hardware**, selecting **Scanners and Cameras**, and then double-clicking the icon of your camera, such as the **Fujifilm FinePix A210**.

1 Connect the Camera to Your Computer

2 Run the Camera and Scanner Wizard

4 Choose a Destination and Name for Your Pictures

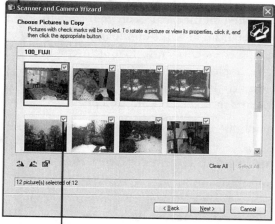

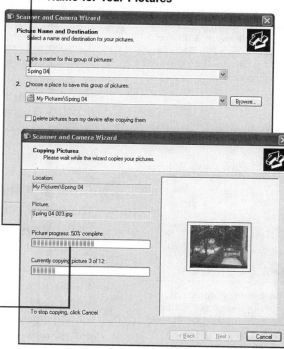

3 Choose the Pictures You Want to Copy

5 Copy the Pictures

6 Order Prints or Publish the Pictures Online

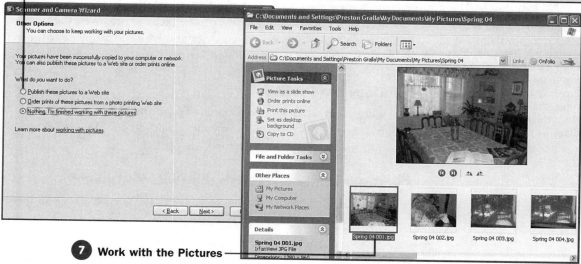

7 Work with the Pictures

The first screen of the wizard appears, telling you that the wizard is running. Click **Next**.

3 Choose the Pictures You Want to Copy

A screen appears, displaying all the pictures on your camera. There will be check marks in small boxes on the upper-right corner of each picture. When there is a check next to a picture, it means that you want to copy that picture to your PC. Uncheck any pictures that you don't want copied, and make sure that there are checks next to each picture that you do want to copy.

When you've selected all the pictures you want to copy, click **Next**.

4 Choose a Destination and Name for Your Pictures

The **Picture Name and Destination** page of the wizard appears. From here you will choose the folder to which you want to copy the pictures and provide a base name for the pictures.

You can also give your group of pictures a name. When you give the pictures a name, two things happen. First, a folder is created underneath the destination folder you chose. For example, if you store pictures in your **My Pictures** folder, and you give the pictures the name **Spring 04**, a new folder called **Spring 04** is created underneath your **My Pictures** folder and the pictures are stored in that new folder. Additionally, all the pictures are given the name **Spring 04**, and then ordered sequentially; for example, **Spring 04 001.jpg**, **Spring 04 002.jpg**, and so on.

5 Copy the Pictures

Click **Next** when you've chosen a folder and name. The wizard now copies the pictures from your camera to your PC and shows you the progress as the pictures are copied.

6 Order Prints or Publish the Pictures Online

After the pictures are copied to your PC, the wizard gives you three options:

- **Publish these pictures to a Web site**
- **Order prints of these pictures from a photo printing Web site**
- **Nothing. I'm finished working with these pictures**

If you choose one of the first two options—publishing the pictures to a website or ordering prints from a photo-printing site—click **Next** and a new wizard will launch. You can first choose which of the pictures you want to publish or have developed from a photo-printing website.

⑦ Work with the Pictures

The last option offered by the wizard, the "**Nothing**" option, is confusing because it makes it sound as if once the pictures are copied, there's nothing you can do with them any longer. That is not the case, however. You can now view the pictures on your PC and use them in the same way you can use any other picture: by printing them, sending them to family and friends as email attachments, using them in newsletters, and so on. When you select the **Nothing** option and click **Next**, the final screen of the **Scanner and Camera Wizard** appears. On that screen, there is a link to the folder that contains your pictures—for example, **My Pictures\Spring 04**. If you want to immediately view and work with your pictures, click that link. If you want to work with the images later, click **Finish**. When you want to work with the images, open Windows Explorer and go to the folder, in this instance, **My Pictures\Spring 04**.

You can now work with the pictures as you can with any others. For more information about working with pictures, see **107** Convert Between Image Formats, **108** Change Photo Resolution and Size, **111** Create An Online Photo Album, and **112** Put Any Picture on Your Desktop.

106 Scan In Photos

Scanning pictures with Windows XP is as easy as importing pictures with a digital camera. As with a camera, before you can scan pictures, you must first install the scanner so that it works with your PC, and install the scanner's software, if it has any. To do that, follow the scanner's instructions. You can also turn to **113** Install New Hardware for more details about how to install hardware.

In this task, you'll learn how to scan pictures into your PC using Windows XP's built-in software. Many scanners also include software that lets you import scanned images, so you can instead use that

NOTE

If you've chosen to publish the pictures to a website, you'll be given a choice of a number of sites on which you can publish the pictures, and you then follow the wizard's instructions for publishing them. If you've chosen to order prints, you'll be given a choice of sites from which to order your prints, and can then follow the wizard's instructions for ordering prints.

Before You Begin

✔ **113** Install New Hardware

See Also

→ **107** Convert Between Image Formats

→ **108** Change Photo Resolution and Size

→ **111** Create An Online Photo Album

→ **112** Put Any Picture on Your Desktop

software to do it. The quality of the software that comes with scanners varies widely, though, so you might want to use XP's built-in software instead of the software that ships with your scanner.

❶ Connect the Scanner to Your Computer

Before you can scan pictures into your PC, you must connect the scanner to your computer. Unless you have a very old scanner, connect it to the USB port. After you've installed the scanner, even if you disconnect it from the USB port, Windows XP will automatically recognize the scanner the next time you plug it in.

❷ Run the Scanner and Camera Wizard

When you plug your scanner into the USB port of your PC, the **Scanner and Camera Wizard** might start up automatically. If it doesn't, you can force the wizard to run by clicking the **Start** button, choosing **Control Panel**, choosing **Printers and Other Hardware**, selecting **Scanners and Cameras**, and then double-clicking the icon of your scanner, such as the **Hewlett-Packard ScanJet 4100C**.

The first wizard screen appears, telling you that the wizard is running. Click **Next**.

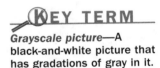

KEY TERM

Grayscale picture—A black-and-white picture that has gradations of gray in it.

❸ Select Your Scanning Preferences

The **Choose Scanning Preferences** screen appears, letting you choose whether you are scanning a color picture, a *grayscale picture*, or a black-and-white picture or text. Enable the button next to the option that best applies to the image you want to scan.

❹ Preview Your Picture

Before actually performing the scan, you'll want to get a sense of its quality before proceeding. Click the **Preview** button, and the scanner will scan the picture and show you a preview of what the picture will look like.

If you're scanning a picture that is much smaller than the size of the scanner's image area, it might appear very small when you preview it. You can see a close-up of the picture by clicking the **Enlarge** button—the one just to the right of the **Preview** button. To see the picture in its normal size, click the button to the right of it.

1 Connect the Scanner to Your Computer

2 Run the Scanner and Camera Wizard

4 Preview Your Picture

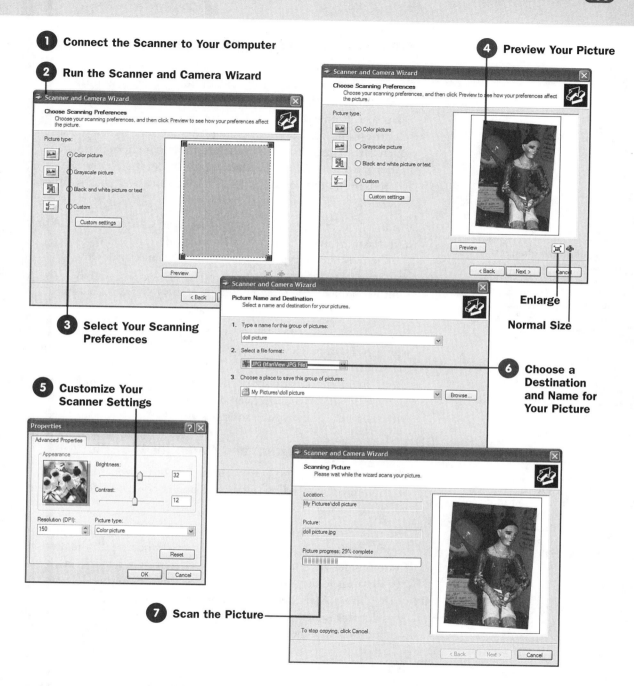

3 Select Your Scanning Preferences

5 Customize Your Scanner Settings

6 Choose a Destination and Name for Your Picture

Enlarge

Normal Size

7 Scan the Picture

⑤ Customize Your Scanner Settings

If the preview looks too dim, too bright, does not have contrast, is fuzzy, or has some other problem with it, you can customize the scan settings. Click the **Custom Settings** button to open the **Advanced Properties** dialog box. From here you can change the brightness and contrast of the image, and change its resolution, which is measured in dots per inch (dpi). The higher the dpi, the higher the quality of the image (and the larger the picture file). The maximum dpi you can choose is determined by your scanner's capabilities.

NOTE

As you make changes in the **Advanced Properties** dialog box, you'll see the effect your changes have on a sample image—a picture of daisies—not on your actual photo.

Use the sliders to change the **Brightness** and **Contrast**, and the up and down arrows to change the **Resolution** (dpi). You can also change the **Picture type** by selecting color, black-and-white, or grayscale from the drop-down list. As you make the changes, the sample image on the screen changes, so that you can see how your customizations will affect the picture.

When you're done, click **OK**. You'll be sent back to the screen where you can preview your scan. Click the **Preview** button again to see how your scan will look. Click the **Custom settings** button again if you're not yet happy with your scan, make changes, and preview the picture again. Keep doing this until you're satisfied with the scan. When you're satisfied with the preview, click **Next**.

⑥ Choose a Destination and Name for Your Picture

TIP

By default, the picture is placed in your **My Pictures** folder. If you want to place it in a different location, click the **Browse** button, choose the new location, and click **OK**.

The **Picture Name and Destination** page of the wizard appears. From here you can name the picture and choose a the folder where you want to store it.

You will also give your picture a name. When you give it a name, two things happen. First, a folder is created underneath the destination folder you chose. For example, if you store pictures in your **My Pictures** folder, and you give the pictures the name **doll picture**, a new folder called **doll picture** is created underneath your **My Pictures** folder, and your picture is stored in that new folder. Additionally, the picture is given the name **doll picture.jpg**.

⑦ Scan the Picture

Click **Next** when you've chosen a folder and name. The picture is now scanned, and you'll see the progress as the picture is scanned.

After the picture is scanned, the steps involved in using your pictures are exactly as described in steps 6 and 7 of **105** **Import Photos from a Digital Camera**, so turn to those steps for more details about how to work with your pictures after they're scanned in.

107 Convert Between Image Formats

Pictures come in a wide variety of image formats—there are literally dozens of them, including JPG, GIF, BMP, TIF, PCX, and many others. One problem with the variety of formats is that certain formats can be used for only certain purposes. For example, if you want to use pictures on the Web, they must be in JPG, GIF, or PNG format.

But what if you have a picture in one format and want to change it to another—if you have a picture in the PCX format and want to use it on the Web, for example? You can convert the image from one format to another. That's what you'll learn in this task.

Before You Begin

✔ **105** Import Photos from a Digital Camera

✔ **106** Scan In Photos

See Also

→ **108** Change Photo Resolution and Size

1 Download and Install IrfanView

The best way to convert files between different formats is to use the free program IrfanView, which lets you view graphics files, convert them between formats, and has some basic image-editing tools, as well. It's one of the best all-around graphics utilities you can find, and it's free to download and use.

To download it, go to **www.irfanview.com**, click the **Download** link, and follow the instructions for downloading. After you download it, follow the instructions for installing it.

2 Run IrfanView

After you install IrfanView, open it by double-clicking its desktop icon, or by clicking the **Start** button, choosing **All Programs**, and then choosing **IrfanView** from the menu.

3 Open the File You Want to Convert

Choose **File, Open** from the menu, navigate to the folder that has the file you want to convert, and then double-click the file. IrfanView shows you a preview of the file in the **Open** dialog box, so it's easy to make sure that you've selected the correct file before you open it.

NOTE

When you use IrfanView, if you want to see information about each file before you open it, such as the date it was created and the file size, enable the **Details** check box in the **Open** dialog box. You can then see that information about each file.

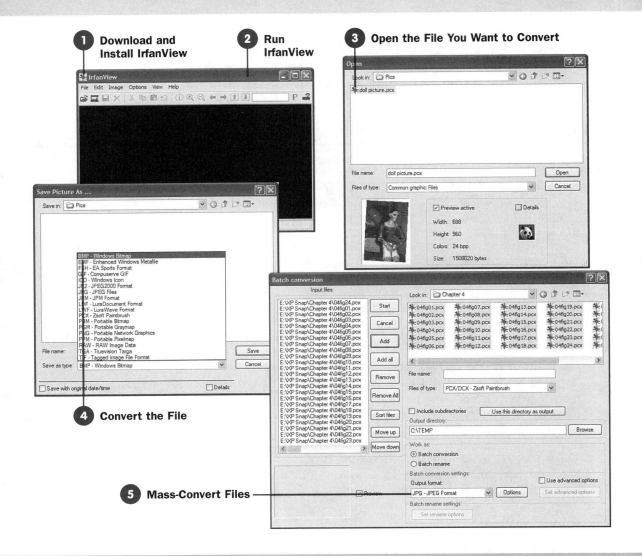

1 Download and Install IrfanView

2 Run IrfanView

3 Open the File You Want to Convert

4 Convert the File

5 Mass-Convert Files

4 Convert the File

After you open the file, choose **File, Save As** from the menu. From the **Save as type** drop-down list at the bottom of the dialog box, choose the file type you want to save the file as, such as BMP. Type a new name in the **File name** text box if you want. Then click **Save**. Your file will now be converted to the new file type.

⑤ Mass-Convert Files

One of IrfanView's better features is its capability to convert an entire group of files from one format to another. To do it, open IrfanView and choose **File**, **Batch Conversion/Rename** from the menu. The **Batch Conversion** dialog box shows a list of all the graphics files in the selected folder. Navigate to the folder that holds the files you want to convert. Highlight all the files you want to convert and click the **Add** button. From the **Output Format** drop-down list, choose the file format to which you want to convert the files. Then click **Start** to convert the files.

108 Change Photo Resolution and Size

You need pictures of different *resolutions* and sizes for different purposes. For example, if you're going to have your digital pictures printed, you want them to be as high quality and in as high resolution as possible. But if you want to send that same photo to someone as an email attachment or post it on the Web, you don't want it to be of that high a resolution, because it will take too long to download.

The solution? You can easily resize images and change their resolution so that you can use any picture for any purpose, and make sure that it's at the right size.

① Download the Image Resizer

The best tool for resizing images is free and available from Microsoft. It's called the **Image Resizer**, and it's one of a suite of free utilities that Microsoft calls **Microsoft Power Toys**. To find it, go to **www.microsoft.com/windowsxp/pro/downloads/powertoys.asp**. Look in the list on the right side of the window for the **Image Resizer** utility. Click the **ImageResizer.exe** link to download the file, choose a folder location where you want to save it, and start the download.

② Install the Image Resizer

After you download it, look for the file named **ImageResizerPowertoySetup.exe** in the folder where you saved it, and double-click it. This action launches an installation program. Click the **Next** button when the first screen appears and then follow the simple installation instructions.

Before You Begin
✔ **105** Import Photos from a Digital Camera
✔ **106** Scan In Photos

See Also
→ **107** Convert Between Image Formats

🔍 KEY TERM

Resolution—The quality of a picture, measured in *pixels*, which are small dots.

🖎 NOTE

Even though the link on the website calls the file **ImageResizer.exe**, the actual filename is **ImageResizerPowertoySetup.exe**.

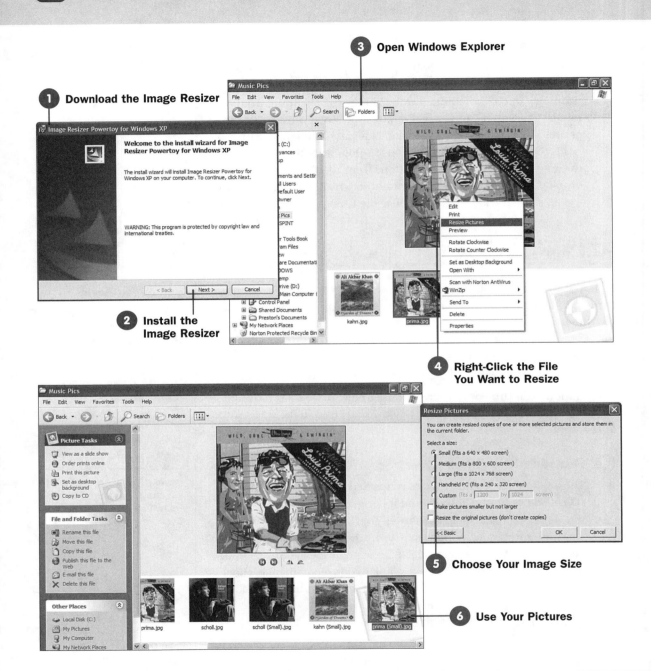

3 Open Windows Explorer

1 Download the Image Resizer

2 Install the Image Resizer

4 Right-Click the File You Want to Resize

5 Choose Your Image Size

6 Use Your Pictures

③ Open Windows Explorer

The Image Resizer isn't a program that runs by itself. Instead, it integrates directly into Windows Explorer's right-click context menu. Open Windows Explorer and locate the file you want to resize.

④ Right-Click the File You Want to Resize

Right-click the file you want to resize. Choose **Resize Pictures** from the context menu to run the Image Resizer. Note that you can select multiple pictures and resize them all in a single operation. To select multiple pictures, **Ctrl**+click each file until you've selected all that you want to resize, right-click any of the files to open the context menu, and choose **Resize Pictures**.

⑤ Choose Your Image Size

The **Resize Pictures** dialog box appears, allowing you to change the picture size. You can choose any of the preset image sizes, or you can choose a custom size by selecting the **Custom** option and entering the size you want the image or images to be. After you make your selection, click **OK**. Keep in mind that if you resize a picture to make it larger than its original size, the quality of the resized picture will often not be very good—and might even be unusable. However, making a picture smaller will not adversely affect the picture quality.

NOTE

It's not a good idea to select the **Resize the original pictures (don't create copies)** option. If you choose that option, your original picture will be deleted, and if you don't like the new size of the picture, there's nothing you can do about it—you're stuck with it.

⑥ Use Your Pictures

The Image Resizer resizes the images and puts them in the same folder in which your original pictures are stored. The program labels the new pictures by appending their new size to the filename; for example, **(small)**. Keep in mind that the pictures won't look smaller in the thumbnail view in Windows Explorer, but the actual *file* is smaller. You can now use the resized image file in the same way you use any picture.

109 Capture a Screenshot

See Also

→ **107** Convert Between Image Formats

There are times when you'll need to capture a screen in Windows XP. You might need it to illustrate a work report or a school report. You might want to capture a picture of a web page to send to a friend. For whatever reason, there will be times when you'll want to save a screen.

There is an awkward way to do it in Windows XP. First press **Shift+Print Scrn**. That action captures the entire screen to the Windows XP Clipboard. Then you can open a graphics program such as Paint. (To open Paint, click the **Start** button, choose **All Programs, Accessories, Paint**.) When Paint opens, paste the screen from the Clipboard into it by choosing **Edit, Paste** from the menu. Now that the screen is in Paint, you can save it.

There are several problems with this process, though. When you save a screen this way, you can only save the *entire* screen—you can't save a portion of one. You also don't get a wide range of graphics formats to which you can save. And the whole thing is very awkward and kludgy.

There's a better way. Use downloadable software to save screens. The best for the purpose is SnagIt, as you'll see in this task.

NOTE

SnagIt is shareware, which means that you can try it out for free, but if you continue to use the program, you're expected to pay $39.95. You can pay directly on the website.

1 Download and Install SnagIt

Go to **www.snagit.com** and click the **Try SnagIt** link. Follow the instructions for downloading and installing the program.

2 Run SnagIt and Choose Your Profile

Double-click the SnagIt icon on the desktop, or choose it from the **Start, All Programs** menu. When SnagIt runs, you'll see a list of what the program calls **Basic Capture Profiles**. Each profile allows you to do a different kind of screen capture. For example, the first one, **A region to File** lets you capture a portion of a screen and then save it as a file in a wide variety of graphics formats. **The Entire screen** profile captures your entire screen to a file.

To find out the details about a profile, click it and look in the **Capture Settings** area on the right side of the screen for information about that profile. You'll see the following information for each profile:

- **Hotkey.** The key combination you press to activate that particular profile. For a start, you use the same hotkey for each profile. To choose which profile to use when you press that hotkey, you first click the profile to highlight it. When you press that hotkey, you'll capture a screen using that profile. To capture a screen with a different profile, open SnagIt, highlight a different profile, and then press the hotkey. You can instead assign different hotkeys to different profiles. To assign a hotkey to a profile, right-click a profile, select **Set Hotkey** from the context menu, press the hotkey combination you want to use, and click **OK**.

- **Mode.** This setting determines whether you'll capture the image from the screen, the text from the screen, a video of several screens, or a website.

- **Input.** This setting determines what portion of the screen you'll capture: for example, the entire screen, only the currently active window, a rectangular portion of the screen, and so on.

- **Output.** This setting determines what happens when you capture the screen—do you send it to the printer, for example, or capture it as a file. If you do capture it as a file, you can set which file format the capture should be in.

- **Filters.** This option lets you apply a kind of filter to the screen capture—for example, you can change its resolution, add a border to it, add special effects to its edges (such as waves and fades), and so on.

- **Options.** Here you can choose your final options for the screenshot, such as whether to include the mouse pointer, and whether you should view your screenshot in a preview window before you save it.

After you look through the profiles, choose the one you want to use and then minimize the SnagIt window by clicking the **Minimize** button in the upper-right corner of the title bar.

NOTE

A particularly useful feature of SnagIt is its capability to specify a delay time before the screen is captured (for example, if you want to arrange windows or menus before the screen is captured). To use it, click the **Timer Setup** icon (it looks like a stopwatch) at the bottom of the right side of the screen and fill in the form.

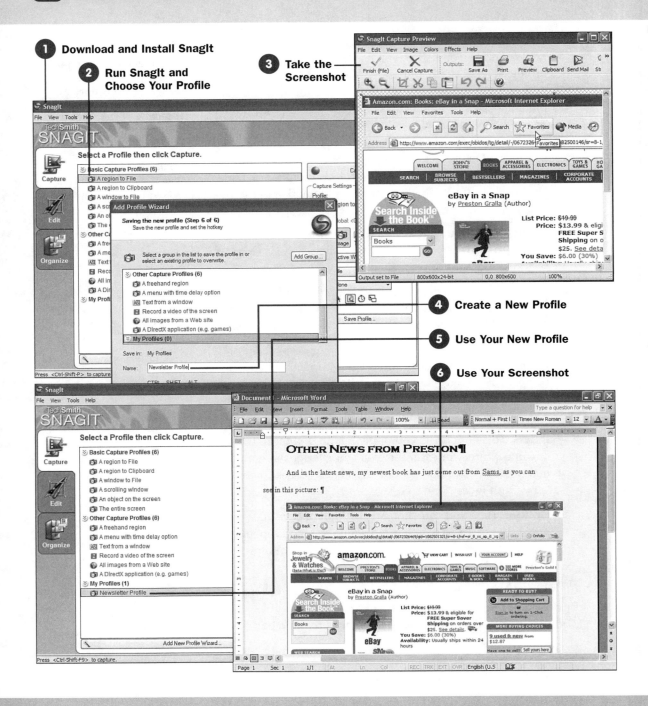

1 Download and Install SnagIt

2 Run SnagIt and Choose Your Profile

3 Take the Screenshot

4 Create a New Profile

5 Use Your New Profile

6 Use Your Screenshot

③ Take the Screenshot

Arrange the screen in whatever manner constitutes the screenshot you want to capture (for example, a website). Press the SnagIt hotkey, which by default is **Ctrl+Shift+P**. If you've chosen to capture an entire screen or the current window, the **SnagIt Capture Preview** window appears, letting you preview your file. If you want to save the capture, click the **Finish (File)** button in the toolbar at the top of the window, navigate to the place on your hard disk where you want to save the file, give the file a filename, and click **Save**.

If you've chosen an option such as capturing a portion of the screen, a cropping tool appears, letting you define the portion of the screen you want to capture. After you stop dragging the area to crop, the **Capture Preview** window appears. Save the screenshot as explained in the previous paragraph.

④ Create a New Profile

To create a new profile, go back to the main SnagIt screen (the one that lists all the profiles). Click the **Add New Profile Wizard** button at the bottom of the list. A wizard runs, first asking you what type of capture mode you want to use. Make your selection and click **Next**. The wizard will walk you through every step of choosing all the options for a new profile—the options described in step 2 of this task.

In the final step, you'll be asked to name the profile and to choose a hotkey for it. Make sure that you choose a hotkey that isn't used by any other program or by Windows XP. Don't forget to give the profile a descriptive name, as well.

⑤ Use Your New Profile

To use your new profile, minimize the SnagIt window (click the **Minimize** button in the upper-right corner of the title bar) and go to the screen you want to capture. Press the hotkey you've defined for your new profile, and use SnagIt as outlined earlier in this task.

⑥ Use Your Screenshot

After you've saved your screenshot, you can use it as you would any other graphics file; for example, in a newsletter, in a report in a Word document, to send as an email attachment, and so on.

Before You Begin

✔ **105** Import Photos from a Digital Camera

✔ **106** Scan In Photos

See Also

→ **107** Convert Between Image Formats

→ **108** Change Photo Resolution and Size

⚓ TIP

If the folder is not a Photo Album folder, it's easy to turn it into one. Select **View, Customize This Folder** from the menu and click the **Customize** tab. From the **Use this folder file as a template** drop-down list, select **Photo Album** and click **OK**.

Windows XP doesn't only make it easy to get pictures into your computer using a digital camera or scanner—it also makes it easy to print photos. Your best bet is to print photos using the **Photo Printing Wizard**.

1 Select the Folder with Pictures You Want to Print

Open Windows Explorer and navigate to the folder that has the pictures you want to print. To use the wizard, the folder must be designated as a Photo Album folder. You'll know that the folder is a Photo Album folder if the **Print Pictures** option is included in the **Tasks** list on the left side of the screen.

2 Launch the Wizard

First select the picture or pictures you want to print. To select multiple pictures, select one, hold down the **Ctrl** key, and click the others you want to select.

When you've selected all the pictures you want to print, click **Print pictures** (or, if you've chosen only one picture, click **Print picture**) in the **Picture Tasks** list on the left side of the window. The Welcome screen of the **Photo Printing Wizard** appears. Click **Next**.

3 Confirm Your Picture Selection

The **Picture Selection** screen of the wizard appears, with thumbnails of all the pictures you've chosen to print. Each thumbnail has its box checked. If there are any photos you don't want to print, disable their check boxes. When you've finished making your picture selection, click **Next**.

4 Choose Your Printer and Paper

The **Printing Options** page of the wizard appears. Select your printer from the **What printer do you want to use** drop-down list. If you're using paper other than normal paper—for example, if you're using photo paper—click the **Printing Preferences** button and choose the kind of paper you're using. After you've made your selections, click **Next**.

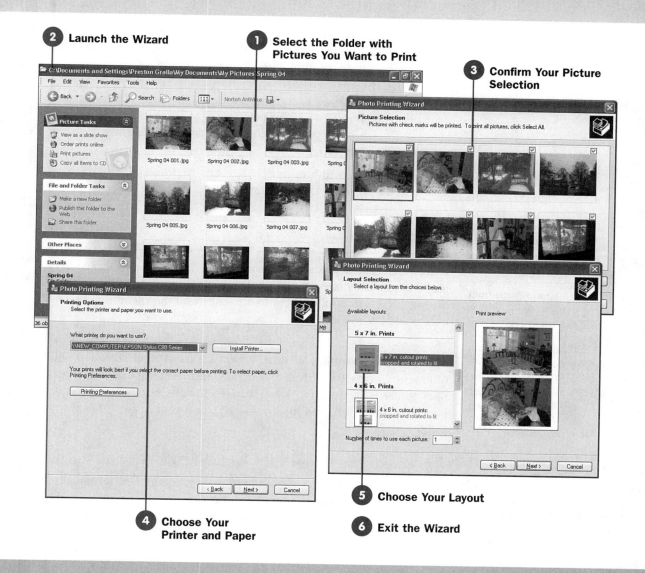

2 Launch the Wizard

1 Select the Folder with Pictures You Want to Print

3 Confirm Your Picture Selection

4 Choose Your Printer and Paper

5 Choose Your Layout

6 Exit the Wizard

5 Choose Your Layout

The **Layout Selection** page of the wizard appears. Choose the type of layout, for example, 5×7-inch prints, full-page prints, contact sheet prints (with 35 small pictures per page), and so on. When you're done making your selections, click **Next**.

Remember to turn on your printer before telling the wizard to print. A surprising number of times, people forget to turn on their printers before printing. If you're using the wizard and get an **Internal Error** message, you've most likely forgotten to turn on your printer. Another common cause for this error is a loose cable between your PC and your printer.

6 Exit the Wizard

Your pictures will now print. After they've printed, click **Finish**, and the wizard screen will vanish.

111 Create an Online Photo Album

Before You Begin

✔ **105** Import Photos from a Digital Camera

✔ **106** Scan In Photos

See Also

→ **107** Convert Between Image Formats

→ **108** Change Photo Resolution and Size

NOTE

You must be connected to the Internet to complete the wizard and publish your photos, so make sure that you're connected before starting the wizard.

With the advent of digital photography, the days of the old-fashioned photo album are long gone. If you want to show your photos to others, the best way is to publish them to a website and then send the site location to friends and family.

The easiest way to create an online photo album in Windows XP is to use the **Web Publishing Wizard**. When you use it, you'll create a photo album on Microsoft's MSN site. You'll get 3MB of storage space for your photos. The wizard will walk you through the free registration process. If you want more storage, you can pay $20 for a year to get 30MB of space.

1 Select the Folder with Pictures You Want to Publish

Open Windows Explorer and navigate to the folder that has the pictures you want to publish on the Web. To use the wizard to publish your pictures, the folder must be designated as a Photo Album folder. You'll know that the folder is a Photo Album folder if the **Print Pictures** option appears in the **Tasks** list on the left side of the screen.

If the folder is not a Photo Album folder, it's easy to turn it into one. Select **View**, **Customize This Folder** from the menu and click the **Customize** tab. From the **Use this folder file as a template** drop-down list, select **Photo Album** and click **OK**.

2 Select Publish This Folder to the Web

3 Select the Pictures to Publish

1 Select the Folder with Pictures You Want to Publish

4 Select MSN Groups

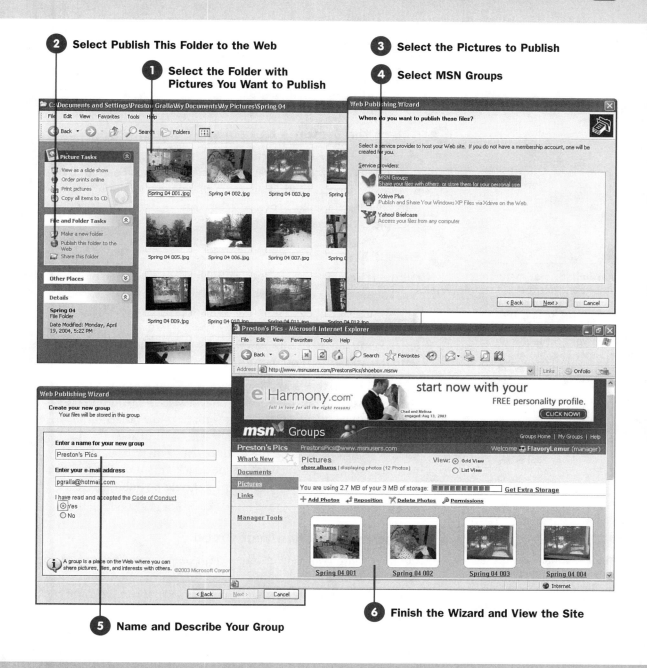

6 Finish the Wizard and View the Site

5 Name and Describe Your Group

2 Select Publish This Folder to the Web

Click the **Publish this folder to the Web** link in the **Tasks** list on the left side of the window. The Welcome page of the **Web Publishing Wizard** appears. Click **Next**.

3 Select the Pictures to Publish

The **Change Your File Selection** page of the wizard appears, with thumbnails of all the pictures in the selected folder. Each thumbnail has its box checked. If there are any photos you don't want to print, disable their check boxes. When you've finished making your picture selections, click **Next**.

4 Select MSN Groups

On the **Where do you want to publish these files** page of the wizard, choose the **MSN Groups** option. That's the best site for publishing photos from Windows XP. Click **Next**. To access the MSN site, you must log on with a Passport account. If you already have an account, log on. If you don't, follow the online instructions for setting up a Passport account.

After you log in to the MSN site, click the **Create a new MSN Group to share your files** option on the wizard screen and click **Next**. You'll be asked whether you want to allow others on the Web to view the pictures, or whether you want to keep them private. If you want to share the pictures with others, click **Shared**. If you want to keep the pictures private, click **Personal**. When you've made your choice about how the files should be published, click **Next**.

5 Name and Describe Your Group

On the **Create your new group** wizard page, type a name for your group, type your email address, select the **Yes** radio button indicating that you've read and understand the code of conduct, and click **Next**.

On the next screen that appears, type a description of your group. This description will be used when others are searching and looking for groups on MSN. If you want to list your group in the **MSN Directory**, select the **Yes** radio button. Doing this makes it easier for others to find your photo site. When you're done, click **Next**.

6 Finish the Wizard and View the Site

A screen appears, giving you the web address of your photo site. You don't have to write it down, though, because it will be emailed to you at the address you used for your Passport account.

You'll be asked whether you want to add the site to your Internet Favorites. If you want to do this, select **Yes**; if not, select **No**. Then click **Next**.

A screen reminds you where your pictures can be found on the Web; click **Next**. The following screen gives you basic information about your photo site; click **Next** again.

Another screen asks whether you want to resize your pictures, and if so, what size you want them to be (small, medium, or large). Unless there is a specific reason you want to resize your images— for example, if they are very large, and it will take a long time for people to download them to view them when they visit your site— don't resize the pictures, and so don't check any boxes. If you resize them, click the **Yes** box and select your preferred picture size.

Click **Next**. The wizard now uploads your pictures to the MSN site. After they're uploaded, you'll get confirmation. Click **Next**; from the final page of the wizard, click **Finish**. Your photos are now available for anyone to see. Just email the web address for your MSN site to someone, and he can view all your pictures online in his browser.

112 Put Any Picture on Your Desktop

Another great use for photos: You can set them to be your desktop background. So you can take a picture of friends or family and use it as the background image (also called the *wallpaper*) for your Windows XP desktop.

But you're not confined to using only the pictures you take as your background images. You can use other pictures as your background, as well.

1 Open Windows Explorer

Open Windows Explorer and go to the folder that has the picture you want to use as your background.

Before You Begin

✔ **105** Import Photos from a Digital Camera

✔ **106** Scan In Photos

✔ **107** Convert Between Image Formats

See Also

→ **13** Use a Picture from the Web as Your Background/ Wallpaper

1 Open Windows Explorer

2 Use the Picture as Your Desktop Background

5 Select Your Picture Position

3 View the Picture on the Desktop

4 Open the Properties Dialog Box

6 View the Picture on the Desktop

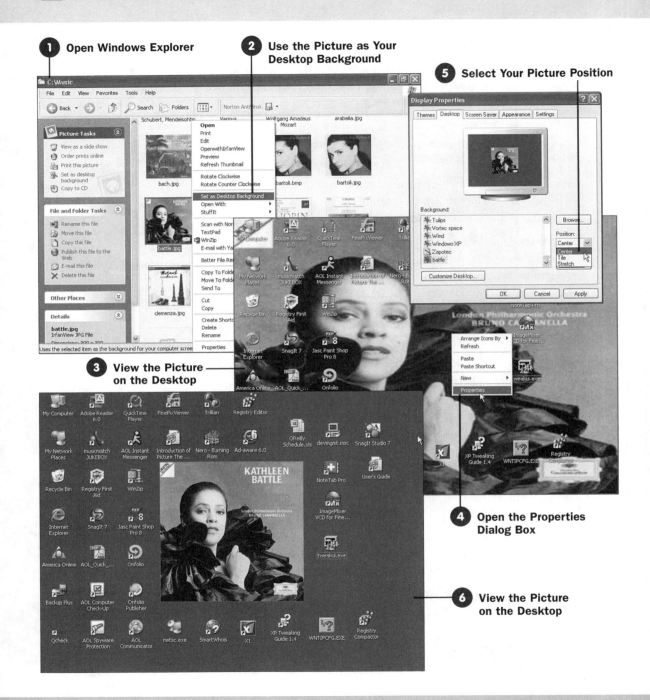

② Use the Picture as Your Desktop Background

To use a picture as your desktop background, right-click it in Windows Explorer and choose **Set as Desktop Background** from the context menu.

③ View the Picture on the Desktop

Minimize Windows Explorer (click the **Minimize** button in the upper-right corner of the title bar) and go to your desktop. You'll see the selected picture there. But frequently, the picture will appear distorted because Windows XP stretches the picture to fit on the desktop, distorting both its size and dimensions. You'll probably want to change the way that the picture is displayed.

④ Open the Properties Dialog Box

Right-click a blank spot on the desktop and choose **Properties** from the context menu. When the **Properties** dialog box opens, click the **Desktop** tab. This tab has options that change the presentation of your desktop picture.

⑤ Select Your Picture Position

From the **Position** drop-down list, choose **Center** or **Tile**. (The third option, **Stretch**, is the default setting, and so is the one that you currently have.) If you center the picture, it is displayed at its normal size, in the center of the screen. From the **Color** drop-down list, you can choose what color to surround it with. If you tile the picture, multiple copies of the image at its original size are displayed in bathtub-tile fashion on your screen.

When you're done making your selection, click **OK** to close the dialog box.

⑥ View the Picture on the Desktop

Your picture is resized on the desktop. Go to the desktop to view it. if you want to change its position again, repeat steps 4 and 5.

PART IV

Troubleshooting and Optimizing XP

IN THIS PART:

13

Solving Hardware Problems

IN THIS CHAPTER:

What makes most Windows XP users tear their hair out in frustration? Hardware problems: Installing digital cameras, scanners, and many other pieces of hardware, or when things go wrong with existing hardware.

However, hardware needn't be so hard. As you'll see in this chapter, there's a lot you can do to handle hardware problems in Windows XP. So before you tear your hair out the next time you have hardware problems, start here.

113 Install New Hardware

See Also

→ **114** Uninstall Hardware

→ **115** Troubleshoot Hardware Problems

One of Windows XP's great strengths is how easy it is to install a new piece of hardware. Although things don't always go according to plan, there's enough smarts built into the operating system that it should generally be relatively easy to install a new piece of hardware.

Most hardware, including printers, digital cameras, scanners, and much other equipment, connect to your PC using a USB port, which makes attaching it very easy. Windows XP frequently automatically recognizes the device as soon as you plug it in.

Still, there are a number of "gotchas" along the way. Follow these instructions whenever you install a new piece of hardware, and you should be relatively problem free.

 TIP

After you install the software, you might have to restart your PC. Double-check whether you must do so, because if you don't restart it and you're required to, the hardware installation might not work.

 Install the Software

Depending on the hardware you're going to install, you may or may not have to install software along with it. For example, scanners, digital cameras, and some printers almost always require that you install software. However, many network cards might not require any additional software.

Follow the hardware manual's instructions for installing the software. In some instances, you'll plug in the device first, but usually you install the software first.

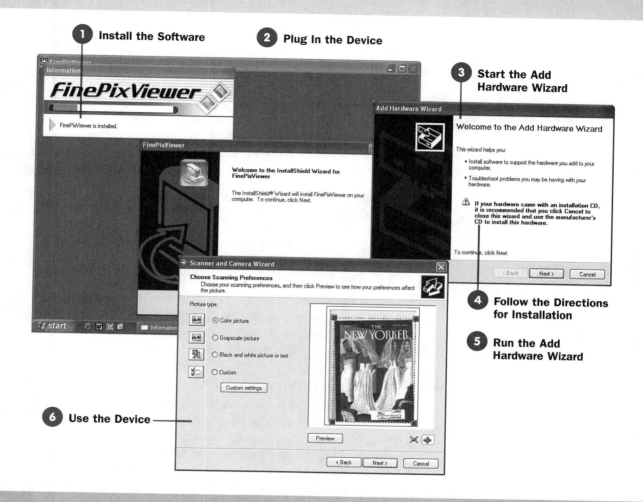

1 Install the Software

2 Plug In the Device

3 Start the Add
Hardware Wizard

4 Follow the Directions
for Installation

5 Run the Add
Hardware Wizard

6 Use the Device

2 Plug In the Device

After you've installed the software, connect the hardware to your
computer. Most, but not all, hardware connects to your computer
using a USB port. If the device requires power, make sure that you
plug in the power cord and turn the device on. If it's a device such
as a digital camera that uses batteries, install the batteries and
turn on the device.

Find the USB cord for the device and plug one end of the cord into the device's USB port and the other into the USB port of the computer. The plugs will fit only one way, so don't try to force them.

3 Start the Add Hardware Wizard

When you plug in your device, Windows XP might recognize it immediately. If it does, you'll get a notification in the **Notification Area** in the lower-right corner of the desktop that the hardware is installed and ready to use.

If Windows XP doesn't automatically recognize your new hardware, the **Add Hardware Wizard** should automatically launch. Click the **Next** button to run the wizard. It will search your computer and automatically recognize your new device.

4 Follow the Directions for Installation

Complete the wizard, following its step-by-step directions. At some point, it might ask you for the location of a piece of software. Place the installation disk for your hardware in your computer and browse to the disk. When the wizard has concluded, click **Finish**.

5 Run the Add Hardware Wizard

If your device was not automatically recognized when you plugged it in and the **Add Hardware Wizard** didn't launch, you will have to manually run it. To get to it, choose **Control Panel** from the **Start** menu. Then choose **Printers and Other Hardware** and click **Add Hardware** on the upper-left side of the screen. When the hardware wizard launches, follow the directions as outlined previously for installation.

6 Use the Device

You can now use the hardware, and it should run without problems. As you can see here, I installed a new scanner and tested the installation by scanning in a *New Yorker* magazine cover.

114 Uninstall Hardware

There may come a time when you want to uninstall a piece of hardware; perhaps an external device such as a scanner or printer or an internal device such as a CD drive. Windows XP does a good job of handling hardware, so it should be relatively easy to do, but there might be a few "gotchas" along the way. Uninstalling a piece of hardware is not a matter of simply unplugging it from your computer. You must remove software and change settings as well.

Before You Begin

✔ 113 Install New Hardware

See Also

→ 115 Troubleshoot Hardware Problems

1 Turn Off the Device

Before uninstalling most devices, you should turn off the power to them. This will not only make uninstalling them easier, but it can make sure that you don't damage the device or your computer.

2 Unplug the USB Device

If you're uninstalling a USB device, after turning its power off, unplug it. Frequently, with a USB device, this is all you'll have to do—no more steps need to be taken to uninstall it. You might have an **Unplug or Eject Hardware** icon on the Taskbar; if you do, click that icon before removing the USB device.

3 Take Out the Internal Device

If you have an internal device, you'll have to remove it. Read your computer manual and the manual of the device for instructions about how to remove the device.

Before doing anything, turn off your PC and unplug the power cord. Then remove your PC's case, according to your manufacturer's instructions. Remove the device or card as instructed, and put the case back on your PC.

At this point, uninstallation might be complete, and you might not need to do anything else. If your PC runs without problems or conflicts, the uninstallation is complete. If not, follow the next steps.

NOTE

Read any special uninstallation instructions that might have come with the device before you uninstall it. Some devices have special instructions that require that certain steps be taken in an exact order.

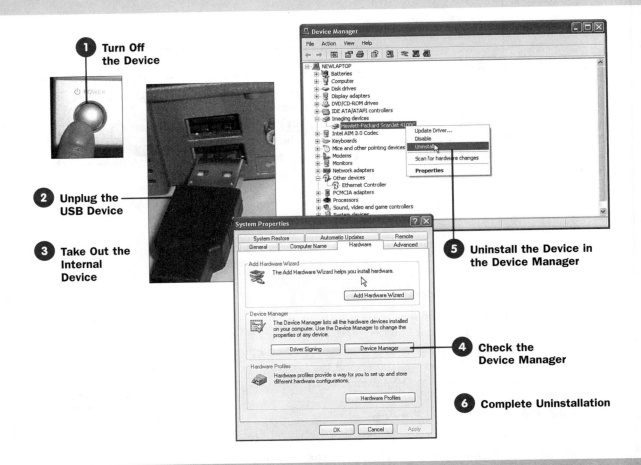

1 Turn Off the Device

2 Unplug the USB Device

3 Take Out the Internal Device

5 Uninstall the Device in the Device Manager

4 Check the Device Manager

6 Complete Uninstallation

KEY TERM

Device Manager—A Windows XP utility that lets you view and manage your hardware.

4 Check the Device Manager

The *Device Manager* is a Windows XP utility that lets you view and manage your hardware. After you unplug or remove a device, you should check this utility to make sure that XP thinks that the device has been removed. There is a possibility that even though you physically removed the device, Windows XP might still think it is present. In that case, you could have system problems and hardware conflicts.

To get to the **Device Manager**, right-click the **My Computer** icon on the desktop and choose **Properties** from the context menu. Click the **Hardware** tab and then click the **Device Manager** icon.

5 **Uninstall the Device in the Device Manager**

When the **Device Manager** launches, look for the device that you just uninstalled. You might have to click one of the + signs to see it. For example, if you are looking for a scanner or digital camera, click the + next to **Imaging devices**. If you see the device that you just removed listed there, it means that Windows XP still believes that the device exists.

Right-click the device in the list and choose **Uninstall** from the context menu.

6 **Complete Uninstallation**

The **Confirm Device Removal** warning box appears, warning you that you are about to remove the device from your system. Click **OK** and the device will be completely removed.

115 Troubleshoot Hardware Problems

We've all lived through them—hardware problems. You've been using a piece of hardware for six months with no problems and suddenly it stops working—and there seems to be no good reason for it—or a piece of hardware simply won't install.

There are many reasons why hardware might go on the fritz, and there's no way to cover every one of them here. But this task will lead you through the most common hardware problems and how to fix them.

1 **Check That the Power Is On**

You'd be surprised at how many supposed hardware problems can be fixed by simply plugging the hardware into a power outlet and making sure that it is turned on. Technical support departments report that a common printer "problem" can be solved by telling callers to plug in the printer and turn on the power.

2 **Make Sure That All Connections Are Secure**

A second common problem is caused when the connection between your PC and the hardware is loose. Check all cables, such as USB cables and printer cables, to make sure that the connection is tight.

Before You Begin

✔ **113** Install New Hardware

✔ **114** Uninstall Hardware

See Also

→ **117** About Updating Drivers

1 **Check That the Power Is On**

2 **Make Sure That All Connections Are Secure**

4 **Start the Hardware Troubleshooter**

3 **Restart Your PC**

5 **Answer Troubleshooter Questions**

6 **Update Your Drivers**

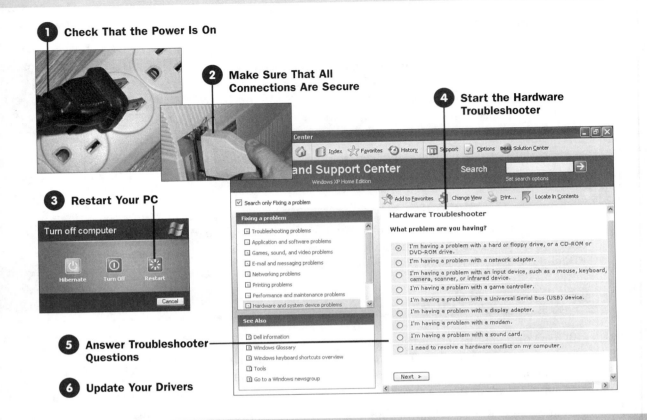

The problem might be a loose connection inside your computer—a memory chip might have gotten loose, for example. Turn off your PC and unplug the power cord. Remove your PC's case according to your manufacturer's instructions. Check all the internal connections to make sure that they're tight. Put the case back on your PC and plug it back in.

3 Restart Your PC

Strange, but true: A common way to fix a hardware problem is to turn off the device and then restart your PC. A surprising number of hardware problems vanish when you do this. What caused the problem, and why did restarting fix it? You'll probably never find out. But you'll have fixed the problem, and that's all that's important.

4 Start the Hardware Troubleshooter

Windows XP has an excellent set of built-in troubleshooters that will automatically check hardware problems and fix any that they find. To start a hardware troubleshooter, choose **Help and Support** from the **Start** menu. Toward the bottom of the list, click the **Fixing a problem** link. A new screen appears. From the **Fixing a problem** list on the left side of the screen, choose the hardware problem you're having, such as **Printing problems** or **Hardware and system device problems**.

5 Answer Troubleshooter Questions

Continue to make choices that describe your problem—for example, if you're having problems with your printer, choose **Fixing a printer problem**. You'll be walked through a series of screens, and you'll make choices that describe the problem. At the end, the troubleshooter might fix your problem. Sometimes it will ask that you reboot.

6 Update Your Drivers

A *driver* is a piece of software required by hardware to work with Windows XP. Whenever you install a new piece of hardware, you also install a driver for it, although that installation might happen invisibly to you.

Hardware problems can be caused by old drivers, so it's a good idea to keep them up to date. For information about how to do it, see **117 About Updating Drivers**.

see **117** About Updating Drivers.

TIP

To make sure that you don't run into problems in the future, it's a good idea to perform regular maintenance on your PC. Buy canned air from a computer store, and once a month turn off and unplug your computer, open up your computer case, and blow out accumulated dust. Swab any areas that show accumulated grime and grit. When your computer is unplugged, spray canned air through the power supply to make sure that dust or grime won't interfere with it.

116 Get System Information

Often, when things go wrong, you'll have to call a technical support department. If you have to call, a technician will most likely want you to provide a good deal of information about your computer, including what kind of chip it has, how much memory it has, the exact version of your operating system, and similar information. In this task, you'll learn how to find out all that information.

Before You Begin

✔ **113** Install New Hardware

See Also

→ **115** Troubleshoot Hardware Problems

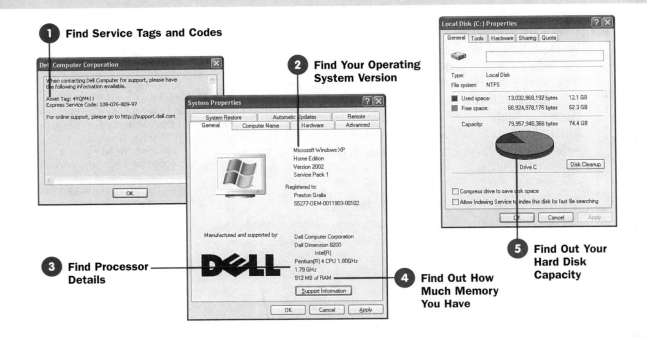

1 Find Service Tags and Codes

2 Find Your Operating System Version

3 Find Processor Details

4 Find Out How Much Memory You Have

5 Find Out Your Hard Disk Capacity

1 Find Service Tags and Codes

Some hardware manufacturers, such as Dell, give you numbers called *service tags and codes* that uniquely identify your computer and you. When you call technical support, a technician will ask for those numbers. Providing them will help the technician identify exactly what hardware you have, and will go a long way toward helping solve your problem.

The service tag and code are affixed to your computer somewhere. On a laptop, they are frequently at the bottom. On a desktop, they might be at the back.

Those tags can be hard to find and read. In some instances, you'll be able to find that information without having to look on your physical computer. The information might be available on your PC. To find out, right-click the **My Computer** icon on the desktop and choose **Properties** from the context menu. Click the **General** tab of the **System Properties** dialog box. If you see a button titled **Support Information** at the bottom of your screen, click it. You might see the service tags and codes there.

2 Find Your Operating System Version

It's important that the technician know the exact version of Windows XP that you have—whether it's the Home Edition or Professional Edition, and whether you have a *Service Pack* installed. You might have installed a Service Pack without realizing it using Automatic Updates. And even if you never installed a Service Pack, you might have one on your computer because they are automatically applied to new computers when the packs become available, so any new computer sold after the pack was released will have it installed.

To find out which version of Windows XP you are running, right-click the **My Computer** icon on the desktop and choose **Properties** from the context menu. The **System Properties** dialog box appears. Click the **General** tab. At the top, you'll see the version of Windows XP you have on your system.

3 Find Processor Details

The technician might also want to know what processor is in your PC, and how fast it is. On the **General** tab of the **System Properties** dialog box, look toward the bottom of your screen. You'll see the name and speed of your processor.

4 Find Out How Much Memory You Have

The technician might want to know how much memory you have in your PC. On the **General** tab of the **System Properties** dialog box, look toward the bottom of your screen. You'll see the total amount of RAM you have installed.

5 Find Out Your Hard Disk Capacity

Problems can be caused if your hard disk is too full, and a technician might want to know the size of your hard disk and how much data is on it. You should monitor this as well, to make sure that your hard disk does not become too full.

Open Windows Explorer, right-click your hard disk, and choose **Properties** from the context menu. In the **Local Disk Properties** dialog box, click the **General** tab. You'll see information about your hard disk, including its capacity and how full it is.

KEY TERM

Service Pack—A patch to an existing version of Windows that updates it with new features or fixes bugs with it.

NOTE

You should have at least 256MB of RAM for use with Windows XP. Microsoft says that you can use 128MB, but if you have that little memory, the system will operate very slowly.

TIP

Don't wait until you have to call technical support to have this information at hand. It will be time-consuming to gather it all. More importantly, if you have a computer problem, you might not be able to start your computer to gather this information. Write it down on a piece of paper and keep it in a safe place.

117 About Updating Drivers

Before You Begin

✔ **113** Install New
Hardware

See Also

→ **115** Troubleshoot
Hardware Problems

KEY TERM

Driver—A piece of software
required by hardware to
work with Windows XP.
Whenever you install a new
piece of hardware, you also
install a driver for it,
although that installation
may happen invisibly to you.

NOTE

You must be connected to
the Internet for Windows
XP to search the Web for a
driver.

For hardware to work, it requires a *driver*, a piece of software that acts
as a mediator between Windows XP and the hardware. Whenever you
install a new piece of hardware, you also install a driver for it, although
that installation may happen invisibly to you.

A surprising number of hardware problems are caused by old drivers.
The problem is not that the drivers themselves get old. It's that you
might have installed a new piece of hardware or software that causes
problems with the old driver. Hardware manufacturers are constantly
updating drivers to take care of these problems, and to also give hardware new features.

Because of that, it's a good idea to update your drivers, even if you
aren't having any hardware problems. Keeping them updated can help
ensure that you won't run into any problems in the future.

The best way to update your drivers is to regularly check the websites of
your hardware's manufacturer. Manufacturers regularly post updated
drivers on their websites. Look in the **Support** or **Downloads** area—
that's where new drivers are usually found.

When they post new drivers, hardware manufacturers include an installation program that will install the new drivers. Follow the download
and installation information you find on the site.

You can also ask that Windows XP check whether new drivers are available for your hardware, and then have Windows automatically install
the new drivers for you. You'll make this request of Windows XP from
the **Device Manager**. Right-click the **My Computer** icon on the desktop
and choose **Properties** from the context menu. In the **System Properties**
dialog box, click the **Hardware** tab and then click the **Device Manager**
button.

Scroll to the piece of hardware whose driver you want to check for
updates. Right-click the entry and choose **Update driver** from the context menu. The **Hardware Update Wizard** appears. Choose the **Install
the Software Automatically** option, click **Next**, and follow the wizard's
instructions. The wizard will search for a new driver, and if it finds the
driver, it will automatically install it for you.

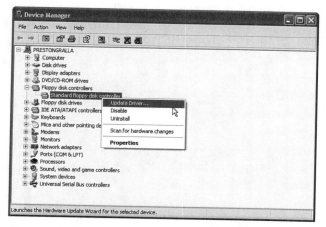

To update a driver, start with the **Device Manager** and choose the hardware whose driver you want to update.

When the **Hardware Update Wizard** appears, tell it to install the software (driver) automatically if it finds a new version available.

14

Fine-Tuning, Optimizing, and Protecting Your PC

IN THIS CHAPTER:

PCs always need fiddling with. Perhaps you want to make yours run faster, or you want to get more life out of your laptop's battery. You certainly want to make sure that it has the latest software protection. And if something goes wrong with it, you want to make sure that you can fix it.

Windows XP offers many built-in tools for doing all that and more. In this chapter, you'll learn how to fine-tune, optimize, and protect your PC using XP's built-in tools.

118 Balance Performance and Visual Effects

See Also

→ **119** Turn Off Unneeded Programs and Services

TIP

Another way to open the **System Properties** dialog box is to click the **Start** button, choose the **Control Panel** option, click the **Performance and Maintenance** icon, and then click the **System** option. If you don't see the **Performance and Maintenance** icon in the **Control Panel** list, choose the **System** icon to launch the **System Properties** dialog box.

NOTE

The **Performance Options** dialog box lists the various special effects that Windows XP can perform. The check boxes next to the ones currently in use are enabled. Those options without check marks are not currently being used.

One of the many things that makes Windows XP unique is its special visual effects—menu items fading in and out, showing shadows under menus, and so on.

One problem with those special effects is each takes a toll on system performance. Your computer has to work harder to use them. If you have an older computer, or if you think your computer is slower than it should be, you can turn off some or all of these special effects.

❶ Right-Click My Computer

The **My Computer** icon might be located in several places depending on how your computer has been set up. You might find an icon for it on your desktop. If not, you'll find it on the right side of the **Start** menu after you click the **Start** button.

Right-click the **My Computer** icon and choose **Properties**. The **System Properties** dialog box appears.

❷ Open the Performance Options Dialog Box

In the **System Properties** dialog box, click the **Advanced** tab. In the **Performance** section, click the **Settings** button to open the **Performance Options** dialog box.

❸ Adjust for Best Performance

If you care more about having your system run as quickly as possible than about the appearance of the screens, choose the **Adjust for best performance** option and click **OK** twice. When you do this, Windows XP disables all the options in the dialog box and uses no special effects. The performance boost takes place immediately.

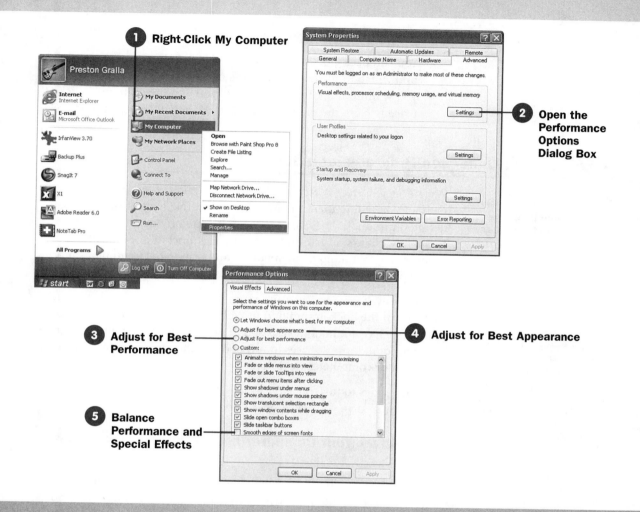

1 Right-Click My Computer

2 Open the Performance Options Dialog Box

3 Adjust for Best Performance

4 Adjust for Best Appearance

5 Balance Performance and Special Effects

---

4 **Adjust for Best Appearance**

If you care more about your system using all of XP's special visual effects than about performance, choose the **Adjust for best appearance** option and click **OK** twice. When you do this, XP enables all the check boxes in the **Performance Options** dialog box and uses all its available special effects. The improved appearance occurs immediately.

 TIP

There are too many effects to detail them all here, so the best advice is to disable check boxes next to some effects and use Windows XP for a while; if you're pleased with the results, leave those effects disabled.

CHAPTER 14: Fine-Tuning, Optimizing, and Protecting Your PC

⑤ Balance Performance and Special Effects

You can decide on an effect-by-effect basis which options to use and which to turn off. Enable the check boxes next to those effects you want to use, and disable those you don't want to use. Click **OK** twice to close the dialog boxes. The effects take place immediately.

119 Turn Off Unneeded Programs and Services

See Also

→ **30** Stop Programs from Running on Startup

→ **118** Balance Performance and Visual Effects

🔍 KEY TERM

Services—Computer processes that run invisibly on your PC to provide your computer with important capabilities, such as managing your computer's sound system.

Whenever you start Windows XP, programs might run automatically without you telling them to launch. For example, your instant messenger program might launch on its own. If you don't use those programs frequently, there's no reason to have them launch automatically, because they're taking away memory and using your computer's processor for programs you do want to run.

Additionally, some *services* run automatically at startup. Services run invisibly in the background and provide your PC with a variety of capabilities, such as managing your sound system. However, you don't necessarily need all those services to run because they take up memory and occupy your computer's processor.

There are ways to turn off services and programs that run on startup, and therefore give your PC a power boost.

① Restart Your Computer and Examine the Notification Area

Restart your computer (click the **Start** button, choose **Turn Off Computer**, and then click the **Restart** button) to make sure that the programs you see in the **Taskbar** are those that launch automatically on startup. The **Notification Area** is on the far right of the **Taskbar** at the bottom of your screen. It displays icons of most of the programs that launch when you start your computer. To see all the icons there, click the small left-pointing arrow.

Hover your mouse over each icon. A balloon tip pops up, which almost all the time displays the name of the program, and might give more information as well. For example, an antivirus program might not only tell you its name, but also whether an important feature is turned on.

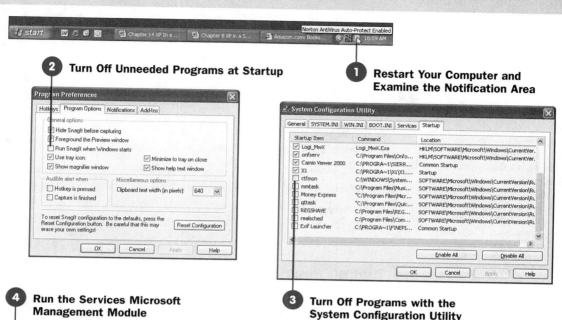

2 Turn Off Unneeded Programs at Startup

1 Restart Your Computer and Examine the Notification Area

4 Run the Services Microsoft Management Module

3 Turn Off Programs with the System Configuration Utility

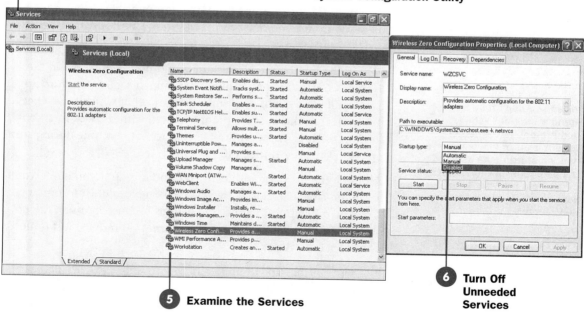

5 Examine the Services

6 Turn Off Unneeded Services

CHAPTER 14: Fine-Tuning, Optimizing, and Protecting Your PC

TIP

Each program has a unique way of launching itself at startup, so there is no way to give specific instructions for how to stop every program from automatically launching. However, you can stop most programs from launching automatically using an **Options** or **Preferences** dialog box. Often the **Options** or **Preferences** dialog box can be accessed from the program's **Tools** menu (double-click the program's icon to open the program so that you can access its menu bar).

TIP

When you don't fully understand a program listing, and are not sure whether to turn it off or leave it running on startup, the safest bet is to leave it running. It might be a program your computer requires to function properly.

If any icons don't display information, double-click the icon. This action runs the program so that you'll know exactly what the program is.

2 Turn Off Unneeded Programs at Startup

If you identify programs you don't need running all the time, such as an instant messenger program that you rarely use, you should stop it from running every time you start your PC.

Find the **Options** or **Preferences** dialog box for the program you want to stop from launching and look for an option that lets you determine whether the program should run when Windows starts. When you find it, disable the check box for that option and click **OK**. (Again, this may vary according to each program.)

3 Turn Off Programs with the System Configuration Utility

Not all programs show themselves in the **Notification Area** when they run on startup. Some programs run invisibly. To see a list of these programs, you must run the **System Configuration Utility**.

Click the **Start** button and choose **Run** to open the **Run** dialog box. In the text box, type **msconfig** and press **Enter**. When the **System Configuration Utility** screen appears, click the **Startup** tab. You'll see a list of programs, most or all of which have check marks next to them. Every program listed with a check next to it runs on startup. Those without checks ran at one time during startup, but were later turned off.

Examine the list of programs. If you find any that you don't want to run on startup, disable the check box next to it. Unfortunately, it can be difficult to decipher the listings because many of the programs are not listed by their actual names—it may be just a filename, such as **qttask**.

It can be difficult, and at times almost impossible, to track down what the programs listed here do. Your best bet is to look at the information in the **Command** column (drag the right edge of the **Command** column heading to widen the column so that you can read all the information there). That column lists the exact location and filename of the program. Examine the folder name and filename to see whether that helps you know what the program is and does.

Disable all the check boxes for programs you don't want to run on startup. When you're done, click **OK**. Windows XP displays a message telling you that the changes won't go into effect until you restart your computer, and asks whether you want to restart now. There's no need to restart now, so restart only if you want to see the effects of your changes. To restart, click the **Restart** button in the dialog box Windows XP displays. Otherwise, click the **Exit without Restart** button. The changes will take effect, even if you don't restart now.

4 Run the Services Microsoft Management Module

You've now identified programs you don't want to run at startup and turned them off, but you haven't done anything about services. To do that, you'll have to run the **Services Microsoft Management Module**. Click the **Start** button and choose **Run** to open the **Run** dialog box. In the text box, type **services.msc** and press **Enter**.

5 Examine the Services

The **Services Microsoft Management Module** lists all the services available on your computer, identifies which are currently running, shows how each starts, and lets you control how each service works.

To see what a service does, click the service name in the list, and make sure that you click the **Extended** tab at the bottom of the screen. When you click the **Extended** tab, whenever you highlight a service, you'll see a description of the service in the large area to the left of the services listing.

The **Startup Type** column tells you whether the service is started automatically by Windows XP, whether it is disabled so that it cannot run, or whether it must be started manually.

TIP

To see which services are currently running, look in the **Status** column. Any that are running have a listing of **Started**. Those that aren't running have that column blank.

6 Turn Off Unneeded Services

It can be difficult to identify which services you need and which you don't because the descriptions can be cryptic. Be careful about which services you decide to turn off.

However, if you use a desktop PC, and it doesn't have a wireless network adapter, and you don't plan to install one, it's a good idea to turn off the **Wireless Zero Configuration** service because it serves no purpose unless you have a wireless network adapter.

To turn off a service, double-click it in the services list. A **Properties** dialog box for that service opens. From the **Startup Type** drop-down list, choose **Disabled** and then click **OK**. The service will not start from now on when you start Windows XP.

120 Create and Use Power Schemes for Laptops

See Also

→ **121** Use ClearType for Better Laptop Resolution

KEY TERM

Power scheme—A profile you apply to Windows XP that determines, for example, how a laptop uses power (whether it turns off the LCD screen or hard disk after a certain amount of time elapses) to save electricity and increase battery life.

Laptop computers are extremely convenient because you can carry them wherever you go and work with them on airplanes, coffee shops, and other locations. But they also pose a problem—too often, they run out of battery power—for example, when you're on a cross-country flight.

The best way to preserve battery life is to create different power profiles, which Windows XP calls *power schemes*. With these schemes, you control how much power Windows XP uses for different functions. For example, you can create a scheme for when your laptop is plugged into a power outlet, and another for when it's running on batteries. For the plugged-in scheme, you can specify no power-savings features, but when it's unplugged, you can have XP turn off your hard disk after several minutes when it hasn't been accessed.

1 Open the Power Options Properties Dialog Box

Click the **Start** button and choose **Control Panel**. From the **Control Panel**, choose **Performance and Maintenance** and then choose **Power Options**.

2 Select a Scheme to Modify

Click the **Power Scheme** tab and from the **Power schemes** drop-down list, choose a scheme you want to modify. There are a number of preset schemes from which you can choose, including **Home/Office Desk**, **Portable/Laptop**, **Presentation**, **Always On**, **Minimal Power Management**, and **Max Power**.

3 Modify the Scheme

After you've selected a scheme, you can modify how it uses power. For this example, I've decided to modify how my laptop uses power when it's plugged in and when it's running on batteries.

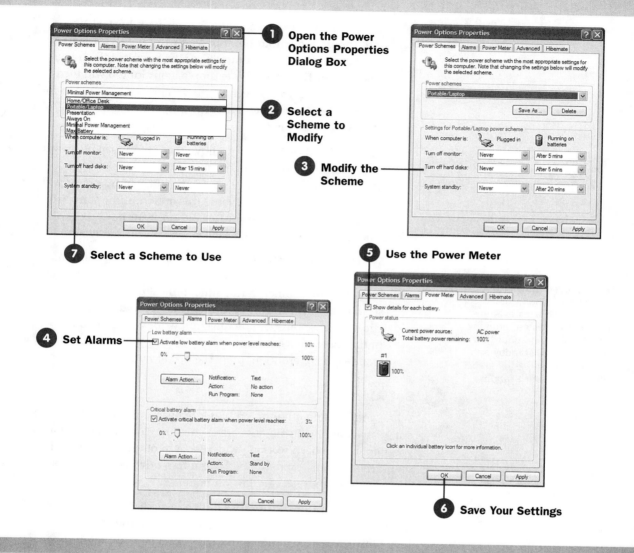

1 Open the Power Options Properties Dialog Box

2 Select a Scheme to Modify

3 Modify the Scheme

7 Select a Scheme to Use

4 Set Alarms

5 Use the Power Meter

6 Save Your Settings

For each power scheme you modify, you have the following choices:

- **Turn off monitor.** You can have the laptop turn off the monitor after a set amount of time. The laptop will still function, and your work won't be lost, but no power will be sent to the laptop screen. Screens use a great deal of power, so this can be a big electricity saver. In the **Running on batteries** section, choose the amount of time you want your laptop to wait before turning off your screen when you're idle. If you choose **After five mins**, for example, your laptop will turn off the power to your screen if you do not use your laptop for five minutes. Your screen automatically comes back to life when you press any key.

- **Turn off hard disks.** You can have the laptop turn off power to the hard disk after a set amount of time. The laptop will still function, and your work won't be lost, but no power will be sent to the hard disk. Choose this option in the same way you chose the **Turn off monitor** option. Your hard disk will automatically come back to life when you press any key.

- **System standby.** Your laptop can automatically go into a state of suspended animation after you don't use it for a certain amount of time. In this state, almost all the power is shut off to it. From the **System standby** drop-down list, choose the amount of idle time you want your laptop to wait until it goes into system standby. To bring your PC out of standby or hibernation, press the power button.

NOTE

You can also have your laptop go into hibernation mode, which uses even less power than system standby. For information about how to use system standby and hibernation, see **10** Use Hibernation and Standby.

4 Set Alarms

When you're using a laptop on battery power and the battery runs out, your laptop will shut down and you'll lose any unsaved data you might have been working with. Because of that, you should set alarms so that you're notified enough in advance of the laptop shutting down that it's very low on batteries.

In the **Power Options Properties** dialog box, click the **Alarms** tab. In the **Low battery alarm** section, enable the **Activate low battery alarm when power level reaches** check box; drag the slider to select the percent of battery life that you want to trigger the alarm. Click the **Alarm Action** button to select what action should be taken, such as a text pop-up notification and a sound alarm.

TIP

When your alarm goes off, you should close all the files you're working on, close all your programs, and then shut off your laptop. If you want to continue working, either put a fresh battery into the laptop or connect the laptop to a power outlet.

Doing that sets the basic alarm, but you set a second alarm as well to provide a second notification. In the **Critical battery alarm** section, enable the **Activate critical battery alarm when power level reaches** check box; drag the slider to select the percentage of battery life that you want to trigger this second alarm.

5 Use the Power Meter

You'll most likely want to know about your battery level not just when you're about to run out of power, but at all times, so that you can gauge how much working time you have left on your laptop.

To do this, you can have a power meter always display in the **Notification Area** in the **Taskbar** when your laptop is running on battery power. A small icon shows how much battery power is left, and when you hover the mouse pointer over the icon, it will report the percent of battery life left. If you double-click the icon, it will report the total amount of time you have left before the computer shuts down.

To have the power meter display on your laptop, click the **Power Meter** tab in the **Power Options Properties** dialog box, and enable the **Show details for each battery** check box.

6 Save Your Settings

When you're done modifying power schemes, alarms, and the power meter, save your settings by clicking **OK** at the bottom of any tab in the **Power Options Properties** dialog box. Your new power scheme settings are now in effect.

7 Select a Scheme to Use

To change to a new power scheme at any time, go to the **Power Schemes** tab of the **Power Options Properties** dialog box and choose the scheme from the **Power schemes** drop-down list.

121 Use ClearType for Better Laptop Resolution

Laptop screens can be very hard on the eyes, especially because many laptops are designed to work at very high screen resolutions. When you have a high screen resolution, the type on the screen appears very small.

As laptop screens get larger, resolutions increase and type gets smaller. In addition, the LCDs used to make laptop screens can be hard on the eyes. The problem isn't confined to laptops—increasingly popular desktop flat-panel LCD screens have the same problem.

TIP

If you use have a wireless network adapter that you plug into your laptop when you travel so that you can connect to *HotSpots* on the road, only plug in the adapter when you actually need to connect to a HotSpot. The adapter requires power to run, so if you plug it in when you don't need it, you're reducing your battery life. For details about how to connect to HotSpots, see **63** **Connect to a HotSpot or Wi-Fi Network.**

See Also

→ **120** Create and Use Power Schemes for Laptops

1 Open the Effects Dialog Box

3 Go to the Web to Fine-Tune ClearType

2 Turn On ClearType

5 Choose Final Settings

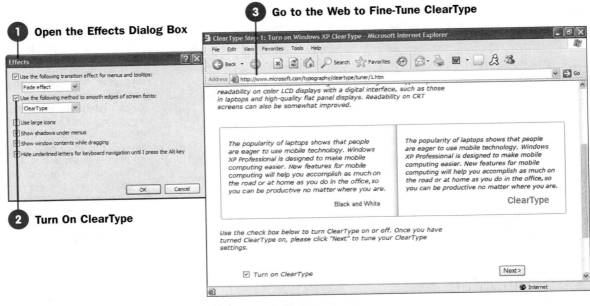

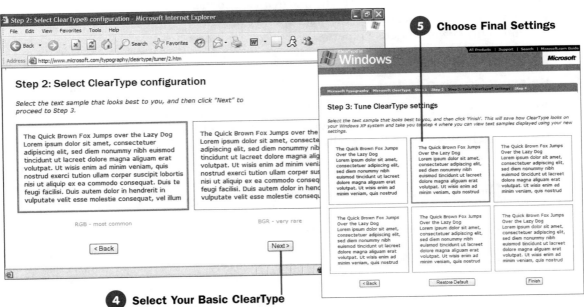

4 Select Your Basic ClearType Configuration

There is a fix for the problem, however. You can use a built-in feature of Windows XP called ClearType, in which text is smoothed, making it much easier to read and much easier on the eyes.

① Open the Effects Dialog Box

Right-click the desktop and choose **Properties** from the context menu. When the **Display Properties** dialog box opens, click the **Appearance** tab and then click the **Effects** button to open the **Effects** dialog box.

② Turn On ClearType

Enable the **Use the following method to smooth edges of screen fonts** check box. Select the **ClearType** option from the drop-down list and click **OK** twice. The ClearType feature is now turned on.

③ Go to the Web to Fine-Tune ClearType

Although the ClearType feature is now turned on, you can't fine-tune the way it looks on your screen. It's important that you fine-tune it, because LCD screens are very different from one another, and you should customize it for your screen. You must go to a web-site to fine-tune its appearance. Connect to the Internet and go to **http://www.microsoft.com/windowsxp/pro/using/howto/ customize/cleartype/tuner**.

You'll be asked whether you want to install and run the **Microsoft ClearType Tuning Control**. Click **Yes**. There are two versions of the control; depending on your version of Windows XP and whether you have certain XP service packs installed, you will see one or the other of the controls. In one of them, from the opening page, click **Next**, and in the other, from the opening page, click **Move on to Step 2: Tuning ClearType Settings**.

④ Select Your Basic ClearType Configuration

Depending on the version of the control the site has provided you with, the next page displays two versions of the same text and asks which looks better. Choose the text that looks better and click **Next**. (One version of the control skips this page entirely, so you might not see it.)

TIP

You can use ClearType on a normal (non-LCD) PC monitor, but it often makes the text appear blurry. Additionally, people have complained that it gives them headaches.

⑤ Choose Final Settings

You'll next come to a page that displays a block of text six different ways. Click the text block that looks best and then click the **Finish** button. You're done; you've tuned ClearType so that it looks best for your LCD.

122 Get System Updates Automatically

See Also

→ **124** Protect Your System with System Restore

 TIPS

To check whether you have Windows XP SP-2 installed, right-click the **My Computer** icon, choose **Properties**, and click the **General** tab in the **System Properties** dialog box. At the bottom of the **System** area, read about your precise version of Windows XP. If it reads **Service Pack 2**, SP-2 is installed; otherwise, it isn't.

Another way to open the **System Properties** dialog box is to click the **Start** button, choose the **Control Panel** option, click the **Performance and Maintenance** icon, and then click the **System** option. If you don't see the **Performance and Maintenance** icon in the **Control Panel** list, choose the **System** icon to launch the **System Properties** dialog box.

Microsoft is constantly updating Windows XP by issuing new fixes and patches. Sometimes it issues them because it finds security vulnerabilities that must be repaired. Other times, Microsoft finds bugs. And still other times, it adds new features.

It's especially important to keep your system up to date with these fixes because without the updates, your computer could be vulnerable to hackers and Internet dangers. You can have Windows XP automatically check for updates and install them using **Automatic Updates**—the safest way for getting system updates. When you use **Automatic Updates**, XP accesses the Internet to check the Microsoft site for updates and then downloads and installs them on your PC. You can customize the **Automatic Updates** settings in a variety of ways.

① Check Whether Automatic Updates Is Turned On

If you're running Windows XP Service Pack 2 (SP-2) or later, a small **Security Center** icon is in the **Notification Area** in the **Taskbar**. Click the icon to open the **Security Center**. Look in the **Automatic Updates** area. If this feature is turned on, you will see a green **On** button. If it is not turned on, you will see a red **Off** button.

If you don't have Windows XP SP-2, you can check to see whether **Automatic Updates** is turned on by right-clicking the **My Computer** icon, choosing **Properties**, and then clicking the **Automatic Updates** tab in the **System Properties** dialog box. If the **Keep my computer up to date** check box is enabled, **Automatic Updates** is turned on.

1 Check Whether Automatic Updates Is Turned On

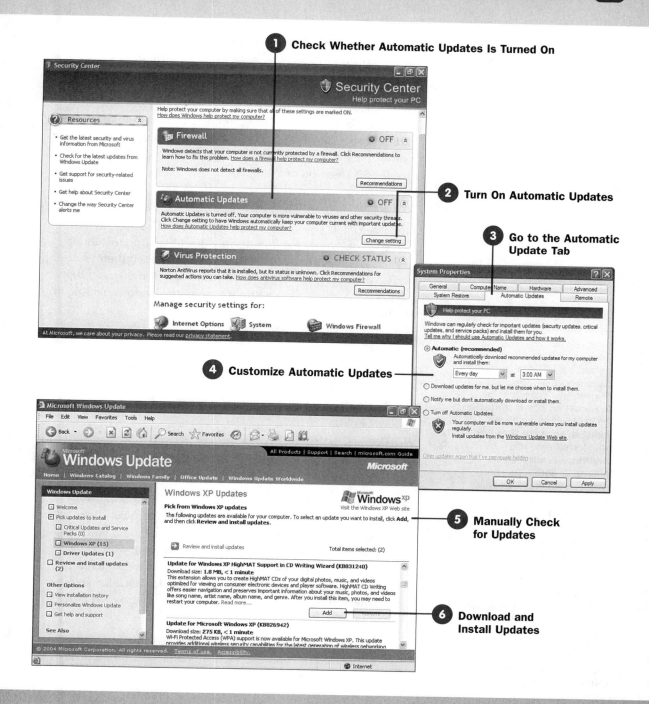

2 Turn On Automatic Updates

3 Go to the Automatic Update Tab

4 Customize Automatic Updates

5 Manually Check for Updates

6 Download and Install Updates

CHAPTER 14: Fine-Tuning, Optimizing, and Protecting Your PC

② Turn On Automatic Updates

To turn on the **Automatic Updates** feature, click the **Change setting** button. The red **Off** button changes to a green **On** button, and automatic updates are turned on.

If you don't have SP-2, in the **Automatic Updates** tab of the **System Properties** dialog box, enable the **Keep my computer up to date** check box. (Note that this option does not show up if you have the SP-2 version of Windows XP.)

③ Go to the Automatic Updates Tab

Windows XP lets you control how **Automatic Updates** are handled. You can have XP automatically download and install all updates, you can have it download the updates but then let you choose when to install them, or you can have it notify you that updates are available but without automatically downloading or installing them.

To customize how the **Automatic Updates** feature works, you need to get to the **Automatic Updates** page of the **System Properties** dialog box. In the **Security Center**, click the **System** icon at the bottom of the screen to open the **System Properties** dialog box, and then click the **Automatic Updates** tab.

④ Customize Automatic Updates

The **Automatic Updates** tab presents these options for customizing how the updates occur:

- **Automatic.** If you choose this option, XP automatically checks for updates, downloads them, and installs them without your intervention. If you choose this option, you must also choose the interval and time when you want XP to check for updates from the drop-down boxes; for example, every day at 3 p.m. It's not a bad idea to check for updates daily, just in case an important security update has been released.

- **Download updates for me, but let me choose when to install them.** If you choose this option, XP automatically checks for updates and downloads them. But it won't

TIPS

You must be connected to the Internet to receive updates, because they are transferred over the Internet. Because downloading update files can take a substantial amount of time over a dial-up connection, be patient.

You might want to download system updates but not install them. The installation procedure can take some time, might interfere with your current work, and might require you to reboot your computer. You might want to do the actual installation at a time when you're not doing anything else on your computer.

automatically install them. Instead, it alerts you that it has downloaded an update, and asks whether you want to install it. You can choose to install it at the time of the alert, or tell XP to remind you at a later time.

- **Notify me but don't automatically download or install them.** If you choose this option, XP checks for updates automatically, but won't download them. Instead, it alerts you when an update is ready, and asks whether you want to download it. You can choose to download it at the time of the alert, or tell XP to remind you at a later time. You can then install it, or tell XP to remind you to install it at a later time.

- **Turn off Automatic Updates.** If you choose this option, XP won't automatically check for updates.

⑤ Manually Check for Updates

If you turn off the **Automatic Updates** feature, you can manually check for updates yourself and choose which to install. First connect to the Internet. When you're connected, click the **Start** button and choose **Control Panel**. From the left side of the screen, click **Windows Update**.

You'll be sent to the **Windows Update** website. To check whether there are any updates, click the **Scan for Updates** link in the middle of the welcome page.

⑥ Download and Install Updates

Windows XP checks the site to see whether any updates are available. It then lists all the potential updates. Scroll through the list and click the **Add** button next to any you want to install. If there are any listed as critical updates, you should make sure to install those.

After you have chosen all the updates you want to install, click the **Review and install updates** link. You'll see a list of all the updates you've chosen. To remove any, click the **Remove** button. To install your updates, click **Install Now**. All the selected updates are downloaded to your computer and installed.

 TIP

You should always install critical updates, but whether you want to install others is a personal decision. Many updates fix only a very specific feature of a program—and you might never use that program or feature. If you locate a large update that would take a long time to download and install, it doesn't always make sense to install it because you wouldn't use it anyway. Read the description of each update carefully, and then use your judgment about how important that update is to you.

About Backing Up Your Hard Disk

See Also

→ Protect Your System with System Restore

 TIP

How often you should make a backup depends on how important your files are to you. If you use your computer for work, you should make a backup every day, if at all feasible. But no matter what, you should back up at least once a week at a minimum.

It's an unfortunate fact of life that hard disks and computers sometimes crash. That means you can lose all your files, data, and programs.

There is a way to protect yourself against these dangers, though. You can use a backup program that makes copies of what's on your computer and stores the data somewhere else (on a CD, another hard drive, and so on). If your computer crashes, you can get the data back from wherever it is stored.

When you use a backup program, you have a choice of backing up your entire computer, just your files and not your programs, or only selected folders and files. Your programs are very large, and it can take a very long time and a large amount of storage space to store them. As a general rule, there's really no reason to back them up, not only because of how long it will take to back them up, but also because you have copies of the programs on the original installation discs, and it's easy to reinstall them from those discs if necessary.

Hard disks are large, and you most likely have a lot of files you want to back up. If you have a CD-R or a DVD-R drive, your best bet is to back up to CDs or DVDs. These storage media have large capacities, are inexpensive, and are easy to store. If you have a network at home, you might want to back up your hard disk from one computer to another.

Which backup program to use is a more difficult problem. Windows XP includes a built-in Backup program. To run it, click the **Start** button, click the **All Programs** button, and choose **Accessories**. Then choose **System Tools** and from there, choose **Backup**. From the **Backup Utility** screen that appears, you can choose to use a wizard to back up your hard disk, or you can customize the backup yourself.

However, there's a very serious problem with the Windows XP backup program: It can't back up to CDs or DVDs. In addition, it's not particularly easy to use, either when backing up your files or if you need to recover them.

Because of that, it's a good idea to buy a separate backup program. There are a variety of good ones, including **NTI Backup Now!** available in stores and online at **www.ntibackupnow.com**, and **Backup Plus**, available in stores and online at **www.backupplus.net**.

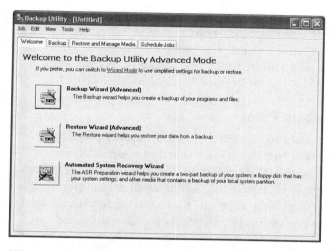

Windows XP's built-in Backup utility has some problems with it, most notably that you can't use it to back up to CDs or DVDs.

124 Protect Your System with System Restore

The software you install on your PC isn't always particularly well behaved. There may be times when you install a new program that does some kind of harm to your system, or interferes with other programs. The same holds true when you install a piece of hardware. There's a chance that it could damage your computer as well.

To protect against that kind of damage to your system, Windows XP includes an excellent form of protection called **System Restore**. At regular intervals, **System Restore** takes snapshots of your system. Then, if you run into a problem—for example with a piece of software or hardware—you can restore your system to the state it was in when that snapshot was taken. These snapshots include only the software and settings on your computer. They don't include data. Let's say that you install a piece of software, then create new files or edit existing ones, and afterwards realize that the piece of software has created problems for your computer. When you restore your computer using **System Restore**, it won't touch the files you created or edited, it will only touch the damaging software.

See Also

→ **123** About Backing Up Your Hard Disk

 TIP

To protect your data files, back them up using a reliable backup program, as described in **123** About Backing Up Your Hard Disk.

TIP

Another way to open the **System Restore** window is to click the **Start** button, choose **All Programs, Accessories, System Tools**, and then click the **System Restore** option.

NOTE

When you scroll through the calendar, you'll find more system restore points than you created. That's because Windows XP automatically creates restore points at certain times and in response to certain events. For example, it creates a restore point whenever you install a program that uses the installation program **Windows Installer** or **Install Shield Pro** version 7.0 or later, when you install an update using the **Automatic Updates** feature (see **123** Get System Updates Automatically), or when a piece of hardware is installed that XP can't verify is safe. Windows XP also creates a restore point every 24 hours if the computer is turned on, or if it has been 24 hours since the last restore point was created.

① Run System Restore

Click the **Start** button, choose **Control Panel**, click the **Performance and Maintenance** icon, and click **System Restore** in the left pane. The **System Restore** welcome window opens.

② Create Restore Point

From the welcome screen, select the **Create a restore point** option and click the **Next** button. On the screen that appears, type a description of the restore point you are about to create. Make sure that it's descriptive enough so that its name will remind you why you created it. You don't have to include the date because you can see the dates and times on which all your restore points were created.

After you name the restore point, click **Create**. When the screen appears telling you that the restore point has been created, click **Close**. If you want to go back to the main screen for creating and managing restore points, click **Home**.

③ Use a Restore Point

If your computer starts running into problems, and you want to restore it to a time when it was running properly, first get back to the **Welcome to System Restore** screen. Get there by following the directions in step 1.

Select the **Restore my computer to an earlier time** option and click the **Next** button. The screen that appears is a calendar; listed on the calendar are all the restore points on your system. Click any date on the calendar to see what restore points were created that day, along with their names and times of creation.

Click the restore point you want to use and click **Next**. You'll be told that you're going to restore your computer to an earlier time, and that you should save all your open files and close your open programs. Save your files, close your programs, and click **Next**. You will be logged off, and your computer will be restored using the selected restore point. Windows XP displays the progress of the operation. Your computer will then turn off and restart, and you'll get a message telling you that the restoration was complete. Click **OK** and use your computer.

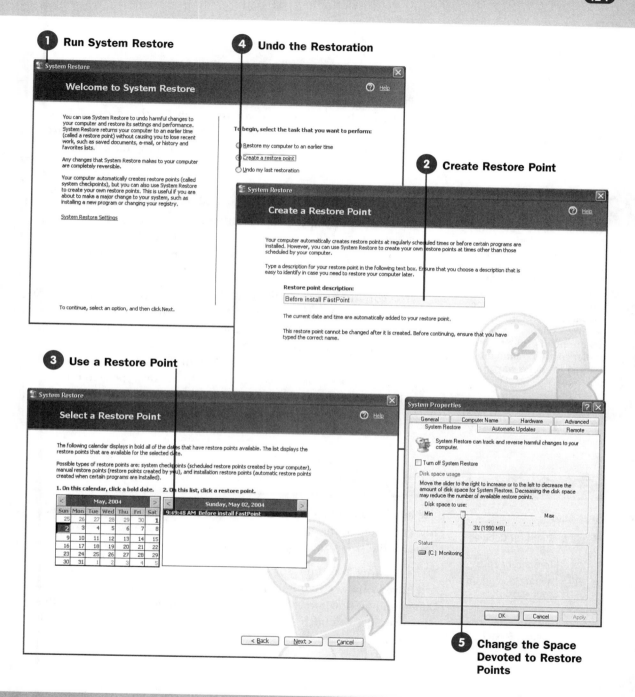

1 Run System Restore

4 Undo the Restoration

2 Create Restore Point

3 Use a Restore Point

5 Change the Space Devoted to Restore Points

4 **Undo the Restoration**

If you've made a mistake and used the wrong restore point, or for some other reason want to undo the restoration, you can put your PC back into the state it was in before you applied the restore point. Get back to the **Welcome to System Restore** screen following the directions in step 1. Then click the **Undo my last restoration** option and click **Next**. Follow the same procedure outline in step 3 for using a restore point.

5 **Change the Space Devoted to Restore Points**

Restore points can take up a substantial amount of space on your hard disk. In fact, XP devotes several gigabytes or more of your hard disk space to restore points, depending on your total hard disk size.

You can increase or decrease the hard disk space devoted to restore points. Go to the **Welcome to System Restore** screen following the directions in step 1. On the left side of the screen, click the **System Restore Settings** link. In the **System Properties** dialog box that appears, click the **System Restore** tab (if it is not already selected) and move the slider to the left to devote less disk space to it (and "lose" some of the restore points you might have already set); move the slider to the right to devote more space to it. When you're done, click **OK**; the new settings go into effect immediately.

NOTE

The more space you have devoted to restore points, the more of them you can have on your computer, but the less space you have for your files and programs. When the amount of space allocated to restore points becomes filled, as new restore points are created, earlier restore points are deleted to make way for new ones.

---

125 **Free Up Space on Your Hard Disk**

See Also

→ **54** Clean Up Cookies and Delete Temporary Files

→ **123** About Backing Up Your Hard Disk

→ **124** Protect Your System with System Restore

The longer you use your computer, the less hard disk space you have. You install programs, you create files, and pretty soon what looked like a large hard disk isn't so large any more.

There is a way to reclaim some space on your hard disk, however. You can have Windows XP automatically delete unnecessary files. Depending on how many unnecessary files you have on your disk, this action can get you back either a little space or potentially hundreds of megabytes of space.

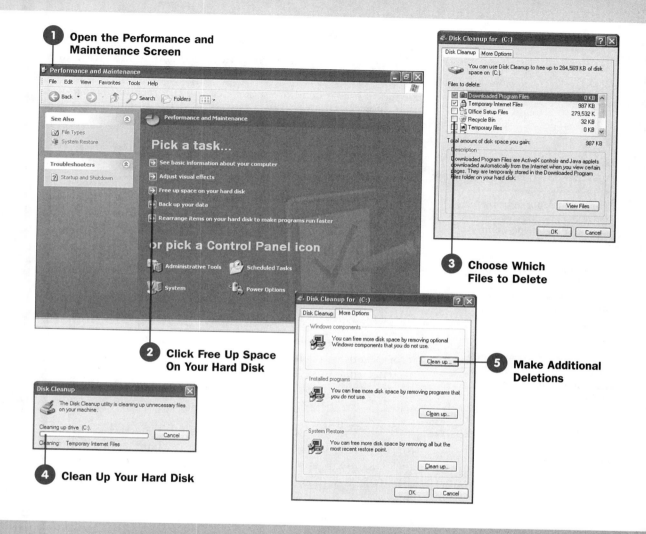

1 Open the Performance and Maintenance Screen

2 Click Free Up Space On Your Hard Disk

3 Choose Which Files to Delete

4 Clean Up Your Hard Disk

5 Make Additional Deletions

❶ Open the Performance and Maintenance Screen

Click the **Start** button and choose **Control Panel**. Click the **Performance and Maintenance** icon to open the **Performance and Maintenance** screen.

② Click Free Up Space On Your Hard Disk

Click the **Free up space on your hard disk** link in the **Pick a task** list. XP examines your hard disk, looking for unneeded files, and calculates how much hard disk space you can reclaim. This process might take a few minutes, depending on the size of your hard disk. A small **Disk Cleanup** window appears, telling you the progress of the search.

TIP

If you want more information about the files you're about to delete, you can try to view them by highlighting the file type and clicking the **View Files** button. This action launches Windows Explorer and puts you into the folder where the files are located. You'll have to browse through the files with Windows Explorer. Be forewarned: Most of the files identified for potential deletion will have incomprehensible names, and not all can be viewed. Although viewing files before you delete them is a good idea in theory, in practice it often won't help you.

③ Choose Which Files to Delete

After the **Disk Cleanup** utility does its calculations, it shows you its findings and asks which files you want to delete. It lists the types of files it can delete, such as **Temporary Internet Files** (files your computer creates when you browse the Web, but which you don't need), files in the **Recycle Bin**, and so on. For each type of file, you'll see how much space you can save by deleting those types of files. You'll also see the total of all the space you'll save, based on all the file types selected for deleting.

Disk Cleanup enables the check boxes next to the types of files it recommends you delete. As a general rule, it's a good idea to follow **Disk Cleanup**'s recommendations, unless you're a very experienced user.

④ Clean Up Your Hard Disk

After you've selected the check boxes for the types of files to delete, click **OK**. You'll get a warning box asking whether you want to delete the files. Click **Yes**. The **Disk Cleanup** utility cleans out those files and reports its progress as it's doing its work. When it finishes, the dialog box goes away.

⑤ Make Additional Deletions

The **Disk Cleanup** utility can clean other types of files from your hard disk as well. Run **Disk Cleanup** as explained in steps 1 and 2. When the **Disk Cleanup** dialog box opens, click the **More Options** tab. Here are three more options for additional disk cleanup:

- **Windows components.** You can delete various Windows utilities and programs, such as **Windows Media Player** and **Windows Messenger**. Click the **Clean up** button in the **Windows components** section of the dialog box. The **Windows Components Wizard** appears to walk you through the process of removing whatever components you no longer want.

- **Installed programs.** You can delete any of the programs installed on your hard disk. Click the **Clean up** button in the **Installed programs** section of the dialog box, and the **Add/Remove Programs** utility launches. To remove a program, highlight it and click the **Change/Remove** button.

- **System Restore.** You can delete all your restore points except the most recent one. (For more details, see **124** Protect Your System with System Restore.) Click the **Clean up** button in the **System Restore** section of the dialog box, and a warning screen appears asking whether you want to delete all but the most recent restore point. Click **Yes** to delete them.

126 Defragment Your Hard Disk

As you use your computer, it slows down over time because your hard disk becomes *fragmented*. Files on your PC are stored in different sections on the hard disk, and as you open and close them, the sections are not stored next to one another on the hard disk—the files become fragmented. That means that when Windows XP opens a file, it must take extra time to find it, because the fragments are spread over your hard disk rather than being found contiguously.

The same thing happens with programs. As you use them, the files needed to run them become fragmented and are slower to load and run. The upshot is that your computer gradually runs slower and slower.

You can speed up your PC by defragmenting your hard disk so that the parts of files are stored next to one another once again. You do this by using XP's built-in defragmentation utility.

See Also

→ **123** About Backing Up Your Hard Disk

KEY TERM

Fragmentation—When the different sections of files and programs on your PC are stored far apart from each other on your hard disk. This leads to a slower operating PC.

① **Open the Performance and Maintenance Screen**

② **Run the Disk Defragmenter**

③ **Analyze Your Hard Disk**

④ **Defragment Your Hard Disk**

⑤ **View the Defragmentation Report**

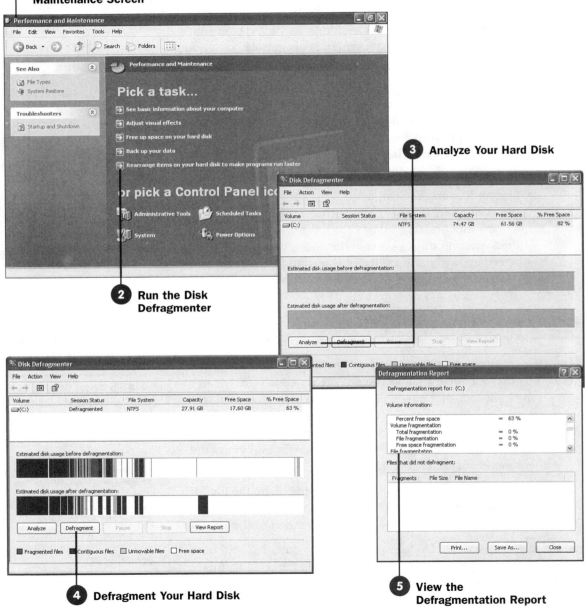

① Open the Performance and Maintenance Screen

Click the **Start** button and choose **Control Panel**. Click the **Performance and Maintenance** icon to open the **Performance and Maintenance** screen.

② Run the Disk Defragmenter

Click the **Rearrange items on your hard disk to make programs run faster** link in the **Pick a task** list. The **Disk Defragmenter** screen opens.

③ Analyze Your Hard Disk

Instead of defragmenting your hard disk right away, you can have Windows XP examine your hard disk and tell you whether your hard disk needs defragmenting. To do this, click the **Analyze** button. XP examines your hard disk and reports back to you. If it determines that your hard disk should be defragmented, it pops up a screen telling you that you should defragment your hard disk. If it determines that your hard disk does not need to be defragmented, it pops up a screen telling you so.

④ Defragment Your Hard Disk

To defragment your hard disk, click the **Defragment** button. Windows XP begins defragmenting your hard disk and displays its progress on the **Disk Defragmenter** screen. The top part of the screen shows the state of your hard disk before defragmentation. The bottom part shows the state of your hard disk as XP defragments your hard disk.

At the end of the defragmentation process, you'll get a notice that defragmentation is complete. The notice may also note that not all your files could be defragmented. Click **Close**.

When defragmentation is complete, the bottom part of the screen shows you the final state of your hard disk after defragmentation, while the top part shows you the state before defragmentation.

 NOTE

Note that the **Defragment** button appears whether or not Windows XP recommends that you defragment your hard disk. You can defragment the hard disk even if XP does not recommend defragmenting it.

5 View the Defragmentation Report

If you're interested, you can view a report that gives you details about your hard disk, including defragmentation information. Click **View Report** at the bottom of the screen to display it. You'll see a variety of information about your hard disk, including its size and how much disk space is used, as well as information about how much of the hard disk, if any, remains defragmented.

Index

copying
folders, 18
music to MP3 players (Windows Media Player), 335
critical updates, 395
custom toolbar, creating (TweakUI utility), 199-202
customized startups, multiboot menu creation, 26-31
customizing
desktop, 4-5
TweakUI utility, 96-97
icons (System Tray), 85
Internet Explorer toolbar, 197-199
Outlook Express, 258-262
bar options, 258-261
mail-checking frequency settings, 262
Preview pane, 261
toolbar layout options, 261-262
Windows Messenger sign-in deactivation, 262
Start menu, item additions/deletions, 78-83
system settings (Control Panel), 15-16
Welcome screen (Stardock LogonStudio), 31-35
Windows Explorer (TweakUI utility), 154-157

D

date/time
behaviors, customizing, 93-95
synchronizing with Internet server, 95
deactivating
programs for performance reasons, 382-384
services for performance reasons, 385-386

decompressing files/folders (Windows Explorer), 142
decryption (Windows Explorer)
files, 138
folders, 138
default file folders, saving to, 152-154
deleting
cookies (Internet Explorer), 191
icons from desktop, 68-70
programs
from Scheduled Tasks folder, 119
from Startup folder, 117
temporary files (Internet Explorer), 192
desktop
appearance, 4-5
modifying, 56-61
backgrounds, selecting personal photos as, 359-361
buttons
color schemes, 57-59
styles, 57-59
clock
time zones, 95
turning on/off, 93-95
colors
16-bit, 61
32-bit, 61
customization tools (TweakIU utility), 96-97
date/time behaviors, 93-95
effects
fade, 59
scroll, 59
fonts, smoothing, 60
icons, 12
changing, 70-73
cleaning up, 68-70
.dll file type, 71
.exe file type, 71
.ico file type, 71
size of, 60
website download sources, 73
keyboard shortcuts, creating, 110-111

menus
hiding underlined letters for keyboard navigation, 60
shadows, 60
transition effects, 59
Notification Area, 11
customizing, 85-86
Quick Launch toolbar, 10
activating, 91-93
icon deletion, 93
icon rearrangement, 93
spacing issues, 92
screen resolution, changing, 60-61
screensavers
creating, 61-64
previewing, 64
size of, 64
time frequencies, 64
Start button, function of, 10
Start menu, 12
All Programs icon, 14
Classic Windows appearance, 83
Connect To, 14
Control Panel, 13-16
elements of, 13-14
frequently used programs list, 13
Help and Support Center, 14
Log Off icon, 14
My Computer, 13
My Documents, 13
My Network Places, 13
My Recent Documents, 13
pinned programs list, 13
rearranging, 78-83
Run option, 14
Search, 14
Turn Off Computer icon, 14
User Account icon, 14
System Tray, 11
Taskbar, 83
Address Bar activation, 88-90
autohiding, 85
buttons, grouping, 85

How can we make this index more useful? Email us at indexes@samspublishing.com

409

How can we make this index more useful? Email us at indexes@samspublishing.com

411

G - H

How can we make this index more useful? Email us at indexes@samspublishing.com

413

J - K

Start menu, 12
system folders, 125
system sounds, 102
Task pane (Windows Explorer), 122
Taskbar, 83
themes (desktop), 73
toolbars, 86
vCard, 265
wallpaper, 12
Wi-Fi, 208
Windows Explorer, 122
wireless routers, 208
key-loggers (spyware), 240
keyboard shortcuts
Alt+Tab (open window cycling), 22
creating for opening programs, 110-111

L

laptops
batteries
low status alarms, 388
power meter usage, 389
mouse options
pointing sticks, 107
touchpads, 107
power schemes
Hibernation mode, 388
using for performance reasons, 386-389
text resolution, readability improvements (ClearType), 389-392
launching
programs with automatic start-ups, 113-115
Start menu, 10
left button (mouse operation), 20-21
Limeware, music file-sharing software, 336
Limited user account, 39

Linksys routers, installing, 213
List view (Windows Explorer), 127
Log Off icon (Start menu), 14
logons, 24
automatic, configuring, 44-46
passwords
creating, 35-38
selecting, 35-38
process, 25-26
Welcome screen, customizing (Stardock Logon Studio), 31-35
Lycos.com website, picture/image searches, 67

M

MAC addresses (routers), 165
mailboxes
configuring (Outlook Express), 270-273
rules, creating (Outlook Express), 274-276
mapping network drives (Windows Explorer), 176-178
maximizing windows, 22
memory
Fast User Switching feature, hardware requirements, 46-49
RAM (Random Access Memory), 47
system information, retrieving, 375
menus
desktop, hiding underlined letters for keyboard navigation, 60
shadowing effect, 60
messages
anti-spam software, 284
blocked senders list, 283
email rules, spam blockage, 284
emoticons (Windows Messenger), 295

flagging (Outlook Express), 271
font options (Windows Messenger), 295
importing from other programs (Outlook Express), 285-287
saving (Windows Messenger), 296
searching (Outlook Express), 273
sending (Windows Messenger), 295-296
spam blockers, 283
metadata
graphics file formats, 149
music file formats, 149
searching (Search Companion), 148-150
microphones
built-in, 103
jack connections, 103
purchasing, 103
recording guidelines, 103
Microsoft MSN website, online photo albums, space availability, 356-359
Microsoft.com website, desktop customization tools, 96
minimizing windows, 22
modems, DSL, 165
mouse
buttons, reassigning, 108
cursor selection, 75
custom settings (TweakUI utility), 109
double-click speed, changing, 109
dragging options, changing, 109
laptop options
pointing sticks, 107
touchpads, 107
left button operation, 20-21
motion, changing, 106-107
Mouse Properties dialog box, 105-107
pointer shapes
changing, 106
schemes, 106
port connections, 105

How can we make this index more useful? Email us at indexes@samspublishing.com

415

How can we make this index more useful? Email us at indexes@samspublishing.com

417

Q - R

restoring system settings, snapshots (System Restore), 397-400
retrieving system information
hard disk capacities, 375
memory amounts, 375
OS version, 375
processor details, 375
service tags and codes,
373-374
right button (mouse operation), 21
ripping CDs to PCs (Windows
Media Player), 322-326
root folders for hard disks, 17
routers, 162
configuring, 164
connecting to PCs, 165
firmware, 179
high-speed Internet, connecting,
162-164
home installation, 162-165
IP addresses, 164-165
MAC addresses, 165, 213
selection guidelines, 162
settings, selecting, 164
wireless, 162, 208
cost of, 208
installing, 210-213
Rover the Search Dog (Search
Companion), 145-147
rules for email folders, creating
(Outlook Express), 274-276
Run box, 44
Run option (Start menu), 14

S

Safe Mode, startups, 26
saving
desktop themes, 75
file searches (Search
Companion), 150
files, default folder changes,
152-154
system sound recordings, 104

Scanner and Camera Wizard
photos
copying, 338-340
ordering prints online,
340-341
scanners, preference settings,
342
scanners
connecting, 342
display settings
brightness, 344
contrast, 344
resolution, 344
photos, 341-345
default storage folder, 344
name creation, 344
previewing scanned image,
342
preference settings (Scanner
and Camera Wizard), 342
Scheduled Tasks, deleting from
folder, 119
screen fonts, smoothing option, 60
screen resolution, changing, 60-61
Screensaver.com website, 62
screenshots, capturing, 350-353
screensavers
creating, 61-64
desktop themes, 75
previewing, 64
size of, 64
time frequencies, 64
website sources
Download.com, 62
Screensaver.com, 62
Tucows.com, 62
scroll effect (desktop appearance),
59
Search Companion (Internet
Explorer)
Advanced Search feature,
147-152
character animation, changing,
145-147
displaying, 188
files, searching, 144-145
hiding, 190

Indexing Service, usage guidelines, 151-152
search terms
entering, 188
highlighting, 190
search types, 145
searches, saving, 150
wildcards, file search criteria,
150
search engines, selection option
(Internet Explorer), 190
Search option (Start menu), 14
searching
current website with Google
toolbar (Internet Explorer),
196
messages in mailboxes
(Outlook Express), 273
Web images as wallpaper,
65-67
security
cookies
blocking on site-by-site
basis, 249
privacy protection, 246-249
encryption, file/folder access
(Windows Explorer), 135-138
Internet Explorer categories,
244-245
online safety
ActiveX controls, 243-244
downloadable software, 244
email worms, 253-256
firewalls, 226
firewalls, built-in, 227-232
firewalls, port blockage, 226
firewalls, Trojan horse protection, 226
firewalls, ZoneAlarm,
232-236
pop-ad blocking, 236-239
spyware, detection of, 239
spyware, protection meas-
ures, 240-243
viruses, 250-253
passwords, file/folder access
(Windows Explorer), 132-135
shared folders, 169

How can we make this index more useful? Email us at indexes@samspublishing.com

419

T

How can we make this index more useful? Email us at indexes@samspublishing.com

421

U - V

W

How can we make this index more useful? Email us at indexes@samspublishing.com

423

X - Y - Z

in a Snap

Jump In Anywhere!

Organized into a series of **short, clearly written, well-illustrated** lessons, all *In a Snap* books in the Sams Teach Yourself series let you **zero right in** on that one particular task you need to accomplish right now—and then they let you get back to work.

Learning how to do new things with your computer shouldn't be tedious or time-consuming. It *should* be quick, easy, and maybe even a little bit fun.

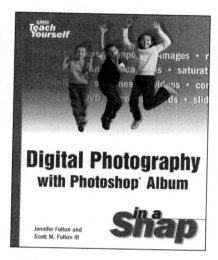

Digital Photography with Adobe Photoshop Album in a Snap

Jennifer Fulton and Scott M. Fulton III
0-672-32568-3
$24.99 US/$35.99 CAN

Mac OS X Panther in a Snap

Brian Tiemann
ISBN: 0-672-32612-4
$24.99 US • $35.99 CAN

eBay in a Snap

Preston Gralla
ISBN: 0-672-32646-9
$19.99 US • $28.99 CAN

Macromedia Contribute in a Snap

Ned Averill-Snell
ISBN: 0-672-32516-0
$24.99 US • $35.99 CAN

iLife '04 in a Snap

Jinjer Simon
ISBN: 0-672-32577-2
$24.99 US • $35.99 CAN

SAMS Teach Yourself

When you only have time for the answers

www.samspublishing.com

Key Terms

Don't let unfamiliar terms discourage you from learning all you can about Windows XP. If you don't completely understand what one of these words means, flip to the indicated page, read the full definition there, and find techniques related to that term.

.NET Passport   A Microsoft technology that uniquely identifies you, and that you'll need to use Windows Messenger. With the Passport, you can sign into multiple Microsoft sites and features, such as Hotmail.   **287**

ActiveX control   A small piece of software that downloads from a website to your PC and runs inside your browser, often to add interactivity to websites.   **244**

Address bar   A toolbar on the Taskbar that lets you type a web address, a command, or the name of a file or folder, and then sends you to the address, runs the command, or opens the file or folder.   **89**

Basic Input Output System (BIOS)   Built-in software that handles the hardware's basic functions, such as controlling the keyboard, screen display, and disk drives.   **25**

Bit rate   The rate at which digital music is recorded, measured in kilobytes per second. The higher the bit rate, the higher the quality of the recorded music, and the larger the file.   **323**

Buddy list   The list of people in Windows Messenger (or another instant messaging program) with whom you frequently communicate, and about whom you want to be notified when they log on to their instant messenger program.   **291**

Central Processing Unit (CPU)   The main brains of your PC, this chip does all the computing and processing.   **51**

Compression   A technique that shrinks files and folders so that they take up less hard disk space.   **139**

Control Panel   The primary place to go when you want to change or customize XP settings.   **15**

Cookie   A small bit of data that a website puts on a PC so that it can track the person's use of the site or to provide services such as customized views or automatic logins.   **191**

Desktop   The main screen that appears when you start XP and log in. It includes all the important components of the operating system.   **10**

Device Manager   A Windows XP utility that lets you view and manage your hardware.   **370**

Dialog box   A screen in Windows XP in which check boxes, buttons, and text boxes are used to control a particular feature or function of XP, such as how your mouse should work.   **15**

Domain   In reference to corporate networks, a domain is a group of network resources such as printers, folders, and corporate applications. On the Internet, a domain is a top-level location such as samspublishing.com.   **9**

Driver   A piece of software required by hardware to work with Windows XP.   **376**

Email worm   A malicious program that takes over your email program and mails copies of itself to people in your address book without your knowledge.   **253**

Encryption   A technique that scrambles data, files, and folders so that only the person who encrypted them can read them.   **135**

Favorites   A collection of Internet sites stored in Internet Explorer so that you can easily revisit them without having to remember the URLs.   **182**

Filename extension   The letters at the end of a filename, to the right of the period (.).   **125**

Filmstrip view   A view in Windows Explorer that displays pictures as if they were in a filmstrip, including links to easy-to-accomplish tasks in the Task pane.   **128**

Firewall   A piece of software that can stop unwanted intruders from gaining access to your computer.   **226**

Fragmentation   When the different sections of files and programs on your PC are stored far apart from each other on your hard disk. This leads to a slower operating PC.   **403**

Frequently Used Programs List   A list of programs you use frequently, located just below the Pinned Programs List. The programs are moved in and out by XP automatically.   **78**

History list   A list of sites you've recently visited.   **185**

IMAP server   A computer that receives email from people and then lets you retrieve the mail using your email software.   **269**

Indexing Service   A feature that lets you do quick searches by indexing your hard disk.   **151**

Instant messaging   Chatting with others live over the Internet using instant messaging software, such as Windows Messenger.   **258**

IP address   A number such as 136.87.23.45 that uniquely identifies any computer or device connected to the Internet.   **164**

Java applet   A small piece of software written with the Java language that downloads from a website to your PC and runs inside your browser to add interactivity to websites.   **244**

MAC address   A number, such as 00-90-4B-0E-3F-BD, that uniquely identifies a piece of hardware, such as a router or a network card.   **213**